ROUTLEDGE LIBRARY EDITIONS: POSTCOLONIAL SECURITY STUDIES

Volume 1

MILITARY POWER AND POLITICS IN BLACK AFRICA

MILITARY POWER AND POLITICS IN BLACK AFRICA

Edited by
SIMON BAYNHAM

LONDON AND NEW YORK

First published in 1986 by Croom Helm

This edition first published in 2021
by Routledge
2 Park Square, Milton Park, Abingdon, Oxon OX14 4RN

and by Routledge
52 Vanderbilt Avenue, New York, NY 10017

Routledge is an imprint of the Taylor & Francis Group, an informa business

© 1986 Simon Baynham

All rights reserved. No part of this book may be reprinted or reproduced or utilised in any form or by any electronic, mechanical, or other means, now known or hereafter invented, including photocopying and recording, or in any information storage or retrieval system, without permission in writing from the publishers.

Trademark notice: Product or corporate names may be trademarks or registered trademarks, and are used only for identification and explanation without intent to infringe.

British Library Cataloguing in Publication Data
A catalogue record for this book is available from the British Library

ISBN: 978-0-367-70773-6 (Set)
ISBN: 978-1-00-314791-6 (Set) (ebk)
ISBN: 978-0-367-67726-8 (Volume 1) (hbk)
ISBN: 978-0-367-67727-5 (Volume 1) (pbk)
ISBN: 978-1-00-313257-8 (Volume 1) (ebk)

Publisher's Note
The publisher has gone to great lengths to ensure the quality of this reprint but points out that some imperfections in the original copies may be apparent.

Disclaimer
The publisher has made every effort to trace copyright holders and would welcome correspondence from those they have been unable to trace.

Military Power and Politics in Black Africa

Edited by

SIMON BAYNHAM

CROOM HELM
London & Sydney

©1986 Simon Baynham
Croom Helm Ltd, Provident House, Burrell Row,
Beckenham, Kent BR3 1AT
Croom Helm Australia Pty Ltd, Suite 4, 6th Floor,
64-76 Kippax Street, Surry Hills, NSW 2010, Australia

British Library Cataloguing in Publication Data

Military power and politics in black Africa.
   1. Africa, Sub-Saharan — Politics and government,
  — 1960-   2. Africa, Sub-Saharan — Armed
Forces — Political activity
I. Baynham, Simon
322'.5'0967   JQ1875.A1
ISBN 0-7099-3280-4

Printed and bound in Great Britain by Mackays of Chatham Ltd, Kent

CONTENTS

List of Tables
The Authors
Preface and Acknowledgements

1. INTRODUCTION: ARMED FORCES IN AFRICA   1
   Simon Baynham

2. MILITARY RULE IN AFRICA: ETIOLOGY AND
   MORPHOLOGY   38
   Samuel Decalo

3. MILITARY DISENGAGEMENT FROM POLITICS?:
   INCENTIVES AND OBSTACLES IN POLITICAL
   CHANGE   67
   Claude E. Welch, Jr.

4. ARMIES AND POLITICS IN CIVILIAN REGIMES   97
   David Goldsworthy

5. REVOLUTIONARY ARMIES OF AFRICA:
   MOZAMBIQUE AND ZIMBABWE   129
   Annette Seegers

6. PAX AFRICANA?   166
   Dennis Austin

7. ARMIES ON LOAN: TOWARD AN EXPLANATION
   OF TRANSNATIONAL INTERVENTION AMONG
   BLACK AFRICAN STATES: 1960-85   177
   Arnold Hughes and Roy May

8. FOREIGN INTERVENTION IN AFRICA   203
   Anthony Clayton

9. ARMS CONTROL IN AFRICA 259
   Abbott A. Brayton

10. SOUTH AFRICA'S MILITARY RELATIONS WITH
    ITS NEIGHBOURS 291
    J.E. Spence

Index 317

LIST OF TABLES

4.1	African States Ranked by *Per Capita* Income...	118
8.1	The Supply of Arms by Non-African Countries to Sub-Saharan Africa (Excluding South Africa)....................	228
9.1	World Socio-Economic Trends, 1960-79.......	261
9.2	World Military Trends, 1960-79.............	262
9.3	Regional Military Expenditures (MILEX): 1977 Actual Figures (and percentile increase, 1969-78)........................	264
9.4	African Military Expenditures (MILEX): 1977 Actual Figures (and percentile increase, 1969-78)........................	267
9.5	Size of African Armed Forces, 1983.........	272
9.6	Arms Transfers to African States, 1974-78..	274
9.7	Value of Arms Transfers as a Percentage of Total Arms Levels	276

Strategic Studies (London).

Anthony Clayton, who is Senior Lecturer at the Royal Military Academy, Sandhurst, earned his doctorate at St. Andrew's University after a career in the Kenya Colonial Government. He is co-author (with D.C. Savage) of Government and Labour in Kenya 1895-1963 (1975) and author of The Zanzibar Revolution and its Aftermath (1981) and Counter-Insurgency in Kenya 1952-56 (1985). Currently writing two books on British and French military forces in Africa, A Super-Power at Work: The British Empire 1919-39 and France, Soldiers and Africa, Dr. Clayton previously served in the British Territorial Army, reaching the rank of Lieutenant-Colonel in the Intelligence Corps.

Samuel Decalo is Professor and Head of the Department of African Studies at the University of Natal. Since obtaining his Ph.D. at the University of Pennsylvania in 1970, he has taught at the University of Botswana and the University of the West Indies. He has carried out extensive field research in many parts of Africa and is author of Military Rule in Africa: Studies in Military Style (1976) as well as several other books and dozens of other articles on African politics and international relations.

David Goldsworthy is Reader in Politics at Monash University and Secretary of the African Studies Association of Australia and the Pacific. Educated at the University of Adelaide and Oxford University, Dr. Goldsworthy currently specialises in Development Theory and African Politics. In addition to many other publications, he has written Colonial Issues in British Politics (1971) and Tom Mboya (1982).

Arnold Hughes is Lecturer in Political Science at the Centre of West African Studies, University of Birmingham, where he teaches African Nationalism and Contemporary African Politics. Over the past two decades he has travelled and researched extensively in West Africa. Apart from an interest in the role of the military, he has published numerous articles in learned journals and contributed to several books on Gambian and Nigerian politics, pan-Africanism and modernisation theory. He is currently preparing a book on Gambian politics.

THE AUTHORS

Dennis Austin is Emeritus Professor of Government at the University of Manchester and was formerly a research fellow at the Institute of Commonwealth Studies and at the Royal Institute of International Affairs. He is the author of several books and numerous articles on Africa including <u>Politics in Ghana 1946-60</u> (1964), <u>Britain and South Africa</u> (1966), <u>Commonwealth in Eclipse</u> (1972) and <u>Politics in Africa</u> (1978).

Simon Baynham, who received his doctorate from the London School of Economics in 1982, is Senior Lecturer in the Department of Political and Social Studies at the Royal Military Academy, Sandhurst. He spent a year at the University of Ghana in the mid-1970s and has recently returned from two years at the University of Cape Town where he taught Third World Politics and from where he undertook extensive fieldwork on the security forces of South Africa, Namibia and the 'frontline' states. Author of <u>The Military and Politics in Nkrumah's Ghana</u> (1986), he has written numerous articles on African politics and civil-military relations.

Abbott A. Brayton, who obtained his Ph.D. from the University of Arizona in 1971, is Professor of International Politics in the Department of Political Science at East Tennessee State University. He is also Staff Officer/Strategist with the Politico-Military Division, Department of the Army, in the rank of Lieutenant-Colonel, U.S. Army Reserve. Author of <u>The Politics of War and Peace</u> (1981) and <u>Allied Policy-Making in the Middle East 1935-45</u> (forthcoming), Dr. Brayton is also Consultant to the International Institute for

Roy May is Principal Lecturer in the Department of Politics and History at Coventry (Lanchester) Polytechnic where he teaches African and Comparative Politics. He originally served with the 1 Sierra Leone Regiment (Royal West African Frontier Force) in Freetown. His current areas of research cover the contemporary role of France in Africa and the political situation in Chad, subjects on which he has presented numerous papers.

Annette Seegers obtained her bachelor's and master's degrees from the University of Pretoria, completing her doctorate through the Fulbright Hays Exchange Programme at the Loyola University of Chicago in 1983. Prior to her appointment as Lecturer in the Department of Political Studies at the University of Cape Town in 1986, Dr. Seegers taught at the University of South Africa. She has written a number of articles and chapters on Southern Africa security issues.

Jack Spence is Professor of Politics and Pro-Vice-Chancellor at the University of Leicester. He has taught at several universities in South Africa, North America and Britain. His numerous publications include <u>Republic Under Pressure: the Study of South African Foreign Policy</u> (1965), <u>Lesotho: the Politics of Dependence</u> (1968) and <u>Investment in South Africa: the Political and Military Framework</u> (1975).

Claude E. Welch, Jr., is Professor and Chairman in the Department of Political Science at the State University of New York, Buffalo. Educated at Harvard College (B.A.) and Oxford University (D.Phil.), Professor Welch's books include <u>Dream of Unity</u> (1966), <u>Political Modernization</u> (1967), <u>Soldier and State in Africa</u> (1970), <u>Revolution and Political Change</u> (1972) and <u>Anatomy of Rebellion</u> (1980). In addition, he has published chapters in more than 20 books, and over 30 articles in academic journals. He is also associate editor of <u>Armed Forces and Society</u> and consultant to the Ford Foundation Programme on Human Rights.

PREFACE AND ACKNOWLEDGEMENTS

The impetus for this collaborative venture came from my research at the London School of Economics and from Peter Sowden at Croom Helm, who invited me to edit a volume on the military in Africa with a number of experts offering a contribution each on a subject of their specialisation. Thematic in character and relevant to a variety of disciplines, the book aims to provide a comprehensive overview of military power in black Africa, from the period since independence but with considerable emphasis on quite recent and contemporary events. It is not limited to the military's purely domestic role, thus providing scope for a less restricted review of armed forces in the sub-continent.

The first chapter is a synoptic commentary on military power and politics in Africa south of the Sahara. Chapters 2-5 focus on the internal influence of the military establishment; Chapters 6-10 on the international dimensions of military force in the region. I am uncomfortably aware that the choice of subjects, wide-ranging as they are, will not suit every reader's requirements. Nevertheless, it is hoped that some sort of balance has been achieved within the limiting constraints of these pages.

Primarily for use as a reader at university level, this compilation of essays is also directed at other bodies and individuals whose professional predilections encompass African politics, conflict and peace studies, international affairs and civil-military relations.

In the preparation of this enterprise, I have benefitted greatly from discussions and correspondence with numerous colleagues in various parts of Africa, Australia, Britain and the United States. My grateful appreciation goes firstly of course to the contributing authors; it is also extended to three other friends, Alan Cooper, Matt Midlane and Alan Ward, for their helpful comments during the initial stages of this project. Thanks also to Sally Creed and Lauren Moser for cheerfully typing successive drafts of the manuscript and to Jeanne Cope for preparing the index. Last but not least, to Nina and our daughters, Anja and Camilla, who tolerated my long absences at a desk and in the field.

Lilongwe, Malawi, 1986   Simon Baynham

Dedicated to my parents and in memory of
my brother, Christopher

Chapter One

INTRODUCTION: ARMED FORCES IN AFRICA

Simon Baynham

This volume is concerned with the larger portion of the African continent usually referred to as black or sub-Saharan Africa. As a rough rule of thumb, it is generally accepted that the Sahara constitutes the northern boundary of the region. Enclosed by this encroaching desert waste to the north and the Atlantic and Indian oceans to south, west and east, this vast territory of over 40 states[1] may be differentiated from North Africa which has been closely linked to the Mediterranean, the Middle East and Mohammedism for thirteen hundred years.
 Certainly the Sahara has served as a bridge to much trade and cultural interchange - and the Sudan's million square miles straddles and is torn, almost literally, between the two parts - but today it also represents something of a barrier to political relations, Gaddafi's Libya notwithstanding. Most of the territory south of the desert has developed with little knowledge of the rest of the world. In turn, much of the area was little known to outsiders until comparatively recently. But in spite of this relative isolation the presence of Moslem majorities or significant Moslem minorities in countries such as Senegal, Ivory Coast, Cameroon, Kenya, Madagascar and Mozambique, and the gradual spread southwards of Islam as well as the activities of the OAU may be reducing the distinction between the respective sub-continents.[2]
 For the most part, however, the contributing authors do not address their commentary to those countries with Mediterranean coastlines (Morocco, Algeria, Tunisia, Libya and Egypt) except where the activities of these states impinge on security and politico-military issues further south. On

the other hand, the Republic of South Africa is included within these pages, the vast majority of its 30 million population - including the counterfeit TBVC states[3] - being black. For white South Africa is not a place; it is an idea, a denial of reality. To paraphrase Trollope's words expressed before the Berlin Conference: It is a land of black men; it has been so, it is so, and it will be so.

It is true, of course, that Africa south of the Sahara is itself an area that defies rigorous description. With a population exceeding 400 million - double the figure existing in 1960 - and growing at three per cent per annum - there are inordinate disparaties between black Africa's constituent parts in terms of size (the Sudan and Zaire on the one hand, Burundi and Equatorial Guinea on the other), population (Nigeria with 90 million citizens, Guinea-Bissau and Swaziland with less than one million apiece) and *per capita* income (over US $4,250 in Gabon, less than a fortieth of that in Chad). Culturally and linguistically, the continent is doubly divided: firstly, between the legacy of deposited European institutions and ideas (Anglophone, Francophone, Hispanophone and Lusophone); in the second place, as between indigenous cultural traits and tongues. And in political terms the region embraces multi-party parliamentary democracies (Botswana, the Gambia and, for the moment, Zimbabwe), traditional monarchies (Swaziland), single-party mobilisation machines (Kenya, Malawi, Togo) and an assorted mixture of military and quasi-military[4] dictatorships of both conservative (Guinea, Nigeria) and radical (Burkina Faso, Ethiopia) ideological orientations.

There are also overriding similarities: Contact with the West and the capricious carve-up of the continent a century or so ago, subjugation and formal empire, a brief high noon of colonial rule and, for the most part very suddenly, independence - or at least 'political independence'. Then dependence, debt and instability. Today, this part of the continent is the poorest region in the world. It faces a crisis of unprecedented proportions. The physical environment is deteriorating (deforestation, overgrazing and desertification); *per capita* production of food is declining; population growths are the highest in the 'developing' world and rising; civil strife and hunger stalk the region. In 1984, Africa's arms imports exceeded

Introduction: Armed Forces in Africa

the value of grain imports to the famine-stricken continent for the first time since independence. And as with the rest of the Third World, sub-Saharan Africa confronts common circumstances by virtue of its economic peripherality in which it has become subordinated to a world-system dominated by the industrialised states of the North.[5]

The evidence suggests that the level of violence and the use of armed force both within the sovereign states and as directed from across their borders has clearly escalated since the 'year of independence' in 1960. However, these and related phenomena preceded and did not post-date the attainment of modern statehood. For not only were acephalous societies, like the Nuer of Sudan, and more formalised polities, such as the Hausa city-states, frequently in a state of conflict - the 'dark continent' was patently no paragon of peace - but the European imperial powers deployed military force to probe, then to impose and finally to consolidate their occupation. Also, contrary to earlier assessments, these processes were accompanied by significant instances of resistance: from the Fulani emirates and Samori Touré to British and French incursions respectively in West Africa on the one hand, to the violent Maji Maji rebellion against German intrusion in Tanganyika on the other.[6] In addition, the experiences of African troops during World War II, and the difficulties of demobilisation and readjustment in the post-war colonial economies, meant that ex-soldiers contributed in developing a sense of political and national consciousness. In the Gold Coast, for instance, ex-servicemen played a part in the 1948 disturbances which influenced the British government's decision to proceed more quickly with the pace of decolonisation.[7] But to many political pundits the prominence of the military in the era after independence came as something of a surprise. Why was this?

In his 1962 preface to *Black Mischief* Evelyn Waugh wrote: 'Thirty years ago it seemed an anachronism that any part of Africa should be independent of European administration. History has not followed what then seemed its natural course.'[8] Similarly, some quarter of a century back, when the 'white man's burden' yielded to indigenous political and bureaucratic elites,[9] few observers predicted a prominent role for the post-colonial military forces. At an Ibadan University conference in 1964, for example, Lloyd declared that 'in few of the independent [African] states is the military elite much in evidence in the social and political life.'[10] This evaluation was not challenged (in fact it was endorsed) by several leading commentators of the day.[11] And within these territories the dilatory pace of officer Africanisation and the late transfer of responsibility 'encouraged both apathy and ignorance about the armed forces among the emerging African elite.'[12]

Yet looking back on African events at the present time, it seems surprising that the potential significance of the army was not more fully anticipated. Given Third World, and especially Latin American, experience elsewhere, military uprisings in black Africa should have come as no great shock. The small size and limited expertise of the region's armies led scholars to minimise the military threat but rebellion - whether a *golpe de estado (coup d'état)* or *golpe cuartelazo* (palace revolt) - has frequently involved only a few hundred troops. In Ghana the army-police National Liberation Council came to office in 1966 when 500 soldiers from an army of 10,000 toppled the regime of Kwame Nkrumah; in the Congo (now Zaire) Mobutu 'neutralised' the conflict between Lumumba and Kasavubu in 1960 by taking Leopoldville (Kinshasa) with 200 men; and President Soglo of Dahomey (Benin from 1975) was removed from power in 1967 by 60 paratroopers.[13]

In short, early predictions to the effect that the imperial legacy in Africa was likely to create armies in the image of the colonial powers - and as such unlikely to interfere in politics - have been hastily revised. Throughout much of the continent today militaries, no matter how small, represent the only disciplined organisations at large. As such, even if not ruling directly, they are virtually unchallenged umpires of who should govern and under what conditions and terms.

Indeed, during recent years, as the soldiers have vacated camp quarters for cabinet rooms, the word 'praetorianism' has been articulated with increasing currency. The term (as with the elusive concept of military professionalism) has become a somewhat blurred piece of descriptive shorthand in the vocabulary of political scientists; it is deployed in a variety of hazily defined and loosely conceptualised ways, thereby defying attempts to endow it with a fixed value. Nevertheless, it is generally taken to imply a state of affairs where the armed services have become major determinants - if not the ultimate arbiters - in the political environment, exercising a high degree of autonomous power. For Nordlinger, it conveys an implicit message, one that 'refers to a situation in which military officers are major political actors by virtue of their actual or threatened use of force.'[14] More recently, Perlmutter has emphasised as a particularly important indicator of a praetorian polity, civilian institutions lacking in legitimacy[15] - a key variable in earlier and more sophisticated analyses of the civil-military nexus advanced by Luckham and Finer in 1971 and 1962 respectively.[16]

Today, almost one half of black Africa's states are governed, in one form or another, by their armies;[17] while in some countries (Mozambique comes to mind) although the military does not rule at the centre, there is an overlap and symbiotic relationship between the senior ranks of the armed forces and the top officials of the hegemonic vanguard party.[18] Most of the *coups d'état* from the modern-day men on horseback have been directed against civilian targets - often for a second or third time as the cases of Uganda and Benin so graphically illustrate - but an increasing proportion are staged from *within* the military, by one set of khaki-clad soldiers against another: as in Nigeria (1966, 1975, 1985), Ghana (1978, 1979) and the Sudan (1985). In numerical terms, there has been an average of three successful coups a year since 1963 (there were six in 1966 but only one, Amin's, in 1971) as well as a rash of attempted but abortive rebellions throughout the sub-continent. Congo-Brazzaville, for instance, hosted seven attempted *coups d'état* between 1966 and 1977. More recently, in November 1985, Liberia's General Doe survived a bloody attempt from elements of the military to unseat him from office. All this in addition to a continuous run of guerrilla insurrections, civil wars, cross-border confrontations and other manifestations of violent disturbances including riots, assassinations, massacres and strikes.

It would be superfluous to document such occurrences at greater length here since they constitute much of the subject matter of the following chapters. What is clear, however, is that the deployment of armed force in post-independent Africa is to a large extent the legacy of the manner in which the continent was divided during the last part of the nineteenth century. It is also intimately linked to the celerity with which the metropolitan powers withdrew from the artificial states they had created. Critical issues relating to the distribution of power and the resources associated with the occupancy of political office were left unresolved. No wonder, then, that so many of the new African armies were sucked into the political centre-stage.

Frequently, too, institutional instability within the armed forces was engendered by the progressive and rapid indigenisation of the officer corps in the immediate aftermath of independence.[19] The result of political as opposed to military imperatives, localisation led to an erosion of skill and in many cases to a breakdown in discipline. The accelerated elevation of inexperienced officers to high executive posts generated unrealistic career aspirations at lower levels; and in most cases such expectations were not borne out following the initial wave of promotions. Had recruitment and advancement been more carefully regulated (both before and after independence), promotional bottlenecks - a breeding ground for discontent and conspiracy - might have been largely avoided. These and related dislocations had wider repercussions since a lack of coherence within the armed services themselves lessens constraints upon military adventurism in the political sphere. Indeed, indiscipline within the security services is a constant problem for all regimes, both civilian and military, that rely principally on force to survive.

Hence the requirement to mesh the 'internal characteristics' approach to the analysis of civil-military relations with that which stresses the wider social and political circumstances in which armed forces operate.[20] While the former school of thought (in which explanations of military participation in politics are mainly restricted to the inner characteristics and dynamics of the armed forces) has been traditionally associated with the name of Janowitz,[21] and the latter model (that emphasising the socio-political environment) with those of Huntington and Finer,[22] there is a general consensus that both traditions in civil-military relations analysis are important, that the explanatory force of stressing the internal qualities of the armed forces to the exclusion of the external sphere, or vice versa, is limited.

On top of the question of the relative qualities and strengths/weaknesses of military and civilian institutions, it is also important, following Luckham, to consider the character of the boundaries, and the nature of the transactions between armed forces and their societal context.[23] This volume is premised on the viewpoint that the vast majority of sub-Saharan militaries exhibit a 'fragmented' (rather than an 'integral' or 'permeated') relationship with their environment. That is they are caught up in, and are susceptible to, wider social forces because intra-military communal cleavages (ethnic, regional, religious etc.) - and, to a lesser but growing extent, vertical (class) alignments which cross-cut traditional horizontal affiliations - coincide with societal divisions, making it possible for patron-client networks to be forged between civilian actors and soldiers. The military's structural differentiation is especially vulnerable once the barracks have been abandoned for political office. For as First noted, once armies step beyond the barracks to engage in public policy-making, 'they soak up social conflicts like a sponge.'[24]

Any attempt to assess the nature and impact of military rule, however, must begin with the causes, or Eckstein's 'preconditions,'[25] of coups although it hardly needs mentioning that the *coup d'état* is merely one manifestation of military intervention. Economic crisis, persistent poverty, regional/ethnic rivalries, government corruption and repression, maladministration, 'contagion' ... In Africa the list, as well as the literature on the subject, seems endless.[26] One early effort to classify armed intrusion into a simple typology was that drafted by Lefever in 1970. He categorised intervention into four recurring demands reflecting the dominant motivation of the soldiers: the 'security' coup, undertaken to replace a regime judged incapable of defending the state from internal or external challenges; the 'reform' coup, prompted by a dissatisfaction with the character or policies - as opposed to the competence - of the regime; the 'punitive' coup, the result of grievances within the military establishment against a regime which is accused of slighting the prestige of the armed forces; and, fourthly, the 'new elite' coup, motivated primarily by ambitious men who use the army to gain power and the material rewards and societal status associated with the occupancy of office.[27] This last factor brings us to the first of our contributing authors, Samuel Decalo.

As he points out in Chapter Two, much of the literature on intervention deals with the structural vulnerabilities of the new African states. And while he does not attempt to minimise the causal linkages between wider societal conditions and political action - indeed, in his view they can never be ignored - his emphasis is on the *behavioural* motivations that propel soldiers into political action. The distinctive mark of 'behaviourism' has been its focus on the study of individual actors in the social system and the unity of political science with the social or behavioural sciences as a whole.[28] When the social scientist observes people in society, he wants to know why the individual behaves as he does - what meaning his action has for him. It is an approach, therefore, which dwells on processes and events; and it is concerned with individual and group patterns of expectation and the related sociological notion of subjective definition of situation.

Decalo's treatment of military rule is similarly premised on a behavioural approach in which he argues that soldiers in office are not dissimilar to their civilian counterparts, opportunistically exploiting power for their own narrow sectional purposes. Concurring with Jackman (whose quantitatively-inclined aggregate-data analysis of key structural variables in the Third World is quite different from his own[29]), Decalo concludes that the difference between sub-Saharan military and civilian regimes 'is not systematically that very different'. And as with civilian administrations, the political fortunes of the junta are inextricably knitted to fluctuations in global primary commodity prices (cocoa, copper, cloves etc.) over which it has very little or no control. The economic levers that move or brake black Africa are not within the region's borders, but beyond them.[30] Not everybody will favour Decalo's methodological approach. Indeed, not a few readers will criticise it on the lines that its focus on the subjective perceptions and actions of autonomous actors at the expense of the socio-economic material base is excessively narrow. Others, by contrast, will commend it as a sorely needed balance to structuralist analysis.

Given their putative strength in relation to civilian groupings and institutions, what then

Introduction: Armed Forces in Africa

induces the armed bureaucrats to head back to the barracks? In an early study of military rule and demilitarisation, to take just one instance, Pinkney argued that one country (Ghana) 'provided an example, rare so far in Africa, of a military government keeping to the timetable it had set itself for restoring civilian rule.'[31] But he failed to appreciate that this had more to do with threats to the cohesion of the army - police National Liberation Council and the military in the barracks (following the junior ranks' abortive counter-coup in April 1967) than with the NLC's commitment to early abdication. At a higher level of originality, Price claims

> that the training process undergone by the officer corps of many of the new [African] states is such as to produce reference-group identifications with the officer corps of the ex-colonial power and concomitant commitments to its set of traditions, symbols, and values.[32]

However, in maintaining that the NLC (or any other junta for that matter) withdrew because 'Reference-group identification with the British officer corps acted as a counterforce to the perquisites of political office, pushing or pulling the Ghanaian officers to give up the power they had earlier seized,'[33] Price exaggerated the impact of external socialisation processes. Despite any appearances to the contrary, African officers and ranks are not primarily governed by an historical tradition or professional ethos which deposited their embryonic forces in the wake of empire. Rather, their actions conform to traditions and *mores* prevailing in their own cultures. In particular, reference is being made here to the soldiers' susceptibility to, and participation in, an indigenous milieu that stresses the primacy of politics as a means of achieving, protecting and advancing private, corporate and communal material advantages and advancement.

In point of fact, abdication is invariably *forced* on soldiers - assuming of course that they survive the praetorian proclivities of their own primary constituents, the troops in the barracks. For as noted earlier, coups within coups have become a secondary growth industry in themselves. It is now commonplace to remark that military disengagement from overt rule occurs through the cumulation of three conditions: first, the disintegration of the original conspiratorial group; second, a growing divergence of interests between the ruling junta and the barracks; and in the third place, the political and economic difficulties faced by the regime.[34] Abdication, however, is not the only way out; recivilianisation - an incremental transfer of power from a semi-civilianised military government to a civilianised one, as envisaged by the senior command responsible for ousting General Nimairi in 1985 - or decompression, to use a term borrowed from Latin American studies,[35] offers an alternative mode of withdrawal.

In one 1985 issue of *Third World Quarterly* devoted entirely to the question at hand, Finer returned to the subject by reminding us that any military regime is faced with two alternatives, institutionalisation or abdication. 'Clearly the more imperfect the former, the more likely, sooner rather than later, is the latter.'[36] But the road back to barracks is strewn with uncertainties: by surrendering office (although not necessarily power given the experience that disengagement in Africa is frequently formal or conditional, and thus a matter of degree, rather than definitive or absolute[37]) soldiers not only lose direct control over the ideological orientation of the state and the allocation of public resources from which they had previously benefitted so lavishly, but they also risk retribution from vengeful civilians. For these reasons, as General Zia ul Huk of Pakistan put it so cogently, 'It is damned difficult for a military regime to hand over power.'[38]

In his chapter on military disengagement, Claude Welch examines the incentives and obstacles to successful withdrawal in five West African states: Ghana, Liberia, Nigeria, Sierra Leone and Upper Volta (Burkina Faso). As with any analysis of military rule, Welch is fully aware that in order to understand disengagement (which is itself part and parcel of the ruling process), there is a clear imperative to examine the original motivations of rebellious soldiers and the policy objectives of the resulting administrations. Drawing upon Perlmutter's dichotomy between 'arbitrator' and 'ruler'-style military government,[39] - the return to barracks being infinitely more testing for the latter type than for the former - he argues that the hurdles to disengagement are much more severe if the military's original political incursion stemmed from 'environmental' or 'interactional' rather than 'internal' issues. Despite some instances of short-term withdrawal (Togo, 1963-67; the Sudan, 1964-69; and Uganda, 1980-85) and one major example of long-term success (17 years in the case of Sierra Leone, following the restoration of civilian rule by the rank and file in April 1968), Welch provides little evidence to suggest that black Africa will deviate from the cyclical or *perpetuum mobile* pattern of successive interventions and disengagements so common to Latin America.[40] It is an assessment reached elsewhere by 'Bayo Adekanye in his recent study of politics in the 'post-military states':

> It is rare for the process of demilitarisation to lead to any stable pattern of civilian rule. Much more often, the military's return to barracks is the prelude to a period of weak civilian government which sooner or later ends in reintervention ... Re-entry takes place because there is no longer anything to prevent it.[41]

On the other hand, the armed forces have not been politically ascendant throughout sub-Saharan Africa. Far from it in fact. For as David Goldsworthy points out in his essay, 'Armies and Politics in Civilian Regimes', a significant number of mainland regimes have maintained civilian control over their armed forces for periods exceeding 20 (and in some cases 25) years: Ivory Coast, Cameroon, Senegal, Gabon, the Gambia, Tanzania, Kenya, Malawi and Zambia. What is more, with the addition of seven other countries, well over one third of black Africa's states have remained free of military domination. In a number of cases, civilian control has remained intact despite top-level leadership successions: for instance, Kenya in 1978 and, more recently, Nyerere's handover to President Ali Hassan Musinyi in November 1985. Some background commentary might be in order, however, before returning to the central issues contained in Goldsworthy's chapter.

The maintenance of internal law and order and necessary provision for protection against external threats are the primary tasks of any political grouping, be it a technologically primitive people surrounded by hostile neighbours or a modern, industrialised and militarily-powerful state in the modern age. But there is, paradoxically, a danger inherent in this civil injunction. For while there is much in Bonaparte's maxim that without an army there is neither independence nor civil liberty, it is equally important to stress Burke's warning that an armed disciplined body is in its essence dangerous to liberty.[42] The potential threat to an incumbent regime, and to the wider society, is further emphasised because armies use force to achieve their objectives. In this respect, they have three crucial advantages over civilians: 'A marked superiority in organization, a highly emotionalized symbolic status, and a monopoly of arms,' which thereby give them 'overwhelming superiority in the means of applying force.'[43]

These points made, we are presently concerned not so much with military intervention *per se* but rather with the other side of the coin, with the question of civilian *control* of armed force - of how regimes mobilise resources and mechanisms to protect themselves from their own security forces - a subject of key importance but one that has received inadequate attention in the study of African civil-military affairs. This said, it follows that explanations for the frequency of military intervention are critically linked to the difficult task of implementing a system of control: an observation that appears unexceptionable at first but one that has important implications. For one thing, ineffectiveness in this regard may provide the *opportunity* to seize power; for another, efforts to subordinate armed forces to governmental authority may imbue the military, or sections within it, with the *disposition* to intervene.

At some risk of simplification, conceptualisations of civilian control as related to military institutions tend to be of three types, the first of which, the traditional model, may be soon discarded for our purposes since it is premised upon the absence of differences between civilians and soldiers (Luckham's 'permeated' boundaries noted earlier) exemplified by seventeenth century European monarchies where the 'aristocracy simultaneously constituted the civilian and military elite ... The same men wore both hat and helmet.'[44] In this model, civilian supremacy is maintained because the differentiation between military and non-military elites is insignificant or absent, the corollary of which is no armed intervention. Since the traditional system is a mainly historical phenomenon and therefore of marginal or no applicability to black Africa, the theoretical interest here is on the alternative liberal and penetration models which roughly replicate Huntington's 'objective'/'subjective' pattern variable. Such an analytical framework provides the present point of departure for examining strategies of control in independent Africa.

In his classic text on the theory and politics of civil-military relations, Huntington gives considerable attention to the question of how civilian supremacy over the armed forces might be assured.[45] He begins by delineating a conceptual distinction between what he calls objective and subjective control. In the former, the officer corps is disciplined by its own professionalism, the most important constituent involving service to the community. He concludes that the more professional an army (that is the more it saw itself serving society), the less of a threat it would pose. According to the subjective model, civilian supremacy is ensured by the denial of an independent military sphere. Here the army becomes an integral, though subordinate, part of the political authority and is inculcated with civilian values and interests. In short:

> Subjective civilian control achieves its end by civilianizing the military, making it the mirror of the state. Objective control achieves its end by militarizing the military, making them the tools of the state.[46]

The subjective format is most clearly identified with absolutist or totalitarian regimes such as Nazi Germany and the USSR where policy is ultimately determined by force and coercion. In such states, internal military power is checked by breaking up the officer corps into competing groups, establishing political armies and special units (*Waffen*-SS and the Soviet MVD security troops), infiltrating the armed services with alternative political chains of command (commissars), indoctrination and surveillance. This sytem approximates to Nordlinger's penetration (as well as Luckham's apparat) model where civilian dominance is ensured through the widespread deployment of ideological controls and surveillance founded upon a dual structure of authority in which military officers are subordinate to political officers.[47] It also encompasses the system of control described by van Doorn. He suggests a series of options available to the leadership of new states: alter the system of recruitment, promotion and discharge; control through indoctrination and political education; direct regulation using party leaders and political commissars within the military.[48]

By contrast, Huntington's objective (like Nordlinger's liberal) model is closely associated with the OECD parliamentary democracies (UK, USA, Norway, New Zealand, etc.) where control is instituted through the maximisation of military professionalism, thus 'rendering them politically sterile and neutral ... A highly professional officer corps stands ready to carry out the wishes of any civilian group which secures legitimate authority within the state.'[49] As one analyst has stated, however, this formula needs to rest on something more substantial than civilian assertions and warnings. For if soldiers are to become attitudinally disposed to their own subordination, they need to internalise the 'civilian ethic' in propitious circumstances and over time. Concomitantly, the politicians must exhibit due regard for the internal autonomy of the fighting forces.[50]

In previous discussion and in Chapter Four of this volume, Goldsworthy shows that civilian control in Africa owes most of what success it has had to the subjective rather than to the objective formula outlined above. Civilian control in a number of states (in Gabon and Djibouti, for instance) is additionally underwritten by the presence of foreign troops. A central theme of Goldsworthy's earlier work was that civilian control was closely enmeshed with the dominating role of a particular national leader: Kaunda in Zambia, Houphouët-Boigny in Ivory Coast, Banda in Malawi, and so on. Yet as he admits early in his essay here, the stress 'on strong leadership as a significant correlate of civilian control, while very well supported by the circumstantial evidence, seemed ultimately unsatisfactory in that it always hovered close to tautology: a strong leader survives because he is a strong leader.'

To confront this dilemma, Goldsworthy's approach is to seek a more analytical view of the character of civilian political leadership vis à vis African armed forces. In searching for the key to civilian *survival* - for we should be reminded that at least half of the coup-free countries

Introduction: Armed Forces in Africa

have experienced coup plots and/or abortive military rebellions - the author conceptualises the nature of 'personal rule' as a *system* of governance that can be differentiated from 'personalist rule'. Personal rule has certain systemic properties; the latter term, by contrast, is associated with 'arbitrary governance at the whim of an individual.'

In personal-rule systems, soldiers are among the players of the political game. Their relationships with civilian politicians are based on clientelistic considerations in which alliances are forged according to a variety of informal criteria. But as Goldsworthy demonstrates in his major casestudy (Kenya), it is a relationship lodged within a social context: fidelity to the ruler is in part a consequence of shared social interests and affiliations. 'All of which', to return to our earlier discussion, 'is to reassert the essential subjectiveness of control.'

Of course, the question of civilian control might be qualitatively influenced according to the nature of a regime's ideological persuasion. In capitalist-inclined regimes such as Kenya, officers have been enabled to accumulate wealth (in the form of land, farms and private businesses), thereby binding them to the acquisitive values of the ruling political class. By contrast, the role of ideology needs to be understood differently in socialist-minded countries (Tanzania, Mozambique, etc.) where deliberate efforts are made to subject soldiers 'to overt indoctrination in radical participatory values.' While this line of enquiry sheds some interesting light on the issue of military subordination to civilians, Goldsworthy surmises that such an approach should be treated gingerly since it cannot be demonstrated that one kind of ideology provides a surer base for control than the other. Both socialist and capitalist regimes place a high premium on personal loyalties to the political leadership.

In Annette Seegers's chapter on Mozambique and Zimbabwe, the thorny question of civilian control also receives attention. Her contribution is especially useful since she focuses on an aspect of African civil-military relations that has received too little deliberation to date, that is on the metamorphosis of guerrilla liberation armies into conventionally-styled military forces in the aftermath of independence. All military organisations are in large measure the product of their countries' political history. In Africa, most armies were (more or less) peacefully transferred from the European powers to the nationalist leadership but in a number of cases - in Algeria, Angola, Guinea-Bissau, Mozambique and Zimbabwe - the state apparatus was wrenched from colonial or white-settler control in wars of national liberation.[51] During the course of these protracted periods of guerrilla warfare, revolutionary militaries were born that were strikingly different from those Western-styled armies inherited as a result of struggles led by purely political movements and parties.[52] Where revolutionary armed struggle took the place of more peaceful constitutional accommodation, the security services of the former colonial administration were largely eliminated and replaced by the fighting forces of the irregular guerrillas.[53] However, in the case of Zimbabwe, whose colonial antecedents stood in some contrast to the experiences of other African states (because of the illegal UDI of November 1965), the armed services were integrated from the ex-Rhodesian forces (after the disbandment of some 'notorious' units such as the Special Air Service and the Selous Scouts) and the ZANLA and ZIPRA guerrillas of Mugabe and Nkomo.[54]

As an instrument of anti-colonialism, the revolutionary soldier's role in the liberation struggle is greatest in the period leading up to the new regime's installation.[55] But as Seegers has noted in earlier work, revolutionary armies have profound consequences for the direction of the revolution *after* the transition to independence:

> Although the new regime may decide to sustain its revolutionary momentum and seek to transform the society, it also acquires the defence needs of a state, such as the protection of territorial integrity. These different needs often produce tension in civil-military relations.[56]

Such strains have certainly manifested themselves in both Mozambique and Zimbabwe, not least as a consequence of internal security operations against the Mozambique National Resistance (the MNR or RENAMO) and the activities of Zimbabwean dissidents in Matabeleland.

In both instances, as Professor Spence discusses in Chapter Ten, the shadowy hand of Pretoria has been much in evidence. The Republic of South Africa is, of course, an economic and military giant in Africa, producing one third of the continent's steel, half of its electricity, three-quarters of southern Africa's GNP and a high proportion of locally-manufactured materiel, the latter through the Armaments Development and Manufacturing Corporation (Armscor), today the world's tenth-largest arms export industry and the biggest in the southern hemisphere.[57] During the past two decades, there has been an enormous rise through a process of quantum leaps in the manpower, capability and budget of the South African Defence Force: today the military budget stands at over R4 billion (it was R217 million in 1964/65) and the SADF is staffed by approximately 85,000 regulars and national servicemen. To this can be added almost 250,000 Citizen Force and Commando reserves, giving a grand manpower total of 335,000.[58] At the same time, South Africa's economic and strategic significance is underlined by enormous mineral wealth and by it geographical positioning at the juncture of the Atlantic and Indian oceans.

Before 1974, the RSA could rely on other countries to act as a buffer between itself and the hostile states further north. But the erosion of South Africa's *cordon sanitaire* following Portugal's eviction from Angola and Mozambique in the mid-1970s and Zimbabwe's independence in 1980 altered the balance of power in southern Africa. These events marked a major watershed in regional affairs, with profound repercussions for South African and contiguous states' security. Nevertheless, these shifts still leave South Africa as the paramount power in the region, able to impose its will, if necessary, on all its neighbours. International attempts to damage the RSA by boycotts and embargoes have - to date at least - all failed; indeed, it is the Republic that has meted out a concoction of punishments and rewards in a militarised foreign policy of destabilisation designed to intimidate adjacent (and entirely surrounded in Lesotho's case) territories into submission, a strategy described as the imposition of dependency based on instability.[59] The dependency and subordination of the 'frontline' states has an additional, economic, profile since in volume terms, for instance, vast amounts of trade - 80 per cent and 50 per cent respectively in the cases of Zimbabwe and Zambia - pass through South African territory.[60] To take just one more example, 40 per cent of Lesotho's national income is derived from the remittances of Lesotho nationals working in

Introduction: Armed Forces in Africa

South Africa.

As Spence points out, the first clear indication of a more aggressive outward strategy came with the deep incursions of South African forces into Angola in 1975 during the civil war. The objective was to ensure a friendly regime (the UNITA faction of Jonas Savimbi) in the Angolan capital of Luanda. The humiliating subsequent withdrawal to the south in early 1976 led to an unprecedented build-up of South African military forces in Namibia, presently estimated at 40,000 men. Ranged against them are approximately 8,500 SWAPO guerrillas, operating principally from bases in neighbouring Angola.[61] Military developments in Angola remain the main stumbling-block to ending the Namibian war after 19 years of sporadic fighting. It seems clearer now than ever before that a settlement is unattainable until the military situation in the two countries has been sorted out. There is little sign of this happening soon. Far from being a simple issue, the wider hostilities on both sides of the border are an almost insoluble labyrinth of conflicting strategic and tactical interests.

Since 1975, South Africa has extended its cross-border raids (against ANC targets) into Mozambique, Botswana and Lesotho. The Republic is also involved in low-intensity clandestine operations in Matabeleland. At the same time, and especially since the early 1980s, South African 'tit-for-tat' destabilisation, part of a wider 'Total Strategy' designed to counter a 'Total Onslaught' against the RSA, has involved the devastating support for the MNR (presently playing a Frankenstein's role over which the Republic has limited leverage) which has destroyed FRELIMO's authority in much of south and central Mozambique. And whereas Mozambique appears to have carried out its undertakings in terms of the Nkomati Accord - banishing ANC insurgents from its territory - South Africa has openly reneged on its fulfilment of its treaty obligations. In short, it seems that South Africa's continued support for rebel movements in southern Africa confirms that the Republic has no intention of relaxing the military overlordship of the sub-continent which it has secured, *inter alia*, through pre-emptive attacks on insurgent bases in neighbouring states and through surrogates such as UNITA and the MNR.

However, the view that Pretoria's policy makers have 'an unchanging commitment to grandiose external visions of the future,' as some analysts posit, is an argument challenged by Spence. In his evaluation, South Africa's military relations with its neighbours have been governed by 'a ruthless pragmatism ... designed to buy time to put the Republic's house in order ... [so that] the task of internal reform can be undertaken free of external attempts at disruption.' Whether or not the military elite will exercise a reformist as opposed to a reactionary influence on policy in the present climate of domestic unrest is, in Spence's opinion, a matter for speculation.

Dennis Austin's interest in Africa's boundaries and the forces that compete to threaten and alter the map on the one hand and to uphold the borders on the other (Chapter Six) also extends to discussion on the region just mentioned. While Pretoria might have to go along with an independent Namibia to ensure its own security, such an arrangement would be unlikely to alter the international map of Africa (although the vision of a separate Ovambo state embracing northern Namibia and southern Angola still remains a flicker in the minds of some Pretoria strategists). But the possibility of South Africa's partition through constitutional consensus or civil war remains one possible scenario for the future - as does Austin's suggestion that the borders of southern Africa could be refashioned by a powerfully endowed 'Azania'.

It is a century since the Berlin Conference of 1884-85 sought agreement on the principles for partitioning Africa, providing a framework for resolving European conflicts that grew out of the scramble. In Sir John Scott Keltie's words, the Partition was 'one of the most remarkable episodes in the history of the world.'[62] More than ten million square miles of territory and over 100 million Africans had fallen to European control in the space of not much more than a decade. Yet despite the grossly arbitrary manner in which the continent was divided,[63] the boundaries delineated by the imperial powers are essentially those of today's independent states. The reason for this is that Africa's governments are primarily concerned, in Austin's words, 'to uphold their national claims to govern within their colonial borders.' Or as Julius Nyerere explained in a speech to the second Pan-African seminar at the World Assembly of Youth in 1961: 'There are obvious weaknesses on the African continent. We have artificial "states" carved out at the Berlin Conference:

we are struggling to build these nations into stable units of human society.'[64] Hence, with one or two minor exceptions, the post-Berlin state structures have remained sacrosanct; so far, no African boundaries have been forcibly redrawn and no forcible or unilateral secessions have been permitted to succeed. Within the OAU, the belief is cultivated that if just one secessionist group is successful in its objectives, it may herald the dissolution of many other states. In such an eventuality it is argued, chaos and disorder would sweep through Africa on an unprecedented scale.

The main thrust of Austin's thesis is that 'force is employed not to alter the map but to hold it together,' a view supported by the evidence in the Hughes/May chapter discussed at more length below. Few African leaders are free from the threat of secessionist movements - in the Shaba region of Zaire, in the western part of Uganda and in the Agni sector of Ivory Coast, to take just three examples. As such, they face a common predicament, 'a need to preserve the partition of Africa ... which keeps alive a shared interest among what are otherwise disparate regimes.' In any case argues Austin, the majority of black African states have neither the motive nor the technical and logistic resources to wage wars with other states.

External annexation or absorption is not the only method, however, by which crudely-designated borders might be rearranged. Balkanisation or disintegration of both pygmies and giants is also threatened, as we have noted, by a variety of secessionist movements. These Austin separates into three recurring categories: neo-traditionalists, proto-nationalists and revolutionary populists. However, rebel groups' efforts to increase the number of states by division are similarly confronted with a myriad of external and domestic obstacles, ranging from problems of international recognition to the strength of the colonially-bequeathed state (and sometimes by the intervention of external patrons).

Austin's 'Pax Africana' therefore serves as a useful introduction to Anthony Clayton's 'Foreign Intervention in Africa' (Chapter Eight), and the earlier contribution by Arnold Hughes and Roy May (Chapter Seven) which deals with the military involvement of African states with each other. It is true that the subject matter of

Introduction: Armed Forces in Africa

these two essays overlaps in some respects since - to mention just one example - intervention on the part of say China or Belgium is in some cases linked to the transnational activities of African countries. Also, in many instances latent irredentist or separatist issues 'invite' outside involvement in the first place.

Clayton's chapter addresses itself to one of the most fundamental aspects of military power in the region, that is to the question of non-African action in the sub-continent during the past quarter century. Intervention is taken to include all overt and covert forms, covering formal military intrusions, invited or uninvited; clandestine operations; the provision of training, equipment and armaments; defence treaties; and intelligence gathering. These interwoven activities are set against the backdrop of global confrontation between the Soviet bloc and a revolutionary ideology on the one hand and the interests of Western capitalism on the other. This is not to suggest that political motivations and rivalry with regard to the ideological orientation of African regimes are paramount in outside powers' designs. Purely economic and strategic considerations relating to sources of energy, markets, raw materials, investments, military base facilities and so on, have never been absent in the wider interactions between the players concerned.[65] In reality, all of this is inextricably joined to the wider network of dependency - initiated during the age of mercantilism and extended through the rise of formal empire but not severed with political independence - in which foreign military assistance is merely one facet, albeit a crucial one, of the neo-colonial equation. Together with financial, technical, political, diplomatic and cultural resources, the military factor represents a further vehicle for perpetuating outside influence and control over the most impoverished region of the world.

With the possible exception of Cuba, French military policy in Africa has attracted the greatest international attention. In its Africa policy, France appears to have a very different concept of its role and a qualitatively contrasting post-colonial commitment than have the other former metropolitan powers. In Zartman's appraisal, there are four ingredients to this commitment: a cultural element, a moral element, an economic element and a power element. 'All but the economic element are absent from the attitudes of other European countries - including Great Britain, which might have been expected to hold similar views.'[66]

In pursuit of its objectives, France has developed substantial mobile forces. As Clayton points out, these have been trained and equipped for general Third World use but they are especially suited for deployment in Africa. On top of this, France has continued to barrack permanent military forces in client-states such as Djibouti and Gabon. Another theme emphasised both here and in the wider literature is the remarkable continuity with which France has single-mindedly upheld and pursued its African interests. Thus, despite some dilatoriness at first, the socialist administration of Francois Mitterrand has continued to play an energetic and dynamic role on the continent - a role first pressed by 'the Man of Brazzaville,' Charles de Gaulle, who did not hesitate to despatch French military forces to Chad, Niger, Gabon, Cameroon, Congo-Brazzaville and Mauritania for a variety of purposes during the 1960s. Such actions have been closely coordinated by French intelligence networks which permeate all of Francophone Africa, a reflection of the economic and political dominance that France exerts in its former colonies. The largest of France's intelligence services is the SDECE employing 2,000 personnel in seven departments, the seventh being responsible for intelligence and military intervention in Africa.[67] This agency, and the associated *Service d'Action Civique*, have kept Paris well-informed of Soviet - and other powers' - activities and France has constantly warned that Africa should look to France rather than to the superpowers for solutions to its difficulties.

While it has no historic ties with Africa, the Soviet Union - together with its principal surrogate, Cuba - is the only other power to match French military activities on the continent. Clayton argues that black Africa is low in Soviet overall priorities: 'Policy tends therefore to be pragmatic.' On the whole, the USSR appears to have been most successful where it has supported a liberation movement during a period of colonial conflict (for instance, in Mozambique), but the massive increase in Soviet arms transfers to the continent appears to be as much related to the acquisition of hard currency as to anything else.

Although United States involvement in sub-

Introduction: Armed Forces in Africa

Saharan Africa has grown since the mid-1970s, US influence has always remained piecemeal compared to its military interests and interventions in other Third World areas. Nevertheless, it has invested considerable resources in Africa's two largest states, the Sudan and Zaire, and Clayton identifies as especially significant the formation (in 1980) of the Rapid Deployment Joint Task Force, for which transport and access facilities have been arranged with Kenya and Somalia. More recently, there have been worrying signs that armed conflict in southern Africa might escalate as a consequence of the USSR's increased support for Angolan troops fighting UNITA and hints of renewed US military assistance to Savimbi's guerrilla units.

Other states whose activities receive individual scrutiny are Israel (whose rescue operation at Entebbe in July 1976 demonstrated the ease with which a small but developed country could intervene in an African state), North Korea and China. There is also some material on Great Britain whose military profile on the continent - with the major exceptions of armed intervention by invitation to restore law and order in a number of newly-independent states in the 1960s - has been very low key. Yet British training activity has been very considerable and there is widespread demand for such assistance on the part of at least a dozen sub-Saharan countries. A good deal of general and specialist training takes place within the British Isles, but much of it is done on African soil. And despite an ideological gap of some proportions, Mozambique began to send military personnel to Britain for training in 1985. This followed President Machel's request for British assistance in 1983.[68] Mozambique's Marxist leadership also concluded a similar deal with the United States in 1984. Thus, just as outside powers have jostled to capture new clients in Africa, so African regimes have attempted to diversify sources of military assistance. This enables them to maximise the amount of aid proffered and to lessen their single-dependency (usually on the former colonial power), thereby stressing their autonomy and non-alignment.[69]

The term 'intervention' has usually been confined to actions on the part of extra-African powers. However, despite the OAU principle of non-interference in the internal affairs of member states, African governments have periodically

23

Introduction: Armed Forces in Africa

intervened in each others' territories. Such intrusions have received very little systematic attention. For this reason it is hoped that Chapter Seven of this volume is acknowledged as breaking fresh frontiers in this respect. Directing their attentions to one manifestation of the use of military power in inter-African relations, namely 'the deployment of elements of the armed forces in open support of foreign policy objectives on the territory of other countries in the region', Hughes and May note that over 30 black African states have been involved as providers or recipients of such actions. The authors separate their analysis of transnational military intervention into three major divisions: Objectives, Modalities and Motivations. The bulk of their investigation is devoted to the question of objectives which is, in turn, sub-divided into three further categories: interventions that are either Regime-Supportive (accounting for an absolute majority of the 30 or so cases examined, these are designed to provide assistance to a threatened regime or government), Regime-Opposing (the aim here is to undermine or overthrow the regime/government in question), or State-Supportive (in which the purpose of intervention is to ensure the very survival of the state).

Suprisingly, perhaps, Guinea emerges as the leading exponent of the external use of military power, having intervened to support endangered neighbours no less than five separate times; but Tanzania comes a close second with military assistance to governments in the Comoros, the Seychelles, Mozambique and Zambia. Nyerere's forces were also responsible for the best-known instance of regime-opposing armed intervention: the overthrow of Idi Amin in 1979. On that occasion, 20,000 Tanzanian troops invaded Uganda. Another surprise given the size of its military establishment (currently in the region of 138,000) is the paucity of such actions on the part of Nigeria which 'seems more committed to an OAU defence force, and to a general opposition to settler power in South Africa and external intervention in black African affairs', than to bilateral interference in individual states.

However, in terms of sheer numbers (and excluding South Africa's military occupation of Namibia), the largest commitment at the present time remains Zimbabwe's military aid to Mozambique. At least 8,000 (and possibly up to 12,000) Zimbabwean soldiers have been deployed in the former Portuguese colony to guard the vital road through Tete province to Malawi; to protect the road and rail links with the port of Beira and the oil pipeline from Beira to the refinery outside Mutare. On 29 August 1985, Zimbabwean and Mozambican forces stormed the MNR rebel base at Gorongoza. Preceded by an aerial bombardment, it appears to have been the nearest thing to a set-piece conventional battle involving black troops in the region since the 1914-18 campaign against the elusive German askari of General Von Lettow Vorbeck which was itself fought partly in Mozambique. In one ironic twist to southern African hostilities in 1984, Zimbabwean forces collaborated with the South African Defence Force on at least one occasion to help President Machel's hard-pressed army against MNR rebels in Mozambique - an extraordinary *dénouement* given Mugabe's international stance against apartheid and his refusal to allow any minister-to-minister contact with the South Africans.[70]

The majority of interventions in black Africa are thus regime-supportive, a natural enough situation as Clapham has explained elsewhere:

> In the context of the state-centred politics of [Africa], external intervention on behalf of regimes established in power at the centre acquires a legitimacy which similar intervention on behalf of their opponents lacks. This is logical enough: in an area of potentially very high instability, one is stabilising, the other destabilising; governments which themselves are heavily dependent on external assistance, are quick to denounce any such assistance to their opponents, and to claim that essentially domestic opposition ... is externally directed.[71]

Collective or multilateral intervention in sub-Saharan Africa is much less common than bilateral assistance, although Hughes and May qualify this conclusion by noting that bilateral measures can involve clandestine support from third African parties. Of course, transnational multilateral interventions may also involve extra-African powers, sometimes by proxy. One major example of this was the 1977 airborne attack on Benin. As the present writer documented some years ago, the abortive raid involved, *inter alia*,

Introduction: Armed Forces in Africa

Morocco, Gabon and France as well as Beninois exiles and European mercenaries.

Multifarious motivations lie at the heart of interventionist African states: ideological affinities, threats from a common enemy, racial solidarity in the face of racialist or colonial regimes, personal friendships, and so on. Yet as the authors demonstrate, transnational interventions very rarely have as their direct object an increase in the national territory of the interventionist state itself. One explanation for this, as Dennis Austin notes in his chapter, is that 'the burden of annexing, say, Benin to Nigeria or Mali to Senegal, is hardly worth the candle: it would only add the problems of the destitute to those of the poor.' In fact, to anticipate one of the unexpected revelations of the Hughes/May study the most interventionist states are economically impoverished. The authors also disclose that radical states have been more actively involved in such adventures than moderate ones and - perhaps the biggest surprise of all - that civilian governments are more likely to deploy their armed forces on external missions than military regimes.

Intervention is almost universally condemned by the international community, but few countries will refrain from interfering in other countries when their interests call for it. Frequently, however, accusations of intervention are strenuously denied; for example, Ethiopian support for Colonel John Garang's Sudan People's Liberation Army, which operates from rear bases in Ethiopia and which has created a state of near anarchy in southern Sudan, has never been acknowledged by Addis Ababa. The ultimate intervention is the use of force; but if a government invites or welcomes foreign intrusion (as with Cuban troops and East German technical specialists in Angola and Ethiopia), this is not viewed by scholars and politicians in the same light. However, we are confronted with a further dilemma: when does assistance become intervention? The point is highlighted by the non-African cases of Soviet 'fraternal assistance' to Hungary, Czechoslovakia and Afghanistan. As has been seen, the question is implicit in the two chapters previewed above since Clayton and Hughes/May subsume military assistance in the shape of training aid and arms transfers under the broader category of intervention.

Introduction: Armed Forces in Africa

As noted previously, all states must take steps to guarantee their national security against external and internal challenges and this necessitates the acquisition and maintenance of military power. The search for such power has encouraged many African states to seek substantial military assistance from weapon-producing states in the industrialised world.[73] Repeated charges that the continent is being rapidly militarised, and that a new arms race has been unleashed in Africa, have stemmed from detailed documentation on the massive increase in the volume of armaments transfers to Africa.[74] Certainly, the statistics would seem to confirm that such assertions are unanswerable. And in his chapter on 'Arms Control in Africa', Abbott Brayton concedes that military expenditures on the African continent *as a whole* rose 154 per cent during the decade after 1969. All the same, some caveats are in order according to Brayton if the figures since independence are to be seen in perspective.

Utilising a framework of analysis in which four major indicators of militarisation are presented (the ratio of military expenditures to GNP and to central government spending, *per capita* military expenditure, and armed forces per 1,000 people), Brayton writes that there is a common misperception about the magnitude of African, and especially black Africa, military spending. For one thing, since no significant arms were bought before independence, 'any subsequent purchase would cause a dramatic percentile increase' thereafter. For another, the primary importers of military equipment on the continent have been the Arab states bordering the Mediterranean (Egypt, for instance, imported almost half of the US $6 billion in arms transferred to Africa between 1965 and 1974) and not the states south of the Sahara. Ethiopia, Nigeria and South Africa provide the exceptions to the rule. More recently during the past two decades, one quarter of all African states accounted for approximately 90 per cent of imported armaments. On the other hand, whereas Africa accounted for only four per cent of the world's arms trade during the 1965-74 period, that figure has now mushroomed to over 17 per cent today. Here again the figures hide as much as they reveal since not one of the 20 largest Third World major-weapon importing countries is in black Africa. But Libya, Egypt, Algeria and Morocco *are* in the top twenty.[75] Who, then, are the main suppliers?

In sub-Saharan Africa, the two major ex-colonial powers, Britain and France, dominated the arms trade market until the early 1970s. Since then, in what has been described by Landgren-Bäckström as 'a general commercialisation of the arms trade',[76] international competition for lucrative sales contracts has pushed the Soviet Union to the number one position: During the past decade, approximately half of all armaments transfer deliveries to the continent have been supplied by the USSR.[77] For South Africa, the pattern of weapons procurement has been dramatically altered by the UN arms embargo, which has had the unintended result of accentuating the domestic prominence of the SA Defence Force and making the country largely self-sufficient in, and an exporter of, materiel.[78] Together with other types of military assistance, arms exports may provide an additional indicator of a state's militarisation, by reflecting reliance on military production capacity to achieve foreign policy objectives. The case of the Soviet Union - and within the continent, of South Africa - serves to illustrate this point in unambiguous terms.

On the basis of a mass of data assembled in his article, Brayton concludes that, with a handful of exceptions, very few African states have been engaged in significant military expansionism 'especially among the independent states south of the Sahara.' Pressing socio-economic needs and limited national resources have constituted the major deterrent to arms escalation. This is not to ignore the possibility of some additional African states embarking on an arms race in the face of significant threats to their security. Seriously at risk from both internal (UNITA) and external (South African) challenges to its authority, Angola presently appears to be moving in just such a direction. In this regard, Brayton suggests that the major powers could perform a responsible role in reducing African inter-state hostilities and concomitant levels of militarisation by providing technical verification services (on the withdrawal of military forces from border areas, for instance) to an appropriate OAU monitoring body. There is also the suggestion that larger security forces would be obviated by regional security arrangements 'such as that of the Francophone countries.'

Yet - to conclude - for all of the above there

are few grounds for believing that the OAU member states[79] or the major powers are, in the first place, predisposed and, secondly, in a position to settle their disputes along such conduits. Unfortunately, the considered consensus of opinion as presented in this volume of essays leads to the inexorable conclusion that the deployment of military power in the overlapping and blurred arenas of African international and domestic politics is more likely to escalate than to subside. Against a backdrop of the continent's satellite status in the global economic order and rapidly deteriorating financial circumstances, great power rivalries will remain interlocked with African transnational friction and intra-state fragilities: continuing military interference from without; armed interventions and guerrilla insurgency from within. In this regard, the prognosis would seem to undercut any basis for optimism about future levels of militarism on the continent as the twilight years of the twentieth century give way to the twenty-first. As in the past, the political life of black Africa will ultimately be decided vi et armis.

NOTES

1. The island states of the OAU, such as Madagascar, the Comoros and Sao Tomé, are also included within the confines of these pages.
2. Phillips, C.S., The African Political Dictionary (Santa Barbara, California: ABC-CLIO Information Services, 1984), pp. 14, 16.
3. The four homelands which opted for 'independence': Transkei (1976), Bophuthatswana (1977), Venda (1979) and Ciskei (1981).
4. A quasi-military regime may be described as one in which the chief leader is (theoretically) a civilian, yet rests his rule upon the military as in Mobutu's Zaire and General Siyad Barre's Somalia.
5. In the words of one commentator, 'Economic peripherality has meant separation from, and subordination to, the dominant industrial economies which have developed especially in Europe and North America.' Clapham, C., Third World Politics: An Introduction (London: Croom Helm, 1985), p. 3. A large and growing literature (associated with the names of Frank, Rodney, Amin, Wallerstein etc.) on centre-periphery relations exists, some of which is touched on by a number of contributing

authors in the following chapters.

6. For examples from one part of the continent, see Crowder, M. (ed.), West African Resistance: The Military Response to Colonial Occupation (London: Hutchinson, 1971).

7. A fuller discussion on Ghana (and Uganda) is provided by Schleh, E., 'The Post-War Careers of Ex-Servicemen in Ghana and Uganda', Journal of Modern African Studies, 6, 2 (June 1968), pp. 203-20. See also, Killingray, D., 'Soldiers, Ex-Servicemen, and Politics in the Gold Coast, 1939-50', Journal of Modern African Studies, 21, 3 (September 1983), p. 534. For the role played in these respects by former soldiers in two other states, see Miners, N., The Nigerian Army 1956-1960 (London: Methuen, 1971), ch. II and Cox, T.S., Civil-Military Relations in Sierra Leone (Cambridge, Mass.: Harvard University Press, 1976), ch. Two.

8. Waugh, E., Black Mischief (Harmondsworth: Penguin, 1962), p. 5.

9. By the end of 1960, more than half of Africa's states had attained political independence; by the end of 1965, the figure was almost three-quarters.

10. Lloyd, P.C. (ed.), The New Elites of Tropical Africa (London: Oxford University Press, 1966), p. 9.

11. See, for instance, Pye, L.W., 'Armies in the Process of Political Modernization', in Johnson, J.J. (ed.), The Role of the Military in Underdeveloped Countries (Princeton, N.J.: Princeton University Press, 1962), p. 69; and Gutteridge, W.F., Military Institutions and Power in New States (London: Pall Mall, 1964), pp. 141-4.

12. Welch, C.E., 'Praetorianism in Commonwealth West Africa', Journal of Modern African Studies, 10, 2 (June 1972), p. 206.

13. First, R., The Barrel of a Gun: Political Power in Africa and the Coup d'Etat (London: Allen Lane, 1970), p. 5.

14. Nordlinger, E.A., Soldiers in Politics: Military Coups and Governments (Englewood Cliffs: Prentice-Hall, 1977), p. 2.

15. Perlmutter, A., Political Roles and Military Rulers (London: Frank Cass, 1981), p. 13.

16. Luckham, A.R., 'A Comparative Typology of Civil-Military Relations', Government and Opposition, 6, 1 (Winter 1971), pp. 5-35; Finer, S.E., The Man on Horseback: The Role of the Military in Politics (London: Pall Mall, 1962). A fuller discussion on the relative qualities of,

and linkages between, military and civilian institutions follows later in this chapter.

17. Benin, Burkina Faso, Burundi, Central African Republic, Chad, Congo-Brazzaville, Equatorial Guinea, Ethiopia, Ghana, Guinea, Guinea-Bissau, Liberia, Madagascar, Mali, Mauritania, Niger, Nigeria, Rwanda, Somalia, the Sudan, Togo, Uganda and Zaire.

18. The model is discussed in greater detail (using the examples of the Ba'ath parties in the 'military regimes' of Iraq and Syria) by Finer, S.E., 'The Retreat to the Barracks: notes on the practice and the theory of military withdrawal from the seats of power', Third World Quarterly, 7, 1 (January 1985), p. 20.

19. The armed forces of many African states had to be almost completely recreated after the colonial withdrawal; this was especially the case in the former French territories. As one writer has noted, 'the armies of the ex-French countries ... were created from scratch within a very short space of time ... Or they were new in the sense that indigenous personnel were injected in very great haste into an existing military organisation, especially its officer corps, in order to replace the expatriates of the colonising power, as happened in almost all the ex-British countries.' Luckham, A.R., The Nigerian Military (London: Cambridge University Press, 1971), p. 90.

20. The former model focuses on the social organisation of the armed forces: structural format and techniques of control, hierarchy and authority, recruitment and assimilation of military roles, skill patterns and career development, sources of cohesion and cleavage, and professionalism. The 'external or "environmental" variables include the actions of civilian executives, the performance and legitimacy of civilian government, the politicization of workers and peasants, the severity of communal conflicts, the extent of socio-economic modernization, and the rate of economic growth.' Nordlinger, Soldiers in Politics, p. xi.

21. Janowitz, M., The Military in the Political Development of New Nations (Chicago: University of Chicago Press, 1964). However, Janowitz has never ignored the other side of the coin, as demonstrated in his earlier Sociology and the Military Establishment (New York: Russell Sage, 1959), p. 8.

22. Huntington, S.P., Political Order in

<u>Changing Societies</u> (New Haven: Yale University Press, 1968), p. 194: 'the most important causes of military intervention in politics are not military but political.' In his earlier work, Finer also maintained that military interference is largely regulated by - and inversely related to - what he called the degree of public attachment to civilian institutions or the 'level of political culture.' <u>The Man on Horseback</u>, chs. 7, 8 and 9. The genesis of the changing theoretical and methodological shifts in civil-military analysis are crystallised in Horowitz, D., <u>Coup Theories and Officers' Motives</u> (Princeton: Princeton University Press, 1980), pp. 31-33.

23. 'A Comparative Typology of Civil-Military Relations', p. 18.

24. <u>The Barrel of a Gun</u>, p. 436.

25. Eckstein, H., 'On the Etiology of Internal Wars', <u>History and Theory</u>, 4, 2 (June 1965), pp. 133-63.

26. Wider reference to the literature is made in especially the following three chapters. However, one early summary of 'causes' is provided in Welch, C.E., 'The Roots and Implications of Military Intervention', in his edited volume, <u>Soldier and State in Africa</u> (Evanston: Northwestern University Press, 1970), pp. 17-35. For quantitative analyses of coup causes see, for instance, Jackman, R.W., 'The Predictability of Coups d'Etat: A Model with African Data', <u>American Political Science Review</u>, 72, 4 (December 1978), pp. 1262-75; and Johnson, T.H., Slater, R.O. and McGowan, P., 'Explaining African Military Coups d'Etat, 1960-1982', <u>American Political Science Review</u>, 78, 3 (September 1984), pp. 622-40.

27. Lefever, E.W., <u>Sword and Scepter</u> (Washington, D.C.: Brookings Institution, 1970), pp. 28-9.

28. Kirkpatrick, E.M., 'The Impact of the Behavioural Approach on Traditional Political Science', in Ranny, A. (ed.), <u>Essays on the Behavioural Study of Politics</u> (Boston, D.C.: Heath, 1962), p. 12.

29. Jackman, R.W., 'Politicians in Uniform: Military Governments and Social Change in the Third World', <u>American Political Science Review</u>, 70, 4 (December 1976), pp. 1078-97.

30. First, <u>The Barrel of a Gun</u>, p. 17.

31. Pinkney, R., <u>Ghana Under Military Rule 1966-1969</u> (London: Methuen, 1972), p. ix.

32. Price, R., 'A Theoretical Approach to Military Rule in New States: Reference-Group

Theory and the Ghanaian Case', World Politics, 23, 3 (April 1971), p. 407.

33. Ibid., p. 427.

34. Finer, The Man on Horseback, p. 191.

35. See, for instance, the whole-issue survey, 'From Authoritarian to Representative Government in Brazil and Argentina', edited by Ionescu, G., Government and Opposition, 19, 2 (June 1984).

36. Finer, 'The Retreat to the Barracks', pp. 16-30. The reader is also presented with a novel and arresting proposition in which Finer argues that 'even feeble institutionalisation implies that the military has retreated from its ruling position.' (p. 18). The case hangs of course on Finer's own definition of institutionalisation and his distinction between an institutionalised 'military regime' (the soldiers put their men in power - but themselves relapse into a support role) and stratocracies (unadulterated military regimes, with neither parties nor legislatures, in which the state is directly ruled by a small group of officers).

37. A classic case of conditional withdrawal was Flight-Lt. Jerry Rawlings's handover to Ghana's President Limann on 24 September 1979. Addressing Limann at the ceremony inaugurating the Third Republic, Rawlings articulated his 'fervent hope that you will develop sensitivity to the tenets of the revolution.' Earlier in the speech, he had cautioned: 'You must be prepared to do justice to all our people. The whole nation is watching you.' Ghanaian Times (Accra), 25 September 1979. Rawlings has the distinction of being the only man in Africa who has overthrown both a military and a civilian regime, all in the space of 30 months. Matatu, G., 'Ghana - the future in another country', Africa, 126 (February 1982), p. 13. For a more comprehensive discussion of demilitarisation in Ghana, see Baynham, S.J., 'Divide et Impera: Civilian Control of the Military in Ghana's Second and Third Republics', Journal of Modern African Studies (forthcoming 1986).

38. Cape Times (Cape Town), 12 March 1985.

39. Perlmutter, A., The Military and Politics in Modern Times (New Haven: Yale University Press, 1977), pp. 104-14.

40. Colombia, Mexico and Venezuela provide the handful of exceptions where civilian successor regimes have lasted beyond a decade.

41. Adekanye, J., 'The Politics of the Post - Military State in Africa', in Clapham, C. and

Philip, G. (eds.), <u>The Political Dilemmas of Military Regimes</u> (London: Croom Helm, 1985), pp. 64, 76-77. The central thesis of his chapter 'is that prior intervention breaks down the previous boundaries between the "civil" and "military", tilts the parallelogram of social forces towards the military side, and makes subsequent interventions more and more difficult to resist.' (p. 87).

42. This military imperative is given wider treatment in Ralston, D.B., <u>Soldiers and States: Civil-Military Relations in Modern Europe</u> (Boston, N.J.: Heath & Co., 1966), pp. vii-viii.

43. Finer, <u>The Man on Horseback</u>, p. 6.

44. Nordlinger, <u>Soldiers in Politics</u>, p. 11.

45. Huntington, S.P., <u>The Soldier and the State</u> (New York: Random House, 1957).

46. Ibid., p. 83.

47. Nordlinger, <u>Soldiers in Politics</u>, pp. 15-19; Luckham, 'A Comparative Typology of Civil-Military Relations', pp. 23-24.

48. van Doorn, J., 'Political Change and the Control of the Military', in van Doorn, J. (ed.), <u>Military Profession and Military Regimes</u> (The Hague: Mouton, 1970), p. 13.

49. Huntington, <u>The Soldier and the State</u>, p. 84.

50. Nordlinger, <u>Soldiers in Politics</u>, pp. 13, 18. But as Finer has noted in <u>The Man on Horseback</u> (p. 15), the problem with the objective model is that the army might accept the formula, then distinguish between the good of the state and the performance of a particular government. Professionalism may then actually lead to armed intervention. See, too, Janowitz, <u>The Military in the Political Development of New Nations</u>, whose discussion on the subject (pp. 63-67) underlines the narrow and 'essentialist' definition of professionalism expounded by Huntington.

51. 'Wars of liberation are the almost inevitable result of a refusal to decolonise ... Such wars provide the clearest possible basis for a nationalist alliance between the urban intelligentsia and an often exploited peasantry ... [but] Guerrilla warfare does not automatically produce a revolution.' Clapham, C., <u>Third World Politics: An Introduction</u> (London: Croom Helm, 1985), p. 164.

52. Such revolutionary armies should, in turn, be differentiated from the avowedly radical armies that have seized power after independence in countries like Burkina Faso and Ethiopia.

53. Welch, C.E., 'Emerging Patterns of Civil-Military Relations in Africa: Radical Coups d'Etat and Political Stability', in Arlinghaus, B.E. (ed.), African Security Issues: Sovereignty, Stability and Solidarity (Boulder, Colorado: Westview, 1984), p. 127.

54. For a deeper understanding of the issues that made this mutual antagonism so difficult to overcome, see Cilliers, J.K., Counter-Insurgency in Rhodesia (London: Croom Helm, 1985).

55. Perlmutter, A., The Military and Politics in Modern Times (New Haven: Yale University Press, 1977), p. 115.

56. Seegers, A., 'The Development of the Armed Forces in Mozambique', paper read at a symposium on The Implications of Ideological and Institutional Change in Angola and Mozambique, Institute for the study of Marxism, Stellenbosch University, 12 October 1984, p. 4.

57. Frankel, P.H., Pretoria's Praetorians: Civil-Military Relations in South Africa (London: Cambridge University Press, 1984), p. 82.

58. Midlane, M., 'South Africa', in Keegan, J. (ed.) World Armies (London: MacMillan, 1983), pp. 525-26, 530. According to one South African report, 'by mobilizing all its reserves at once the Defence Force would have about 404,500 trained men.' Cape Times (Cape Town), 19 December 1984.

59. Jenkins, S., 'Destabilization in Southern Africa', The Economist, 16 July 1983, p. 28.

60. Sunday Times (Johannesburg), 10 November 1985.

61. Baynham, S.J., 'Interview with Major-General Georg Meiring, General Officer Commanding SWA/Namibia', Indicator South Africa (Political Monitor), Vol. 3, No. 3 (Summer 1985), p. 15. Independent estimates of these strengths have an overall consistency and are not thus in dispute. For a recent analysis of the SADF in Namibia, see Toase, F., 'The South African Army: The Campaign in South West Africa/Namibia since 1966', in Beckett, F.W. and Pimlott, J. (eds.), Armed Forces and Modern Counter-Insurgency (London: Croom Helm, 1985), pp. 190-221.

62. Quoted by MacKenzie, J.M., The Partition of Africa (London: Methuen, 1983), p. 1.

63. Consider, for instance, Lord Salisbury's words following the signing of the Anglo-French Convention of 1890: 'We have been engaged in drawing lines upon a map where no whiteman's foot ever trod; we have been giving away mountains

and rivers and lakes to each other, only hindered by the small impediment that we never knew exactly where the mountains and rivers and lakes were.' Asiwaju, A.I., 'The Berlin Centenary: 2', West Africa, 4 March 1985, p. 417.

64. Quoted in Goldthorpe, J.E., The Sociology of the Third World (London: Cambridge University Press, 1975), p. 257.

65. Economic and strategic factors in East-West rivalry are discussed in greater detail by Aluko, O., 'African Response to External Intervention in Africa Since Angola', African Affairs, 80, 319 (April 1981), pp. 159-79.

66. Zartman, W.I., 'Africa and the West: The French Connection', in Arlinghaus, African Security Issues, p. 40. In his analysis, Zartman introduces a geopolitical framework of French interests and activities based on three zones: Active, Passive and Mixed.

67. Pateman, R., 'The Role of Western Intelligence Services in Nation Building, Africa, 1952-1984,' paper read to the eighth annual conference of the African Studies Association of Australia and the Pacific, Australian National University, 24-26 August 1985, p. 6.

68. In a variant of training assistance using the territory of a third party, groups of Mozambican officers and NCOs began a series of British-run short courses in Zimbabwe in January 1986.

69. The question of 'developing' states' leverage in this respect is discussed by Kolodziej, E.A. and Harkavy, R.E., 'Developing States and Regional and Global Security', in Kolodziej and Harkavy, (eds.), Security Policies of Developing Countries (Lexington: D.C. Heath & Co., 1982), pp. 353-4.

70. A convoy was handed over by SADF drivers to the Zimbabwean National Army at Beit Bridge, to be taken to Mutare's border post for the Mozambican security forces. Cape Times (Cape Town), 20 June 1985. South African interventions are not included in the Hughes/May chapter since they are dealt with by Spence (and, to a lesser extent, by Seegers).

71. Clapham, Third World Politics, pp. 115-16.

72. Baynham, S.J., 'Praetorian Politics and the Benin Raid', The Army Quarterly and Defence Journal, 107, 4 (October, 1977), pp. 422-34.

73. Orwa, D.K., 'National Security: An African Perspective', in Arlinghaus, African Security Issues, p. 208.

74. See, for instance, many of the chapters in Eide, A. and Thee, M. (eds.), Problems of Contemporary Militarism (London: Croom Helm, 1980), especially the respective contributions by Signe Landgren-Bäckström, 'Arms Trade and Transfer of Military Technology to Third World Countries', and Miles Wolpin, 'Arms Transfers and Dependency in the Third World.'

75. For details, see Stockholm International Peace Research Institute, Armaments or Disarmament? (Stockholm: SIPRI, 1984), p. 26.

76. Landgren-Bäckström, S., 'Arms Trade and Transfer of Military Technology', p. 231.

77. US Arms Control and Disarmament Agency, World Military Expenditures and Arms Transfers, 1985 (Washington, D.C.: US Arms Control and Disarmament Agency, 1985), p. 43.

78. Baynham, S.J., 'On Praetorianism - A Note with Reference to South Africa', Social Dynamics, 11, 1 (June 1985), p. 85.

79. The OAU is not in any case united on many issues and some African states do not belong to the organisation at all. Zaire, for example, has left the OAU and has launched its own plan for a league of black African states, excluding the Arab countries of the continent.

Chapter Two

MILITARY RULE IN AFRICA: ETIOLOGY AND MORPHOLOGY

Samuel Decalo

INTRODUCTION

Nearly two decades ago Zolberg made his gloomy observation that the most striking patterns in independent Africa were those of conflict and instability.[1] Soon after, another scholar noted 64 instances of unrest and upheaval since decolonisation.[2] More recently, in assessing the record of 25 years of independence, *West Africa* noted that 'nowhere, apart from Mauritius in 1982, has a ruling party been voted out of office in an election ... change has happened for the most part through military intervention, either by straight *coup d'état* in numerous countries, or by popular demonstrations of the kind that have obliged the military to intervene'.[3]

Capable yet of rivalling Latin America's record of instability (over 1,100 coups in 180-odd years) the *coup d'état* has become for much of Africa the functional equivalent of elections, and military rule the most common modality of governance. At any particular moment in time, over 40 per cent of the continent is under military administration and - given Nigeria's record of instability - well over 60 per cent of its population. For better or for worse, the military sociology of Africa has become a dominant sub-field within African studies, itself rivetted to issues related to stability and instability, civil-military relations and military rule.

A truly voluminous literature has developed as scholars have attempted to come to grips with the phenomenon of the Man on Horseback (or more properly, Colonels on Command Cars) and the salient characteristics of military rule. Yet much of this academic out-pouring, whether based on theoretical, statistical or empirical analysis of the roots of instability in Africa, is often mutually contradictory and lacking in predictive powers, foundering as it does against an empirical reality resilient to easy generalisation. Zolberg's early conclusion that 'it is impossible to specify as a class countries where coups have occurred from others which so far have been spared'[4] appears paradoxically still very much valid today even though, as Finer notes, 'the causes, courses, and immediate consequences of the military coup have been reasonably well established'.[5]

Coups, however popular, seemingly 'justifiable', and bloodless (as most are in Africa), are sharp extra-legal seizures of power backed by the threat of force and triggered by specific considerations.[6] Coups do not erupt without reason, though their true causes may at times be difficult to perceive, or appear petty in relation to the dramatic sequence of events they set into motion, and the societal forces they may unleash. And even when the *coup d'état* does not appear to change much in society, by its very occurrence - if not by any specific policy embarked upon by the new junta - it does bring about a fundamental rearray of civil and military power with profound systemic implications for the future.

Coups, at inception, are secretive, selective and limited conspiracies. The original core clique cannot involve the entire officer corps in the plot, and frequently does not wish to do so, since the rebellion oftentimes is also against a segment of the military leadership. Success, which is quite easy in relatively weak, unstructured African states, catapults to power a junta that may not be - and often is not - the most senior in rank, shattering the formal military hierarchy and power balance. It is this clique and its allies, rather than 'the military' (a reification of a corporate structure) that emerges in power, sets policy and constitutes the core of the 'military regime'. Moreover, the rise to prominence of a military junta - even if they establish collegial rule - of necessity spawns personal grievances and a host of intra-military rivalries - that - again within societies that cannot easily contain strife - tend to manifest themselves in the form of subsequent military upheavals. Knowledge of the precise composition, predisposition and the overt and covert coup motivations of the original conspirators is thus an important first step in any analysis of the military regime that ensues. A fundamental overview of the etiology of military coups is a necessary prerequisite to any analysis of military rule in Africa.

THE ETIOLOGY OF MILITARY COUPS

Early assessments of the conditions encouraging military seizures of power traditionally stressed the structural weaknesses of African states as the key explanatory variable. Though scholars varied in assigning priority and weight, the immediate and specific 'causes' of coups in Africa were usually seen as stemming from two conditions: (1) the various failings of civilian leadership set against the context of, *inter alia*, the destabilising effects of social mobilisation, ethnic pluralism and rapid modernisation;[7] and (2) the professional and organisational characteristics of African military hierarchies that allegedly sharpen their motivations to usurp political power from civilian elites.

The first school of thought stressed the failure in office of antecedent civilian elites against a socio-economic background of stresses and strains of weak political systems. Huntington summarised the underlying assumptions of this approach when he categorically declared that 'the most important causes of military intervention in politics *are not military* but political, and reflect not the social and organizational characteristics of the military establishment but the political and institutional structures of society'.[8] Or, as another scholar put it slightly differently, 'in every country, the issues which best account for the ease of military access to power relate to economic circumstances and their social consequences'.[9] Despite a revisionist trend in the structuralist school, the approach has remained more or less intact. Perlmutter, writing as recently as 1982, was to note that 'political interventionism ... is an effort (mostly unsuccessful) by the military institution to surrogate for absent or politically underdeveloped regulative instruments'.[10]

If armies intervene in political voids occasioned by societal strains and stresses to correct, or compensate for, failings of civilian rule, then their motivations are instrinsically altruistic, and their subsequent political role essentially positive. The military is perceived from this vantage point to be reacting, unwillingly, to societal conditions that call for firmer and more astute leadership, and succour from rapacious or inept civilian politicians. The purpose of the coup is 'to accomplish mission impossible - create stability, order and legitimacy'.[11]

The second school of thought, lodged in organisational theory, stressed that African armies possess certain attitudinal traits and characteristics that impel them to enter the political centre-stage. Idealised as conforming to the Western model of apolitical military forces, African armies were seen as their society's most modern, unified, non-ethnic structures, inculcated with an *esprit de corps* and the values of self-effacement, nationalism, professionalism, duty, patriotism, etc.[12] Despite a similar commitment to an apolitical role under the supremacy of civilian control, African armies are driven to rebel against inept or corrupt civilian governments out of a sense of patriotic pride and duty, aware that they can provide more effective government.

Here even more there is a very clear-cut, positive underlying assumption about the attributes and characteristics of military hierarchies, and by extension about the likely benefits of rule under such enlightened and dedicated soldiers. Moreover, since the military has the monopoly of coercive power (while civilian elites only have access to it through their control of the military), military rule may even be seen as possibly the most appropriate for societies in the process of modernisation, where democratisation has to take a back seat (being a costly luxury) in conditions of instability and underdevelopment. As Marion Levy cogently put it, the military is the organisation best capable of 'combining maximum rates of modernization with maximum levels of stability and control'.[13] A very prevalent viewpoint in the 1950s and 1960s in Latin American studies, when transferred to the study of Africa, 'so self evident did the virtues of soldiers seem that two scholars appeared dismayed that armies in Black Africa were too small to overturn their governments should the latter fail'.[14]

Though both approaches are quite distinct in terms of fundamental assumptions and emphases, in concrete analyses of specific coup situations, the differences tended to blur. The early academic consensus was, therefore, that coups arose out of a host of structural weaknesses and/or failings of antecedent civilian regimes that triggered a largely reactive intervention by patriotic, apolitical and relatively unified national armies willing to 'clean up the mess'.

Needless to say most of the academic perceptions of the failings of civilian elites and the structural weaknesses of African states closely mirrored actual military indictments of the civilian regimes being toppled. There thus appeared to be a close (and gratifying) congruity between scholarly analyses and military justifications for intervention. Against a destabilising background of social mobilisation, mass-elite gaps, low political institutionalisation etc., patriotic military hierarchies were moving to oust inept or authoritarian civilian regimes that were either corrupt, politically paralysed, ethnically biased, overly ideological or attempting to jeopardise the corporate autonomy of the armed forces - failings meticulously enumerated by several scholars.[15]

The facile conceptualisations of the 1960s faded as a healthier pessimism (by now maybe even overdone) seeped in about the inevitability and unidimensionality of the developmental process, hitherto very ethnocentrically and unidirectionally defined. More recently, an increased awareness of the myth-reality syndrome of African politics[16] similarly brought about a shift in emphases and a re-examination of fundamental premises. A more empirical analysis of the internal dynamics of African military hierarchies, coupled with a more critical and meticulous examination of overt and covert military motivations in specific coup situations, eroded much of the determinism of the structural approach, and completely discredited theories of military intervention stressing organisational theory. And as the actual record and long-term heritage of military rule began to be assessed in a more critical fashion, old quasi-predeterministic assumptions about the *necessarily* positive contributions of military rule were largely laid to rest.

Structural explanations for instability, useful as they are in pin-pointing fundamental sources of stress in 'developing' countries, often throw very little light on what are basically personal and/or power relationships. At most they may provide partial explanations and insights on the societal background that might encourage military upheavals. Previous conceptualisations of African armies, coups and military rule have largely been developed in an empirical vacuum as extensions of analyses of other geographical regions or as adjuncts to 'grand theory' by scholars with primarily theoretical credentials. But coups may in reality have very simple *behavioural* origins and motivations quite independent of other societal conditions, or in tandem with them. Structural explanations for systemic instability cannot, and should not, be ignored: to do so would suggest lack of causal relationships between societal characteristics and social action, even total randomness of social phenomena - theoretical and empirical improbabilities if not impossibilities. But as Africanists and African field work came of age, a greater awareness developed of human motives in power-contexts; motives, it should be noted, given their due and commonly ascribed to civilian politicians, but hitherto denied to their more 'saintly' military counterparts.

All African states may be seen as afflicted with most of the systemic weaknesses allegedly creating coup conditions. Scarcity, corruption, ethnic rivalry, low levels of political institutionalisation, stresses of modernisation etc., are found in virtually every African country even if in differing doses and combinations. They often form, however, the backdrop against which the civil-military drama unfolds, not the triggering causes. Otherwise disenchantment with civilian rule should have resulted in military upheavals long before 1975 in Chad, 1974 in Niger, 1966 in Ghana, 1979 in Equatorial Guinea and 1984 in Guinea - to cite but a few instances - and maybe not at all in some states where coups indeed did erupt.[17]

Conceptually many African armies were at independence little more than structural umbrellas only loosely and superficially encompassing a multiplicity of internally divided, feuding, armed camps, each owing primary clientelist allegiance to a number of mutually antagonistic officers of different (and not necessarily senior) rank. Within this semi-praetorian[18] setting an assault on civilian authority may indeed be an actual attempt by a sincere military junta to set the ship of state on an even keel; but it could also be nothing more than (1) a power grab for societal plunder or status; (2) the 'resolution' of some intra-military personal or corporate rivalry by the seizure of the ultimate fount of authority - the state; and (3) a pre-emptive 'strike' by a threatened or aggrieved faction or soldier. A few concrete examples might be in order.

On 25 January 1971, General Idi Amin seized power in Kampala, publishing an 18-point *J'accuse* against the government of President Milton Obote, that was for some time taken at face value by many observers. Virtually every single one of the accusations against Obote's regime could not be disputed, but none to any degree truly formed the motivation for the coup. Although the general malaise in Uganda may have suggested that Obote's overthrow might be popular in many circles, Amin's takeover was a classic 'pre-emptive' strike by an officer facing imminent dismissal and imprisonment on a host of charges from embezzlement to murder and possibly high treason.[19] Purely personal considerations (fear) triggered the coup, and the utterly sterile, murderous and rudderless eight years that followed were but a natural consequence of a coup with no ulterior or societal goals.

Similar coups, though without the same devastating consequences, have occurred in many other states. In the Central African Republic, the New Year's Day 1966 coup of Jean-Bedel Bokassa had strong personalist overtones (ambition, vanity) within the context of an internal power rivalry between him and the chief of the police and a society weary with the inept leadership of David Dacko.[20] The coups of 1966 and 1968 in Ghana and Mali respectively, included very powerful corporate rivalries and purely intra-military antagonisms stemming from the erection and better treatment accorded to ancillary armed formations (the President's Own Guard Regiment and the popular militia); and in the case of Ghana also, frustration with the demeaning 'non-British' manner President Nkrumah was treating his officer corps.[21] In coup-prone Dahomey (after 1974 Benin), most military upheavals, successful or not, have had roots in personal power conflicts and ambitions, hurt pride and intra-military rivalries within the officer corps. The published rationalisations have usually been *ex post facto* justifications. And in Chad the army overthrew the long established authoritarian, corrupt and politically inept regime of Ngarta Tombalbaye only after a purge of the military threatened careers of officers who did not wish early retirement.

An empirical examination of the internal dynamics of African military hierarchies, and a much more critical analysis of formal justifications for coups, thus reveals a bewildering array of very strong personal and corporate motivations for power grabs, that supplement, or are camouflaged beneath, the more noble justifications offered by coup leaders. Jackman's recent statistical work indicating a moderate (20 per cent) effect of 'idiosyncratic variables' (as I have phrased it elsewhere)[22] on military coups, is a very welcome attempt at statistical examinations of behavioural motivations in what have been hitherto largely structural equations of stability and instability.[23] The correlation, it can be argued however, could have been much higher - as empirical research by those engaged in field work suggests - were all the relevant variables adequately identified, isolated and quantified for analytical purposes, which they were not in Jackman's design, where they formed instead an amorphous non-empirical 'residual' element to specific enumerated structural variables.

Official pronouncements by military juntas about their 'reluctant' reaction to conditions of socio-economic decay are no longer accepted uncritically since they have been clearly observed on numerous instances to intervene in the political process as prime actors on their own corporate behalf. Indeed, in a number of countries military unrest itself has been the prime destablising variable, not socio-economic stress. No longer saints immune to temptations of power, prestige, or money - nor that indifferent to the pulls of greed, fear, hate and the quest for revenge - armies are now no longer reified as eiptomising the best in society.

Slowly, even reluctantly, African armies began to be perceived for what they were: relatively malintegrated structures, frequently internally fractured on a multiplicity of planes, mirroring society's own cleavages, and often seething with a host of personal intra-military rivalries and/or civil-military tensions that, given the proper pretext (different in each country), could erupt in the form of a power grab to be *ex post facto* rationalised in a manner more flattering to the military junta assuming power.

Viewed from what may be termed a 'realpolitik' perspective, some African militaries are indeed responding to the crisis of civilian leadership (a fact that should not be lost sight of either!); but others are opportunistically utilising it.

The task of the scholar is to separate the sheep from the goats, for the nature of the impetus to the Presidential House will axiomatically determine the nature and class interests of the policies that will emerge from the new regime. Thus the *coup d'état*, a 'short-circuit of power-conflicts in a situation where arms do the deciding',[24] becomes analytically a more complex political occurrence with multiple possible motivations and outcomes. A rephrasing of the no longer valid Huntingtonian maxim would read: *purely* military considerations and motivations - corporate, parochial and personal - are *always* present in African military upheavals to different degrees their unfettered expression and successful execution is assisted by the multitude of structural and political weaknesses of African states.

AFRICAN ARMIES AND MILITARY COUPS

African armies never conformed even loosely to the ideal model of 'politically sterile and neutral' forces committed to the defence of the civil *status quo*,[25] if only due to their acute malintegrated composition and the myth of civil-military values transmitted to largely unlettered forces of coercion during the colonial era. Nor were African armies ever, for much the same reasons, complex organisational structures, the most Westernised, nationalist, non-ethnic ones in largely traditional parochial societies.

At inception African military forces were overwhelmingly recruited from among the more backward and/or 'martial' ethnic groups for whom a military career usually meant a measure of otherwise unattainable modern social status, economic security and upward mobility.[26] The troops were by definition forces of colonial control and repression (at home and in other colonies) and pools of military manpower for intra-European conflicts. While physical training tended to be arduous and the stress on instant obedience to command absolute, actual *military* training was spotty, materiel minimal and service conditions quite primitive and brutal.

The colonial powers expended little or no effort in the direction of either preparing indigenous leadership cadres (most actually barred Africans from crossing the NCO barrier at least until the 1950s) or building true cohesion in the colonial armies. Neither were seen as necessary, or for that matter advisable, from the colonial point of view. The forces were thus preponderantly headed by European officers and a pool of indigenous NCOs, with the latter frequently drawn from the more advanced (and/or minority) ethnic groups. The alleged *esprit de corps* of the colonial (and immediate post-independence) forces - propounded mostly by ex-colonial (i.e. metropolitan) military historians - was invariably the very much romanticised reification of the iron discipline on which colonial forces operated, perceived from the rarified stratosphere of the higher reaches of the expatriate officer corps. It was, moreover, this strict discipline, the bleak employment prospects in the civilian sphere, and the overt and covert benefits of military service, that kept the forces servile, rather than the effect of civic training and/or the inculcation of civil-military 'traditions' - the colonial myth to the contrary notwithstanding. (The latter in any case usually commenced only in the 1950s when independence was on the horizon).

The approach of independence shattered the military *status quo* - a fact not given sufficient stress - just as it transformed the entire political balance of power in each colony. It triggered nationalist pressures for at least a measure of Africanisation of the officer corps, a process many colonial officers resisted but could not stem. Other colonial officers, aware that they enjoyed much higher rank, status, and better terms of service abroad, and that decolonisation might lead to functional unemployment or premature retirement (if repatriated), began to 'adjust' to the realities of the emerging new order by supporting objectively unnecessary expansions of armed forces and/or major intakes of sophisticated materiel, both of which would require their continued presence beyond independence for technical and/or training reasons.[27] And with accountability shifting to indigenous elites much more sensitive to complaints from the ranks, decolonisation also meant a loosening of the tight (and summary) discipline of colonial forces and a certain 'democratisation' of the colonial 'old boys' informal decision-making process, and the military hierarchy. Since the armies were not in reality cohesive national units, these otherwise healthy military reforms actually spelled the beginning of the disintegration of whatever corporate integrity the forces ever had.

The post-independence African armies were thus indeed 'lineal descendants'[28] of colonial armies, but hardly the idealised cohesive and intrinsically loyal formations the literature sometimes suggests. And even then, their 'lineal descent' was only chronological, since the new national army that emerged bore little resemblance to the colonial force. (In French Africa the new armies were to a significant extent the demobilised, utterly unintegrated national segments of large colonial forces of repression, used in Algeria, Indo-China and elsewhere). And the tight discipline that kept colonial forces intact as instruments of social control was already breaking down, while Africanisation of the officer corps was introducing new inter-ethnic strains into the already malintegrated forces.

The first drives to recruit local personnel for the newly created and extremely well-paying officer-slots brought about a flood of candidates.[29] The relatively high (for that era) educational prerequisites stipulated assured, however, that the new officer-cadets tended to be drawn from an entirely different social and ethnic strata for whom only now had a military career become financially attractive compared to civilian (mostly commercial/administrative/technical) employment. Thus a major ethnic/regional split developed, separating the officer corps from the rank and file, remaining to this day potentially the most problematic source of tension and intra-military strife in many African states. While in some coutries (e.g. Nigeria) concerted efforts were mounted to create an ethnically balanced officer corps (without, it must be added, spectacular success), in many others this was either impossible (due to lack of interest or the educational criteria) or crassly negated by political favouritism of civilian elites packing the armed forces with their own kinsmen (e.g. Uganda).

Since decolonisation proceeded faster than originally anticipated, promotions to officerhood from the NCO ranks were necessary in order to assure at least token national control of the armed forces at independence. From these ranks emerged many of the first Chiefs of Staff of independent Africa. The rise of Christophe Soglo (Dahomey), Jean-Bedel Bokassa (Central African Republic) and Idi Amin (Uganda) are but a few instances where prolonged (10-20 years) experience as colonial NCOs temporarily replaced formal educational and technical qualifications due to the exigencies of the times. Whether the appointments ultimately turned out well (Soglo) or not (Amin, Bokassa), a second major strain was introduced in the budding indigenous officer corps, as destabilising internal rivalries were later to emerge between the 'intellectuals' (i.e. staff college and university graduates) and the 'peasants' (ex-NCOs), as they often referred to each other perjoratively.

After independence the process of localisation accelerated since very few nationalist elites could tolerate an army staffed with expatriate officers. Only 10-14 per cent of the officer corps of Ghana and Nigeria had been localised by independence, and the figure was even lower in some other countries such as Chad.[30] The exploding demand for staff academy officer-training slots, and the desire on the part of some African leaders to diversify ('decolonise') sources of military training and aid, resulted in the virtual internationalisation of some African armies and their materiel,[31] at times - as in Uganda and Ghana, but elsewhere too - to the detriment of the already fragile corporate integrity of the corps.

Moreover, the accelerated departure of expatriate military officers dramatically increased the number of leadership slots vacant, triggering consecutive waves of extraordinary promotions. The net result often was that young personnel moved from cadet status to senior command in the space of a few years; many 'first generation' officers (whether ex-NCO or academy graduates) certainly advanced from the rank of lieutenant, to colonel or higher in less than seven years (as opposed to a European norm of at least twelve) subject to suitability and/or passage of various training programmes. Heightened expectations of continued career advancement clashed, however, with the massive promotion bottlenecks that developed after the initial wave of Africanisation. With hardly any attrition, youthful officers seeking to emulate the meteoric rise of their predecessors faced slow and uncertain advance to higher ranks occupied by equally youthful personnel, all within miniscule armies precluding a multiplicity of senior posts. (In coup-prone states the rapid turnover of military staff consequent to post-coup purges 'assured' rapid professional advancement for second, even third generation officers who indeed might find themselves zooming up the ranks to be retired on full pension before the age of

49

40 - witness Nigeria!).

The net effect of these and a host of other factors was that very seriously malintegrated national armies frequently emerged on the ashes of equally unintegrated colonial forces. Already divided internally on a multiplicity of planes, the cleavages were aggravated, sharpened and politicised with the removal of the coercive 'social glue' (or 'integrative grid'[32]) of the colonial era, and attempts by insecure post-independence political elites to subvert the army's corporate autonomy and monopoly of force.

The basic cleavage in many African armies tends to be the ethnic one, much as the civilian tug-of-war also often manifests ethnic overtones. Stemming from pre-colonial rivalries exacerbated by differential modes of socio-economic reaction to, and advancement under, the colonial order,[33] ethnic sub-nationalism is at the root of much strife in Africa. Empirically visible in various intra-military rivalries in Africa (Benin, Congo-Brazzaville, Ghana, Uganda, Chad, Togo etc.), ethnic divisions exercise a 'strong linear destabilizing influence' in general as correlational analysis suggests,[34] with distinctions between civilian and military regimes hardly being salient insofar as socio-economic change is concerned.[35]

However, ethnicity and sub-nationalism subsume, camouflage or overlay, many other planes of division and sources of conflict in African armies; regionalism (where ethnicity is not the dominant cleavage); inter-generational tensions; educational cleavages (separating the largely illiterate rank and file from the officer corps, and the latter internally between the 'intellectuals' and the 'peasants'); ideological (between apolitical and/or Europhile elements and the politicised 'new' African officer, increasingly Afro-Marxist[36]). Even graduation from different foreign officer training academies has created major tensions in some armed forces, notably in the pre-1971 Ugandan army.[37]

Needless to say, not all African military forces were originally so acutely fragmented, though as Nordlinger noted in the late 1960s only one-third of the armies were ethnically balanced[38] - only one plane of division. In some countries the ethnic breakdown of the force resembled data drawn from completely different states, and the split between the officer corps and the rank and file was absolute. In the Sudan, for example, every single officer - in a complex multi-ethnic country - was northern, Moslem and Arab; in Dahomey over 80 per cent of the officer corps was southern, and over 80 per cent of the rank and file was northern; in Chad only two of the army's relatively large officer corps came from the northern two-thirds of the country (and 60 per cent of the population), while entire regiments were drawn from these ethnic groups.

Some independent states - whether or not inheriting relatively cohesive national armies - *appear* to have succeeded in containing the fissiparously destabilising tendencies of their military forces. The time-honoured practice of 'purchasing' the loyalty of the army by assuring officers and the rank and file adequate levels of finance, materiel, prestige and routinised promotions, certainly seems to have worked in some African states (e.g. Ivory Coast, Gabon) even if at the expense of scarce resources. Yet for every such quiescent army there are two others where these tactics have failed.

Moreover, as the military upheavals in Cameroon and the Gambia, and the coups in Guinea-Bissau and Guinea (until recently viewed as 'inherently stable') have strikingly illustrated, even existing images of loyalty and cohesion can be misleading. Assumptions about the allegedly stabilising effect of militant ideology (Guinea-Bissau), absence of military establishments (the Gambia) and a history of charismatic leadership need to be re-assessed as these and other military upheavals underscore.[39] The contemporary pattern of military stability and instability in Africa is so muddled, defying generalisation and theorising as in Zolberg's day, that probably all that really prevents the overthrow of many 'stable' civilian regimes (e.g. Senegal, Ivory Coast, Gabon) may be nothing more than the physical presence of French troops in these countries and/or the known commitment of France to the preservation in office of the existing civilian hierarchies - a subject discussed by David Goldsworthy elsewhere in this volume.

THE MORPHOLOGY OF MILITARY RULE

The implications of the foregoing analysis of African armies and the etiology of military coups is fundamental to an understanding of the morphology of military rule. Cause and effect, etiology and morphology, are axiomatically inter-related. The study of the characteristics of military rule cannot be divorced from the analysis of underlying motivations for the original seizure of power. The prevalence of diverse and multiple motives for military takeovers clearly implies that there will be dramatically different preoccupations and policy-priorities among military juntas once in office. Political power will obviously be used for different purposes and with different goals depending in part upon the reasons for which it was sought. And while objective socio-economic limitations such as scarcity of resources, neo-colonial relationships, underdevelopment etc., may well stultify reformist efforts of well-intentioned coup-leaders, to juntas catapulted to power with less altruistic motives, they will only serve as *ad hoc* rationalisations for mediocre performance.

Since idiosyncratic factors (personal and corporate) play such an important role in triggering many coups, then the identification of political systems especially afflicted by conditions encouraging upheaval becomes quite problematic, if only because all are susceptible and none truly immune - as has already been noted. Moreover since military juntas at times seize power not so much to 'tidy up the mess' but rather to feather and protect their personal or corporate nest, the most common characteristic of military rule is likely to be preoccupation with the army's own narrow class-interests, and only secondarily the amelioration of the various failings of the antecedent regime. In this self-seeking orientation and opportunistic utilisation of political power, military regimes are quite similar to their civilian counterparts, further sustaining contentions and statistical correlations suggesting that the differences between the two and their ultimate mark on society is not systemically very different.[40] As one observer put it bluntly, 'the simple civil-military government distinction appears to be of little use in the explanation of social change ... military governments have no unique effect on social change, regardless of level of economic development'.[41] Finally, since so many African armies are internally fragmented along the lines previously outlined, the coups, just by upsetting the inertia of the command hierarchy *status quo*, are quite likely to set loose highly destabilising praetorian impulses.

Early expectations of dynamic, progressive and efficient rule from military leadership, anchored as they were in the by now discredited idealisations of the corporate characteristics of African armies, have largely disappeared. Occasionally analysts may still see merit and utility in that military juntas at least possess 'organizational characteristics of coercion', necessary corollaries of effective government in multi-cleavaged societies.[42] Yet though it is obvious that direct control of the means of coercion may be marginally more functional than indirect control (as in a civilian regime) especially in turbulent societies (e.g. Zaire, CAR, Congo-Brazzaville etc.), deriving from this expectations of social-economic change under military auspices is both myopic and in opposition to empirical evidence. Coercive power can be used for the securement of different goals. The military regimes of Doe (Liberia), Amin (Uganda), Kountché (Niger), Sankara (Burkina Faso), Mobutu (Zaire), Buhari (Nigeria) and Rawlings (Ghana) are simply not comparable even though all possess(ed) coercive powers.

What then are the salient characteristics of military rule in Africa? *West Africa* - despite its usually rosy outlook on Anglophone military regimes - cogently summed it by noting that

> the truth that has been demonstrated again and again in Africa (and elsewhere, going back to ancient Rome) is that military men rarely make good rulers. Power corrupts them as quickly as it corrupts others; ... the bankruptcy of their ideas becomes painfully obvious. Soldiers are trained to kill people, not govern them; sensitivity and subtlety do not thrive in the barracks.[43]

As already noted in its overall systemic effect (whatever its other more superficial peculiarities) military rule is not significantly different, nor necessarily better or worse than civilian rule. In any specific country a shift from military authority (or vice versa) may indeed result in profound change, either good or bad. But if assessed across a whole spectrum of states experiencing military governance, existing empirical evidence suggests little significant differentiation. This is by definition a negative verdict or assessment of the role of the military, since armed forces theoretically move into the political centre stage to correct civilian misrule.

The equally mediocre (or more properly speaking, undistinguished) performance of military rule stems - apart from the general factors suggested by *West Africa* above - from (1) the nature of the covert motivations for the military takeover that might not have been reformist to start with, and (2) the far greater role of external factors in promoting or retarding socio-economic change and development in essentially weak unicrop states.

If inspirations for coups are not primarily reformist and the army is catapulted to power out of parochial and/or particularistic considerations, little change is likely to occur in those areas of direct concern to most citizens. This is not to imply that such military administrations will necessarily be purely retrogressive. Much good did stem out of the early leadership of Eyadema in Togo, and even Mobutu's in Zaire, where a balance was briefly struck between the corporate (and personal) interests of the ruling clique and the national interests. Still, it is a cardinal rule in politics (if not in all social relations) that each group tends to look after its own interests above all else; thus it should not be surprising that in every instance that the miltiary has come to power - irrespective of the nature of the motivation - virtually the first issue that tends to capture their attention involves increases in the size of the armed forces and its budget, military salaries, fringe benefits and new materiel - even when the absence of fiscal stringency and improper setting of national priorities constituted the butt of the criticism leading to the overthrow of the antecedent government.^{44} Needless to say, a self-seeking military leadership unaccountable to anyone, will promote its interests above all else. If venal (Zaire) or brutal (Amin's Uganda) enough, it can bring a nation to its knees economically.

As noted before, a significant number of the coups and attempted coups in Africa have had such particularistic motivations, resulting consequently in uninspiring and self-centred leadership. Reference has already been made to Amin's coup in Uganda that, despite its 18-point critique of civilian rule, was nothing more than a preemptive act of self-defence of a military leader (Amin) who knew little, cared not at all and subsequently did nothing whatsoever about Uganda's pressing socio-economic problems. Indeed,

Amin's brutal nine year reign left nothing but massive social and economic devastation and dislocation that taxed the resources of the successor Obote regime until its own collapse in July 1985.

The 1966 coup in the Central African Republic stemmed from Bokassa's ambitions, vanity and ennui within the stagnant backwaters of Bangui, set against the background of intra-military rivalry between him and the police chief. Military rule, stemming from such motivations could hardly be expected to be progressive. And indeed after Bokassa consolidated his rule and grew tired of his boring role as a statesman, the state was harnassed to provide the stage against which his flights of fancy could be enacted, culminating in his Napoleonic-style coronation.[45]

Not all personalist coups have such colourful motives and/or outcomes, though all tend to be socially arid, intellectually sterile and programmatically venal. In pre-revolutionary Dahomey (Benin) much of the military unrest and most of the coups stemmed from personalist rivalries and/or ambitions. The principal coup-maker at the time - Colonel Maurice Kouandété - when interviewed in 1971 could not name a single specific policy, innovation or reform that he had in mind at the time of his former power gambits except for a vaguely expressed need for 'strong' government, unfortunately associated in his mind with the venal regime of Mobutu in Zaire.

In Ghana - both in 1966 and 1972 - mixed motives underlay the coups sponsored by Harlley/Kotoka and Acheampong respectively, explaining their preoccupations, sins of omission and commission and subsequent negative assessments of their years in office. The military was catapulted to power in Sierre Leone in 1967 solely due to personal rivalries at the head of the force, resulting in sophomoric and contradictory justifications for the takeover; not surprisingly, little of import resulted from the muddled leadership that percolated into office. Lieutenant Moussa Traoré's own 17-year rather uninspiring tenure as Head of State in Mali owes its origins to ugly competitions within the military and a tug-of-war with the militia, erected by Modibo Keita as a bulwark against the army. One might even question Sergeant Samuel Doe's true motivations in toppling the Americo-Liberian political dynasty in Liberia. Though the upheaval had very legitimate societal goals, nothing since the 'revolution' has been aimed at either alleviating Liberia's socio-economic plight or restructuring the internal array of power between the various population groups. Virtually all policy coming our of Monrovia seems to underscore the manner in which the 'revolution' in Liberia was perverted or sidetracked by the emergence of personalist ambitions on the part of Doe himself.[46]

The second factor that militates against a more positive military performance in political office is the objective weakness of African states and African regimes (civil and military) that prevents much internal change even by reformist military administrations. While many military regimes came to power on the wake of significant popular acclaim, and some remained relatively untainted after exposure to political office, very few may be said to have either attained their self-defined goals, or to have passed on to successor civilian administrations a truly healthy socio-economic heritage.

Corruption is a cogent case in point since it is by far the most common complaint raised against civilian regimes being overthrown. Often striking is the helplessness and timidity of even reform-minded military administrations faced with inherited cesspools of corruption. Despite forcefully-enunciated commitments, popular support, and a free hand to punish the culprits of yesteryear, few military regimes in actual fact undertake thorough purges of society. Every Nigerian and Ghanaian coup, for example, has had as its prime goal the elimination of deeply ingrained corruption from society; yet not one military administration has made truly consistent efforts in that direction, scored significant inroads against the insidious social malady, or for that matter remained immune to it itself.

The Acheampong administration made much ado about corruption when it came to power; but in reality its concern was primarily with having been by-passed in the original distribution of largesse by the preceeding army-police regime (for which it amply compensated for once in office). The latter, despite its original acclaim in toppling Nkrumah, and popular support for a clean sweep of the corruption that had permeated society under Nkrumah, attained extremely modest results; and by the time it handed over power to civilian authority it was itself increasingly the subject of corruption scandals. Jerry Rawlings's meteoric rise to power and crusade against corruption during his first brief tenure, chopped a few heads but left the monster alive; and during his current stint in office the eradication of corruption, still rampant, has had to take a back seat to more threatening economic maladies plaguing Ghana.

Anti-corruption drives under military auspices have proven to be too socially traumatic, destabilising, time-consuming and very often self-incriminating.[47] And it should be remembered that all African states have very weak regulative and administrative capabilities, the image of omnipotence sometimes projected notwithstanding. Their real ability to implement and/or monitor policy and/or change is quite limited. Military forces are modest; the number of officers 'seconded' to political duties is very small (one major exception being the NRC/SMC regime in Ghana between 1972 and 1979) and basic policy preoccupations demands their attention, while the power, pull and social function of 'dash' is too ingrained. Consequently even regimes that come to power on the wake of anti-corruption planks are forced to be content with merely publicising the sins of the previous regime rather than in mass punishment, and certainly not in the elimination of the phenomenon.

Many military regimes 'forgive and forget' rather than arouse animosities and threaten the social strata (civil service; police) vital to their remaining in office. In Chad, despite token rhetoric, the Malloum government did not even identify or shunt from office the most notorious plunderers of billions of CFA francs of state funds or of the international drought relief programme. In Ghana, after all the publicity about the corruption of the Nkrumah administration, the end result of over three years of activity by the Ankrah/Afrifa administration was less than 200 convictions. The only exception to this spotty record of military rule seems to be the current mass trials in Ouagadougou of virtually every participant in the country's preceding civilian and military administrations; yet here the purpose is cathartic, educational and ideological - while corruption has seeped into the new regime itself even as it purges members of the old one.

As *West Africa* has put it, 'the sins of the politicians [find] their way into the military regimes'[48] with corruption permeating the most pristine military government, and swamping the already tainted. In two of the more recent military regimes - Guinea and Burkina Faso - nepotism and accumulation of wealth commenced the very day the officer hierarchy took office. Less than six months after the Burkinabé revolution, the first military personnel were being hauled in on a host of offences - at the height of mass public trials of members of the preceding governments, vividly underscoring the one thread running through all Ouagadougou administrations. In Guinea, less than a year after the historic 1984 coup in Conakry the Conté regime, staffed by 'people in hurry for personal gains'[49] finally having their day in the sun, was thoroughly discredited; administration was soft-pedalling the punishment of the key figures of the Touré regime, granting pardons and self-exile to those formerly convicted of theft, embezzlement, mismanagmeent and/or human rights offices.

In Mauritania, to take yet another recent example, Ould Haidallah was toppled in December 1984 because of the 'alarming proportion' of corrupt personnel in his government; he himself had been involved in the overthrow of the antecedent Mauritanian regime in July 1978 for much the same reason, which in turn had toppled its antecedent again on charges of corruption![50]

As with corruption, so in matters relating to socio-economic development military regimes have proven to be largely undistinguished. The slight amelioration of conditions at times visible at the outset of military rule usually turns out to be transitory - a result of procedural, fiscal and administrative caution and greater accountability in the immediate aftermath of coups. This plus belt-tightening, some elimination of waste, voluntary civic labour etc., are very important in setting the tone of new administrations, but seldom are they the solution to fundamental social and economic problems which military regimes are very rarely capable of providing. The very simple biting of the economic bullet - Draconian fiscal and foreign exchange measures such as introduced by Rawlings in Ghana (including the 'Holy War'[51]) and Buhari in Nigeria - are very rare in military regimes as in civilian regimes. And even these do not really address the central economic problems but simply constitute painful, costly and necessary corrective economic wrenches preparatory for real development.

Military rule also at times coincides with economic upturns, though not causing them. In Togo the 'economic miracle' of the 1970s had nothing to do with the emergence of the Eyadema military regime in Lomé. The roots of the economic upturn (phosphate exports) were laid during the antecedent much maligned civilian administration; the plant only came of age after the fall of Grunitzky, with the Eyadema regime garnering the credit for the sudden infusions of state royalties and the development these allowed. Niger's even more dramatic economic success story was virtually identical to the Togolese one, except that the local export was uranium, not phosphates. General Kountche's regime came to power in time to supervise the distribution of the valuable fruits of the Saharan desert, but had nothing to do with their development.

Fortuitous increases in global commodity prices, coinciding with the rise of military regimes, project the false image of military-sponsored stabilisation of flagging economies, as in Ghana after the 1966 coup, in the CAR after the 1966 coup and even in Uganda after Amin's coup. Moreover, sharp gyrations in global market prices of primary commodities often do more to make or break economies than any leadership (civilian or military) may do or strive to attain with short-run solutions. The post-1974 quadrupling in the global price of oil bankrupted many already shaky African economies, at one stroke wiping out export gains of the post-independence era, as in Ghana and Sierra Leone specifically. With expenditures on oil imports for some by far the prime fiscal outlay, a decline in the global spot price of oil can stabilise these economies more than any domestic economic attainments.

Finally, military rule is also not particularly stable, compared to civilian rule, though - with the slow accretion in the military-headed Afro-Marxist camp - military rule may be becoming a permanent fixture of some African states. The relative instability of military regimes stems partly from the malintegrated nature of most African armies and the growth of personalist ambitions within its officer corps, as previously noted. Civilian politicians, shut out of power by the military interregnum, may also conspire with disgruntled elements in the army to effectuate a comeback. The praetorian politics of Congo-Brazzaville in the 1960s and 1970s vividly illustrate the turbulance of this free-for-all in contradistinction to expectations of at least stability, social tranquility and political quietism under military rule.

CONCLUSION

But it could be argued that military rule axiomatically praetorianises society, or at the very least sets loose praetorian impulses that may not be restrained in some countries. Armies have been conceptualised here as coteries of armed factions in a temporary and dynamic state of relative balance. As Rapaport so aptly puts it 'insurrections have enormous divisive potentials for a military body ... every *coup d'état* must create hostilities, anxieties and suspicions'.[52] In malintegrated societies and armies every coup is assessed to some extent at least in terms of its effect on the ethnic/regional balance of power, and the intra-military tug-of-war. In very few instances has the army been sufficiently united, disciplined or truly under the control of its official military leaders; internal rumblings and/or upheavals against the leadership in office has thus been a characteristic of military regimes as well. All too often the hostilities, anxieties and suspicions referred to by Rapaport have translated themselves with great ease into constant internal power grabs (e.g. Dahomey/Benin, Congo-Brazzaville, the Sudan etc.) that rocks society, discredits the army and negates the last possible reason for military rule. The intrusion of the military in the political scene may lead to its own possible disintegration along existing lines of division. Catapulting the military into the political vortex of competing influences and pulls (that do not disappear just because the army is in office) politicises, polarises and civilianises the ethos and perspective of soldiers, eroding existing military discipline even as the civil-military boundaries become fluid. Existing intra-military competitions become politicised and resolve themselves along existing power-relationships. In Mali (in 1966), Ghana (in 1966), Congo-Brazzaville (in 1969), Chad (in 1974), Guinea (in 1984) and elsewhere coups were followed by fractricidal clashes with, and the disbandment of, militias or other ancillary armed formations set up by politicians as buffers against the army itself. In Congo-Brazzaville both the police and the gendarmerie (and earlier, the paramilitary

JMNR youth) formations had to be totally dissolved, and even then conflict and strife did not cease.

The above fissiparous tendencies in African armies notwithstanding, a trend seems to be developing in Africa as military rule begins to acquire an aura of permanence. Unlike the situation in previous decades, the majority of the continent's military regimes in the 1980s are no longer essentially interim administrations of limited duration that may be expected to ultimately usher in civilian rule albeit with differing degrees of reluctance or alacrity. The number of military juntas that view themselves either intrinsically better fit to govern, or with a mission to steer their countries, has slowly inched upwards; utilising complex epistemological gyrations and rationalisations, and various (frequently corporative) constitutional adjustments, they contrive to transform themselves into integral and permanent fixtures of political life in their state.

To date there have been few military autocracies where officers entrenched themselves in political office primarily out of considerations of self-aggrandisement and/or societal plunder. With the overthrow of Bokassa and Amin (both within the space of one year in 1979) possibly the only military regimes that could be regarded as clear-cut venal autocracies may be those currently in Zaire and Equatorial Guinea, though Doe's in Liberia may also be developing in that direction. But elsewhere military rule is developing a permanent stranglehold over local political life, rationalising the necessity of its continued presence on either ideological grounds (Benin, Congo-Brazzaville, Libya, Ethiopia, Madagascar, Somalia, the Sudan, Burkina Faso) or not (Togo, Mali, Mauritania, Niger). Even Ghana and Nigeria - hitherto (especially the latter) - seemingly immune to the militarisation of life, may be moving in this direction as well, though it is too early to tell.

Herein lies the real danger of military rule, if the trend is truly there. Not so much the army's unaccountability to anyone and equal susceptibility to the temptations of office; nor its simplistic way of viewing socio-economic problems, and its inability to resolve all except the immediate and those relating to the changing of the Guard. Through weariness, disenchantment, disillusionment and constant friction and strife - within society and the army alike - an attitudinal metamorphosis transforms the possibly unavoidable 'neither better nor worse' temporary military interregnum into a permanent authoritarian non-participatory modality of governance with little possibility of qualitative change. As military hierarchies shed some of their earlier sources of division, and disencumber themselves of personal rivalries, they become more stable. (Witness, for instance, the former coup-prone Benin and Congo-Brazzaville and their relative stability in the late 1970s). Stable, permanent, widespread, authoritarian and uninspiring military rule spells the end to the lofty African political dreams of a global role of yesteryear.

NOTES

1. Zolberg, A.R., 'Creating Political Order: The Party-states of West Africa' (Chicago: Rand McNally, 1966). See also that author's 'The Structure of Political Conflict in Africa', American Political Science Review, 62, 2 (June 1968).
2. Grundy, K.W., Conflicting Images of the Military in Africa (Nairobi: East Africa Publishing House, 1968), p. 7.
3. West Africa, 28 January 1975.
4. Zolberg, A.R., 'Military Intervention in the New States of Africa', in Bienen, H. (ed.), The Military Intervenes (New York: Russell Sage Foundation, 1968), p. 71.
5. Finer, S.E., 'The Morphology of Military Regimes', in Kolkowicz, R. and Korbonski, A. (eds.), Soldiers, Peasants and Bureaucrats (London: George Allen & Unwin, 1982), p. 281.
6. The seminal work on coups remains that by Finer, S.E., The Man on Horseback: The Role of the Military in Politics (London: Pall Mall, 1962). See also Janowitz, M., The Military in the Political Development of New Nations (Chicago: Chicago University Press, 1964).
7. See, among others, Deutsch, K.W., 'Social Mobilization and Political Development', American Political Science Review, 55, 2 (June 1961), pp. 483-514; Geertz, C., 'The Integrative Revolution: Primordial Sentiments and Civil Politics in the New States', in his The Quest for Modernity in Asia and Africa (New York: Winston, Holt & Rinehart, 1963), pp. 105-57; and Huntington, S.P., Political Order in Changing Societies (New Haven: Yale University Press, 1968).

8. Huntington, ibid., p. 194.
9. Nelkin, D., 'The Economic and Social Setting of Military Takeovers in Africa', Journal of Asian and African Studies, 2, 2 (1967), p. 231.
10. Perlmutter, A., 'Civil-Military Relations in Socialist Authoritarian and Praetorian States: Prospects and Retrospects', in Kolkowicz and Korbonski, Soldiers, Peasants and Bureaucrats, p. 313.
11. Ibid., p. 314.
12. For a good comparative survey of the corporate features of military hierarchies see Perlmutter, A., The Military in Modern Times (New Haven: Yale University Press, 1977) and Abrahamsson, B., Military Professionalization and Political Power (Beverly Hills: Sage, 1972).
13. Levy, M. Modernization and the Structure of Societies (Princeton: Princeton University Press, 1966), p. 603.
14. Rapoport, D.C., 'The Praetorian Army: Insecurity, Venality and Impotence', in Kolkowicz and Korbonski, Soldiers, Peasants and Bureaucrats, p. 252. The reference is to Coleman, J.S. and Brice, B., in their contribution in Johnson, J.J. (ed.), The Role of the Military in Underdeveloped Countries (Princeton: Princeton University Press, 1962), p. 359. See also Huntington's earlier view that was in a similar vein: Huntington, S.P., The Soldier and the State (New York: Random House, 1964) and Janowitz, The Military in the Political Development of New Nations.
15. See in particular, Zolberg, A.R., 'Military Intervention' in Bienen, The Military Intervenes; Welch, C.E., 'Soldier and State in Africa', Journal of Modern African Studies, 5, 3 (October 1967), pp. 305-22; and Eleazu, U.O., 'The Military and Political Development: A Reconsideration of Existing Theories and Practices', Journal of Developing Areas, 7, 2 (April 1973).
16. Decalo, S., Coups and Army Rule in Africa: Studies in Military Style (New Haven: Yale University Press, 1976). See also Erny, P., 'Parole et travail chez les jeunes d'Afrique centrale', Projet (September-October 1966).
17. Decalo, Coups and Army Rule in Africa, ch. 1.
18. See Rapoport, 'The Praetorian Army', in Kolkowicz and Korbonski, Soldiers, Peasants and Bureaucrats; also Rapoport's earlier Praetorianism: Government without Consensus (unpublished Ph.D. dissertation: University of California, Berkeley, 1959). A very useful article even though

dealing with the Middle East, is Perlmutter, A., 'The Praetorian State and the Praetorian Army', Comparative Politics, 1, 3 (April 1969), pp. 382-405.

19. Decalo, Coups and Army Rule, pp. 207-11.

20. Decalo, S., 'African Personal Dictatorships', Journal of Modern African Studies, 23, 4 (December 1985, forthcoming).

21. See, inter alia, Price, R.M., 'Military Officers and Political Leadership: The Ghanaian Case', Comparative Politics, 3, 3 (April 1971), pp. 361-81 and 'A Theoretical Approach to Military Rule in New States: Reference Group Theory and the Ghanaian Case', World Politics, 23, 2 (April 1971), pp. 399-430; and Baynham, S.J., 'Quis Custodiet Ipsos Custodes?: the case of Nkrumah's National Security Service', Journal of Modern African Studies, 23, 1 (March 1985), pp. 87-103.

22. Decalo, S., 'Corporate Grievances and Idiosyncratic Variables in African Military Hierarchies', Journal of African Studies, (Summer 1975).

23. Jackman,, R.W., 'The Predictability of Coups d'Etat: A Model with African Data', American Political Science Review, 72, 3 (September 1978), pp. 1262-75.

24. First, R., The Barrel of a Gun: Political Power in Africa and the Coup d'Etat (New York: Pantheon Books, 1970), p. ix.

25. Huntington, S.P., 'Civilian Control of the Military: A Theoretical Statement', in Eulau, H., Eldersveld, S., and Janowitz, M. (eds.), Political Behaviour: A Reader in Theory and Research (Glencoe: The Free Press, 1956), p. 391.

26. For the British practice see, inter alia, Miners, N.J., The Nigerian Army, 1956-1966 (London: Methuen, 1971), ch. 2., and Cohen, S.P., The Indian Army: Its Contribution to the Development of a Nation (Berkeley: University of California Press, 1971), pp. 49-56.

27. In Togo, for example, expatriate French officers strongly supported the expansion of the country's miniscule army at a time when President Olympio actually favoured its elimination altogether.

28. For a discussion of the colonial army see, among others, Gutteridge, W.F., The Military in African Politics (London: Methuen, 1969), ch. 2; Obichere, B. (ed.), African States and the Military, Past and Present (London: Frank Cass, 1980); Van den Berghe, P., 'The Military

and Political Change in Africa', in Welch, C.E. (ed.), <u>Soldier and State in Africa</u> (Evanston: Northwestern University Press, 1970) and, of course, Finer, <u>The Man on Horseback</u>.

29. For some comparative data, especially for British Africa, see Lee, J.M., <u>African Armies and Civil Order</u> (New York: Praeger, 1968).

30. Coleman and Brice in Johnson, <u>The Role of the Military in Underdeveloped Countries</u>, p. 445.

31. The early military donors included Israel, India, Yugoslavia, West Germany as well as China and the Soviet Union.

32. Feit, E., 'The Rule of the Iron Surgeons: Military Government in Spain and Ghana', <u>Comparative Politics</u>, 1, 3 (July 1969), pp. 2-31; see also Feit's 'Military Coups and Political Developments: Some Lessons from Ghana and Nigeria', <u>World Politics</u>, 20, 2 (January 1968), pp. 179-93.

33. Legum, C., 'Tribal Survival in Modern African Political Systems', <u>Journal of Asian and African Studies</u>, 14, 1 (1979), pp. 102-12. See also Enloe, C.H., <u>Ethnic Soldiers: State Security in Divided Societies</u> (Harmondsworth: Penguin, 1980).

34. Jackman, 'The Predictability of Coups d'Etat', p. 1273.

35. Jackman, R.W., 'Politicians in Uniform: Military Governments and Social Change in the Third World', <u>American Political Science Review</u>, 70, 4 (December 1976), p. 1096.

36. See Decalo, S., 'The Morphology of Radical Military Rule in Africa', <u>Journal of Communist Studies</u> (forthcoming 1986).

37. First, R., 'Uganda, the latest coup in Africa', <u>The World Today</u>, 27, 3 (March 1971), p. 133.

38. Nordlinger, E.A., <u>Soldiers in Politics: Military Coups and Governments</u> (Englewood Cliffs: Prentice Hall, 1977), p. 39. See also Nordlinger's earlier 'Soldiers in Mufti', <u>American Political Science Review</u>, 64, 4 (December 1970), pp. 1131-49.

39. See, for example, the positive outlook in Pachter, E.F., 'Contra-Coup: Civilian Control of the Military in Guinea, Tanzania and Mozambique', <u>Journal of Modern African Studies</u>, 20, 4 (December 1982), pp. 595-612. Pachter's interesting point (p. 595) that 'In the long run it may even be that the vast majority of military coups in Africa simply mark a period of Africanising, nationalising, and integrating the army', not only ignores the

continuing empirical record of personalist coups in armies that may be regarded as satisfying these criteria, but also was undermined by the eruption of the coup in Guinea - one of her key studies.

40. Jackman, 'Politicians in Uniform', p. 1097.
41. Ibid., pp. 1096-7.
42. Odetola, T.O., Military Regimes and Development (London: George Allen & Unwin, 1982), p. 181.
43. West Africa, 15 June 1981.
44. Nordlinger, 'Soldiers in Mufti', pp. 1135-6.
45. Decalo, S., 'African Personal Dictatorships'.
46. See Momoh, E., 'Civilian Rule Politics', Parts 1 & 2, West Africa, 20 and 27 August, 1984. See also his 'Liberia: Doubts About Democracy', West Africa, 18 March 1985.
47. The best example of many that may be cited is that of Major Hachémé, the Quartermaster General of Dahomey. Following the 1967 coup, he strongly propounded the idea and became the president of an anti-corruption Tribunal to investigate abuses of power under the former (military) regime. When the Tribunal convened, however, Hachémé himself was the first victim of its investigations. See Decalo, S., 'Regionalism, Politics and the Military in Dahomey', Journal of Developing Areas (April 1973), pp. 449-78.
48. 'December 31 and all that', West Africa, 24 December 1984, p. 2615.
49. Momoh, E., 'Guinea: Past, Present and Future', West Africa, 26 November 1984, pp. 2370-1.
50. Doyle, M., 'Haidallah Ousted,' West Africa, 17 December 1984, p. 2564; Schissel, H., 'Challenges After the Palace Coup,' West Africa, 13 May 1985, pp. 934-5.
51. 'The Holy War,' Africa Report, (May-June 1982).
52. Rapoport, 'The Praetorian Army,' in Kolkowicz and Korbonski, Soldiers, Peasants and Bureaucrats, p. 257.

Chapter Three

MILITARY DISENGAGEMENT FROM POLITICS? : INCENTIVES AND OBSTACLES IN POLITICAL CHANGE

Claude E. Welch, Jr.

INTRODUCTION

The exit of the armed forces from the political stage has been far less frequent in Africa than their entrance. Indeed, the majority of the successful *coups d'état* detailed in the appendix to this chapter have been mounted against governments already dominated by the military. Yet, for all the alarums and drama surrounding the arrival of new governing juntas, attention must be given to the conditions that might foster successful disengagement south of the Sahara.

In this chapter, I shall examine five states in West Africa after placing 'disengagement' within the general context of civil-military relations, to illustrate how interactions among inherited patterns of armed forces' involvement in politics (primarily but not exclusively the result of colonial administration), indigenous political and social pressures, economic factors and leadership have resulted in a variety of patterns of returns to the barracks. As will quickly become apparent, the record is neither extensive nor encouraging for those hoping civilians will regain the paramount political positions they held at independence.

At the outset, it must be noted that disengagement is both an elusive goal and a slippery concept. Given the ease of subsequent re-engagement, how firm a commitment by military and political leaders is necessary for long-term success? If the armed forces remain the *eminence grise* of politics, can they in fact really remove themselves from the political stage, or do they hover in the wings, using any slip by their successor to justify yet another seizure of power?

Military Disengagement from Politics

The literature on civil-military relations abounds with examinations of why and how individual *coups d'état* occurred.[1] The body of scholarly work dealing with how coup-initiated governments rule is growing.[2] By contrast, few, if any, academic generalisations exist for military disengagement from politics for the simple reasons that (1) most instances appear to arise from *ad hoc* combinations of circumstances, and (2) it is often difficult to determine when disengagement can in fact be deemed 'successful.' Unlike a *coup d'état* - a quick, decisive event - disengagement is a process that is often protracted, always complex and rarely analysed from within. Hence, the process (or, perhaps better, the processes) of military disengagement from politics is liable to interruption or reversal. I find appealing Finer's observation: 'In most cases the military that have intervened in politics are in a dilemma: they cannot withdraw from rulership nor can they fully legitimize it. They can neither stay nor go.'[3] Nonetheless, it behoves us to examine, in comparative fashion, the incentives and obstacles to successful military disengagement from politics.

Finer has set forth four necessary conditions for long-term military disengagement: (1) the leader imposed as a result of intervention must strongly desire that his troops quit politics; (2) he must be able to establish a regime capable of functioning without further military support; (3) there must be continuing support of the armed forces by the new regime; and (4) the military must have confidence in the individual leader who ordered them back to the barracks.[4] Problems exist with this initially straightforward presentation. Closer examination suggests that Finer's points may be necessary but not sufficient conditions. The examples he cites - France (Napoleon I, Napoleon III and de Gaulle), Turkey (Ataturk), Mexico and (potentially) South Korea - are all societies characterised by relative ethnic and linguistic homogeneity; all but South Korea experienced revolutionary upheaval, in which nationalist armies played important roles in restructuring the political systems; only South Korea gained independence after World War II, contemporaneous with much of the Third World. How many states in tropical Africa can claim analogous heritages of extensive social integration, revolutionary restructuring and prolonged periods of self-government? Are the above necessary (if not in themselves sufficient) conditions?

Huntington follows a slightly different path in discussing how military leaders become 'builders of political institutions ... most effectively in a society where social forces are not fully articulated.'[5] Like Finer, he is attentive to leadership, cites essentially the same examples and considers the impact of social mobilisation on the functioning and legitimacy of government organs. Only by institutionalisation of major political values might junta leaders (as in Mexico, Turkey and South Korea) bring about lasting disengagement; only by means of 'sustained military participation' in politics, as contrasted with intermittent military intervention in politics, could stronger, more effective government institutions be assured.[6] As societies become more complex and the nature of social differentiation changes, Huntington argues, the political role of officers changes, from one potentially of radical moderniser to one of conservative guardian. Successful disengagement would appear far easier to achieve, as the initial quotation in this paragraph suggested, in states at relatively early stages of modernisation.

Speaking to the broad issue of 'redemocratisation' from within authoritarian regimes (a category broader than that of military-based governments) Stepan finds a limited number of examples, again all from outside Africa.[7] He divides the category into three subtypes: (1) redemocratisation initiated by the civilian or civilianised political leadership (e.g., Spain after Franco); (2) redemocratisation initiated by the military acting as the government (a category in which Stepan feels liberalisation but not redemocratisation can occur); and (3) redemocratisation initiated by the military acting as an institution (e.g., Greece in 1973; Portugal in 1974). Stepan's category represents a more far-reaching category than liberalisation. Redemocratisation requires a willingness to tolerate dissent and political organisation greater than most African military governments to date have been willing to tolerate; at most they seem to tolerate a degree of liberalisation, as will be suggested below when we look briefly at selected cases.

In an early issue of *Armed Forces and Society* several authors probe the issue of political participation under military regimes in various countries. Janowitz presents a sage introductory comment: 'It is more and more apparent that the underlying question is not the conditions under which the military will "exit from power" but rather how the long and twisted process of the transformation of the military regimes will take place.'[8] Let me sample the conclusions reached by three authors: (1) 'military disengagement as such is a rather infrequent, complicated, and difficult process ... A more important, permanent, and significant ... pattern of civilianizing [than abrupt withdrawal] is the gradual model';[9] (2) 'the Thai experience suggests that gradual evolution of a civil-dominant structure requires the country's military leaders to be able to function in the new political environment, and to feel that their role of governing the nation is not threatened with extinction by new civilian decision makers';[10] (3) 'while military leaders may acquiesce in civilian control of certain policies, there is little evidence from the case of the Sudan and Uganda to suggest that bringing civilians back into the political arena is likely to result in a military exit from power.'[11] As these citations make abundantly clear, area specialists have little confidence that gradual restoration of elected government will restore long-term civilian power, and even less confidence that abrupt restoration of civilian rule will endure.

This author, in earlier writings on military disengagement from politics, suggests a variety of contributing factors without indicating whether they are necessary and/or sufficient. An earlier contribution points to the key roles of (1) commanding officers firm in their resolve to step aside, (2) forceful, articulate civilians pressing for withdrawal, and (3) a belief that military unity and effectiveness would be further impaired by remaining in power.[12] Focusing on the attitudes and perceptions of governing officers, Welch proposes examining (1) the cohesiveness of ruling juntas, (2) the scope of their political objectives, and (3) the relative 'fit' with a potential successor group to assess the relative likelihood of long-term returns to the barracks.[13] In a subsequent essay, he distinguishes between conscious extrication of governing juntas and pressured breakdown of military-based governments. The former requires attention to intra-military cohesion, the size of the officer corps relative to the upper civil service, the objectives and outlook of the governing junta, affinities with potential successor groups and salience of social divisions; the latter requires attention, in addition to the factors noted above, to duration of time governing, economic factors and exacerbation of internal strains.[14] In a brief recent paper on West Africa, Welch stresses the need for additional research on regional dynamics, on consequences of economic development and on inherited patterns of civil-military relations.[15]

Let me summarise the conclusions of the above writings. Removal of the armed forces from politics appears more likely to succeed if it is voluntary rather than coerced. Long-term disengagement rests fundamentally on military willingness to reduce the scope of their political involvement. In this task, a trusted military leader plays a key role, being both symbol and agent of recivilianisation. As Goldsworthy suggests elsewhere in this volume, attention to the 'system of personal rule' provides an avenue for explanation.

Adopting a strict definition of successful disengagement - a minimum period of five years during which at least one successful 'regular' executive transition has occurred following public efforts by the ruling military groups to reduce their levels of political involvement - one would be hard pressed to find any examples in sub-Saharan Africa. The main examples in tropical Africa have been few in number and limited in their impact. This should be expected. As Kirk-Greene has commented, scarcely one-tenth of successful military changes in government in tropical Africa have brought about handovers to civilians.[16] And most of these have failed. Indeed, the chief examples from Africa are both Maghrebian (Algeria and Egypt); there, continuity in governing juntas has been extensive, and succession of leaders has been carried out with a modicum of popular consultation.[17]

The vaunted transitions in Ghana and Nigeria in 1979 came to naught respectively on New Year's Eve 1981 and New Year's Eve 1983; the less-studied attempt in Upper Volta to restore elected government started in 1970, collapsed in 1974, was revived in 1977 but once again failed. The Tanzanian ouster of Idi Amin and subsequent installation of Milton Obote constitutes an externally imposed redemocratisation markedly different from the internally generated restoration of electoral politics in the three West African states just cited; it seems too early as yet to judge the efficacy of the Uganda transition. As for such countries as Burundi, Congo-Brazzaville or Rwanda, in which original military leaders have been replaced by other officers who have sought electoral mandates, or states such as Togo or Zaire in which the original coup leader remains in power but with a veneer of civilianisation, redemocratisation remains limited, despite the organisation of political parties to bolster the leaders' claim to legitimacy. The recivilianisation brought about in Sierra Leone by the misnamed 'Sergeants' Revolt' remains distinctive, as will be shown below, in terms of its speed of transition and its apparent success.

Given the restricted record to date, what insights can be gained by efforts that have largely been abortive? If what Finer has termed disengagement of a 'contingent and temporary nature' rather than genuine neutralisation is the case for most of tropical Africa, is scholarly enquiry served by looking at a seemingly dismal record?[18]

Clearly, I believe so. Examination of attempts at military withdrawal from politics, though these may have been short-lived, has several values: (1) civil-military relations in individual societies can be shown as a series of dynamic, changing relationships; (2) additional perspective is provided on governmental ability to implement policy choices; (3) observers can better determine whether the demands of ruling fundamentally change the nature of the military *qua* institution; and (4) analysts can better determine the relationship between presumed 'causes' of military intervention and policy outcomes.

To better understand disengagement, one should first examine the factors that led to particular *coups d'état* and the policy objectives of the resulting governments. Disengagement is a far easier task for 'arbitrator' as contrasted with 'ruler'-style military governments.[19] Disengagement is also far easier for armed forces whose original greater political involvement stemmed from 'internal' rather than 'environmental' or 'interactional' issues.[20] Conceivably, militaries with a heritage that 'Politics is not for soldiers' are relatively reluctant to intervene and comparatively willing to disengage.[21] The greater the 'fit' in values and outlook between governing officers and their would-be successors, it further stands to reason, the less difficult a hand-over of power will be.[22]

CASE STUDIES FROM WEST AFRICA

To put flesh on the bones of these points, let us give brief attention to efforts at recivilianisation in five West African states: Ghana, Liberia, Nigeria, Sierra Leone and Upper Volta (Burkina Faso).

Sierra Leone

Military intervention in Sierra Leone in March 1967 initially resulted from boundary fragmentation, encouraged by civilians and carried out by an unpopular military commander whose ethnic and personal loyalties overrode his institutional responsibilities. Military disengagement in Sierra Leone in April 1968 was designed to take the army out of politics, and politics out of the army. It was far more akin to a mutiny of enlistees against their superior officers than to an elaborately staged *coup d'état*. The result was by far the simplest and longest-lasting disengagement in West Africa.

As Cartwright, Cox and (earlier) Kilson have recounted,[23] no single nationalist party dominated the political scene in the early years of independence. The SLPP (Sierra Leone People's Party) gained the upper hand as political participation expanded in rural areas; it drew its major support from the Mende, coopted traditional leaders, and members of the bourgeoisie. An increasing challenge to it came from the APC (All People's Congress), which garnered support from the Creole population of the Western Province (Freetown) and the Temne, in particular. The freewheeling, corrupt style of Prime Minister Albert Margai aroused discontent, while the SLPP's narrow basis of support (in Cox's words, the party was little more than 'a loose association of elites'[24]) portended trouble. The March 1967 elections were marked by ineffectual manipulation by the SLPP, anxious to maintain its hold on power. With most but not all parliamentary seats decided, the Governor General asked the APC leader Siaka Stevens to form the government. Within an hour of being sworn in, Stevens had been deposed by Brigadier David Lansana, likely on the basis of a 'deliberate precoup strategy'[25] inspired by SLPP civilians. Lansana himself was quickly elbowed aside and the National Reformation Council (NRC) took shape. And, under the impact of Lt.-Col. Andrew Juxon-Smith, what had been a 'military holding action in favour of a particular group of civilian leaders [became] a kind of Calvinist vendetta against prevailing value systems, tribalism, and political institutions.'[26] An especially strong personality, in other words, came to dominate Sierra Leone, in the process besmirching the reputation of the armed forces as a whole.

The NRC carried out little planning to restore civilian rule - while at the same time doing practically nothing to build support for itself. It was

> a hastily constructed band of men with little or no political program ... Lacking a concept of how to govern or of how to cultivate popular support, the NRC could do little more than flounder from one threat of reprisal against civilians to another ... the NRC's 'politics of reformation' was mere window-dressing, designed to conceal the regime's fundamental insecurity and lack of goals.[27]

The group became increasingly polarised, most of its members tending toward disengagement, while Juxon-Smith, in Cox's words, 'appears to have regarded himself as destined to rule Sierra Leone even in a post-NRC era ... he created a self-image of more than a humble army officer on a "rescue mission."'[28] Pressures for recivilianisation grew, though the NRC attempted to deflect them by establishing a National Advisory Council. But what NRC leaders probably viewed as a minor commission of inquiry dropped a political bombshell in September 1967 (six months after the coup) by asserting the APC had fairly won the aborted election and that the military, in effect, wrongfully denied them the right to rule. The NRC, by extension, had no legitimate role in governing. The regime was placed on the defensive.

The ouster of the National Reformation Council by the military rank and file in 1968 restored to power a party unjustifiably deprived of it just over a year earlier. Initiative for change finally came from the privates. On 23 April 1967, almost all officers of the police and armed forces were imprisoned; defining themselves as the Anti-Corruption Revolutionary Movement, the military rank and file restored civilian rule, under Siaka Stevens, a little over 13 months after the initial military seizure of power. Only the armed forces could have maintained the discredited system symbolised by the SLPP in power; only the military could remove its own members from power. Stevens remains in power at the time of writing in 1985.

Ghana

Bearing some similar hallmarks to what has just been described was the 1979 disengagement of the Ghanaian military from politics, though this process was far more protracted than the rapid rise and fall of the Sierra Leone Anti-Corruption Revolutionary Movement; at the same time, this disengagement, the second in Ghana, resembled the carefully planned return to the barracks of 1969. Both merit brief discussion.

The initial entrance of the Ghanaian armed forces and police onto the political stage occurred in February 1966, in a process chronicled by many scholars and several protagonists.[29] If a single explanation for this *coup d'état* had to be identified, it would be reaction against the policies and style of governing of President Kwame Nkrumah. As Austin has written, 'What was needed ... was ... a return to the past, or rather to a "reformed past." [Coup leaders] could also talk not only of reform but of withdrawal ... since they believed that alternative leaders were available.'[30] The military- and police-based National Liberation Council (NLC) that was established by the *coup d'état* saw its role in relatively restricted, 'curative' terms.[31]

Having encouraged expectations of a speedy return to civilian rule, the NLC was both subject to pressures from would-be civilian successors and ready to take initiatives on its own. It established a series of advisory groups dominated by the best-known opponent of Nkrumah, Dr Kofi Busia. It ousted its own Chairman, General Joseph Ankrah, when he became involved in political activities his colleagues deemed inappropriate for an active duty officer. And, most important for this analysis, the NLC set in motion a deliberate process of disengagement. Civilians (though primarily bureaucrats rather than politicians) were named to the Executive Council and given titles as Commissioners; a Constitutional Committee was appointed and its report presented; a timetable for a 15-month transition was officially announced in May 1968; an indirectly elected Constituent Assembly was established (its product being, in one Ghanaian's terms, 'a Constitution by Lawyers for Judges'[32]); political parties were permitted to emerge and campaign officially; competitive elections were held on 29 August 1969; and a new civilian government under Busia took office a month later.[33] The NLC thus succeeded as a political midwife in bringing to term a regime headed by civilians, though it was far less successful in reshaping the economic and social legacy of the Nkrumah period.

The second protracted process of disengagement was initiated in the spring of 1977 under General Ignatius Acheampong (garbed in the guise of 'Union Government' or 'Unigov'), was accelerated in the summer of 1978 under General Fred Akuffo and was brought to a bloody conclusion the next summer by Flight-Lieutenant Jerry Rawlings. The procedure thus had elements of both careful planning, in which the armed forces attempted to retain initiative over a protracted period, and intra-military factionalism, which made a rapid return to the barracks essential to restore a semblence of military unity.

'Unigov' merits a few words of explanation - and possibly of defence. All so-called 'military regimes' in Africa have functioned, by necessity, with coopted civilians: bureaucrats, political advisers, traditional leaders and the inevitable self-seekers. Although members of the armed forces dominate the top policy-making positions, they cannot function without extensive civilian assistance. The period of planned disengagement itself is an especially delicate time in civil-military relations. Not without reason did the well-known Nigerian politician Nnamdi Azikiwe propose, in October 1972, a combined military and civilian government that would exercise a five-year mandate following the demise of the Federal Military Government. (As we shall see shortly, such a five-year transition was taking place at that point in Upper Volta.) In the fragmented Ghanaian setting, however, Acheampong's proposal for 'Union Government' seemed to camouflage continued control by the unpopular Supreme Military Council (SMC), rather than bring a real sharing of power, or - far better in the eyes of influential civilians - a full restoration of civilian government as had taken place nearly a decade earlier. Substantial sectors of the Ghanaian populace (some 44 per cent of those voting, although participation was well below 40 per cent) voted against a proposed non-party union government comprised of civilians, police and military officers.[34] The handwriting on the wall appeared for the SMC. Acheampong, like Juxon-Smith, became increasingly isolated from his military colleagues; they, in turn, were embarrassed by his insistence on 'Unigov' in the face of widespread opposition.

Indeed, a pledge to restore civilian rule gave the government of General Fred Akuffo (who, as Chief of Staff and member of the six-member SMC, forced Acheampong's resignation on 5 July 1978) its basis for legitimacy. The ouster was made not only because of Acheampong's failure to consult his colleagues, but also because of the progress Nigeria was then making (as will be discussed later in the chapter) in its own restoration of civilian control. The process was to be phased, in a fashion reminiscent of the first disengagement in Ghana.

The planned sequences of events in the two Ghanaian disengagements were in fact highly similar. Briefly, they included: (1) internal changes in the governing junta, removing a head whose commitment to redemocratisation was unclear (Ankrah replaced by Afrifa in April 1969; Acheampong supplanted by Akuffo in July 1978); (2) sponsorship of an elaborate set of steps to draft and legitimate a new constitution; (3) clear sympathy by senior military officers toward relatively conservative politicians untainted by prior close association with Nkrumah; and (4) corresponding distrust of mass-based political parties, since they might appeal to lower-class sentiments as had Nkrumah's CPP. The Ghanaian officers tended to view partisan politics with scepticism. They viewed themselves as guardians of a bourgeois political order. They preferred to command rather than to mobilise, to stand above politics rather than to immerse themselves in it.[35]

It was this deliberate scorn for popular movements that brought the downfall of both Akuffo and, 27 months later, of the relatively conservative civilian government that had been installed. The 'Rawlings phenomenon' itself indicated a factor disengaging officers had attempted to avoid, namely the mobilisation of popular sectors. Rawlings's seizures of control in June 1979 and December 1981 suggested a new variety of civil-military relations, hitherto little known in tropical Africa, namely the 'radical' or 'populist' *coup d'état*.[36]

Flight-Lieutenant Rawlings came into public attention when he led an abortive coup attempt on 15 May 1979. Many frustrations of the rank and file had coalesced around him, owing to his willingness to criticise the actions of senior officers more interested in politics than the views of their fellow soldiers. He was imprisoned, escaped and succeeded on 4 June in seizing control. What he did resembled in some respects the explosion of the enlistees that had rocked Sierra Leone in 1968, for it revealed 'the extent of the animosity prevalent among the rank and file against the senior officer corps.'[37] A 'house-cleaning exercise' was announced (the immediate victims being eight senior military officers, three of them former heads of state); on the other hand, Rawlings's Armed Forces Revolutionary Council promised 'a smooth transition to constitutional rule as planned.'[38] Elections went ahead, and the new government of Dr Hilla Limann took control on 24 September – having been warned by Rawlings that 'if people in power use their offices to pursue self-interest, they will be resisted and unseated no matter how unshakeable their position may seem to be.'[39] Rawlings acted on his threat 829 days later. He again took power, this time on New Year's Eve 1981, in the name of the Provisional National Defence Council (PNDC).

The title notwithstanding, the PNDC appeared ready to exercise power for a lengthy period. In common with other coup-installed 'second generation' governments noted in this chapter, Rawlings installed a 'ruler'-type rather than 'arbitrator'-type regime. Governments of the latter type accept the existing social order, are willing to return to the barracks after disputes are settled, have little desire to maximise army rule and set a time limit for military governance; governments of the former type, by contrast, challenge the legitimacy of the existing social order, have no expectation of disengaging due to lack of confidence in civilian rule, and seek to maximise military rule, which its leaders consider the only alternative to political disorder. The PNDC seems installed for the long term. Rather than carry out a brief 'house-cleaning,' Rawlings (like Buhari in Nigeria and Sankara in Upper Volta/Burkina Faso) intends to carry out a major transformation, even (or perhaps particularly) in the absence of major national resources.

Upper Volta

The arbitrator-ruler contrast shows with marked clarity in the third of our cases, Upper Volta. (Since the following paragraphs emphasise the pre-August 1984 period, this title is used rather than Burkina Faso). Secondly, Upper Volta illustrates as well the strong, direct impact a senior officer can have. The two abortive restorations of civilian control owed their initiation to General Sangoule Lamizana, a man whose conduct 'was guided by the objective of surrendering power to the politicians ... even where their actions are not pleasing to the soldiers.'[40] And, thirdly, Upper Volta illustrates the difficulties of transition when the potential successors are themselves riven by personal and ethnic rivalries, thereby exemplifying what military rule was supposed to overcome.

Military intervention in Upper Volta occurred in a seemingly off-hand fashion, as a response to urban demonstrations in January 1966. 'Benevolent neutrality' of the armed forces toward strikes and public protests 'encouraged union leaders to create the conditions under which army officers could intervene without violating their notion of legitimacy.'[41] From the outset, Lamizana encouraged civilian participation in the government he headed. He apparently hoped that contending political movements - for Upper Volta had stumbled to independence with a complex, fragmented party system - would coalesce behind a widely accepted heir-apparent to military rule. The parties did not; yet Lamizana clung to his hope. A new constitution was drafted and approved in a November 1970 referendum, providing explicitly for a mixed military and civilian government during a five year transition period. The senior military officer would serve as president, the civilian leader of the largest party as prime minister.

What appears logical on paper often is not so in practice. The deliberate combination of ten civilians and five officers in the cabinet intensified conflict between the two groups. Further, Voltaic officers who joined in governing risked alienating their own military constituencies, thereby undercutting their power base; at the same time, Lamizana opposed officers' taking steps to create a political movement. The civilians themselves were plagued by animosities. In the face of drought and severe fiscal pressures, the government appeared immobilised. Junior officers felt especially aggrieved by the fruitless politicking and factionalism of their civilian counterparts. With the foundation of military unity threatened, and with civilian leaders paralysed, Lamizana moved in February 1974 to break the deadlock. The cabinet of Prime Minister Gerard Ouedraogo was dismissed and the process of recivilianisation started anew.

The second would-be disengagement ran aground on similar political reefs. Though the Lamizana government was, in the words of *West Africa*, 'perhaps the most benign of all military governments in Africa to date'[42], its rather relaxed style of rule could not still the factionalism or trade union militance to which junior officers objected. Nor, perhaps more significantly, could the regime mobilise support. The population of Upper Volta (one of the most impoverished and seemingly apathetic in tropical Africa) appeared to hold little respect for democracy, at least as envisaged by Lamizana. In the April 1978 elections, less than three quarters of the eligible adult population registered; scarcely 40 per cent participated. Lamizana himself failed to receive a majority in the first round of popular balloting for the Presidency - perhaps a first south of the Sahara! As in the 1970-74 period, the National Assembly was dominated by the UDV-RDA, the overwhelmingly Mossi party whose then leader had been the chief target of the 1966 *coup d'état*. In Voltaic politics, 'Plus ça change ...' was the operative style. Politicians, it appeared, would bicker endlessly; officers, it also appeared, would complain - and, on occasion, act.

In November 1980, the so-called Military Recovery Committee for National Progress assumed control, thus ending the 30 month second experiment in redemocratisation. A period of pronounced instability followed, with three *coups d'état* in nine months, leading by August 1983 to a radical, Rawlings-style government. The armed forces of Upper Volta have thus moved from the arbitrator style exemplified by Lamizana to the ruler style exemplified by Captain Thomas Sankara. Voluntary disengagement appears highly unlikely in the foreseeable future, although intra-military tensions could erupt and lead to Sankara's removal.

Liberia
Before turning to the largest West African instance, the 1979 return of the Nigerian armed forces to

the barracks, a few words about Liberia's hesitant groping for a new political formula should be added.

Master Sergeant Sammy Doe and his 15 Krahn co-conspirators staged their *coup d'état* at a time of rising urban tension. Rice shortages continued to plague the capital; outspoken opponents of the governing True Whig Party were coming up for trial; the Monrovia mayoral election was cancelled because of the possibility of opposition victory: all testified to discontent. The virus of distrust had penetrated the armed forces as well. The NCOs' seizure of power in April 1980 bore a surface resemblance to the April 1968 actions in Sierra Leone, and to the first intervention of Rawlings in Ghana, in expressing profound discontent of the rank and file against commissioned officers and the political elite. The seizure of control opened the floodgates of retribution and greed, affecting not only deposed President Tolbert and his Americo-Liberian entourage, but also ordinary Liberians. 'During the first weeks of the coup,' an observer wrote in June 1980,

> the military, undisciplined, stoned or drunk, terrorised the country, looting houses, arresting people en mass [sic], demanding money and stealing cars ... it's becoming clear to most Liberians that the army, looked down upon and ignored in the past, is intent on taking, by whatever means, anything it has been deprived of ... It has become increasingly obvious that members of the military are anxious to consolidate their power ... Sergeant Doe and his PRC [Peoples Redemption Council] intend to remain in power for an unspecified time, despite popular demand that they name a date [for disengagement].[43]

Given these conditions, little wonder should exist as to why the Liberian armed forces were hesitant in taking formal steps toward recivilianisation. What was done occurred under pressure, domestic and to some extent international, notably from the United States. The procedure was standard enough, and the process was subject to a number of unexplained or weakly rationalised delays. A constitutional drafting committee was appointed, its report being submitted in March 1983; a July 1984 popular referendum approved the draft constitution (although the required majority of registered voters did not give their support, leading the head of state to declare a majority of votes cast sufficient); Doe nominated a 57-member interim national assembly, which included all 17 members of the PRC; it chose Doe as provisional president a few hours later; Decree 75A was issued, in effect barring parties or candidates who 'at any time whatsoever have engaged in activities or have otherwise expressed converse and/or ideological aims and objectives that are repugnant to our intrinsic values and republican form of government.'[44] In short, as opposition politicians were arrested or threatened, it was abundantly clear that Doe wished to remain in power.

Tensions doubtless will rise further before the November 1985 elections, especially given the negative views about disengagement held by many officers fearful of political eclipse and loss of prestige.[45] No active duty officer can stand for President - and given Doe's absence of a power base outside the military, can he afford to resign his commission and pursue the presidency in an open fashion? Or is he likely to reinforce his personal grip on power, attempting to relegate potential rivals within the armed forces to the sidelines? The prospects for easy recivilianisation appear dim in Liberia.

Nigeria
Contrasted with the hesitancy of disengagement, the obvious personal interest of the military head of state in retaining power, and the steps against viable potential oppponents of Doe, the process of disengagement in Nigeria marched ahead with martial efficiency. From almost any perspective, the phased return to civilian rule of Africa's most populous state represented an impressive accomplishment. Yet questions remain. To what extent can the seeming success be attributed to strong leadership by senior officers? What role did rising petroleum revenues play? Did the protracted period of military rule, and the extensive reforms undertaken in the late 1970s, correct the problems of regionalism, corruption and political incompetence that had prompted the initial *coup d'état* of 1966?

In the 1975-79 process of recivilianisation, the Supreme Military Government of Murtala and Obasanjo coupled elements of prescription for the successor system with substantial reorganisation of the armed forces. The disengaging officers had little desire to see Nigeria return to the narrow politicking of the past; hence, they took several explicit steps to design the shape of the emergent political institutions. They inherited a military bloated by the civil war; they sought to reduce its size while raising its efficiency and level of force modernisation. Elements of both 'arbitrator' and 'ruler' thus appeared in the SMG's policies.

Disengagement from politics, to be certain, had been broached within the Nigerian military long before 1975.[46] The removal of the Gowon government in July 1975 permitted a group of no-nonsense officers to write their own prescription for political health. The elements emerged quickly. Barely two months after the *coup d'état*, Murtala sketched a five-stage programme 'to forge a viable political system which will be stable and responsive enough to the needs and realities of [Nigeria].'[47] The steps included: (1) creating new states (by April 1976) and drafting a constitution (by September 1976); (2) reorganising local governments and holding elections for them and a constituent assembly (by October 1978); (3) preparing for higher-level elections, by delimiting constituencies and lifting the ban on political party activities (starting October 1978); (4) holding state-level elections; and (5) holding federal-level elections for the presidency and houses of parliament. Murtala insisted that the emergent system be based on a limited number of 'genuine and truly national political parties,' an executive president and a cabinet reflecting the 'Federal character' of Nigeria, an independent judiciary, new corrective institutions for corruption and a constitutional restriction on the number of new states to be created.[48]

A fair amount of success attended the reform efforts - though specialists, as might be expected, reach mixed conclusions. The key accomplishments, as summarised by Oyediran (a member of the constitutional drafting committee), include restructuring the public service, redistributing federal revenue to local governments and making them the third tier of administration, pursuing a far more activist foreign policy, implementing elections at the local level (with, for the first time in much of the North, female suffrage), mandating indigenisation of most of the economy and, certainly not least, disengaging 'without being partisan in the struggle among competing groups of possible successors.'[49] Some 10,000 civil servants were sacked or retired on grounds of corruption or inefficiency; all military governors under Gowon were dismissed; the 12 states were rearranged into 19; and an ambitious programme of military modernisation was announced.[50]

Underlying these alterations were financial resources unmatched in any other West African state under military control. The Murtala-Obasanjo government benefited from the intersection of three factors: a doubling of petroleum production between 1970 and 1974 (from 1.08 million barrels per day to 2.25 million); a major increase in Nigerian share participation in oil production (from a maximum of 35 per cent in 1971 to a minimum of 60 per cent by 1979[51]); and the OPEC price hikes of 1973-4 and 1978-9. A country that had gained 80 per cent of its 1959 export earnings from agricultural products was gaining 95 per cent of these earnings from petroleum 20 years later.

A boom mentality affected all sectors of Nigeria, starting under Gowon but unabated after his ouster. The armed services themselves were major participants. Despite the successful conclusion of the civil war, defence expenditures rose. For example, the 1975/6 and 1976/7 budgets provided the military with one third of recurrent federal expenditures (547 million naira of 1,721 million; 827 million naira of 2,434 million). The Ministry of Defence ordered 16 million tons of cement - more than eleven times the annual unloading capacity of Lagos harbour[52] - and thereby aroused a great deal of hostility for such waste. Implementation of UPE (universal primary education) cost far more than estimated. New universities, extensive irrigation projects and other expensive projects were announced. External borrowing and internal inflation rates mounted. Outstanding federal debt climbed from 375 million naira in 1976, to 1,250 million in 1978, to 2,330 in 1981; with the state debts added in, the total jumped to a staggering 12,237 million naira in 1983. As *West Africa* commented, 'from 1978 caution seemed to have been thrown to the winds and the nation seemed to go on an external borrowing spree.'[53] The burden of debt service, which had been less than one per cent of total export earnings in 1980, jumped to 17.5 per cent in 1983.[54] The disengaging Nigerian officers, and the civilians who followed them, preferred to solve the 'guns vs. garri' question by ordering both. Members of both groups anticipated that a buoyant, oil-dominated economy would permit simultaneous military modernisation, domestic industrialisation, expanded social services and the like. When the precariousness of Nigeria's position became apparent, the resulting strains were immense.

Economic improvement, whether real or presumed, has received little attention from the scholars of military disengagement discussed earlier in this chapter. The case of Nigeria suggests that real increases, and anticipated further growth, in government revenues facilitate recivilianisation. An ever-growing economic pie can be sliced to satisfy many demands.

Of course, it did not: Nigeria, like Ghana, Liberia, Sierra Leone and Upper Volta, found itself after October 1979 with a civilian government incapable either of satisfying popular demands or of ensuring fiscal integrity. Accused by disgruntled officers of profligacy and waste, elected officials in each of the five countries were also confronted by discontented constituents demanding more government services. Pronounced government deficits, inflation, rising unemployment, food shortages and similar economic ills plagued all the West African governments that attempted to recivilianise.

CONCLUSIONS

The following conclusions emerge from the study of West African military disengagements from politics:

1. The act of disengaging, though it may provide limited legitimation, cannot and does not right the fundamental conditions that help incite military intervention. Cosmetic changes may be carried out, as shown particularly in Nigeria, but the period of explicit recivilianisation seems too brief and politicised to restructure the system. In fact, the relaxation of pressures from the armed forces due to disengagement may result in a significant heightening of domestic tensions, as groups, parties and individuals seek to better their

positions in the emergent system.
2. A clearly-defined successor group is essential for phased disengagement to succeed, as shown in the contrasting examples of Ghana or Nigeria on the one hand, and Sierra Leone and Upper Volta on the other.
3. Equally essential is a leader able to carry the armed forces with him. Lamizana, despite his prestige, failed in his second attempt to still intra-military doubts about his policies; Obasanjo, following the line laid down by Murtala, succeeded.
4. Differing colonial heritages appear to have little discernible impact on armed forces' political activities, at least by the time a second or third military government has taken over. The British concept that 'politics is not for soldiers' was better exemplified by French-trained Lamizana than by many of his Anglophone counterparts.
5. The size of the armed forces similarly seems to make little difference: the small Sierra Leone army could step aside, as a result of internal planning. So long as the chain of command remained intact and leaders were bent on returning to the barracks - or conversely, so long as widespread pressures from the armed forces made rapid demilitarisation essential - the number of men under arms had no effect.
6. Internal conflict in the armed forces is the proverbial two-edged sword. As in Sierra Leone, Ghana (Akuffo/Rawlings) or Nigeria, it can hasten returns to the barracks; as in Ghana or Upper Volta, it can result in the installation of a 'ruler'-type government of indefinite duration dedicated to major restructuring.
7. Efforts to follow Huntington's prescription that soldiers 'cannot stand above politics or attempt to stop politics. Instead they must make their way through politics'[55] have yet to be fully implemented in West Africa. The reason may lie in the 'system of personal rule,' discussed elsewhere in this volume. It is not the military as an institution around which parties may be built; it

is individuals, who may have risen through the armed forces to the political heights. However, unless more detailed study is carried out of states such as Benin or Ethiopia, in which 'ruler'-type officers have sought to mobilise public support, the results remain open to question.
8. The processes of liberalisation and redemocratisation ultimately are long-term. The experience of Sierra Leone notwithstanding, the establishment and maintenance of civilian control of the military in tropical Africa will require long-term economic growth and better distribution of government investments, greater national unity and a redefinition of the armed forces' role in more classic defence rather than more modern developmental terms.
9. Economic improvement, be it real or perceived, appears to help the process of disengagement. Conversely, economic adversity - as shown in all the states discussed in this chapter - introduces major strains in civil-military relations. Intense disputes over resources appear both to heighten military perceptions of the need for change, and to increase civilian solicitation for intervention.
10. Finally, attention must be given, as Adeksen aptly notes, to 'psychological' as well as 'physical' withdrawal of governing officers.[56] Not only must the head of state (be he Lamizana or Rawlings in 1979) be prepared to return to the barracks, his colleagues must also be willing to do so. Pay helps; so too do grants of immunity or indemnification; respect for what the armed forces accomplished should mark the wise politician who hopes to remain in power following disengagement; and an emphasis on professionalism in the sense of neutrality toward political movements also appears important.

What the armed forces of Africa are showing, in other words, is a self-perpetuating pattern of involvement that, though not inevitable in its spread and significance, makes short-term disengagement (either voluntary or coerced) possible, but that makes long-term neutrality extremely unlikely. The 'system of personal rule' can be utilised by officers, such as Eyadema or Mobutu, in a fashion that may not lay foundations for future stability. And, where political succession is unclear and social tensions are mounting, the chances for renewing the intervention/disengagement/reintervention cycle increase. 'The most common aftermath of military government,' Nordlinger has concluded, 'is military government.'[57] I concur. Disengagement remains 'provisional and temporary' through most of West Africa. Officers stand on the sidelines as referees of their successors' performance, ready to blow the whistle and potentially change all the rules of the game.

Military Disengagement from Politics

APPENDIX

SUCCESSFUL *COUPS D'ETAT* IN AFRICA: 1958-84

Date	Country
17 Nov. 1958	Sudan
14 Sept. 1960	Zaire
13 Jan. 1963	Togo
15 Aug. 1963	Congo-Brazzaville
28 Oct. 1963	Benin (Dahomey)
12 Jan. 1964	Zanzibar
19 June 1965	Algeria
25 Nov. 1965	Zaire
29 Nov. 1965	Benin (Dahomey)
22 Dec. 1965	Benin (Dahomey)*
1 Jan. 1966	Central African Republic
3 Jan. 1966	Upper Volta
15 Jan. 1966	Nigeria
24 Feb. 1966	Ghana
8 July 1966	Burundi
29 July 1966	Nigeria
28 Nov. 1966	Burundi
13 Jan. 1967	Togo
21-3 Mar. 1967	Sierra Leone
17 Dec. 1967	Benin (Dahomey)
18 April 1968	Sierra Leone
2 Aug.; 9 Sept. 1968	Congo-Brazzaville
19 Nov. 1968	Mali
25 May 1969	Sudan
1 Sept. 1969	Libya
21 Oct. 1969	Somalia
10 Dec. 1969	Benin (Dahomey)
25 Jan. 1971	Uganda
13 Jan. 1972	Ghana
18 May 1972	Madagascar
26 Oct. 1972	Benin (Dahomey)
5 July 1973	Rwanda
8 Feb. 1974	Upper Volta
15 April 1974	Niger
12 Sept. 1974	Ethiopia
25 Jan. 1975	Madagascar
13 April 1975	Chad
29 July 1975	Nigeria
1 Nov. 1976	Burundi
18 March 1977	Congo-Brazzaville
4-5 June 1977	Seychelles
5 May 1978	Comoros

5 July 1978	Ghana
10 July 1978	Mauritania
5 Feb. 1979	Congo-Brazzaville
6 Apr. 1979	Mauritania
4 June 1979	Ghana
4 Aug. 1979	Equatorial Guinea
20 Sept. 1979	Central African Empire
4 Jan. 1980	Mauritania
12 April 1980	Liberia
11 May 1980	Uganda
15 Nov. 1980	Guinea-Bissau
24 Nov. 1980	Upper Volta
1 Sept. 1981	Central African Republic
31 Dec. 1981	Ghana
7 Nov. 1982	Upper Volta
18 May 1983	Upper Volta
4 Aug. 1983	Upper Volta
31 Dec. 1983	Nigeria
23 Apr. 1984	Guinea
12 Dec. 1984	Mauritania

Note: This table does not include abortive *coups d'état* (as in Congo-Brazzaville: February 1972, the Gambia: July - August 1981, the Seychelles: November 1981, Kenya: August 1982, Central African Republic: March 1982, Equatorial Guinea: May 1983 or Ghana: June 1983), but does include changes of personnel in military-based governments brought about by threats of force, as in Mauritania in 1979 and 1980, or Upper Volta in May 1983.

*I have included these and other pre-1972 *coups d'état* in Benin despite Ronen's apt warning that many showed 'no evidence of a plan or scheme or intention to overthrow the civilian government'; he considers counting the two 1965 events separately to be 'too pedantic.' Ronen, D., 'Benin: The Rule of the Uniformed Leaders,' in Mowoe, I.J. (ed.), <u>The Performance of Soldiers as Governors: African Politics and the African Military</u> (Washington: University Press of America, 1980), p. 121.

NOTES

1. Significant quantitative analyses of causes of military intervention include Jackman, R.W., 'The Predictability of Coups d'Etat: A Model with African Data,' American Political Science Review, 72, 4 (December 1978), pp. 1262-75; and Johnson, T.H., Slater, R.O., and McGowan, P., 'Explaining African Military Coups d'Etat, 1960-1982,' American Political Science Review, 78, 3 (September 1984), pp. 622-40.

2. Jackman, R.W., 'Politicians in Uniform: Military Government and Social Change in the Third World,' American Political Science Review, 70, 4 (December 1976), pp. 1078-97; McKinlay, R.D. and Cohan, A.S., 'A Comparative Analysis of the Political and Economic Performance of Military and Civilian Regimes,' Comparative Politics, 8, 1 (October 1975), pp. 1-30, and, by the same authors, 'Performance and Instability in Military and Nonmilitary Regime Systems,' American Political Science Review, 70, 3 (September 1976), pp. 850-64; and Ravenhill, J., 'Comparing Regime Performance in Africa: The Limitations of Cross-National Aggregate Analysis,' Journal of Modern African Studies, 18, 1 (March 1980), pp. 99-126.

3. Finer, S.E., The Man on Horseback: The Role of the Military in Politics (New York: Praeger, 1962), p. 243.

4. Finer, S.E., 'The Man on Horseback - 1974,' Armed Forces and Society, 1, 1 (Fall 1974), p. 19.

5. Huntington, S.P., Political Order in Changing Societies (New Haven: Yale University Press, 1968), p. 261.

6. Ibid, p. 243.

7. Redemocratisation from within constitutes one of eight categories for potential transition. Stepan, A., 'Paths Toward Democratization: Theoretical and Comparative Considerations,' in O'Donnell, G. and Schmitter, P. (eds.), Transitions from Authoritarian Rule: Classes, Institutions, Processes and Choices in Comparative Perspective, (forthcoming).

8. Janowitz, M., 'Preface,' Armed Forces and Society, 1, 3 (Spring 1975), p. 286.

9. Ben-Dor, G., 'Civilianization of Military Regimes in the Arab World,' ibid., pp. 319-20.

10. Morell, D., 'Alternatives to Military Rule in Thailand,' ibid., p. 300.

11. Kasfir, N., 'Civilian Participation

Under Military Rule in Uganda and Sudan,' ibid. p. 360.

12. Welch, C.E., Jr., Soldier and State in Africa (Evanston: Northwestern University Press, 1970), pp. 54-5. In a related writing, note was also taken of international economic and political pressure, a factor 'far less significant and far more difficult to document' than the other three. Welch, C.E., Jr., 'Cincinnatus in Africa: Military Disengagement from Politics,' in Lofchie, M. (ed.), The State of the Nations: Constraints on Development in Independent Africa (Berkeley: University of California Press, 1971), pp. 215-37; quote from pp. 226-7.

13. Welch, C.E., Jr., 'The Dilemmas of Military Withdrawal from Politics: Some Considerations from Tropical Africa,' African Studies Review, 17, 1 (April 1974), pp. 213-27. This framework has been applied to at least two West African states; see Hansen, E. and Collins, P., 'The Army, the State, and the "Rawlings Revolution" in Ghana,' African Affairs, 79, 314 (January 1980), pp. 3-23; Joseph, R.A., 'Democratization under Military Tutelage: Crisis and Consensus in the Nigerian 1979 Elections,' Comparative Politics, 12, 1 (October 1981), pp. 75-100; and Koehn, P. 'Prelude to Civilian Rule: The Nigerian Elections of 1979,' Africa Today, 28, 1 (June 1981), pp. 17-45.

14. Welch, C.E., Jr., 'Long Term Consequences of Military Rule: Breakdown and Extrication,' Journal of Strategic Studies, 1, 2 (September 1978), pp. 139-53.

15. Welch, C.E., Jr., 'Military Disengagement from Politics: Lessons from West Africa,' Armed Forces and Society, 9, 4 (Summer 1983), pp. 541-54.

16. Kirk-Greene, A.H.M. 'Stay by Your Radios': Documentation for a Study of Military Government in Tropical Africa (Leiden: Afrika-Studiecentrum, 1981), p. 18.

17. In Algeria, the December 1979 death of Hourari Boumedienne, who had siezed power in June 1965, made possible the peaceful accession to power of Col. Chadly Benjedid to the Presidency; in Egypt, the direct line of succession from Nasser to Sadat, and thence to Mubarak, suggests decreasing military involvement in politics. For a focus on the central importance of the executive, see Cooper, M.N., 'The Demilitarization of the Egyptian Cabinet,' International Journal of Middle East

Studies, 14, 2 (May 1982), pp. 203-25.

18. Finer, 'The Man on Horseback - 1974,' p. 19.

19. These terms are taken from Perlmutter, A., 'The Praetorian State and the Praetorian Army,' Comparative Politics, 1, 3 (April 1969), pp. 382-404; for further elaboration, see, by the same author, The Military and Politics in Modern Times (New Haven: Yale University Press, 1977), pp. 104-14.

20. By 'internal', I refer to factors that are primarily organisational, such as salaries, factionalism within the military, and promotions; by 'environmental', I refer to factors characterising the surrounding social, economic and political systems, such as declining legitimacy of major political parties or leaders, corruption, domestic violence, or national financial adversity; by 'interactional', I refer to factors that reduce the organisational autonomy of the military and result in the intrusion of cleavages characteristic of the society as a whole into the armed forces, such as conscious solicitation of military intervention by civilian groups, involvement of the armed forces in suppression of domestic opponents of the government, activation of ethnic sentiments, or other forms of 'boundary fragmentation.' For the latter concept, see Luckham, A.R., 'A Comparative Typology of Civil-Military Relations', Government and Opposition, 6, 1 (Winter 1971), pp. 58-9.

21. Welch, C.E., Jr., 'Civil-Military Relations in Commonwealth States: The Transfer and Transformation of British Models,' Journal of Developing Areas, 12, 2 (January 1978), pp. 153-70; for a different perspective, see Price, R.M., 'A Theoretical Approach to Military Rule in New States: Reference-Group Theory and the Ghanaian Case', World Politics, 23, 3 (April 1971), pp. 399-430.

22. Cox gives particular attention to this factor, in explaining why the National Reformation Council in Sierra Leone remained in power until its ouster by the rank and file: no civilian successor group could be identified to whom the NRC could hand over control; and the headstrong leadership of Juxon-Smith fragmented top military leadership. Cox, T.S., Civil-Military Relations in Sierra Leone: A Case Study of African Soldiers in Politics (Cambridge: Harvard University Press, 1976), pp. 177-92.

23. Cartwright, J.R., <u>Politics in Sierra Leone 1947-1967</u> (Toronto: University of Toronto Press, 1970); Cox, <u>Civil-Military Relations in Sierra Leone</u>; Kilson, M., <u>Political Change in a West African State: A Study of the Modernization Process in Sierra Leone</u> (Cambridge: Harvard University Press, 1968).
24. Cox, <u>Civil-Military Relations in Sierra Leone</u>, p. 49.
25. <u>Ibid.</u>, p. 117.
26. <u>Ibid.</u>, p. 146.
27. <u>Ibid.</u>, p. 226.
28. <u>Ibid.</u>, p. 178.
29. For the protagonists' views, see Afrifa, A.A., <u>The Ghana Coup</u> (London: Cass, 1966); Ocran, A.K., <u>A Myth is Broken: An Account of the Ghana Coup d'Etat of 24 February 1966</u> (London: Longmans, 1968); and Nkrumah, K., <u>Dark Days in Ghana</u> (New York: International Publishers, 1968). For a governmental view, see Barker, P., <u>Operation Cold Chop</u> (Accra: Ghana Publishing Corporation, 1967). For views critical of Nkrumah from varying academic perspectives, see Bretton, H., <u>The Rise and Fall of Kwame Nkrumah</u> (New York: Praeger, 1967); Fitch, B. and Oppenheimer, M., <u>Ghana: End of an Illusion</u> (New York: Monthly Review Press, 1966); and Jones, T., <u>Ghana's First Republic 1960-1966</u> (London: Methuen, 1976).
30. Austin, D. and Luckham, R. (eds.), <u>Politicians and Soldiers in Ghana</u> (London: Cass, 1975), pp. 2, 4.
31. Feit, E., 'The Rule of the "Iron Surgeons": Military Rule in Ghana and Spain,' <u>Comparative Politics</u>, 1, 4 (July 1969), pp. 485-97. Also see, by the same author, 'Military Coups and Political Development: Lessons from Ghana and Nigeria,' <u>World Politics</u>, 20, 2 (January 1968), pp. 179-93.
32. Kwesi Lamptey, quoted by Luckham, R. and Nkrumah, S., 'The Constituent Assembly - A Social and Political Portrait,' in Austin and Luckham, <u>Politicians and Soldiers in Ghana</u>, p. 89.
33. For a brief period, a three-member Presidential Commission of ranking army and police officers also served, evidence, it would seem, of some lingering doubts among NLC members of the value of total disengagement.
34. Chazan, N., <u>An Anatomy of Ghanaian Politics: Managing Political Recession, 1969-1972</u> (Boulder: Westview Press, 1983), pp. 245-67;

LeVine, V.T. and Chazan, N., 'Politics in a "Nonpolitical" System: The March 30, 1978 Referendum in Ghana', *African Studies Review*, 22, 1 (April 1979); and Owusu, M., 'Politics without Parties: Reflections on the Union Government Proposal in Ghana,' *ibid*., pp. 89-108.

35. Huntington, *Political Order in Changing Societies*, pp. 243-4: 'The problem in moving societies away from endemic intervention is military opposition to politics ... Military leaders ... condemn political parties ... Their goal is community without politics, consensus by command'.

36. Welch, C.E., Jr., 'Emerging Patterns of Civil-Military Relations in Africa: Radical Coups d'Etat and Political Stability,' in Arlinghaus, B. (ed.), *African Security Issues: Sovereignty, Stability and Solidarity* (Boulder: Westview Press, 1984), pp. 126-39.

37. Chazan, *An Anatomy of Ghanaian Politics*, p. 280.

38. *Africa Research Bulletin*, 16, 6 (July 1979), col. 5307A.

39. *Ibid.*, 16, 9 (October 1979), col. 5400B.

40. Legum, C., (ed.), *Africa Contemporary Record, 1971-1973* (New York: Africana Publishing, 1973), p. B746.

41. Skurnik, W.A.E., 'The Military and Politics: Dahomey and Upper Volta,' in Welch, *Soldier and State in Africa*, p. 71.

42. *West Africa*, 31 October 1977, p. 2193.

43. *Ibid.*, 9 June 1980, pp. 1005-8.

44. *Ibid.*, 30 July 1984, p. 1520.

45. *Ibid.*, 27 August 1984, p. 1715.

46. Bennett, V.P. and Kirk-Greene, A.H.M., 'Back to the Barracks: A Decade of Marking Time,' in Panter-Brick, K., *Soldiers and Oil: The Political Transformation of Nigeria* (London: Cass, 1978), pp. i-xx.

47. Quoted in Adekson, J.B., 'Dilemma of Military Disengagement,' in Oyediran, O. (ed.), *Nigerian Government and Politics under Military Rule 1966-79* (New York: St. Martins, 1979), p. 218.

48. Phillips, C.S., 'Nigeria's New Political Institutions 1975-9,' *Journal of Modern African Studies*, 18, 1 (March 1980), pp. 1-22.

49. Oyediran, O., 'Civilian Rule for How Long?', in Oyediran, *Nigerian Government and Politics*, p. 278.

50. For details, see Bassey, C., *Military Power in Nigerian Foreign Policy: An Analysis and Assessment of Motivation, Goals and Utility*

(unpublished Ph.D. dissertation, Dalhousie University, 1985).
51. Figures from *West Africa*, 29 September 1980, p. 1889.
52. Legum, C., (ed.), *Africa Contemporary Record, 1975-6* (London: Rex Collings, 1976), p. 802.
53. *West Africa*, 3 December 1984, p. 2461.
54. *Ibid.*, p. 2462.
55. Huntington, *Political Order in Changing Societies*, p. 241.
56. Adekson, 'Dilemma of Military Disengagement', p. 231.
57. Nordlinger, E.A., *Soldiers in Politics: Military Coups and Governments* (Englewood Cliffs: Prentice-Hall, 1977), p. 210.

Chapter Four

ARMIES AND POLITICS IN CIVILIAN REGIMES

David Goldsworthy

INTRODUCTION

A received wisdom about African military coups has been accumulating now for some two decades. Explanations of Africa's coup-proneness usually stress such broad contextual factors as economic malaise, political corruption and sectional conflict, along with factors internal to the military such as corporate grievances and an absence of military tradition. But such generalisations seem evident to most of the coup-free states of Africa as well as to the coup-prone, doing little therefore to differentiate the cases. In addition, the sustained focus on military intervention has helped to reinforce the commonly held view that it has become a norm of African political behaviour, with the instances of civilian control being regarded as exceptions to the rule. It is not unusual to encounter the fatalistic attitude that, so fragile is civilian control in Africa, the turn of the coup-free states is bound to come.

No doubt, in some cases, it is. Yet such an approach represents an abdication of scholarship. Fatalism is simply not a substitute for analysis of the achievement of various regimes in maintaining civilian control so far - which means, in several countries, for well over 20 years. To fail to confront the question of why a significant number of African militaries have not usurped their countries' governments, when by all the indications they could have done so had they wished, is to impede our fuller understanding of the dynamics of civil-military interactions in the continent. We take our cue, then, from S.E. Finer: 'Instead of asking why the military engage in politics, we ought surely to be asking why they ever do otherwise ... Why and how do civilian forms of rule persist?'[1]

In an earlier discussion of this theme, I sought firstly to expound some relevant theory built upon the concepts of 'subjective' and 'objective' forms of control, seen in relation to the broad categories of legitimacy and effectiveness in government; and secondly to look at the records of the 17 African mainland states which had maintained civilian control from independence until late 1980. These states, listed here in the sequence in which they attained independence, were Guinea (1958), Cameroon, the Ivory Coast, Gabon and Senegal (all 1960), Tanzania (1961), Kenya (1963), Malawi and Zambia (both 1964), the Gambia (1965), Botswana and Lesotho (both 1966), Swaziland (1968), Mozambique and Angola (both 1975), Djibouti (1977) and Zimbabwe (1980).

From the record, it appeared that civilian control in these states was much more often subjective than objective: that is 'military allegiance to government depends much more on informal linkages, merging of class interests, and so on' than on 'self-restraining military professionalism'. A prime conclusion was that control usually had a lot to do with the dominating role of a particular national leader. In some states - though not many - it was underwritten by the presence of foreign (French, British or Cuban) troops. In addition, governments usually sought to enhance their control by the deliberate use of techniques, for example in the ethnic matching of regime and army; in strategies of recruitment, promotion and retirement; in the cooptation of soldiers into state authority structures, for example by seconding them to ministerial, bureaucratic or parastatal office; in the dispensation of patronage, perquisites and payoffs; in manipulation of the military's 'mission'; and in the prudential use of militias, gendarmeries and security agencies as counter-balancing forces. Most such attributes and devices appeared highly specific to particular incumbent regimes and thereby offered no real assurance that civilian rule would survive a regime change. Nevertheless, it was notable that by late 1980 all five of the civilian-ruled states which had experienced top-level leadership successions (Tanzania in 1962, Gabon in 1967, Kenya in 1978,

Angola in 1979, Botswana in 1980[2]) had managed the task peacefully and indeed constitutionally, with no evident diminution of civilian control. In certain countries, the success of these transitions was arguably correlated with higher than average levels of governmental legitimacy (for example in Botswana) or institutionalisation (for example in Kenya). If this were indeed so, there appeared to be a nascent case for modifying some of our received wisdom about African 'praetorianism', 'the inevitability of instability' and the like.[3]

My argument at that time was very much a preliminary exploration of an under-researched field. On revisiting the field some five years later, I was able to note, firstly, that civilian rule still prevailed in all but one of the 17 countries. The exception was Guinea, where the military takeover of April 1984 followed immediately upon the death of Ahmed Sékou Touré; in Guinea, evidently, no base of control more durable than one man's authority had developed.[4] I noted secondly, and with a certain gratification, three more cases of orderly succession: the transitions from President Senghor to his Prime Minister, Abdou Diouf, in Senegal on New Year's Day 1981, from King Sobhuza to an interim regent in Swaziland in August 1982 and from President Abidjo to his Prime Minister, Paul Biya, in Cameroon in November 1982. In Swaziland the succession was occasioned by the death of the King; in the other two countries, by the voluntary retirement of the incumbent. In all the other states the incumbent leaders of 1980 were still in power in late 1985. Several of them (Houphouët-Boigny, Nyerere, Banda, Kaunda, Jawara, Chief Jonathan) were not only the original independence leaders of their countries but ranked among the longest-serving heads of government in the world. On the face of it, this looked like remarkable testimony to the political stability of these states. This is not of course to argue that stability is necessarily a positive attribute; the long-lived civilian regimes of Africa vary widely along the spectrum from the admirably representative (for example Botswana) to the harshly repressive (for example Lesotho, Cameroon, Gabon). Nor is it to presume any *particular* causal link between the stability and the civilian control. The limits of crude generalisation become fairly evident here. In the task of attaining a clearer understanding of the survival of a specific civilian regime, generalisations can serve as no more than signposts for detailed empirical research.

Overall, I felt no reason to depart from the majority of my earlier formulations. Nevertheless it seemed to me, in the light of the passage of events in Africa and following some further reading in the field,[5] that certain points now stood in need of more extended discussion than I had initially given them.

In the first place, the common stress in earlier writings (including my own) on strong leadership as a significant correlate of civilian control, while very well supported by the circumstantial evidence, seemed ultimately unsatisfactory in that it always hovered close to tautology: a strong leader survives because he is a strong leader. To turn this proposition into a more useful form we should be seeking a more analytical view of the character of civilian political leadership in relation to African militaries. Indeed, following Jackson and Rosberg, we should perhaps be thinking more about the nature of 'personal rule' as a *system* of governance.

In the second place, by late 1985 more than half of the coup-free states had in fact experienced at least one coup attempt, or rumours of at least one coup plot. This would appear significantly to modify the nature of the question. In looking for the key to civilian survival in these states, we should be asking not simply: Why no coups?, but rather: Why no successful coups? And it will be suggested that here again it may be useful to think of government in terms of a 'system of personal rule'.

In the third place, the ideological-cum-structural diversities of contemporary Africa, ranging from capitalist ultra-dependence to 'actually existing socialism', in Bahro's phrase[6], should perhaps be sensitising us to the different ways in which our questions might need to be framed in these varying contexts. Should we expect, for example, qualitative variations in the manner of civilian control according to the nature of a regime's capitalistic or socialistic persuasions? And how might these ideological-structural considerations interact with the notion of the 'system of personal rule'?

This chapter, then, will be organised around these three topics.

CIVILIAN CONTROL IN A SYSTEM OF PERSONAL RULE

The notion of personal rule, with 'personal' usually treated as synonymous with 'personalist', is far from new in African studies. Decalo's 1976 typology of forms of military governance, for example, runs in ascending order of institutionalisation from praetorian via personalist and brokerage to bureaucratic.[7] Jackson and Rosberg's work *Personal Rule in Black Africa*, however, goes well beyond other studies in regarding personal rule as the modal form in the continent and as something distinguishable from personalist rule. Whereas the latter term suggests more or less arbitrary governance at the whim of an individual, personal rule, in their sense, has certain systemic properties. At first sight there is a contradiction, or at least a paradox, here: how can the personal be systemic? A brief exposition is in order.[8]

Colonial rule was built very largely on assumptions and norms of governance that were alien to Africa. Further, colonial territories were seldom coextensive with traditional African societies. Thus the political structures that were transmitted from the colonial order to the new state lacked autochthony; that is they were not rooted in distinctively African notions of authority and legitimacy. Because of this disjunction between the local culture and the inherited political structures, the political life of the new state was carried on without the benefit of well-established normative and institutional bases and guidelines for action. And in Jackson and Rosberg's words, 'In the absence of unifying indigenous institutions, politicians were left with the task of governing with their personal power and authority.'[9] A non-institutionalised politics is a personalised politics.

In such a situation, politics is more usefully perceived as a game (following F.G. Bailey's usage), in which leaders and their clients contest for power and place, than as, say, an arena in which secondary social groups compete over policies and the constitutional right to govern. It is of course a game played for high prizes, chiefly because of the centrality of the public sector in disposing of the material surplus in African countries. Since the game is not yet institutionalised and has no referee, the players 'are not restrained from employing coercion, violence, and other harmful and unfair political means in their struggle'. If these methods are to be minimised, 'the players themselves must see to it without the assistance of a political culture with an institutional tradition'; the avoidance of conflict depends chiefly on 'private and tacit agreements, prudential concerns, and personal ties and dependencies'.[10] In these several respects, contemporary African politics somewhat resembles the palace politics of early modern Europe.[11] Correspondingly, the classical Western political theorist whose work is most apposite for grasping the nature of the game is Niccolo Machiavelli. The African ruler is Machiavelli's Prince; how well he performs and how long he survives are very largely a function of his personal political willpower, skill and *fortuna*.[12] In a strikingly pertinent passage, Machiavelli wrote:

> Governments set up overnight, like everything in nature whose growth is forced, lack strong roots and ramifications. So they are destroyed in the first bad spell. This is inevitable unless those who have suddenly become princes are of such prowess that overnight they can learn how to preserve what fortune has suddenly tossed in their laps.[13]

In what sense, then, can personal-rule politics, thus conceived, be regarded as systemic? Jackson and Rosberg provide two answers. Firstly, in formal and functionalist vein, they describe personal rule as a system in so far as it serves to regulate power in the state and to carry out political functions and provide political goods - peace, order, stability, non-material security - as well as material rewards. This is clearly a relative statement, and the authors allow that personal rule is generally less effective than institutionalised rule in doing these things. Secondly, and closer to our concerns, the personal-rule game, like any other game, can be seen as a system in operational terms: that is as a system of relations. Political relationships link rulers with associates, supporters, sub-patrons (and hence indirectly, through clientelism, with the public), and also with rivals and enemies. The system is structured by these actors and is maintained by their mutual understandings and their rational self-interest in the avoidance of risk or deprivation (such as loss of privileges, freedom, or life). African experience suggests that, so long as such understandings and interests are preserved, 'a relatively stable public life is attainable in large-scale territorial states that are neither institutionalized "civil societies" nor anti-political totalitarian regimes ... a measure of political order has been attained without the complete suppression of politics.'[14]

But of course, the fact that the system is built upon persons rather than institutions is also its great vulnerability. Personal rule is intrinsically more subject to disruption than institutional. Feelings of insecurity are rife. Accordingly people who fear exclusion, not to mention those who have already been excluded or were never included, may well engage in plotting and attempt coups. Similarly, those in power may well resort to intimidation, suppression and purges. Such behaviour must be regarded not as aberrant, but as generic to systems of personal rule. Clientelism, factionalism, plots, coups, purges, succession crises: all these phenomena, so commonly observed in African politics, can be perceived falling into place as *integral elements of a distinctive political system.*[15]

So is the trend towards authoritarianism - the narrowing of the public sphere, the concentration of authority. Yet no personal ruler is ever wholly unrestrained or certain of his power. Precisely because of the weakness of institutions, the ruler must deal all the more directly with other powerful individuals. And a fair measure of his skill as a Prince will be the degree to which he is able to deal with his rivals by methods - such as cooptation and patronage - which fall short of main force.

In the end, almost everything depends upon the ability and fortune of the individual at the top. His position is at once the most commanding and the most vulnerable to the plotting of others. It is therefore hardly surprising that Africa has produced many leaders who have been truly remarkable political tacticians, and that the most outstanding of these have been remarkably long-lived in office. Some of their case histories are used by Jackson and Rosberg to refine the general analytical construct, personal rule, into types. Thus we observe the Princely style proper - conservative, immensely shrewd, ostensibly above the courtiers' rivalries - exemplified by, for example, Kenyatta, Senghor and Seretse Khama; the Autocratic style - managerial, technocratic, domineering - exemplified by Houphouët-Boigny and Banda; the Prophetic style - visionary, hortatory - exemplified by Nyerere; and finally personal rule in its degenerate form, the murderously anti-political Tyrannical style of Amin, Bokassa and Nguema.

To comment on all this. 'Personal rule' is not of course the only way in which African politics might be conceptualised, and it lies open to certain lines of criticism. Some might say that its focus on the techniques of domination and survival is not only cynical and amoral but excessively narrow, drawing attention away from the major issues of policy which ought to be of central interest in politics and political analysis. Others might see it as idealist, treating politicians as if they were autonomous, free-floating game-players somehow separated from the material base; as if there were no larger socio-economic structures and no deeper dimensions of socio-economic conflict governing the roles they play.

In fact, the notion of personal rule can be applied with no great difficulty to both of the analytical objects implied by these criticisms, respectively policy output and socio-economic structure. The connections between styles of personal rule and the varieties of policy output are well covered in both the Jackson-Rosberg volume and in Cartwright's *Political Leadership in Africa*, in their case-studies of, for example, Houphouët-Boigny, Nyerere and Kenyatta. As for the links between the personal-political game and the broader conditions and conflicts of the social formation, three things can be said. First, the social and cultural fragmentation which typifies most African states is foremost among the reasons for the lack of institutionalised consensus in the first place, and hence for the very pervasiveness of personal rule. Second, without question politicians do represent or 'express' socio-economic forces beyond themselves, being powerful, for example, in the degree to which their home regions are powerful (in terms of wealth, population, etc.), or in the degree to which their links with major foreign investors are strong. Third, the scope for any personal ruler's manoeuvrings is in some degree determined by, for example, the forms of economic dependency (*vide* Kaunda's power of reward fluctuating with the copper revenues) or the idiosyncracies of social structure (vide Senghor's political need to accommodate the 'non-political' Islamic marabouts). Such things are simply not in dispute.

We will return to these broader issues of policy and context in a later section. For the present our concerns do not, in fact, extend beyond the issue of survival at the apex of politics, and for this level of analysis, it is submitted, the personal-rule conceptualisation is strongly and consistently illuminating. Indeed it would appear superior to conceptualisations which concentrate heavily on the 'chronic instability' of African politics; for it has the potential to explain both instability and stability, both coup-proneness and coup-freeness, in all the varying degrees in which these phenomena actually occur.

To return, then, to civil-military relations.[16] We have argued that by and large, there are few strongly institutionalised cultural bases for contemporary African politics; there is little evidence of a national consensus expressed in entrenched and legitimate institutions. It follows that political control of the military, where it exists, cannot rest upon such a base. If it did, we would be entitled to regard control as objective, bureaucratised, professionalised, and so on. Since it does not, we must look for the prime determinants of control where we look for the other significant elements of the personal-rule system: that is within the nexus of subjective and personal relationships.

Superficially, an African military may present the appearance of an impersonal, rational and self-contained secondary institution. In practice, as numerous studies of military coups have helped to show, African armed forces are anything but insulated from the cultural *mores*, the social cleavages and the conflicts that pervade the civil society and the polity. African armies, in Lemarchand's words, 'are an integral part of a wider social system with which they interact along different axes and in response to different events.'[17] It cannot therefore be assumed

> that military training and indoctrination in the ideals of discipline and obedience will take precedence over ethnic, familial, or personal loyalty in situations where soldiers are forced to choose between military duty and personal duty ... military commanders

often cannot count on the obedience of soldiers in a crisis situation, and command within military organizations ... must be exercised with the awareness and adroitness of a politician if the command is to be obeyed.[18]

Soldiers, then, and especially officers, are predisposed to think like politicians even in their intra-military dealings. In their dealings with their civilian superiors, such a mode of thinking can only be reinforced. For the relationship between soldier and politician within a personal-rule system is deeply and reciprocally political. High military office, like all appointive office, is a prize in the gift of the ruler; a prize that can be withdrawn as well as bestowed. Thus the fortunes of officers tend to rise and fall with the fortunes of particular politicians. For their part, the political leaders seek to underwrite their personal positions by cultivating selected officers and segments of the armed forces. Here is nothing other than a variant of the familiar reciprocal search of patrons for clients and clients for patrons, with alliances and networks being formed according to all manner of informal criteria having little to do with the formal civilian and military roles of those involved. If the ruler sees to it that an officer's military career prospers, it is likely to be because of his political reliability at least as much as his military virtues. If an officer supports a politician, his support is at least as likely to be based upon sound clientistic considerations as upon the constitutional delineation of roles. We are saying, in brief, that soldiers are among the players - actual and potential - of the political game; and that civilian control may generally be seen as a function of military loyalty to the person of the ruler rather than to the abstraction of the state. The relationship is of course embedded in a social context; frequently, loyalty to the ruler is in part a matter of shared social interests and affiliations (class, communal, familial, and so on). All of which is to reassert the essential subjectiveness of control.

By way of illustration we will draw upon a notable case of prolonged civilian control, that of Kenya. In arguing that civilian control in Kenya has been largely subjective, a matter of loyalty to the ruler, we will stress in particular the ways in which Kenya's rulers have manipulated the variables of ethnicity, personal friendship and material self-interest in their dealings with the security forces.

After the abortive mutiny by military units in January 1964, Jomo Kenyatta determined to absorb the armed forces thoroughly into his system of rule. The army was purged of its mutineers and buttressed by a continuing British 'advisory' presence. At independence, both the rank and file and the officer corps had been composed chiefly of Kamba and Kalenjin recruits; Kenyatta's government began recruiting from other communities and rapidly promoted young, British-trained Kikuyu officers. Kenyatta's goal, precisely as it was in the civilian political game, was to achieve a particular and advantageous kind of balance in which effective Kikuyu dominance would be tempered by much-more-than-token representation of other ethnic and regional communities at leadership level. In December 1966 the (British) army commander was succeeded by the most senior African officer, Brigadier J.M. Ndolo, who was a Kamba; immediately below Ndolo was a mix of Kikuyu, Kamba and Kalenjin officers. Meanwhile the paramilitary General Service Unit (GSU) became all but exclusively Kikuyu, while the police, the special branch and the CID came under mainly (though not entirely) Kikuyu leadership. This organising of ethnic representation, it was observed in 1968,

> is designed to discourage intervention by any of the security forces and keep them under predominantly Kikuyu control. A move by the army as a whole would call for a degree of trust and co-operation between Kikuyu and non-Kikuyu officers beyond what now seems to exist. A move by Kikuyu officers alone would probably bring a reaction from non-Kikuyu in the lower ranks, while intervention by non-Kikuyu officers alone could be expected to bring a counter-move by the General Service Unit and other elements of the police under Kikuyu command.[19]

The officer corps, some 23 per cent Kikuyu by 1967, became increasingly so during the seventies. So did the fledgling air force. The long-serving security ministers - the Minister of Defence, James Gichuru, and the Attorney-General,

Charles Njonjo - were not only Kikuyu but among the President's closest associates. This growing ethnic solidarity at the top of the security apparatus certainly contributed to the strength of Kenyatta's control. But in addition, senior officers were being increasingly absorbed into the circles of privilege. Many were able to use their positions to serve their material interests - acquiring farms, commercial businesses and other forms of wealth - in very much the manner of the politicians.[20] Several of the most important security-force officers, for example Ben Gethi, commander of the GSU, and James Kanyotu, head of the special branch, were personally close to Kenyatta's innermost circle. Where personal ties between officers and civilian big men did not yet exist, they began to be created; during the seventies, the marrying of military officers into the families of the civilian elite became commonplace.[21]

It nevertheless remained Kenyatta's characteristic and prudential policy to qualify this Kikuyu centrality by continuing to recruit junior officers nationwide, and by allowing the post of army commander - like the somewhat analogous post of vice-president in the civilian political system - to remain in non-Kikuyu hands. When Ndolo was retired in 1971 (in circumstances to be noted later), his successor as army commander, Major-General J.K. Mulinge, was another Kamba.

Daniel arap Moi, a Kalenjin, succeeded to the presidency in August 1978. Apparently he lost little time in seeking to provide military personnel with material reason to support him. For example Moi, like Kenyatta,

> used grants of land to keep senior officers loyal. After the first Rawlings coup in Ghana, land grants in Kenya went to junior officers as well. Large areas around Nakuru and Ngong were handed out to keep the armed forces behind the government.[22]

In addition, Moi began carefully and incrementally to dilute Kikuyu power in the highest ranks. Soon after Moi's accession, General Mulinge was promoted to Chief of the General Staff. A Kalenjin, Lt.-General J.M. Sawe, became army commander, with a Somali, Major-General M. Mohammed, as his deputy. By October 1979 the two top Kikuyu army officers had been sacked, in circumstances which remained mysterious.[23] Ben Gethi was transferred to the police, and the GSU came under the command of a European and a Meru. It was reported in October 1981 that General Mulinge was 'close to Moi, who has made a point of keeping officer ranks well cared for'.[24] These moves parallelled a general rise to prominence of non-Kikuyu (especially Kalenjin) in the civilian political elite. However, the vice-presidency and other key ministerial posts remained in Kikuyu hands so that the political game remained, broadly, a 'balanced' one, if with a different centre of gravity; as did the overall composition of the officer corps.

In drawing upon the Kenyan case in this fashion, we have not meant to suggest that objective military professionalism is simply absent in that country. We have nevertheless argued that the more subjective factors which loom large, and are consciously exploited, in systems of personal rule have been extremely relevant to the maintenance of civilian control in Kenya. And much the same could be said of other countries. Though evidence is not always easy to come by, periodicals of record and reportage such as *Africa Research Bulletin, Africa Contemporary Record, West Africa* and *Africa Confidential* do provide indicative material on, for example, patterns of military appointment and promotion across the continent. Among secondary sources, Cox's study of Sierra Leone has documented very fully the close personal involvement of politicians with officers and the salience of subjective factors - particularly kinship and ethnicity - in civil-military dealings during that country's years of civilian control; Luckham has written similarly, if more briefly, with reference to Nigeria in the years 1958-66; and Pachter has described some relevant patterns and relationships in Nyerere's Tanzania, Touré's Guinea and Machel's Mozambique. There are also much briefer analyses of civilian control in various other countries, for example Kaunda's Zambia, Senghor's Senegal and Banda's Malawi, which make some reference to subjective forms of control.[25]

Space constraints prohibit any extended discussion of these countries' experiences. However in one of them, Mozambique, one development has been so apropos that it cannot be left unmentioned. As of 1981, in a quite remarkable effort to personalise civilian control, high military rank had been conferred on nine members of the Mozambique cabinet, 'some of whom have never served in the army.'[26]

But something else must be said about both Kenya and Mozambique. Both have experienced coup attempts: Mozambique on 17 December 1975, Kenya on 1 August 1982.[27] It is time, then, to shift the focus of our discussion. The personal-rule idea has helped to show how civilian control may be maintained in Africa; can it also be used to throw light upon times of crisis in the civil-military relationship?

COUP PLOTS AND COUP ATTEMPTS

We have emphasised that it is very much up to the players themselves to keep the game orderly. But precisely because of this dependence upon persons, rather than institutions or culture, the possibility of degeneration into disorder is ever-present. Occasions do arise when all the resources available to the leading players - patronage, cooptation, dismissal, repression - are simply inadequate to the task of containing the ambitions, suspicions, rivalries, factional disagreements, and the like in the political community; whereupon violence in some form or other is likely to be used. Clearly, when violence becomes an instrument of politics, the security forces hold trump cards. How they will play them is an entirely political decision on their part, and it is governed overwhelmingly by their attitudes towards the civilian players at the time.

Broadly speaking, there are three possibilities. Firstly, the armed forces, or a mobilised segment of them, may exercise their power in support of the ruler against his domestic opponents, real or supposed. This is how Banda's soldiers, for example, have behaved for over 20 years in Malawi, and how Mugabe's soldiers have operated since 1980 in Zimbabwe. It is also the normal pattern for Kenya's GSU, a unit described by Tamarkin as 'a political force, the regime's coercive arm against its internal enemies.'[28] Such behaviour is usually described as loyal, by definition, and it certainly presents an *appearance* of civilian supremacy being maintained. As we have already argued, however, this sort of loyalty often rests heavily upon subjectivities - for example the ethnic matching of the regime of the day and its army - and as such is loyalty of a conditional, and perhaps transient, kind. Moreover, the very fact that the ruler has been unable to deal with his opponents except by resort to armed force underlines the point that he is ultimately as dependent upon his auxiliaries as they are upon him. When force becomes arbiter, the armed clients can decide the patron's fate. Just how conditional their support can be in a personal-rule system is most vividly illustrated by the Ugandan case. In 1966 the military client, Amin, helped buttress the power of his civilian patron, Obote, in a military operation to destroy Bugandan civilian power. Five years later the client overthrew the patron, largely in order to pre-empt a suspected threat to his own position.

Secondly, the armed forces, or a proportion of them, may throw their weight against the ruler in favour of some other civilian player or players: oppositionists or rival ministers, perhaps. This, it appears, was the meaning of the attempted coup in Gabon in February 1964; the soldiers' aim was to transfer power not to themselves, but to the Foreign Minister.[29] The attempted coup in Cameroon in April 1984 has been interpreted similarly, as an effort by a section of the army to seize power from President Biya on behalf of ex-President Ahidjo.[30] This kind of behaviour should be no cause for surprise in a personal-politics system. For one thing, given that the soldiers do hold trumps, it is natural that politicians of all persuasions, oppositionists no less than rulers, should seek to establish their own alliances and/or clienteles in the military forces. For another, as noted earlier, the armed forces are in no way insulated from the cultural and communal subjectivities of the wider society. Thus, in a time of political crisis, some of the soldiers might well place communal loyalties, say, ahead of their presumed loyalty to government. It appears that the attempted coup in Cameroon was of distinctly religious-regional character; the coup-makers' link with Ahidjo was their common provenance in the country's Moslem north, a factor which aligned them subjectively against the non-Moslem southerner Biya.

And thirdly, of course, the soldiers, or some of them, may initiate the use of violence, in an attempt to seize power for themselves. All that will be said here about successful military coups is that their aftermaths usually serve to confirm the personal-political nature of the game.

Confronting the same societal problems as did the civilians, they too must rule as personal politicians; the fact that they are soldiers will have little to do with their success or failure in office. Long-lived military rulers survive not because they dispose of armed force (for they may well be, and often are, the targets of counter-coups by other armed men), but because of the same sorts of political factors - acumen, skill, fortune - which sustain long-lived civilian rulers.[31]

Our concern, however, is with civilian survival, so we are interested in unsuccessful coups rather than successful ones. Coup attempts fail usually because plotters are discovered in time or because rebellious soldiers are subdued militarily by loyalist ones (of either local or foreign origin). In the previous section we concentrated on politically supportive behaviour by soldiers, the kind of behaviour which underlies the first of the three possibilities just outlined; we now turn to some instances of attempted rebellion (the second and third possibilities), in quest of further evidence on the workings of civilian control.

How many attempted military coups have the long-lived civilian regimes actually survived? At least half a dozen attempts have been well documented: in Gabon (1964), Mozambique (1975), Angola (1977), the Gambia (1981), Kenya (1982), and Cameroon (1984). A disturbance in Tanzania - specifically Zanzibar - in 1982 was probably a coup attempt. In addition, coup plots have been discovered, alleged or rumoured on various occasions in recent years, for example in Kenya (1971, 1978), the Ivory Coast (1980), and Zambia (1980, 1981).[32] We have commented already on two of these disturbances: the coup attempts in Gabon and Cameroon, both of which brought out the significance of personal-political ties between rival politicians and their respective military support groups. Here we will focus once again on Kenya, the country where three of the listed disturbances have occurred.

The 1971 plot involved the army commander, Ndolo, with a mixed group of ex-soldiers and political dissidents, the most prominent of whom was a former minister (and fellow Kamba). The plotting, amateurish in the extreme, was easily detected by the government's intelligence apparatus, and Ndolo was duly brought to trial. For our purposes the point of interest is that Ndolo had apparently been paralysed by indecision: he wished to strike against 'the government', but *not against Kenyatta*. It would be hard to find a clearer instance of the mixed and conditional character of loyalty in a personal-rule system. And as Leys has noted, 'Ndolo was treated with remarkable lenience, perhaps because of his consistent expression of reluctance to act against Kenyatta personally. He retired to his 9,416-acre farm ... in Machakos, a latter day Cincinnatus.'[33]

The 1978 plot reflected the tensions within the civilian elite on the issue of the succession to Kenyatta. It appears that the political faction grouped around Njoroge Mungai had been seeking to establish its own private clientele within the armed forces, by exploiting kinship ties and by offering material inducements such as stockholdings in the business enterprises of the Gikuyu, Embu and Meru Association (GEMA). In particular, this faction had built up a close relationship with the so-called Stock Theft Unit, a lavishly well-equipped military group based in the Rift Valley. Allegedly, in the wake of Kenyatta's death members of this unit would assassinate the leaders of the rival civilian faction, led by Moi and Njonjo, so as to ensure the political supremacy of their patrons. In the event the intelligence service, controlled by Njonjo as Attorney-General, uncovered the details and the unit's commander fled the country.[34] Here is a further illustration of points already made, concerning the permeation of the armed forces by civil conflicts and the fashioning of rival political alliances across the civil-military boundaries. The outcome was political triumph for the Moi-Njonjo forces, and, eventually, something of a replay of the Ndolo trial; for like Ndolo, the Stock Theft Unit's commander, once back in the country, was permitted to retire to his farm. Moi's leniency, like Kenyatta's earlier, was presumably a reflection - and indeed a demonstration - of his confidence in his personal political security at the time.

The 1982 coup attempt came from an entirely unexpected quarter, junior officers and senior NCOs of the air force; more specifically, the Ground Air Defence Unit plus a few members of the Air Cavalry battalion. The rising was fairly rapidly put down by army units. It appears that the coup-makers were young, technocratic, well-educated, many of them being in close touch with radically disillusioned university students, and that their main motivation was a genuine conviction that the government's policies for Kenya were bankrupt and that only a coup could bring change. Allied with this was a revulsion against the corrupt, repressive and self-seeking ways of politicians at the top of the personal-rule system: that 'gang of local tyrants' (to quote the coup-makers' radio broadcast) who had 'made life almost intolerable in our society.' They might in addition have been reacting against the very high and growing level of US military involvement in the country, not least in the air force itself. Arguably, communal considerations were involved as well; the Kikuyu who predominated among the conspirators might well have had ethnically subjective reasons for resenting the Moi ascendancy, while the Luo who were involved might well have been driven by the frustration of the Luo's virtual exclusion from power in the system.[35]

There are several points of interest about this uprising. Fistly, it came from the sector of the armed forces often regarded, by virtue of its advanced technical training, as the most highly professionalised, and hence, by implication, as the least likely to step outside the professional sphere into politics. That the airforcemen, of all people, should attempt a coup is eloquent testimony to the fragility of mere professionalism as a restraining influence in the absence of a restraining culture.

Secondly, the attempt came from a fairly junior level of the armed forces. Civilian control of the top brass does not count for much if the junior ranks are prepared to defy the authority of the senior officers, or simply bypass them on the way to a coup. This, in Africa, they sometimes are. In terms of the game metaphor, a rising from the junior ranks can be seen not so much as a violent move within the game as an attempt by a semi-excluded group to enter into it more fully, by force of arms. No personal ruler can eliminate the risk of such attempts being made. For that matter, he can never be sure that his manipulations of the armed forces might not prove counter-productive in some way; one soldier rewarded could easily mean another soldier alienated. Such (once again) are the hazards of control by subjective means.

The third point of interest lies in President

Moi's subsequent actions. Having had his skin saved by the army, the President's dependence upon it - and especially upon his politically reliable senior officers - became visible as never before. Moi not only refused to allow General Mulinge to retire, but kept him 'prominently visible beside him both in Nairobi and on visits around the country',[36] while the no less reliable Lt.-General Mohammed was promptly deputed to preside over the reconstitution of the air force. The Mohammed link was further personalised after the 1983 general election, when Mohammed's brother was appointed a minister in the President's office - the first ethnic Somali to attain cabinet rank in Kenya. At the end of that year it was reported that the top five servicemen (three Kamba, one Kalenjin and one Somali) were 'all considered personally loyal to Moi'; that in the wake of the coup attempt several more officers whom Moi might have had some reason to fear (mainly Kikuyu, and including Ben Gethi) had been sacked and imprisoned; and that the paramilitary GSU, the key coercive unit, was taking on an increasingly Kalenjin complexion, although in the armed forces as a whole the existing ethnic balances were being maintained as carefully as possible.[37]

All these developments can be seen as typical of the moves in a personal-rule game. Civilian supremacy is sought to a large extent in the manipulation of those subjective factors in which, it is fervently hoped, loyalty will take root. Even where a degree of military professionalism does appear to exist, there is little evidence of civilian reliance upon it as a *sufficient* condition of control.

SOCIAL STRUCTURE, IDEOLOGY AND CIVILIAN CONTROL

It might be argued that to focus upon subjectivities, as we have done, is to miss the significance of broader structural and ideological factors in the maintenance of civilian control.

On the matter of broad structure, for example, Saffu suggests that the study of civil-military relations 'must be informed by acute historical analyses of the process of incorporation of the Third World into the present international system ... analyses of the twin processes of colonialism and neo-colonialism are a necessary backdrop.'[38] No less generally, we might seek to trace the underlying connections between domestic, social, political and economic structures in Africa and patterns of order and disorder, including military order (subservience) and disorder (rebelliousness).

Such study may well give us a better grasp of certain elements of civilian control in particular cases. By focusing upon neo-colonialism and dependency, for example, we will probably be better placed to analyse cases in which overseas powers seek to stabilise favoured African regimes by providing valued goods - financial aid, military hardware, training programmes - which those regimes can then disburse to their armies; and we will be better sensitised to the instances of a foreign government taking positive steps to defend a client president against his secessionists (for example the French interventions in Zaire in 1977 and 1978) or even his own troops (for example the French intervention in Gabon in 1964, and on other comparable occasions during the heyday of Jacques Foccart in the Elysée Palace). Today, as Clayton notes in a later chapter, the French continue to show a special interest in protecting the civilian governments of at least four of their client states, Senegal, the Ivory Coast, Gabon and Djibouti, by stationing troops in those countries; as do the Cubans in Angola. In these particular cases it may reasonably be said that relationships with a foreign country not only help set the parameters of the political game in general, but also have a special relevance for civilian control.

Outside these obvious cases, however, it is difficult to regard such macro-level variables as neo-colonialism and dependency as having much general explanatory power in relation to soldiers' domestic political choices. Indeed, the record is so mixed as to suggest a fine impartiality towards the degrees of dependency and clientelism among the governments which soldiers supplant or sustain. And much the same may be said of the macro-level variables of domestic social and political structure (e.g. class patterns; ethnic patterns; political-party patterns). Clearly the domestic social environment helps determine the broad ambit of the political game. No less clearly, social and political deterioration and disorder have in some instances provided the background to breakdowns in civilian control of the soldiery -that is to have so changed the soldiers' perceptions of the state of the game as to prompt them to intervene. Yet any attempt to generalise from such instances will encounter, once again, the problem that in many other cases of civil deterioration and disorder the soldiers have backed their rulers. Both the successes and failures in political control over the military are scattered along the spectrum from the more orderly and socially homogeneous states to the more disorderly and socially fragmented.

One important economic (as distinct from social or political) variable which might seem at first sight to furnish evidence for a hypothesis about coup-proneness and coup-freeness is *per capita* income. If we group sub-Saharan Africa's mainland states, as the World Bank does, into various low-income and middle-income categories, and if we denote sustained civilian rule (lasting, that is from independence to late 1985) with a letter C, we get the picture shown in Table 4.1.

The hypothesis which might appear from this table to be prima facie reasonable is simply that the higher the *per capita* income, the better the prospects for sustained civilian rule. The clustering of civilian-ruled states in the middle-income oil-importing category seems, on the face of it, especially notable. Thus Zartman, for example, asserts:

> It is no accident that the original single-party elites tend to continue in power in the African states with the higher economic growth rates ... It is again no accident that military regimes frequently exist in countries with lower growth rates ... Higher-income states ... are likely to be able to accommodate internal rivals for leadership.[39]

Yet such a hypothesis would have to be treated with caution. For it is surely the case that, cutting right across the income categories, the great majority of the civilian-ruled states are those in which political leadership has been outstandingly able, or dominating, or even, in a few cases, popular; whereas in the great majority of the coup-prone states, these sorts of things simply cannot be said about the civilian leaders who were overthrown. Certainly it might be suggested, as it is by Zartman, that higher levels of national income could give a leader more resources with which to control the political game, to keep the lid on political discontents and, in particular, to keep the military quiet.

Table 4.1: African States Ranked by *Per Capita* Income

Low Income Semi-Arid	Low Income Other	Middle Income Oil-Importing	Middle Income Oil-Exporting
Chad	Ethiopia	Kenya (C)	Angola
Somalia	Guinea-Bissau	Ghana	Congo
Mali	Burundi	Senegal (C)	Nigeria
Burkina Faso	Malawi (C)	Zimbabwe (C)	Gabon (C)
Gambia (C)	Rwanda	Liberia	
Niger	Benin	Zambia (C)	
Mauritania	Mozambique (C)	Cameroon (C)	
	Sierra Leone	Swaziland (C)	
	Tanzania (C)	Botswana (C)	
	Zaire	Ivory Coast (C)	
	Guinea		
	CAR		
	Uganda		
	Lesotho (C)		
	Togo		
	Sudan		

Source for country rankings: *Accelerated Development in Sub-Saharan Africa* (Washington DC: The World Bank, 1981), Statistical Annex. Low income is defined as an income equal to or less than US$370 *per capita* in 1979; middle income is an income greater than US$370 *per capita* in 1979. Countries are listed in ascending order of *per capita* income reading from top to bottom within each category. Djibouti and Equatorial Guinea are excluded from World Bank tables because of lack of data.

The leader nevertheless needs to be astute enough to understand how to do this. Nyerere and Banda have managed it with low national incomes; the Liberian and Congolese (Brazzaville) leaders, with considerably higher national incomes to allocate, could not. In line with the general argument of this chapter, it would appear once again that leadership is a variable of prime significance; the level of national income is probably one of the mediating ones, in some cases.

Having analysed several successful military coups, Samuel Decalo came to the conclusion that

> Notwithstanding enduring structural, ethnic, and economic factors ... conducive to the breakdown of political order (and present in all African systems), the interpersonal dynamics of the officer corps and interpersonal clashes between civil and military elites have been primary causes of political intervention by the armed forces.[40]

Though he is speaking of breakdowns in civilian control and we are concerned with its maintenance, the point is the same in both cases: obverse and reverse of the same coin. In brief, the personal and subjective determinants of the civil-military relationship appear more significant, most of the time, than the structural and objective.[41]

A different kind of argument arises if we focus more specifically on ideology. Namely: to stress subjectivity is to miss the point that socialist-inclined regimes will establish civilian control on a somewhat different basis from capitalist regimes, in that they seek much more deliberately to implant a social ideology in the soldiers' consciousness. Mozambique is said to provide a good illustration. The Mozambican army is not only subordinate to the party, but is meant to be aware of the ideological reasons for this. On Armed Forces Day 1980, President Machel declared that 'no army is neutral, no army is apolitical. The armed forces of any country are the product of the class they serve.' He has repeatedly noted that 'to be a Mozambican military officer, it is first necessary to be a communist.' It is made clear that the army's tasks include not only fighting the enemy (chiefly in the form of the Mozambique National Resistance), but also explaining FRELIMO ideology and policy, mobilising the people,

119

and working for development, especially in regions previously occupied by the MNR. Thus soldiers are expected to play an active role in carrying out the ten-year plan, and are already to be found 'helping to re-establish agricultural production, and assisting in the construction of communal villages.' It is also intended that the soldiers will eventually become the direct producers of their own food.[42]

In Nyerere's Tanzania and Touré's Guinea there have been broadly similar three-pronged strategies of politicising the soldiers, making them activists in economic tasks, and requiring ideological commitment. Pachter has suggested the main implication of this approach for civilian control:

> The three Governments have avoided the Western style of army management, with its tradition of a strong semi-autonomous hierarchy ... [However], Nyerere, Touré and Machel believe that lack of professionalism is a small price to pay for an army that does not feel it has financial and political claims on the state in return for its unquestioned support.[43]

In more capitalist-minded countries, it may be argued, the role of ideology needs to be understood differently. Instead of being subjected to overt indoctrination in radical participatory values and being expected to act as ideologues themselves, the soldiers absorb an 'all-pervasive ... emphasis upon conservative and accumulationist values'.[44] We have noted already in the case of Kenya that officers have been enabled to accumulate wealth and to run private businesses (farms, shops), rather in the manner of the politicians and the bureaucrats, thereby helping to bind them into a common class project with these governing-class fractions. There would thus appear to be good ground for regarding the nature of civilian control as qualitatively different in countries of differing ideological persuasions.

This line of argument does help to bring out interesting points of comparison, and is worth keeping in mind as we look empirically at particular cases of civilian control. And yet it would be difficult to sustain the argument that ideology has any major or determinant bearing upon the soldiers' propensity to intervene, or to abstain from intervening. For a start, we can never be sure of the 'real' salience of ideology in the minds of the soldiers. Nor can the ideological homogeneity of an army be presumed. Every socialist army is likely to contain its reactionary elements (Mozambique's certainly does, to judge by the quite frequent purgings and trials of 'corrupt' and 'materialistic' solidiers since 1975[45]), while capitalist militaries are likely to harbour their socially conscious progressives (for example, arguably, the young air force officers in Kenya). And it would be straining at credibility to suggest that the incidence of military interventions and non-interventions correlates with the *level* of ideological commitment among the various armed forces.

Nor can it plausibly be maintained that one *kind* of ideology provides a surer base for control than another. There is an argument that socialist ideology provides a sounder base than capitalist, since the latter tends to instil in the soldiers a cynically acquisitive drive for more goods - including more power. But in fact, just as some dependent-capitalist countries have experienced frequent military coups and some none, so some socialist and would-be socialist countries have remained under civilian control (Angola, Mozambique, Tanzania), while others have succumbed (Guinea-Bissau, Guinea). In the last-named country, it is clear that the military had been controlled less by an ideology than by a particular individual, since it intervened immediately after his death. And the centrality of a dominant leader is surely significant in other leading cases of sustained civilian control under 'actually existing socialism' - leaders such as Machel in Mozambique and Nyerere in Tanzania. (Tanzania's socialism is very much Nyerere's socialism, and there is no guarantee that it will outlive him.)

It is no less significant that a large part of the reason for the dominance of these socialist presidents is that they are successful personal rulers. In the matter of civilian control of the army, in particular, they leave things neither to ideology nor to chance. Like their capitalist counterparts, they evidently keep the question of the soldiers' political reliability - that is loyalty to the political leadership - much in mind as they manage military affairs. In January 1984, for example, President/Field-Marshal Machel made a linked series of appointments to high defence and security posts. The five appointees had in common the fact that they were 'strong Machel supporters', three of them being described as his former 'personal secretary', a 'staunch Machel man', and a 'former presidential assistant'. Two of them were to share responsibility for the defence of the political centre, Maputo; it was observed that Machel could 'count on a rapid and loyal response to any attack' on the city.[46] Clearly, these appointees were to be seen as reliable primarily because of their personal loyalty to the ruler, rather than because of any abstract attachment to ideological principles. In Tanzania similarly, there is a long record of personnel manipulation in the cause of maintaining political reliability - from the reconstitution of the army after the 1964 mutiny, when the new recruits 'had to have exhibited political loyalty',[47] through to Nyerere's reshuffle of defence ministers and senior officers after what was apparently a coup attempt in Zanzibar in December 1982.[48]

CONCLUSIONS

Richard Hodder-Williams ended his study of President Banda's political longevity by remarking that

> Explanations for political survival in independent Africa are badly catered for in the literature of political science ... 'The Inevitability of Instability' seems a curious vantage point from which to study the present political systems of say, Malawi, and nearby states like Kenya, Tanzania, and Zambia ... Despite the advances made by political scientists in many spheres, the descriptive virtues of the best traditionalists remain central to any understanding [of survival] ... what is needed still is the detailed knowledge of the relationships between named individuals in ... positions of authority and power.[49]

These observations could equally well have flowed from the argument of this chapter. It should be noted, however, that we are not going to the other extreme and arguing for the 'inevitability of stability' in the civilian-ruled states. Civilian control of the military based on personal rule will always be situational and conditional, and obviously less secure than control which rests on an institutionalised culture. And there is no clear prospect of control becoming much less personalised, more institutionalised, in the near future. It may well be, as Jackson and Rosberg suggest, that a growing number of African states 'may be thought of as still highly personal and arbitrary at the top but increasingly bureaucratized at lower levels'[50] - with the Ivory Coast, perhaps, as the vanguard case. If this is so, we may expect a greater stability of, say, administration (bearing in mind that this could be a good or bad thing; if a bureaucracy is repressive, anti-reformist and corrupt, its stabilisation is hardly to be desired). But we could not necessarily expect a consolidation of civilian control over the armed forces. Military interventions are of necessity aimed at the very top of the system. So long as the system remains 'personal and arbitrary' at the top, we must expect control to remain largely a function of the soldiers' loyalty to the incumbent ruler. If, for whatever reasons, this loyalty diminishes, then the ruler's position is at risk.

Clearly leadership successions remain critical testing-points, as the Guinean experience reminds us. Further: whether successor rulers will maintain control over the soldiers cannot be predicted from the record of their predecessors. No doubt Jomo Kenyatta, by dint of his enormous personal authority, did institutionalise the Kenyan presidency in some degree.[51] But that degree, it seems, can be overstated. The fact that his successor survived a coup attempt in 1982 is less important here than the fact that the attempt could be contemplated, and was made. There are now no good reasons for ruling out the *possibility* of further attempts.

Certainly we may believe that in this country or in that, the propects for government remaining in civilian hands are very good, even excellent. But we should recognize that our beliefs rest ultimately on contingent arguments of an 'if ... then' variety.

To conclude on this note might seem to be yielding ground to the 'inevitability of instability' school. But to talk about possibilities is a long way from talking about inevitabilities. What we have attempted, basically, is the delineation and application of a set of ideas about personal rule in Africa; ideas which should help in the understanding of both instability and stability, and not least in the area of civil-military relations.

NOTES

I am grateful to Robert Dowse for his comments on an earlier draft of this chapter.
1. Finer, S.E., <u>The Man on Horseback: The Role of the Military in Politics</u> (London: Pall Mall Press, 1962), pp. 5, 12.
2. The Tanzanian case was <u>sui generis</u>. Nyerere resigned as Prime Minister in January 1962 and was elected President in December 1962; in the intervening period, Rashidi Kawawa served as Prime Minister. In the other four cases, leadership successions were occasioned by the death of the incumbent.
3. Goldsworthy, D., 'Civilian Control of the Military in Black Africa', <u>African Affairs</u>, 80, 318 (January 1981), pp. 49-74, quoted at p. 56.
4. See Momoh, E., 'A Dawn Descends, A Myth Broken', <u>West Africa</u>, 9 April 1984, pp. 756-7.
5. Relevant and useful writings published since 1980 include Enloe, C.H., <u>Ethnic Soldiers: State Security in a Divided Society</u> (Harmondsworth: Penguin Books, 1980); Bienen, H., 'Civil-Military Relations in the Third World', <u>International Political Science Review</u>, 2, 3 (1981), pp. 363-70; Wolpin, M.D., <u>Militarism and Social Revolution in the Third World</u> (Totowa, New Jersey: Allanheld, Osmun & Co., 1981); Jackson, R.H. and Rosberg, C.G., <u>Personal Rule in Black Africa: Prince, Autocrat, Prophet, Tyrant</u> (Berkeley and Los Angeles: California University Press, 1982); Ball, N., 'Third World Militaries and Politics: An Introductory Essay', <u>Cooperation and Conflict</u>, 17, 1 (March 1982), pp. 41-60; Pachter, E.F., 'Contra-Coup: Civilian Control of the Military in Guinea, Tanzania, and Mozambique',<u>Journal of Modern African Studies</u>, 20, 4 (December 1982), pp. 595-612; Cartwright, J., <u>Political Leadership in Africa</u> (London: Croom Helm, 1983); Charlton, R., 'Predicting African Military Coups', <u>Futures</u>, 15, 4 (August 1983), pp. 281-92; Johnson, T.H., Slater, R.O., and McGowan, P., 'Explaining African Military Coups d'Etat, 1960-1982', <u>American Political Science Review</u>, 78, 3 (September 1984), pp. 622-40.
6. Bahro, R., <u>The Socialist Alternative in Eastern Europe</u> (London: Verso, 1978).

7. Decalo, S., Coups and Army Rule in Africa: Studies in Military Style (New Haven: Yale University Press, 1976), ch. 6.

8. Jackson and Rosberg's theoretical presentation is lengthy, occupying pp. 1-82 and 266-86 of their book. The present account seeks only to summarise, in digested and re-written form, certain aspects of the argument considered relevant to understanding civil-military relations. Only direct quotations will be page-referenced.

9. Jackson and Rosberg, Personal Rule in Black Africa, p. 22.

10. Ibid., pp. 19, 1.

11. An image which calls to mind Leys's vivid description of 'Kenyatta's Court': see Leys, C., Underdevelopment in Kenya: The Political Economy of Neo-Colonialism 1964-1971 (London: Heinemann Educational Books, 1975), pp. 246-9.

12. These attributes of leadership are not only much more important than legal-constitutional structures in helping a leader to survive; they are also much more important than 'charisma'. Non-charismatic leaders can survive indefinitely given skilful and fortunate play; charismatic ones can easily fall if they lack the political skill to exploit their charisma in ways relevant to survival.

13. Machiavelli, The Prince, quoted in Jackson and Rosberg, Personal Rule in Black Africa, p. v.

14. Jackson and Rosberg, Personal Rule in Black Africa, pp. 1-2.

15. Ibid., p. 18; authors' emphasis. In treating such phenomena as integral elements, the authors have distanced themselves from earlier systems theorists who would certainly have described these things as dysfunctional. It is apparent from the text that the idea of system is in fact being used in a fairly relaxed way, essentially as a metaphor that is more or less interchangeable with the game metaphor.

16. Oddly enough, Jackson and Rosberg do not treat the matter of civilian control of the military in any depth. Neither does Cartwright; nor, in an earlier discussion of leadership survival techniques, did Wriggins (Wriggins, W.H., The Ruler's Imperative: Strategies for Political Survival in Asia and Africa (New York: Columbia University Press, 1969); in a text of 263 pages, Wriggins devoted just four rather unsatisfactory pages to civil-military relations. From here

on, then, we are more or less on our own.

17. Lemarchand, R., 'African Armies in Historical and Contemporary Perspectives: The Search for Connections', Journal of Political and Military Sociology, 4, 2 (Fall 1976), p. 263.

18. Jackson and Rosberg, Personal Rule in Black Africa, p. 36.

19. Murray, J., 'Succession Prospects in Kenya', Africa Report, 13, 8 (November 1968), p. 47.

20. Tamarkin, M., 'The Roots of Political Stability in Kenya', African Affairs, 77, 308 (July 1978), p. 301; Anon., 'Kenya: The End of an Illusion', Race and Class, 24, 3 (Winter 1983), p. 238.

21. Bienen, H., Armies and Parties in Africa (New York: Africana, 1978), p. 185, n. 66.

22. Anon., 'Kenya: The End of an Illusion', p. 238.

23. Africa Confidential, 20, 20 (3 October 1979), p. 6.

24. Ibid., 22, 21 (15 October 1981), p. 3.

25. Cox, T.S., Civil-Military Relations in Sierra Leone (Cambridge, Mass.: Harvard University Press, 1976); Luckham, R., The Nigerian Military (Cambridge: Cambridge University Press, 1971), esp. pp. 238-46; Pachter, 'Contra-Coup' (see note 5); Pettman, J., Zambia: Security and Conflict (Lewes, Sussex: Julian Friedmann, 1974), pp. 105-13, esp. p. 109; Markovitz, I.L., Leopold Sédar Senghor and the Politics of Negritude (London: Heinemann, 1969), pp. 220-2; Hodder-Williams, R., 'Dr Banda's Malawi', Journal of Commonwealth and Comparative Politics, 12, 1 (March 1974), esp. p. 99.

26. Pachter, 'Contra-Coup', p. 605.

27. A Nairobi joke subsequently had it that 1 August should be declared, along with Kenyatta Day, Jamhuri Day, etc., a 'siku kuu' - day of celebration. 'Kuu' and 'coup' have the same pronunciation.

28. Tamarkin, 'The Roots of Political Stability in Kenya', p. 301.

29. First, R., The Barrel of a Gun: Political Power in Africa and the Coup d'Etat (Harmondsworth: Allen Lane, 1970), pp. 220-1; Gutteridge, W.F., The Military in African Politics (London: Methuen, 1969), pp. 47-8.

30. Africa Confidential, 25, 8 (11 April 1984), p. 6.

31. See e.g. Decalo, <u>Coups and Army Rule in Africa</u>, esp. chs. 1, 6.

32. Documentation will be found in the relevant volumes of <u>Africa Contemporary Record</u>, <u>Africa Research Bulletin</u> and <u>Africa Confidential</u>. The list of attempted military coups is probably complete; the list of plots, almost certainly incomplete.

33. Leys, <u>Underdevelopment in Kenya</u>, p. 243.

34. See especially Karimi, J., and Ochieng, P., <u>The Kenyatta Succession</u> (Nairobi: Transafrica, 1980), Part 3.

35. For further discussion of the coup attempt see Anon., 'Kenya: End of an Illusion', pp. 235-44, and 'Kenya: Post-Mortem', <u>Africa Confidential</u>, 23, 17 (25 August 1982), pp. 1-3. We should note here the persistent rumours that a quite separate coup plot was brewing at the time among certain Kikuyu big men who hoped to use military force to bring themselves to power. Charles Njonjo was specifically accused of this during the 'Njonjo hearings' in Nairobi in 1984. Such a move would certainly not be beyond the bounds of a personal-rule game. We are here concerned, however, only with the attempt that did occur.

36. <u>Africa Confidential</u>, 24, 5 (2 March 1983), p. 8.

37. <u>Ibid.</u>, 24, 25 (14 December 1983), p. 4. See further <u>ibid.</u>, 26, 1 (2 January 1985), p. 7.

38. Saffu, Y., 'Commentary' (on Bienen - see note 5), p. 372.

39. Zartman, I.W., 'Social and Political Trends in Africa in the 1980s', in Legum, C., et al., <u>Africa in the 1980s: A Continent in Crisis</u> (New York: McGraw-Hill, 1979), pp. 82-3.

40. Decalo, <u>Coups and Army Rule in Africa</u>, p. 232.

41. There is of course an extensive literature on the structural correlates of coup-proneness in Africa. The most quantitatively sophisticated of recent discussions is Johnson <u>et al.</u>, 'Explaining African Military Coups d'Etat, 1960-82' (see note 5). Johnson <u>et al.</u> claim to have accounted statistically for some 90 per cent of the variance in the coup-proneness of African states by correlating the incidence of coups with a range of macro-level structural variables. They make no reference to political leadership and almost none to civil-military relations. Obviously their

approach differs a good deal from the one adopted in this chapter. I have discussed some methodological and interpretative issues at stake between the two approaches in Goldsworthy, D., 'On the Structural Analysis of African Military Interventions', unpublished manuscript, 1985.

42. Hanlon, J., 'Mozambique's Battle for Reconstruction', in the *Guardian*, 27 October 1980.

43. Pachter, 'Contra-Coup', pp. 610-11.

44. Goldsworthy, 'Civilian Control of the Military', p. 59.

45. Pachter, 'Contra-Coup', pp. 602, 604-5.

46. 'Mozambique: Politicizing the Ranks', *Africa Confidential*, 25, 4 (15 February 1984), p. 5.

47. Bienen, H., *Tanzania: Party Transformation and Economic Development* (Princeton: Princeton University Press, 1970), p. 375.

48. *Africa Confidential*, 24, 6 (16 March 1983), p. 2.

49. Hodder-Williams, 'Dr Banda's Malawi', (see note 25), p. 110.

50. Jackson and Rosberg, *Personal Rule in Black Africa*, p. 5.

51. This is argued in Goldsworthy, D., 'Kenyan Politics Since Kenyatta', *Australian Outlook*, 36, 1 (April 1982), p. 29.

Chapter Five

REVOLUTIONARY ARMIES OF AFRICA : MOZAMBIQUE AND ZIMBABWE

Annette Seegers

INTRODUCTION

In analysing the military development of sub-Saharan African states scholars avail themselves of established sets of literature on armies inherited at independence, the military's Africanisation, causes and consequences of coups and, more recently, military capabilities and security concerns. The military development of states involved in the 'second wave' of liberation struggles in southern Africa does not, however, readily fit the mould presented by states that achieved independence in the late 1950s and early 1960s, if only because the liberation struggles in Angola, Mozambique and Zimbabwe were characterised by guerrilla warfare. What therefore are the characteristics of such states' military evolution during the second wave of liberation?

This chapter concerns itself with the recent military development of Mozambique and Zimbabwe: What are the important features of the military establishments in these states, and how (or why) did these features develop? The discussion is not intended to be a comparison in the strict or social-scientific sense of the word; it is, rather, a joint discussion intended to identify the overall trends in these states' military development.

BEFORE THE FALL

The roots of the major liberation organisations of Mozambique (the Front for the Liberation of Mozambique or FRELIMO) and Zimbabwe (the Zimbabwe African National Union or ZANU and the Zimbabwe African Peoples Union or ZAPU) of course can be broadly interpreted to be embedded in twentieth century African history or, seen more narrowly, in the post-1945 experiences of southern African states. In Mozambique FRELIMO was created in 1962 as an amalgamation of three exile organisations with subnational constituencies, namely UDENAMO (consisting mainly of Mozambicans living in exile in Rhodesia), MANU (originally a Makonde tribal organisation that later developed nationalist aims) and UNAMI (an organisation with its original constituency based in Tete province).[1] Similarly, the ZAPU that was created in 1962 under the leadership of Joshua Nkomo and its rival ZANU (created in August 1962), were outgrowths of the National Democratic Party (NDP), an urban-oriented party aiming mainly at creating a system of universal franchise in Zimbabwe through the intervention of the British government, and the earlier 'new' African National Congress, which was an amalgamation of the initial ANC and the City Youth League of Salisbury.[2]

In contrast to their organisational predecessors, however, FRELIMO and the two Zimbabwean organisations abandoned existing policy-commitments to non-violence. FRELIMO's First Congress spoke of preparations for an armed struggle and accordingly 200 recruits were sent to Algeria for training in 1962.

Approximately two years after FRELIMO's creation its guerrillas supplied evidence of their presence in the northern provinces of Cabo Delgado and Niassa, attacking Portuguese administrative posts, convoys and patrols.[3] In Zimbabwe the struggle was initiated in an almost haphazard fashion. During 1962 a 'Zimbabwe Liberation Army' started to advertise its existence by distributing leaflets and indeed there were some 'irregular and infrequent'[4] incidents of violence, such as petrol bomb attacks and railroad sabotage, but ZAPU's leaders denied any connection with it.[5] Despite this denial, ZAPU was declared an illegal organisation by the Rhodesian regime and the organisation was forced to withdraw to Lusaka, Zambia, where they were joined by former ANC members released by the Rhodesian Front regime when it came to power in December 1962. In Lusaka ZAPU leaders became divided over issues of leadership and strategy. The move to Zambia was said to be based on reasonable grounds, namely that security legislation made effective action within Zimbabwe impossible; but Nkomo was accused of avoiding altogether a struggle within Zimbabwe, seeking to have ZAPU known as a 'government-in-exile' preferably based in Tanzania. Charges and countercharges were made; soon (on 9 August 1963) ZANU was formed by dissident ZAPU leaders with Ndabaningi Sithole as President, and in the following year ZANU and ZAPU battled each other in the 'worst year on record for violence'[6] in postwar Zimbabwe. Both ZANU and ZAPU prepared for an eventual guerrilla struggle, but the fact that most of the violence was aimed at nationalist rivals - and not the incumbent regime - bode ill for the future. Except for one ZANU attack in July, there were no guerrilla incidents within Zimbabwe in 1964. Indeed, despite some rhetorical differences, ZANU and ZAPU were quite similar in that they both mainly engaged in diplomatic and/or foreign relations activity to secure international assistance and, in particular, attempted to gain British support and possible intervention to prevent a unilateral declaration of independence or at least prevent the British transfer of the former Central African Federation's armed forces to the Smith regime.[7]

Between 1966 and 1970 ZAPU's Zimbabwe Peoples Liberation Army (ZIPRA) and ZANU's Zimbabwe African National Liberation Army (ZANLA) clashed with the regime's security forces on only seven major occasions (with six of these incidents attributed to ZAPU), leading several observers to conclude that neither ZANU nor even ZAPU could wage effective guerrilla struggle within Zimbabwe. More ominously, there was no indication that ZANU or ZAPU between 1965 and 1970 had managed to infiltrate trained recruits as agents of political mobilisation.[8] In Mozambique, FRELIMO fared only slightly better. From bases in Tanzania FRELIMO guerrillas managed some infiltration of the northern provinces, but by 1969 action there could make no further progress and the focus of attention switched to Tete province with the stated intention of halting the construction of the Cahora Bassa dam project.[9]

It could be argued that a major reason for the poor performance of the Mozambican and Zimbabwean liberation organisations in the 1960s lay in the skill with which the incumbent regimes countered guerrilla actions.[10] But for our purposes it is also important to enquire why the guerrillas fought in the way that they did, and to identify the consequences - organisationally and otherwise - of such actions.

Internationalised Guerrilla Struggle

FRELIMO and the Zimbabwean liberation organisations were created at a time when the conditions of African liberation struggle had become internationalised. For example, there were international and regional organisations, such as the United Nations and the Organisation for African Unity, that dedicated themselves to anti-colonialism and the overthrow of white minority regimes. This international arena presented numerous occasions for action, such as the opportunity to call for aid, to participate in international conferences and help the organisations acquire a political profile, and to attack and attempt to politically isolate the Portuguese and Rhodesian regimes and their supporters. Also the Portuguese regime was a colonial one and the pre-UDI Rhodesian governments appeared to have similar status. A diplomatic offensive against colonial-type regimes was thus entirely appropriate, as similar actions by other anti-colonialists in Africa had yielded the desired result of independence. Stated differently, colonial rule could be terminated by organisations without them necessarily establishing a position of coercive military or physical superiority within the territory in question. Colonial regimes can be persuaded, by diplomatic means, to recognise claims of political equality, whereas independent or sovereign regimes are unlikely to fall if they cannot be defeated in physical-military terms.[11]

The benefits the liberation organisations derived from the diplomatic offensives cannot be minimised. FRELIMO, for example, was recognised by the OAU as the sole and legitimate organisation representing the people of Mozambique and it used this recognition to outmanoeuvre its splinter organisation COREMO (the Revolutionary Committee of Mozambique). On balance, however, the costs of diplomatic action outweighed the benefits thereof. These costs manifested themselves in several ways.

First, the cash contributions of the UN, OAU and individual African and other states remained small and, together with the indifference of Western states to their struggle, resulted in the liberation organisations turning to communist states for training and financial aid. In the case of FRELIMO the Soviet Union was the major donor, assisted by other states such as China, Cuba, Czechoslovakia and Yugoslavia,[12] while in Zimbabwe, China emerged as the major contributor to ZANU and the Soviet

Union as the major backer of ZAPU.[13] While this aid was indispensable to develop a guerrilla capability, it endowed the organisations with the stereotypical description of 'communists', thus contributing to the solidarity of the incumbent regimes, who were already bolstered by their ability to counter guerrilla actions and saddled the liberation organisations with the foreign policy objectives of states external to the region. The liberation organisations also came to rely heavily on neighbouring frontline states to grant asylum to political exiles, receive refugees, host political offices and, most importantly, to train guerrillas and make bases available. Although the value of neighbouring safe havens can hardly be overstated, the problem was that the liberation organisations, especially ZANU and ZAPU, struggled to simultaneously adjust to an exile environment and to transform themselves into entities capable of waging effective guerrilla warfare. ZAPU was internally divided; it could not reach any agreement with ZANU as to how the struggle should be waged. Most of ZIPRA activity inside Zimbabwe consisted of sabotage, such as the planting of landmines and ambushes of vehicles in southeastern Matabeleland, but despite an expected increase in these actions, the Smith regime was more worried about possible guerrilla action in eastern Zimbabwe, expressing alarm at the Portuguese failure to contain FRELIMO activity to Tete province.

With the Portuguese coup of April 1974 and Mozambican independence in June 1975 many new avenues of infiltration became available to ZANU and ZAPU, and hopes were further raised when the Rhodesian regime in December 1975 released nationalist leaders in an attempt to negotiate a settlement to the conflict. Yet it was only two years later that the value of Mozambique as a safe haven could be exploited. In Zambia the warfare between ZANU and ZAPU continued and, with the assassination of Herbert Chitepo and an attempted coup within ZANU, Zambian authorities in March 1975 made a sweeping arrest of ZANU and ZAPU supporters, restricting guerrillas to bases and training camps. Tanzanian authorities responded similarly in May 1975 and, in Mozambique, ZANLA guerrillas were confined to their camps and their leaders (such as Robert Mugabe and Edgar Tekere) placed under virtual house arrest in Quelimane. The effect of these arrests were dramatic: in southeastern Matabeleland ZIPRA activity dwindled to almost nothing, and in the east ZANLA activity declined to only three active guerrilla groups within Zimbabwe. Infiltration was to be restarted in January 1976, but then only after the frontline states had forced ZANLA and ZIPRA leaders to merge in an 18-member military committee and the armies united as ZIPA (the Zimbabwe Peoples Army). ZIPA could not resolve the differences between ZANLA and ZIPRA, and eventually the organisations continued as before.[14]

At times when they did not suffer from a lack of recruits, had access to instructors and training bases, and their political and military leaders were at hand, the Zimbabwean organisations' access to their home territory was controlled by Mozambican, Tanzanian and Zambian authorities. When permission to infiltrate was withdrawn, guerrilla activity declined, and when the frontline states dictated unity, ZANU and ZAPU had to oblige. Eventually, ZANU and ZAPU could do little without the blessing of outsiders.

Second, the international arena and the opportunities presented by it distracted the leadership of all the liberation organisations in question and contributed to internal divisions. Within FRELIMO there were intermittent charges that the political or exiled leadership lacked the commitment to wage a protracted struggle within Mozambique. In 1968, for example, FRELIMO's Mozambique Institute (a school in Dar es Salaam) was forced to close amidst charges that its training distracted recruits from essential military tasks. Later Dar es Salaam was also the scene of an attack on senior FRELIMO members who, as overseas representatives of the Executive Committee, were accused of self-indulgence and high living while the rank and file lived in harsh conditions in overcrowded camps in Tanzania.[15] Similar tensions plagued the Zimbabwean liberation organisations. In the early 1960s there was unhappiness over Nkomo's (and by implication senior ZAPU members') apparent preoccupation with foreign travel and later, as more trained recruits returned to Mozambique and Zambia to engage in guerrilla warfare, tensions between ZANU and ZAPU's political and military wings increased. Nkomo became involved with the internal United African National Congress of Bishop Abel Muzorewa and started to espouse a position advocating a negotiated ending to the conflict. Within ZANU tensions between the political and military wings became even more conspicuous. ZANU President

Sithole, on trial for plotting the murder of Prime Minister Ian Smith, made a statement in which he disassociated himself from any form of violence; in other words, ZANU's top leader disavowed any connection with ZANU's guerrillas. In Tanzania guerrillas in fact formalised their grievances in the Mgagao Declaration, charging that the political leadership of ZANU was incapable of leading the struggle. Of the political leaders, only Robert Mugabe escaped serious criticism, and indeed he was later appointed ZANU's overall leader.[16]

Third, recognition from outside tended to obfuscate the difference between organisations' legitimacy and their political support base. The former notion refers to, for example, attitudes and designations of what is considered just, fitting or proper and can be the source of much moral and material power, whereas the latter notion usually describes collectivities of people who are willing to assist, are loyal and give strength to, encourage political organisations by material and other means, and who are in turn incorporated into the administrative body of the organisation. Certainly FRELIMO, ZANU and ZAPU were recognised by international and other outside bodies to be legitimate organisations engaged in a morally just struggle, but this did not necessarily translate into a broad and firm domestic support base.

In Mozambique, FRELIMO managed to turn its defeat in the 'Bust Cahora Bassa' campaign into a victory by establishing itself as a presence in the outlying areas of the Tete province and, from this base, extended its influence southward towards the central provinces of Manica, Sofala and Zambezia. By the end of 1973 FRELIMO thus could - and did - claim to have extended its activities. It is doubtful, however, whether FRELIMO turned the areas in which it was active into liberated areas in the traditional guerrilla sense. Some institutions typical of liberated areas, such as medical clinics and schools, certainly did exist, but FRELIMO more often coopted local leaders, used existing tribal structures and elicited the support of the local populace in order to gain freedom of movement in an area. Thus, instead of introducing new FRELIMO-controlled structures, existing structures were used. Regardless of the nature of FRELIMO's political and military control over the populace, however, their sphere of operations were by April 1974 still mainly focussed on the provinces of Cabo Delagado and Niassa and the northern areas of Tete province.[17]

In Zimbabwe guerrilla infiltration occurred mainly during two periods; the first occurred in the 1972-3 period, when ZANU used FRELIMO's success in Tete as a springboard for actions into northeastern Zimbabwe, and the second between 1976 and 1979 as ZANU activity spread from the eastern border areas towards central and southern areas and ZAPU activity in the west spread eastwards. As regards the years between 1964 and 1971, the style and timing of the actions seem predicated on the OAU's reaction to ZANU-ZAPU rivalry. The OAU stipulated that it would recognise only effective guerrilla organisations and in order to gain recognition ZANU and ZAPU therefore 'had to *seem* to be fighting. So armed men were sent into territories at precisely the time an OAU organ was about to meet ... In other words, revolutionary effectiveness was sacrificed for propagandistic reasons.'[18] During the two ZANLA-dominated infiltration waves of the 1970s, the rugged terrain facilitated guerrilla movement in the eastern areas. After making contact with religious figures (such as spirit mediums), sympathetic chiefs, and ward- and kraalheads, and with the support given by especially the inhabitants of the black reserves (or tribal trust areas) and workers on white farms, ZANLA robbed stores, ambushed security forces, and attacked white farms and property. These actions were undertaken by guerrillas recruited from local villages, some urban areas, and the migrant and refugee communities in Mozambique, who were assisted by women and *mujibas* (landless, unemployed and otherwise available young men). Yet, at any given time, the regime security forces could still detect and pursue guerrilla groups. ZANLA's guerrillas could only escape capture and death as long as they remained highly mobile. Political mobilisation increased dramatically towards the end of 1979, when forthcoming elections were announced, but for the greater part of the 1970s the local population's role in guerrilla activities was designed for military purposes - not incorporation into the administrative structure of ZANU.[19]

Lastly, the progress of the respective guerrilla struggles were interrupted and indeed terminated when FRELIMO and especially ZANU had begun to make substantial progress. As FRELIMO was extending its actions southward, the Portuguese coup and the subsequent Lusaka Agreement recognised FRELIMO as the future government of Mozambique. In Zimbabwe the incumbent Muzorewa regime, weakened by the loss of South African support and the extension of guerrilla activity, consented to the introduction of the long-disputed British authority in Zimbabwe and negotiated an electoral ending to the war. While it is important to note that the curious endings of the respective struggles had much to do with forces external to them, it is also important to stress that the struggles had a short life-span, especially when one considers that guerrilla warfare requires a condition of protractedness in which guerrillas, for example, establish links with the local population, seek sanctuary among the locals, find recruits, and develop political and other structures in areas where their influence is uncontested. The periods of active guerrilla warfare in Mozambique and Zimbabwe were actually quite short: In Mozambique FRELIMO guerrilla actions were confined to the 1972-73 period, while in Zimbabwe guerrilla actions were confined to the 1972-73 and 1976-79 periods. Whether the respective organisations could widen the scope of their activities and solidify their political control over the areas they claimed to have liberated is of course a speculative question but that they did not have the chance to do so is a reality.

Revolutionary Intentions and Divisive Elites

Throughout their respective struggles the Mozambican and Zimbabwean liberation organisations frequently explained their lack of success and internal difficulties by charging that the incumbent regimes used all the powers at their disposal to divide the liberation organisations. Although there is evidence to at least partly support these charges,[20] the regularity and depth of the internal schisms suggest other and perhaps more enduring reasons for the failure to develop united nationalist fronts.

As regard Mozambique, there were tensions within FRELIMO that involved class, racial, regional, strategic and tribal considerations. Class tensions, for example, played a role in the accusations of the rank and file that senior FRELIMO members of especially the external wing were self-indulgent; racial considerations frequently surfaced over the role of *mestiços* (persons of mixed race) in senior positions; regional tensions and tribal loyalties were revealed in views describing southerners as 'aggressive' and 'domineering' and northerners as 'backward', as well as demands by former MANU members and Makonde that they were being used as cannon fodder without adequate representation in top positions; and differences over strategy revealed itself in disputes over whether a lengthy or shorter guerrilla struggle would be the best course of action. Despite the lack of a single dominant cause of these tensions, a pattern revealed itself over time as a southern, *assimilado-mestiço* group with moderate political views came to be opposed by a northern Makonde-dominated and ideologically more radical group.[21] With the death of Mondlane in 1969 and the ascendance of Samora Machel to the position of President of FRELIMO, the tensions seemed to abate and a consensual decision-making style developed among senior FRELIMO members.[22]

Yet, despite the achievement of some internal stability, there were several indications that FRELIMO could not offer a home to most Mozambican nationalists. The former leader of UDENAMO, Adelino Gwambe, was for example not included in FRELIMO's Central Committee and recreated UDENAMO in Kampala (Uganda) under the name of UDENAMO-Monomotapa. Another UDENAMO was established by Paulo Gumane and Joseph Mabunda when they were expelled from FRELIMO. Known as UDENAMO-Mozambique, this organisation merged with the Mozambique Revolutionary Council (MORECO), created by other individuals expelled from FRELIMO. Kampala also was the home of MANC (Mozambique African National Congress), created by Sebastene Sigauke. In 1964 UDENAMO--Monomotapa, MANC and MANU (resurrected by Mathew Mmole and Joseph Millinga after their expulsion from FRELIMO) coalesced to form FUNIPAMO (the United Popular Anti-Imperialist Front of the Africans of Mozambique). FUNIPAMO in turn gave way to COREMO, created by the amalgamation of the two UDENAMOs, MANC, MANU and the erstwhile UNAMI of Lusaka.[23]

Despite its limited guerrilla-effectiveness, COREMO and its predecessors housed individuals with deep-seated animosity towards FRELIMO. Excluded from the rewards offered by FRELIMO's rise to power they would first reassert themselves during the transitional period (1974-75) and later form the nucleus of armed resistance against the Machel regime. In time FRELIMO would offer these individuals yet another motive of dissent, for FRELIMO gradually developed an affinity for the principles of Marxism-Leninism and eventually became an organisation officially dedicated to the restructuring of Mozambican society along scientific-socialist lines.[24]

Although often caricatured as such, the view that the initial split of ZANU and ZAPU was produced by the irrevocable division of Mashona and Matabele political loyalties greatly simplifies matters. In 1963 almost half of ZAPU's executive did leave to join ZANU, but there was not an exodus of local branch leaders or other members of ZAPU. Not only did ZAPU retain most of its membership, but it continued to attract support in urban areas containing large concentrations of Mashona. Even the dissatisfaction with Nkomo cannot easily be explained in tribal terms as Nkomo is a Kalanga, a branch of the Mashona ethno-linguistic confederation.[25] Yet, even if the original split was not primarily due to tribal exclusivism, several factors contributed not only to continued bitterness between ZANU and ZAPU but also later to the division of guerrilla labour (that is ZANU dominance in Mashona and ZAPU dominance in Matabele territory).

First, regime repression forced the liberation organisation into exile where they had great difficulty in waging an effective guerrilla struggle. With mounting morale problems and suffering the anxieties and indignities of exile, individuals resorted to self-promotion, periodically charged other guerrillas with 'treason', 'collusion with the agents of imperialism' and 'revisionism', and frequently engaged in disorderly and drunken activities.[26] In the second place, ZANU and ZAPU were also bureaucratic institutions wherein individuals' demands for roles, positions and status exceeded the supply. This job scarcity led to intense personal competition and candidates' attempts to beat the opposition by questioning their loyalty, commitment and character and, importantly, the use of linguistic, regional and tribal loyalties in order to demonstrate superior political support.[27] Rather than being conceptualised as a swell of tribal exclusivism seeping upwards into liberation politics, the first and second factors mentioned here suggest that the organisations' leadership, while being tribally mixed, contain individuals who use subnational loyalties in order to further personal ambitions. Finally, since there seemed to be no end to ZANU-ZAPU rivalry when both organisations were housed in Zambia, peace could only be obtained by literally separating them. Thus ZANU shifted its headquarters to Mozambique. With ZAPU ensconsed in Zambia the result was a separation of guerrilla labour: ZAPU dominated guerrilla actions in the western areas, while ZANU dominated the action along the eastern border areas.[28] With actions thus divided, there was even less inclination for ZANU and ZAPU to resolve their differences.

Because of the persistent internecine warfare, it was hard for either ZANU or ZAPU to convincingly claim or cultivate an overarching Zimbabwean nationalism. At first the two organisations differed mainly as regards the tone of their rhetoric, with ZANU usually taking the more militant line. Like FRELIMO, however, ZANU under the leadership of Robert Mugabe later developed a commitment to scientific socialism.

Liberation Armies
Originally the Mozambique Peoples Liberation Army was organised along conventional military lines with battalions and smaller subdivisions resorting under the authority of the Central Committee's Department of Defence. With the guerrilla leadership based in Dar es Salaam and with the command difficulties presented by guerrillas operating at long distance from external bases, it later was thought best to divide Mozambique into guerrilla regions. In each region operations were directed by an executive commander (and his assistant), a political officer and an operational commander. The executive commanders, as well as FRELIMO's overall military commander (that is the Minister of Defence), were represented in a national command council chaired by the President of FRELIMO or, in his absence, by the Vice-president of FRELIMO or the Secretary of External Affairs. Functional (or staff-type) personnel remained in Dar es Salaam; they were responsible for matters relating to, for instance, finance, recruitment and weapons procurement.[29] Despite the constitutional chain of command and a central source of authority, however, the remoteness of these command origins endowed the commanders of guerrilla regions with considerable autonomy in making daily decisions. Centralised daily control over the army, estimated at between 4,000 and 10,000 active guerrillas,[30] was impossible; at worst, it encouraged unruly behaviour. Indeed, when the FRELIMO guerrillas emerged out of the bush during the transitional period, they proved to be an undisciplined force,

Revolutionary Armies: Mozambique and Zimbabwe

leading Vice-president Chissano to publicly reprimand them for 'reactionary' activities such as alcoholism, black marketeering, rape and theft.[31]

Authority over ZAPU's 400-man guerrilla contingent resided with a high command, headed by the military commander, but the daily struggle was influenced more by the directives issued by the War Council which included both military and political leaders. At first ZANU's ZANLA was also headed by a military high command (and its commander) with a 16-man Revolutionary Council directing daily operations, but the Revolutionary Council was later replaced by a Supreme Council, also known as DARE (or Dare re Chimurenga).[32] At lower levels organisational arrangements were similar to that of FRELIMO. Guerrilla actions were divided into regional commands operating under the direction of provincial and operational commanders as well as the commanders of regional subsections. These lower level commanders were given wide discretionary powers in daily decision-making, being able to (for example) select their own targets. ZANLA often had problems with adequately training, equipping and commanding their supporters, especially after recruitment increased so drastically towards the end of the 1970s. Many of these recruits came from urban environments and, when sent on missions without adequate training, maps, medicine and other essential equipment, they were ineffective and, moreover, developed morale problems, symptoms of psychological exhaustion, and expressed resentment at superiors by whom they felt betrayed.[33] Compared to ZANLA's decentralised form, ZIPRA was smaller, better equipped and trained (mainly by Soviet advisors), and followed a more conventional organisational style which allowed them to better absorb recruits.[34]

The main guerrilla armies of Mozambique and Zimbabwe thus were similar in organisational and other respects: The Mozambique Peoples Liberation Army of FRELIMO and ZANLA both coopted existing social structures rather than attempting to introduce new ones; they relied on regional spheres of guerrilla operations, decentralised decision-making and, as pointed out earlier, suffered similar tensions between the political and external leaders on the one hand and the internal military leaders on the other, as well as suffering the problems presented by a rank and file often resentful of what they saw as the privileged position of politi-

141

cal leaders. The ideological development of FRELIMO and ZANU also followed a similar pattern, as both organisations developed an affinity for the principles of scientific socialism. Given their organisational nature and internal problems, it was however difficult to envisage FRELIMO, ZANU or their respective guerrilla components as cohesive, disciplined and reliable instruments of societal transformation.

TRANSITION AND THE INDEPENDENCE ERA

The ending of the struggles in Mozambique and Zimbabwe did much to shape the immediate independence experiences of the two countries, and it is also at this juncture that important differences appeared in the conditions that shape military development.

The independence constitution of Zimbabwe was the result of 47 plenary sessions of the parties to the Lancaster House conference. The final product was a compromise since no party could fashion the constitution to suit its exclusive interests. The legislature, for example, included a lower house wherein 20 seats were reserved for whites, while the constitution could only be amended by a two-thirds vote in the Senate and a 70 per cent vote in the lower house. Equally important, the Lancaster House constitution left much of Zimbabwe's existing structures intact: for example, the existing judicial system was preserved, the right to private property and guarantees against expulsion from land recognised in a Bill of Rights, and the public service preserved as regards pensions and other internal regulations. The Lancaster House conference also produced two other important agreements. The first of these concerned the transitional period before an independence date, wherein Britain assumed colonial authority over Zimbabwe; the other produced a ceasefire (effective on 28 December 1979) administered by a Ceasefire Commission composed of a military aide to the new (colonial) governor, a senior commander of the Muzorewa regime's security forces, and a senior commander of the Patriotic Front. All the guerrillas were to assemble in 16 assembly points (APs) by 4 January 1980. This assembly of guerrillas was to be supervised by a 1,200-man Commonwealth Monitoring Force. The forces of the Muzorewa regime and the Patriotic Front would first be demobilised and then integrated, in equal proportions, into a conventionally-styled military force and trained by officers of the British Military and Advisory Training Team (BMATT). The regime's security forces, ZANLA, and ZIPRA each would have a representative on the military high command.[35]

In the internationally-supervised elections, the Rhodesian Front party of Ian Smith won all the reserved 'white' seats in the lower house, while ZANU(PF) won 57 of the 80 remaining 'black' seats, Nkomo's PF (or ZAPU) won 20 seats, and the UANC of Prime Minister Muzorewa took the remaining three seats. Roughly speaking the electoral support of ZANU(PF) and the PF (or ZAPU) coincided with, respectively, the operational areas of ZANLA and ZIPRA. Thus the tenuous PF compromise of the Lancaster House conference disintegrated with ZANU and ZAPU again opposing each other. Within ZANU there was also a shift, as the senior guerrilla commanders, who so strongly had asserted their power in Mozambique prior to the Lancaster House conference[36], were outmanoeuvred by the senior political figures of ZANU. These ZANU leaders used the guerrillas to mobilise electoral support, yet simultaneously relieved senior guerrilla commanders of their operational command as this, ZANU politicians argued, would otherwise be a recipe for a coup. Additionally deprived of their commander and spokesman, Josiah Tongogara, who was killed in a car accident in Mozambique, the senior guerrilla leaders watched as 'the politicians' reasserted their control over ZANU.

The transitional arrangements in Zimbabwe thus both denied and confirmed the legacy of guerrilla warfare. Denial consisted in, among other factors, the transformation of the guerrilla armies into a new military entity, while the disintegration of the PF into ZANU-ZAPU hostility confirmed the continued lack of national unity. Despite this disunity, however, the majority party ZANU (PF) captured an intact set of state structures, as well as a reasonably diversified economy.

In Mozambique a transitional agreement of June 1974 created a temporary and FRELIMO-dominated government for the period until June 1975. A Joint Military Commission, composed of senior FRELIMO and Portuguese military figures, was responsible for the defence of Mozambique during the transitional period, but thereafter there was to be no contact with the Portuguese military, nor any attempt to absorb the approximately 30,000 black Mozambican soldiers of the Portuguese military - who outnumbered FRELIMO guerrillas by three to one - into the new Mozambican security establishment.37 In addition, three other ominous developments marked the transitional period: First, administrative and economic collapse quickly became evident as Portuguese bureaucrats and the skilled white Mozambicans left the territory in increasing numbers. By 1977 the white population - the backbone of Mozambique's fragile economy - would be reduced by 80 per cent.38 Second, while FRELIMO's relationship with South Africa remained stable, their relationship with the Smith regime rapidly deteriorated as FRELIMO allowed ZANU to use Mozambique as a base of infiltration. Third, the hostility toward the Smith regime was fueled by FRELIMO's anxiety that the Smith regime was supporting opposition groups in Mozambique. Indeed, FRELIMO's opposition re-emerged with a vengeance. COREMO still existed and now linked up with FRECOMO (Mozambique Common Front), a splinter organisation of the old GUMO (Mozambique United Group) of Maximo Dias and Joanna Simao, to form the Party of National Coalition (PCN). In Malawi, Matues Gwenjere, expelled from FRELIMO after the dispute at the Mozambique Institute, created the African Independence Front (FREINA), but he later joined the PCN. Another defector of FRELIMO, Lazaro Kavandame, founded UNIPOMO (Union of the Peoples of Mozambique). Yet another source of opposition was the Portuguese secret police (PIDE), especially the elite black counter-insurgency unit (the *flechas*) it commanded, and the links PIDE had with Jorge Jardim, a powerful industrialist, and other important financial-industrial figures in Mozambique.39

After independence FRELIMO was to address these proliferating problems with a new organisational structure. FRELIMO was to be a political party (FRELIMO Partido) after 25 June 1975, and the executive committee of the party was to be the cabinet of Mozambique.40 The armed forces (the Armed Forces of Mozambique or FAM) succeeded the guerrilla army and assumed responsibility for the defence of Mozambique.

The Armed Forces of Mozambique (FAM) : 1975-1985
In ten years of independence the nature and role of Mozambique's armed forces have been shaped by, chiefly, Mozambique's descent into civil war, a condition accompanied and to a large extent caused by economic collapse and Mozambique's troubled relations with its more powerful neighbours.

In the months following independence, the most serious problem appeared to be the growing tension between FAM and FRELIMO Partido. As discussed earlier, FAM soldiers were undisciplined, and the Machel regime now attempted to curb malpractices by arrests, public denunciations of corruption, 're-education' by (among others) political study sessions, and a military identification system. To make matters worse, the regime's austerity programme, which drastically reduced defence spending and required many of the rapidly increasing number of soldiers to work without pay, revived the old charge that FRELIMO's top leadership lived a life of luxury while the rank and file struggled to make ends meet. The climax of these tensions came in December 1975. On December 17 a coup was attempted by an FAM battalion when they seized some installations in Maputo's Machava district and attempted to march to the centre of Maputo. Within 36 hours, however, the coup was crushed by troops loyal to President Machel.[41] The Machel regime explained the coup by downgrading its importance to a plot by 'imperialists ... [and] a small group of officers who had simply been bought over' and emphasised that FAM remained the 'mainstay of the revolution'.[42] But the coup attempt revealed the necessity of strengthening FRELIMO Partido's source of institutional and popular support, and of making FAM more politically subservient to the regime. Accordingly, more purges followed, 'peoples assemblies' organised on a regional basis became vehicles for asserting party authority over military personnel, organisations (such as the Mozambican Organisation of Women) were incorporated into FRELIMO Partido, a recruitment drive strengthened FRELIMO Partido's membership and, on an executive level, two agencies (the political commissariat for the security forces and the central committee for defence and security) were created to strengthen party control over FAM.[43]

By early 1978 there were indications, however, that FRELIMO Partido's suspicions about FAM's political reliability was only one problem that required urgent attention. More serious was FAM's inability to protect Mozambique's territorial integrity against attacks of the Smith regime. While its opposition to South African racial policies and internal dispensation remained muted, the Machel administration made no effort to conceal its hostility towards the Smith regime. Thus Mozambique housed approximately 10,000 ZANU guerrillas in various refugee and military camps in Mozambique, closed the Mozambique-Rhodesia border (including the suspension of the use of Mozambique's ports and rail and road facilities), and confiscated Rhodesian property in Mozambique.

In retaliation, Rhodesia followed a two-pronged strategy: First, the Smith regime's security forces launched cross-border raids on guerrilla and refugee camps, and attacked economic targets and towns often far within Mozambique territory, thereby exposing the military vulnerability of Mozambique to foreign incursions. That the territorial integrity of Mozambique could be violated in at least 350 separate incidents pointed to the need to strengthen FAM in a way that would improve their conventional deterrent against especially airborne raids. As the Soviet Union was the principal supplier of military equipment to FRELIMO prior to 1975, the Soviet Union again stepped in as the major supplier of arms and helped train FAM soldiers. In time FAM started to exhibit a more conventional orientation, with artillery and tank battalions and a general staff system, and an air force was created whereby Mozambique came to possess some combat and training aircraft (including helicopters).[44] This new orientation was the major reason why FAM was referred to in 1980 as a 'new army in terms of organisation and fighting',[45] with a somewhat improved ability to deter foreign incursions.

In apparent contradiction to the conventional trend, however, FAM's ground and air forces of, respectively, 25,000 and 1,000 men were also employed as counter-insurgent forces against the rural opposition to the Machel regime encouraged by the Smith regime as a second component of their two-pronged strategy. The Smith government used a radio station, the Voice of Free Africa, to broadcast to a Mozambican audience, incorporated disaffected Mozambicans (such as former *flecha* commanders) into their security forces, and otherwise provided aid to organisations opposing Machel. Though initially active in only a few areas and discredited by the association with the Smith regime, the rural opposition soon extended its activity beyond Cabo Delgado and Niassa provinces to the central provinces of Inhambane, Manica, Sofala, Tete and Zambesia. This 'rural opposition' was led by an organisation called the Mozambique National Resistance (RENAMO or the MNR), which claimed to be an organisation of wholly Mozambican origin with its membership consisting of Mozambicans ideologically or otherwise opposed to the Machel regime. Indeed, the MNR did attract opponents of FRELIMO. Supporters of organisations like Kavandame's UNIPOMO, FUMO, COREMO, UNAR, and an organisation called the Mozambique Nationalist Movement (MONAMO) joined ranks with the MNR, and repeated purges and defections produced a supply of militarily-trained individuals often bitterly hostile to FRELIMO. Two former FRELIMO soldiers, André Matzangaissa and Afonso Dhlakama, were respectively commander-in-chief and deputy commander of military operations of the MNR but later, upon Matzangaissa's death, Dhlakama assumed the position of the MNR's 'Supreme Chief', assisted by Orlando Cristina (until his death in April 1983) as general secretary and Evo Fernandez as 'public spokesman'.[46] The threat posed by MNR activities was initially described by the Machel regime as the 'Makonde problem' and later as banditry, and required the military to be employed as counter-insurgent forces, assisted by a partially-armed militia. In addition, a set of agreements between Mozambique and Tanzania led to two Tanzanian battalions (approximately 3,000 troops) to be employed in the provinces of Cabo Delgado, Niassa and Tete.[47]

The demise of the Smith and Muzorewa regimes did little to alter the pattern of Mozambique's security problems. The impetus to develop a conventional capability to deter foreign attacks continued as South Africa, angered by Machel support of the African National Congress of South Africa, on two occasions launched attacks deep into Mozambican territory and became the main external supporter of the MNR. Despite the role of the Tanzanian troop contingent and later also a Zimbabwean brigade, as well as several major counter-insurgent offensives, the MNR dramatically expanded its support base and the scale of its activities, forcing the Machel regime by 1983 to admit that between 5,000 and 10,000 MNR soldiers had the countryside 'to themselves. They were not confronted by anyone.'[48] By this time all of Mozambique's provinces had military governors, and defence expenditures became the largest single item in Mozambique's state budget, growing from a modest $ 18m in 1975 to more than $196 in 1982.[49] Convinced that the deteriorating security situation was in major part attributable to South Africa's support of the MNR, the Machel regime in early

1984 opened negotiations with South Africa on matters relating to security (as well as economic relations, the Cahora Bassa dam and tourism), which in March led to the signing of the Nkomati Accord. As Professor Spence discusses at greater length in his chapter on South Africa's Military Relations, included in this accord was a non-aggression pact whereby Mozambique and South Africa undertook to suspend their support of rebels operating in each others' territory or, stated differently, they undertook to halt subversion of each other. Soon the Machel regime publicised the suspension of its military support of the South African ANC.[50]

The Nkomati Accord has had little effect on Mozambique's internal security situation. The MNR continues to receive aid from South Africa and from other states and organisations,[51] and it has become increasingly clear that conditions within Mozambique are amenable to the growth of not only guerrilla opposition, but also lawlessness, banditry and social dislocation. Mozambique's economic problems, worsened by the severe drought gripping southern Africa for the past five years, have deteriorated to the point where 700,000 Mozambicans suffer acute starvation, an additional 5 million being in an only slightly less threatened position. To make matters worse, the MNR attacks on trading posts in rural areas and trucks and convoys have destroyed emergency aid being transported to stricken areas.[52] While the desperate need for food has encouraged banditry, there also is - as acknowledged by the Machel regime - the widespread abuse of power and even criminal activities by members of the military, the militia and police whose actions are mistakenly attributed to the MNR. When dealing with crime, for example, the police often resort to brutal and summary forms of 'justice'.[53] In this environment the MNR has flourished, operating in groups as large as 100 men and apparently able to operate in any corner of Mozambique.[54]

Although the causes of the growing security problem in Mozambique thus are rooted in a variety of circumstances and, by implication, efforts at improving the security situation supersede military actions, the security forces of Mozambique are presently in the forefront of the Machel regime's efforts to stay in power. The security force has grown in numbers, from 10,000 men in 1975 to a figure of well over 30,000 in 1985 (this includes the two border guard brigades and militia).[55] Part of the military has a conventional orientation, trained and supplied with heavy weapons by mostly Soviet and other socialist states. But the main portion of the military in 1985 has a counter-insurgency posture. This portion of the military relies on the leadership of the military governors of the provinces, as well as officers trained at a school in Manica. But it faces an uphill battle with the MNR. Indeed, despite outside assistance, the leadership supplied by trusted political figures[56] and veterans of FRELIMO's guerrilla struggle, the growth in the size of the security forces, the role played by the militia and 'peoples vigilance committees', the Mozambique armed forces seem unable to contain the MNR. There is no indication that this situation is going to be altered, let alone reversed, in the forseeable future.

The Zimbabwe National Army (ZNA) : 1980-1985

At first glance, there are several similarities in Mozambique and Zimbabwe's post-independence military development. For instance, both countries hold that South Africa is their principal external enemy and they tend to see a South African hand in many of the internal problems they experience. Yet, despite these and other similarities, Zimbabwe's military development has been influenced by a set of circumstances radically different from that of Mozambique. Considerations of space do not allow for a discussion of the entire range of conditions influencing Zimbabwe's development since 1980; for our purposes, however, three conditions are highly relevant.

First, the conflict in Zimbabwe ended in an election which did much to clarify the political power distribution in the country. To contest the first election, ZANU and ZAPU campaigned as political parties and in the process demonstrated separate bases of political power. ZAPU further demonstrated that it was a minority party with a power base primarily in Matabeleland, while ZANU showed its strength as majority party by capturing virtually all the parliamentary seats in the rest of Zimbabwe.[57] That ZANU has been unable to make any electoral headway in Matabeleland since 1980 or, put another way, that the political support bases of the major black political parties have hardened since 1980, is of course a cause of strife, but the important point is there is no doubt as to the breadth and legitimacy of ZANU's electoral base. Second, although the Mugabe regime's management of the economy certainly has not satisfied all pre-1980 expectations regarding jobs, income or land-related issues, a combination of the regime's cautious and pragmatic economic policy, the resilience of economic structures inherited from the pre-1980 period, and the lifting of sanctions have - in spite of the drought only recently broken in Zimbabwe - provided a reasonbly stable economic environment.[58] There is indeed considerable continuity between pre- and post-1980 economic policy, particularly as regards the priority accorded to the manufacturing sector,[59] and this continuity has done much to allay whites' and foreign investors' fears about impending economic collapse under ZANU political leadership. Third, the Mugabe regime inherited a set of state institutions whose powers vastly increased during the UDI period. With the removal of discriminatory hiring practices and the accelerated promotion of black and especially ZANU-oriented public servants, the public service for ZANU has become a valued means to manage the economy, distribute patronage, and to strengthen its power base.[60] Public pronouncements in Zimbabwe have often tended to create the expectation of a radical break with the past, but in view of the preceding discussion it is clear that considerable continuity in fact exists between pre- and post-1980 Zimbabwe. It is against this backdrop of relative overall stability that military development has taken place.

In 1980 Zimbabwe's immediate military problems seemed daunting. During the war the Rhodesian Army had increased to 14,000 regulars, assisted by about 60,000 reservists and auxiliary and para-military forces.[61] ZANU and ZAPU together numbered between 35,000 and 40,000 guerrillas.[62] Portions of these military entities, trained in different traditions, with different operational experiences, and regarding the others with mutual suspicion, had to be integrated into a new army intended to be about 45,000 men strong, while the remaining sections of the separate armies had to be demobilised. The task of integration and demobilisation, or 'Operation Merger,' was headed by a Joint Military High Command, consisting of high-ranking officers of the three armies, as well as a representative of the Ministry of Defence. The high command had a small staff of its own (including integrated functional subcommittees to issue orders), but was still forced to rely on the chains-of-command of the respective armies. Also part of 'Operation Merger' was the retraining of the men to be incorporated in the new Zimbabwe National Army (ZNA). This training effort was headed by the British Military and Advisory Training Team (BMATT) of about 100 officers and NCOs, who specialised in leadership, staff and technical training along conventional lines.[63]

By late 1980 it was evident that the Joint Military High Command had made considerable progress in integrating the three armies. As had been requested by ZANU at the Lancaster House conference, the high command dismissed the controversial head of the ZNA, Peter Walls, and disbanded the notorious units of the old Rhodesian Army, such as the Selous Scouts. But other portions of the army were retained, especially the racially-integrated three Rhodesian African Rifles units, the Grey's Scouts mounted infantry unit, the Rhodesian Light Infantry (a crack white paratroop battalion that changed its name to, simply, the Commando Battalion), and logistic and service units. The ZNA was organised into four brigades, each with its support units. In addition, there are the specialised units directly controlled by army headquarters in Harare, such as the armoured and artillery regiments and the parachute battalion, and the various training establishments.[64] The overall military commander initially was Lt.-General Sandy Maclean, but he was later succeeded by former ZANLA commander Rex Nhongo. Each of the brigades are commanded by former ZANLA leaders; indeed, the trend in the ZNA is for ex-ZANLA personnel to dominate the senior and middle level positions, as former ZANLA guerrillas also vastly outnumber both ex-ZIPRA personnel and whites in overall military positions.[65] This trend is partly related to white emigration and reluctance to serve under former enemies and also to political vetting by ZANU, but more obviously it is a consequence of the sheer size of ZANU and its recruiting base among the Mashona.

Despite the progress made in integrating and retraining the ZNA, events during 1981 and subsequently revealed serious domestic security problems within Zimbabwe. The first of these problems to manifest itself was the difficulty in simultaneously demobilising soldiers and giving them a productive role in civil society. By

May 1981 the total armed forces of Zimbabwe had swollen to 65,000, a figure that excluded the number of armed reservists, auxiliaries and para-military forces. Overall, more than 100,000 former guerrillas and soldiers had to be absorbed by civil society.[66] To increase the incentive to return to civilian life, the Mugabe regime (a) developed a programme entitled 'Soldiers Employed in Economic Development' (SEED), administered jointly by the Army Demobilisation Committee and the Ministry of Manpower Planning and Development, that was aimed at employing suitable former military personnel in agriculture, commerce and industry. But with the lack of skills among especially many former guerrillas, poor administration, and the limited appeal of civilian jobs, the SEED programme made little progress. By mid-1981 it had managed to involve only 2,000 former guerrillas. Where SEED failed, the Mugabe regime (b) simply demobilised soldiers who were for two years entitled to regular army pay, but this, while forming a considerable drain on state finances, also made only slow progress. Finding a home in neither civilian nor military life, many former soldiers simply deserted and took to a life of crime. By the end of 1981 banditry, featuring especially ex-ZIPRA guerrillas in the Matabeleland area, had become a serious internal security problem necessitating the re-introduction of the para-military local militia and even some limited army operations, as well as the disarming of many ZIPRA guerrillas still present in assembly points.[67]

The second security problem to manifest itself was politically-motivated armed resistance, again occurring mainly in Matabeleland's rural areas, as well as ZANU-ZAPU fighting that spilled over into urban areas with several deaths caused by attacks on houses, party offices, beer halls and, importantly, fighting in army barracks and assembly points. As guerrillas from the assembly points were moved to military bases near cities, the tension between ZANLA and ZIPRA guerrillas increased, fueled by Joshua Nkomo's demotion in a cabinet re-shuffle and claims that the ZNA treated ZIPRA guerrillas in a 'shabby' manner.[68] Finally the tensions gave way to fierce fighting in the areas around Bulawayo, Gweru and Kwekwe, killing more than 300 people.[69] The fighting, nevertheless, had a random character (partly as ZIPRA guerrilla units were prevented from establishing links with each other[70]) and it resulted in the disintegration of relatively few newly created units.[71] Moreover, mixed ZNA battalions were successfuly employed against the ZIPRA dissidents. Yet, despite the ability of the new ZNA units to maintain their cohesion and their giving proof of their political reliability under difficult circumstances, the Mugabe regime felt that the events of 1981 warranted the creation of a military unit not trained by the BMATT and used specifically against dissidents. Accordingly a team of North Korean officers started to train a fifth brigade, structured around 1,000 ex-ZANLA guerrillas, in the Inyanga district of eastern Zimbabwe. Despite official denials, the Fifth Brigade was an exception to the developing pattern in Zimbabwe's military: the brigade was not trained by British officers and was thus exposed to a different ideology, military traditions and tactics. They were also issued with different weapons (AK-47s instead of the standard NATO rifles used by the other brigades) and, although perhaps not a 'private army' of ZANU, certainly were intended to be used in politically-sensitive situations.[72]

The Mugabe regime did not view the events of 1981 as random occurrences: in their estimation dissidence was a direct result of plotting by ZAPU, who were assisted by outside agents, namely the South African regime.[73] The real problem, therefore, was not the groups of dissidents, but the ZAPU infrastructure that supported dissidence and the plotting of senior ZAPU leaders (that is the so-called Super-ZAPU).[74] Initiated in early 1982, the response of the Mugabe regime was swift and vigorous. In March 1982 caches of weapons found on ZAPU-owned farms quickly led to: the dismissal of four ZAPU ministers from the cabinet, including Nkomo, and the arrests of other ZAPU supporters; action declaring illegal several ZAPU companies and the confiscation of ZAPU property; security operations in Matabeleland; and the arrest of many ex-ZIPRA guerrillas in the ZNA, including former ZIPRA commander Lookout Masuku, Dumiso Dabengwa and Akim Ndlovu. Believing that Nkomo's dismissal and, especially, the arrests of Masuku and Dabengwa provided concrete proof of the ZNA's preference for ZANLA over ZIPRA, ex-ZIPRA guerrillas absconded from the ZNA in increasing numbers.[75] Adding to their numbers were the ZIPRA guerrillas who never sought incorporation in the ZNA, preferring to hold on to their arms and secreting them for future use, and who lived among people in Matabeleland convinced that the ZANU-dominated regime was out to destroy ZAPU. Soon - by June 1982 - it was impossible to travel safely along Matabeleland roads other than highways and the number of armed robberies and murders increased.[76] Dissatisfied with the performance of the security force units in Matabeleland - the civil police, the First and Second Brigades, and the para-military militia - the Mugabe regime assigned the Fifth Brigade to Matabeleland.[77]

Since the end of 1982 the regime has dealt with the 'Matabeleland problem' in a brutal fashion. The means are varied and include: depriving the population of food by way of, for example, a curfew that prohibits outdoor movement during daylight hours, the closing of shops, and the limitation of aid in an area already under severe pressure from the drought; arrests and detentions of ZAPU supporters, either arbitrarily or under the sweeping legal provisions of the emergency powers and the Law and Order (Maintenance) Act inherited from previous regimes; the torture and murder of civilians in order to extract information about, or to discourage support of, ZAPU; and the capture of ZAPU dissidents and bandits.[78]

If the regime's actions were aimed at eliminating ZAPU as a political force, it has failed. On the contrary, it could be argued that the regime's actions had the opposite effect, creating a 'degree of unity in Matabeleland that had not existed before.'[79] ZANU has claimed that its membership in the Matabeleland area has increased from 100,000 in mid-1983 to about quarter of a million at present and that some successes in local elections indicate increased support for ZANU. But the preferences of Matabeleland voters in the 1985 parliamentary elections demonstrate ZAPU's continued support in the area.[80] Furthermore, violence continues to plague the area, with frequent reports of armed robberies, attacks on farmers, murders and, not the least, ZNA and ZANU-instigated 'excesses'.[81] One important consequence of the continued unrest is its effect on national politics, vastly contributing to the Mugabe regime's intolerance of opposition. Another and for our purposes more important consequence is the effect of the unrest on the ZNA. The ZNA after 1980 was intended to be a conventionally-styled army trained by the British, but events have forced major portions of the ZNA

Revolutionary Armies: Mozambique and Zimbabwe

- the First, Fifth and later also a new Sixth Brigade - to be employed as counter-insurgent forces. This shift in military predisposition may, however, prove to be less than traumatic. The past operational experiences of ZNA soldiers, either as guerrillas or those opposing them, reflect a familiarity with counter-insurgency; most former ZANLA guerrillas - the bulk of the ZNA - are not unused to being employed in domestic military operations, and they are unlikely to be dismayed by the practice of assessing and discarding military men according to political criteria.

The impetus for the ZNA to develop a counter-insurgent or even defensive posture is strengthened by Zimbabwe's position in the southern African security context. Although the Mugabe regime has often criticised South Africa's policies, there is little evidence to suggest that Zimbabwe, as a frontline state with a revolutionary guerrilla experience, has joined in the liberation offensive against South Africa. Rather, the principal security obligation of Zimbabwe (and the ZNA) is to defend vital interests, that is the protection of territorial integrity and landlocked Zimbabwe's links with Mozambique, and the cultivation of economic growth and political stability, against hostile South African actions. As the dominant power of the region, South Africa is able and increasingly willing to blunt the liberation struggle by destabilising frontline states that support the ANC. South Africa also is hostile to efforts by the frontline states to extricate themselves from the grip of South Africa's economic dominance by developing an alternative economic system of co-operation, namely the Southern African Development and Co-ordination Conference (SADCC), which for its success relies heavily on Zimbabwe's industrial base and routes of transportation through Mozambique.[82] With South Africa's policy predicated on the need to keep its neighbours dependent and hence vulnerable, Zimbabwe is in an unenvious position. South Africa has indeed pressured Zimbabwe by economic means, including the withdrawal of locomotives and damage (by sabotage) of rail and road bridges when Zimbabwe's maize crop required urgent shipment, the suspension of the preferential trade agreement between South Africa and Zimbabwe, and the repatriation of Zimbabwean contract workers - thus causing the loss of a lucrative source of foreign exchange.[83] Equally serious is the effect of the MNR's activity in Mozambique on particularly the security of the Beira-Mutare railroad, the Sofala-Mutare oil pipeline, and roads that convey vital goods to and from Zimbabwe. To assist Mozambique to protect these links, the Mugabe regime has since July 1982 deployed ZNA battalions in Mozambique, where they can provide escorts for traffic along roads and help guard the oil pipeline, railroad and other important installations in the northern and central provinces.[84]

To summarise: The ZNA has since 1980 played two major security roles, namely the containment of the unrest in Matabeleland and the defence of Zimbabwe's vital interests against South African-instigated subversion. In performing these roles the ZNA uses equipment of varied origin, such as NATO-type rifles, South African-made Eland armoured cars and Soviet reconnaissance vehicles. The BMATT remains in Zimbabwe on request and they feature prominently in training. Since the high point of 1981 the size of the ZNA has been reduced to manageable levels, from 60,000 to about 41,300 in early 1985, though the military personnel are regularly assisted by the para-military militia.[85] The composition of the ZNA conspicuously favours former ZANLA guerrillas, both in overall numbers and in senior positions.

CONCLUSION

What kinds of militaries thus 'emerged out of the bush' in Mozambique and Zimbabwe, and why did they assume these shapes? Further, what happened to these militaries after independence?

The liberation armies of Mozambique and Zimbabwe were products of a type of guerrilla warfare not easily equated with the traditional Maoist notions of guerrilla warfare, with its condition of protractedness and stage-like progression from small-scale actions to conventionalised mobile warfare. The periods of guerrilla warfare actually conducted in Mozambique and Zimbabwe were relatively short in duration, and the conditions of struggle so internationalised that little could be accomplished without the blessing of the outsiders who armed and trained guerrillas, provided the organisations with money, and offered bases in neighbouring countries. When guerrillas did enter their respective territories, they tended to operate under the command of a regional authority, and did not aim mainly at supplanting existing social

structures but rather coopted existing ones to
ensure military freedom of action. Of necessity
guerrilla decision-making relied on local initiative
and, especially when the struggles started to
attract more recruits, commanders had to make
do with an assortment of guerrillas who frequently
were undisciplined and lacked adequate equipment
and training. These difficulties fueled internal
divisions and led to recriminations in organisations
already conspicuously lacking a sense of internal
unity. Divisions were caused by many factors
that divided the elite on the one hand and, on
the other, introduced divisions between guerrillas
and their leaders. Indeed, FRELIMO especially
but also ZANU and ZAPU did not provide a home
for most important nationalist leaders, nor did
they successfully cultivate inclusive or overarching
nationalist traditions.

When the struggles culminated in independence,
it was difficult to foresee the liberation organisations as focal points of revolutionary transformation according to the principles of scientific
socialism; instead this lofty goal was rather
rapidly reduced to the more modest need to maintain
stability and promote economic growth. For Mozambique, even these goals have proved to be elusive,
as mounting economic difficulties, bureaucratic
collapse and foreign-supported opposition soon
placed the Machel regime and its armed forces
in an embattled position. The armed forces have
been thrust in the forefront of efforts to contain
the MNR and the banditry that is intermingled
with MNR activity; in the process they have
developed a counter-insurgency posture that
co-exists with conventional Soviet-supplied
equipment and training developed by the need to
protect Mozambique against foreign incursions.
But the armed forces are also part of the problem
as, first, its political assertiveness and, later,
indiscipline and uneven military performance
contributed to disorder and lawlessness. In
Zimbabwe, military 'excesses' certainly also
contribute to ZANU-ZAPU tension, but overall the
ZNA has demonstrated its ability to maintain its
cohesion and discipline under difficult conditions.
With British training and arms of varied origin,
the ZNA is dominated by former ZANLA guerrillas
who have been able to contain banditry and
politically-motivated unrest to a limited geographic
area. To be sure, this success is in large part
supported by the economic continuity between pre-

and post-1980 Zimbabwe, the breadth and constitutional legitimacy of ZANU's political support base and, not the least, the vast array of repressive measures inherited from pre-1980 regimes.

Finally, the most prominent common denominator of Mozambique and Zimbabwe's military development is their common enemy, namely South Africa and the threat it poses to economic development, political stability and the defence of vital links with the outside world. Upon independence, this threat ironically transformed the liberation armies of southern Africa into entities mainly concerned with counter-insurgency and less interested in participating in the struggle to liberate South Africa than in defending their respective countries. Yet even this defensive posture provides no guarantees in escaping South Africa's reach; ultimately, the best defence lies in the resolution of South Africa's internal political problem.

NOTES

1. On the organisational antecedents of FRELIMO, see Chilcote, R. (ed.), Emerging Nationalism in Portuguese Africa: Documents (Stanford, California: Hoover Institution Press, 1972); Mondlane, E., The Struggle for Mozambique (Middlesex: Penguin, 1969); and Samuels, M.A., 'The Nationalist Parties' in Abshire, D.M. and Samuels, M.A., Portuguese Africa: A Handbook (London: Pall Mall Press, 1969).

2. On the pre-1962 history of black politics in Zimbabwe, see Gibson, R., African Liberation Movements (London: Oxford University Press, 1972) and Ranger, T., The African Voice in Southern Rhodesia (Evanston, Illinois: Northwestern University Press, 1970).

3. Mondlane, The Struggle for Mozambique, pp. 152-54.

4. Barber, J., Rhodesia: The Road to Rebellion (New York: Oxford University Press, 1967), p. 141.

5. Wilkenson, A.R., 'From Rhodesia to Zimbabwe', in Davidson, B., Slovo, J. and Wilkenson, A.R., Southern Africa: The New Politics of Revolution (New York: Penguin, 1976), p. 227.

6. Barber, Rhodesia, p. 210.

7. Day, J., International Nationalism (London: Routledge and Kegan Paul, 1967), pp. 22-111.

8. Gibson, African Liberation Movements,

pp. 164-78; Morris, M., Armed Conflict in Southern Africa (Cape Town: Jeremy Spence, 1974), pp. 28-42; Maxey, K., The Fight for Zimbabwe (London: Rex Collings, 1975); and Wilkinson in Davidson, Slovo and Wilkenson, pp. 232-44.

9. Kilbracken, Lord., 'Confrontations of the War', Africa Today (November 1965), pp. 7-8; Marcum, J.A., 'Three Revolutions', Africa Report, 12 (November 1967), p. 20; Venter, A.J., The Zambezi Salient (Cape Town: Howard Timmins, 1974), pp. 332-33.

10. On Mozambique, see Jundanian, B.F., 'Resettlement Programs: Counterinsurgency in Mozambique', Comparative Politics, 6 (July 1974) and De Arriaga, K., The Portuguese Answer (London: W. & J. Mackay, 1973). On Zimbabwe, see Bowyer Bell, J., 'The Frustration of Insurgency: The Rhodesian Example of the 1960s', Military Affairs, 35 (February 1971), pp. 1-5.

11. On this crucial strategic distinction, see Rejai, M., The Comparative Study of Revolutionary Strategy (New York: David Mackay, 1977), p. 19; Taber, R., The War of the Flea (Suffolk: The Chaucer Press, 1970), pp. 70-71; and Mack, A., 'Sharpening the Contradictions: Guerrilla Strategy in Imperialist Wars', Race and Class, 17 (Autumn 1975), pp. 161-77.

12. Whitaker, P.M., 'The Liberation of Portuguese-held Africa' (paper presented at the annual meeting of the African Studies Association, Montreal, 15-18 October 1969), Tables 2 and 3.

13. Legum, C., 'African National Liberation', Problems of Communism, 24 (January 1975), p. 7 and Day, International Nationalism, pp. 104-11.

14. Gibson, African Liberation Movements, pp. 169-70, 180-83; and Martin, D. and Johnson, P., The Struggle for Zimbabwe (New York: Monthly Review Press, 1981), pp. 15-30, 112, 215.

15. Opello, W.C., 'Pluralism and Elite Conflict in an Independent Movement: FRELIMO in the 1960s', Journal of Southern African Studies, 2 (October 1975), pp. 73-5.

16. See Smiley, X., 'Zimbabwe, Southern Africa and the Rise of Robert Mugabe', Foreign Affairs, 85 (Summer 1980), pp. 1060-83.

17. Davidson, B., 'The Politics of Armed Struggle: National Liberation in the African Colonies of Portugal', in Davidson, Slovo and Wilkenson, Southern Africa, pp. 56-75; Hastings, A., 'Some Reflections on the War in Mozambique', African Affairs, 73 (July 1974), pp. 264-5;

Mondlane, The Struggle for Mozambique, pp. 138-62, 167-71; and Venter, The Zambezi Salient, p. 95.

18. Kapungu, L.T., 'The OAU's Support for the Liberation of Southern Africa', in El-Ayouty, Y. (ed.), The Organization of African Unity after Ten Years: A Comparative Perspective (New York: Praeger, 1975), pp. 138-9.

19. See Seegers, A., Revolution in Africa: The Case of Zimbabwe (1965-1980) (unpublished Ph.D. dissertation: Loyola University of Chicago, 1984), ch. 4.

20. As, for example, in Portuguese attempts to manipulate Makonde-Makua differences in the northern provinces of Mozambique.

21. For a full account, see Opello, 'Pluralism and Elite Conflict'. Assimilado refers to individuals who, under Portuguese rule, acquired voting rights and other entitlements consistent with a higher socio-economic status.

22. Isaacman, A. and B., Mozambique: From Colonialism to Revolution, 1910-1982 (Boulder, Colorado: Westview Press, 1984), p. 143.

23. See Chilcote, Emerging Nationalism in Portuguese Africa; Gibson, African Liberation Movements, pp. 267-290; and Morris, Armed Conflict in Southern Africa, p. 76.

24. For the expression and gradual development of this ideological affinity, see the editions of FRELIMO's mouthpiece, Mozambique Revolution.

25. On the initial split and its causes, see Gibson, African Liberation Movements, pp. 161-2; Nelson, H., Area Handbook for Southern Rhodesia (Washington: United States Government Printer, 1975), p. 179; and Wilkenson in Davidson, Slovo and Wilkenson, p. 228.

26. See Marcum, J.A., 'The Exile Condition and Revolutionary Effectiveness: Southern African Liberation Movements', in Potholm, C.P. and Dale, R. (eds.), Southern Africa in Perspective (New York: The Free Press, 1972), p. 27.

27. This is also the view of Opello regarding the many schisms within FRELIMO.

28. For this division of guerrilla labour, see Martin and Johnson, The Struggle for Zimbabwe, pp. xx-xxi.

29. Mondlane, The Struggle for Mozambique, pp. 152-4, 168-71.

30. See Bruce, N., 'Portugal's African Wars', Conflict Studies, 34 (March 1973), p. 22; Gibson, African Liberation Movements, p. 286; and Martelli, G., 'Conflict in Portuguese Africa', in Abshire

and Samuels, Portuguese Africa, pp. 424-5.
31. Keesing's Contemporary Archives, 21 (28 July-3 August 1975), p. 27245.
32. Martin and Johnson, The Struggle for Zimbabwe, pp. 15-30, 112, 215.
33. Before the 1976-1979 increase in guerrilla activity, ZIPRA numbers were estimated at between 400 and 1,000 and those of ZANLA at between 5,000 and 10,000. Later ZIPRA increased to about 3,000 and ZANLA guerrillas increased to between 13,000 and 15,000. See Gann and Henrikson, The Struggle for Zimbabwe, p. 103; Martin and Johnson, The Struggle for Zimbabwe, pp. xx-xxi; Carter, G. and O'Meara, P., (eds.), Southern Arica in Crisis (Bloomington: Indiana University Press, 1977), pp. 36-7; and Rotberg, R.I., Suffer The Future (Cambridge: Harvard University Press, 1980), p. 262.
34. Gann, L.H. and Henrikson, T., The Struggle for Zimbabwe (New York: Praeger, 1981), pp. 87-90.
35. For more detail, see Wiseman, A. and Taylor, A.M., From Rhodesia to Zimbabwe: The Politics of Transition (New York: Pergamon, 1981), especially pp. 7-13.
36. The prominence of ZANLA within ZANU became obvious with the organisational reforms of 1977, which enlarged ZANLA's representation on the Central Committee. When Robert Mugabe rose to power in the late 1970s, 18 of the 25 members of the Central Committee were either military commanders or men who had at some point undergone military training. See Legum, C., Western Crisis over Southern Africa (New York: Africana Publishing Company, 1979), pp 219-20.
37. Keesing's Contemporary Archives, 21 (28 July-3 August 1975), p. 27245.
38. Africa South of the Sahara, 1978-1979, p. 643.
39. See Fauvet, P., 'Roots of Counter-Revolution: The Mozambique National Resistance', Review of African Political Economy, 29 (July 1984), pp. 108-14.
40. Fifteen of the 19 members of the first cabinet had actually fought in the war.
41. Africa South of the Sahara, 1976-1977, p. 576 and Kaplan, I., Area Handbook for Mozambique(Washington: United States Government Printer, 1977), pp. 202-04.
42. Forbes Pachter, E., 'Contra-Coup: Civilian Control of the Military in Guinea, Tanzania and Mozambique', Journal of Modern African Studies,

20 (December 1982), p. 602.
43. Ibid., p. 600-03; and Isaacman, Mozambique, pp. 121-2.
44. See The Military Balance (London: International Institute for Strategic Studies), issues starting with 1976-1977 up to 1984-85.
45. Forbes Pachter, 'Contra-Coup', p. 602.
46. Fauvet, 'Roots of Counter-Revolution', pp. 116-19.
47. Keesings's Contemporary Archives, 23 (14 October 1977), p. 28620.
48. The Star (Johannesburg), 3 January 1984.
49. See The Military Balance (London: International Institute for Strategic Studies), issues starting with 1976-1977 up to 1984-1985.
50. The Rand Daily Mail (Johannesburg), 9 April 1984.
51. On South Africa's continued support, see (for example) the South African Broadcasting Corporation's interview with General Constand Viljoen on the 'Network' programme (9 October 1985); Africa Now (March 1984), pp. 35-7; The Weekly Mail (Johannesburg), 28-30 June 1985; and The Star (Johannesburg), 11 April 1985. 'Unofficial' aid from South Africa also reaches the MNR. See Sunday Star (Johannesburg), 17 March 1985 and the Sunday Times (Johannesburg), 27 January 1985. For other external supporters, see the discussion of West German and Portuguese individuals and organisations in Africa, 127 (March 1982), pp. 118-20.
52. The Rand Daily Mail (Johannesburg), 5 December 1983. On Mozambique's economic woes, see the report of the International Monetary Fund summarised in the Washington Report on Africa, 3 (1 April 1985), pp. 46-7.
53. Africa Confidential, 25 (1 August 1984), pp. 1-2. See also Africa, 128 (April 1982), pp. 32-3; and Africa Now, 8 (November 1981), p. 24.
54. Reports of MNR actions appear almost daily in South African newspapers. For some examples, see: Sunday Tribune (Johannesburg), 30 September 1984; Pretoria News (Pretoria), 19 October 1984; Sunday Star (Johannesburg), 16 December 1984 and 24 March 1985; The Rand Daily Mail (Johannesburg), 25 April 1985. Little remains known of the MNR as an organisation, though it has a political programme, drawn up in West Germany in 1981, that consists of seven chapters and very generally supports Western and capitalist or free-market notions. As regards guerrilla operations,

Mozambique is apparently divided into regional guerrilla areas headed by military *commandantes*, with overall headquarters located in the Gorongosa Mountains. See Africa Now, 7 (October 1981), pp. 42-43; The Citizen (Johannesburg), 9 and 12 September 1985; Defense and Foreign Affairs (April 1984), pp. 35-6; Pretoria News (Pretoria), 2 January 1985.

55. The Military Balance 1984-1985 (London: International Institute for Strategic Studies), pp. 79-80.

56. Several military governors are members of the Council of Ministers, such as Marcelino Dos Santos (Sofala), Mario Machungu (Zambesia), Mariono Matsinhe (Niassa) and Albert Chipande (Cabo Delgado).

57. See Gregory, M., 'Zimbabwe 1980: Politicisation through Armed Struggle and Electoral Mobilisation', Journal of Commonwealth and Comparative Politics, 19 (March 1981), pp. 62-94.

58. See Hawkins, A.M., 'The Zimbabwean Economy: The First Five Years' Bulletin of the Africa Institute of South Africa, 25 (1985), pp. 37-45 and Gordon, D.F., 'Development Strategy in Zimbabwe: Assessments and Prospects', in Schatzberg, M.G. (ed.), The Political Economy of Zimbabwe (New York: Praeger, 1984), pp. 119-43.

59. This has generated opposition within ZANU. See Libby, R.T., 'Developmental Strategies and Political Divisions within the Zimbabwean State', in Schatzberg, The Political Economy of Zimbabwe, pp. 143-63.

60. For background, see Seidman, R.B. and Gagne, M., 'The State, Law and Development in Zimbabwe', Journal of Southern African Affairs, 5 (April 1980), pp. 149-70.

61. The Military Balance 1979-1980 (London: International Institute for Strategic Studies), pp. 55-6, 95.

62. African Report, 25 (March-April 1980), pp. 22-3.

63. Keegan, J. (ed.), World Armies (Basingstoke: MacMillan, 1983), pp. 681, 683. At the end of 1985 the BMATT consisted of 35 officers and 23 WOs and NCOs. Baynham, S.J., 'Civilian Control of the Military in Botswana, Zimbabwe and Malawi', unpublished manuscript, 1986.

64. The air force maintained its existing structure of seven squadrons. Zimbabwe does not possess a navy. See The Military Balance (London: International Institute for Strategic Studies),

issues starting with 1981-1982 up to 1984-1985.
65. Most whites are found in the air force. To date, brigadier is the highest rank attained by an ex-ZIPRA guerrilla.
66. <u>Africa Now</u> (September 1981), p. 32. See also Carter, G.M., 'The First Year', <u>Africa Report</u> (May-June 1981), p. 65.
67. <u>Africa</u>, 119 (July 1981), pp. 42-3.
68. <u>Africa</u>, 115 (March 1981), p. 25.
69. <u>Africa</u>, 116 (April 1981), p. 19.
70. For example, a convoy of ZIPRA guerrillas from the base near the Gwaai river that sought to link up with ZIPRA guerrillas at Entumbane (near Bulawayo) was turned back by ZNA forces.
71. Between 1980 and 1982 only five of the 46 mixed army units collapsed under the strain of internecine warfare. <u>Africa Confidential</u>, 23 (April 1982), p. 4.
72. <u>Africa</u>, 140 (April 1984), pp. 15-17.
73. South Africa does have a hand in the situation in Matabeleland, but a lack of reliable evidence makes it difficult to gauge the precise nature and extent thereof. Zimbabwe has alleged that South Africa trains dissidents in camps in the northern Transvaal, that South Africa supplies ZAPU with arms and otherwise supports dissidents, and that South Africa's reconnaissance troops are active in Matabeleland. Independent confirmation exists only of a radio station (Radio Truth or the Voice of Free Zimbabwe) that operates from the vicinity of Messina. See <u>Africa</u>, 152 (April 1984), p. 15 and <u>Africa Confidential</u>, 25 (April 1984), p. 2. Allegations of South African subversion has played a prominent role as justification for the retention of repressive security legislation and measures inherited from pre-1980 regimes. The state of emergency has been periodically renewed, and more than 60 new security regulations have been passed since 1980. See Weitzer, R., 'Continuities in the Politics of State Security in Zimbabwe', in Schatzberg, <u>The Political Economy of Zimbabwe</u>, p. 82.
74. See <u>Africa Now</u> (April 1983), pp. 45-46 and <u>Africa</u>, 128 (April 1983), pp. 16-17.
75. Initial ZIPRA desertion was initially estimated at 'hundreds'. Later estimates during 1982 put the figure at 1,800. See <u>Africa Contemporary Record</u>, 14 (1981-1982), p. B882. Overall about 4,000 men deserted from the ZNA during 1982. See Hodder-Williams, R., 'Conflict in Zimbabwe: The Matabeleland Problem', <u>Conflict Studies</u>, 151

(1983), p. 15.

76. Adding to the worsening security situation was the damage of 13 aircraft at Thornhill, a Gweru air base, that resulted in the arrest of several white airmen on charges of sabotage. The resulting trial did much to damage the morale of whites in the ZNA, of whom only about 500 - as against 8,000 in 1980 - presently remain.

77. Although the best-known of the units in Matabeleland, the Fifth Brigade is not the only unit active in the area. Also present are the First Brigade (in Matabeleland North), the Sixth Brigade (a presidential guard unit), the parachute and commando battalions, and police units. It is difficult to at times identify units in action, as they do not wear distinctive uniforms.

78. See Hodder-Williams, 'Conflict in Zimbabwe', pp. 16-18 and Africa Confidential, 25 (April 1984), pp. 1-3 for good summaries of the security operations in Matabeleland.

79. Hodder-Williams, 'Conflict in Zimbabwe', p. 10.

80. See South, 52 (February 1985), p. 82.

81. See The Star (Johannesburg), 27 February 1985 and the Sunday Times (Johannesburg), 3 March 1985.

82. Africa Now, 9 (December 1981), pp. 19-20. See also the discussion of SADCC in Thompson, C.B., 'Zimbabwe in Southern Africa: From Dependent Development to Dominance or Cooperation' in Schatzberg, The Political Economy of Zimbabwe, pp. 197-217.

83. Africa Now, 7 (October 1981), p. 44.

84. By early 1985 there were at least 3,000 ZNA soldiers present in Mozambique. According to observers, a comparison of Mozambique and Zimbabwe soldiers reveals the former to be relatively 'dirty, ill-trained, poorly equipped, badly fed and undisciplined.' The Sunday Star (Johannesburg), 28 April 1985. According to one reliable source, the number of ZNA troops in Mozambique had increased to at least 8,000 by late 1985. Baynham, 'Civilian Control of the Military in Botswana, Zimbabwe and Malawi', p. 17.

85. The Military Balance 1984-1985 (London: International Institute for Strategic Studies), pp. 84-5. Defence expenditure initially remained stable, but rose sharply towards the end of 1983, from $337m to $459m.

Chapter Six

PAX AFRICANA?

Dennis Austin

Cartographically, Africa certainly exists. The partition of the continent would hardly have been possible without the map-marker's art - to such degree that the continent has been imprinted on the mind as on the geographer's map table, an image which encourages the belief that Africa can be given a corporate identity. The notion of a special relationship, of an Africa possessed of a common ancestry and a shared future, still lingers in the language of soldiers and politicians. There are also treaty obligations of an *inter se* nature, enjoined by the OAU, which each of the 50 or more African governments professes to uphold ... Are such commitments to be taken seriously today, and is there a residual meaning to the ideals of a pax-Africana?

The question is not quite so old-fashioned as one might think, although it would be easy to dismiss protestations of peace and unity as belonging to the antiquated vocabulary of colonial nationalism. Is it not the case (one might ask) that civil war, border conflicts, military intervention, brutal dictatorships, public executions, the plight of refugees (by the 1980s, one in every two refugees in the world was an African: five million out of 10 million), famine and the mass expulsions of 'aliens' from one African country to another, have soured early hopes of a peaceful continent? Born in colonial chains, African governments struggled to be free; yet they are everywhere becoming more militarised, whether measured by the purchase of arms, the ambitions of soldier politicians, or the hostility of rival regimes. Since soldiers are usually inclined to use the weapons that they possess as symbols of their power, it is at least arguable that Africa will see foreign war added to its apocalyptic companions: famine, pestilence and death. To understand what may befall the continent, do we need to look further than the history of Latin America, or Europe before 1945, or the aggressive behaviour of present-day governments in Asia? Already the war dead in Africa number many hundreds of thousands in Eritrea, Chad, Ethiopia, the Western Sahara, Nigeria, Rwanda, Burundi, Somalia, Uganda, Zaire, Zimbabwe, Angola, Mozambique and the Sudan.[1] In the light of such events, the OAU is a disgrace, pan-Africanism a farce. The post-independence leaders have neither joy, nor love, nor certitude, nor help for pain; they are indeed on a 'darkling plain, Swept with confused alarms of struggle and fight, Where ignorant armies clash by might.'

Draw closer, and the view is not quite like that. The evidence is examined later, but the conclusion can be set down here. African states are so uncertainly governed that force is employed not to alter the map but to hold it together. OAU injunctions against change mirror the desire of African leaders. They express what is indeed their common predicament, namely a need to preserve the partition of Africa, a need which keeps alive a shared interest among what are otherwise disparate regimes.

There are exceptions, but they too reinforce the overall impression, confirmed over the past quarter of a century, of a continent of uneasy leaders who want only to preserve the map as it is. Consider, for example, the question of aggression by one government against another. The few African wars that have been fought have been largely because the colonial legacy was obscure or muddled, as between Algeria and Morocco over the Western Sahara, or between Ethiopia and Somalia in the Ogaden. Had Spain brought its desert colony clearly into independence, the sovereignty of the new state would have been upheld by the OAU and the international community. But the Spanish never fully made up their mind; they divided the area confusedly between Morocco and Mauritania despite the protests of nomad leaders. The coup in Nouakchott in 1978 put an end to Mauritania's claims, leaving Morocco with the POLISARIO Front guerillas backed by Algeria. Similarly, the Ogaden in southern Ethiopia was tossed from one government to another by different administering authorities during World War II, encouraging Somali hopes that the region could be detached (forcibly if necessary) from Addis Ababa.

There are other partial exceptions. There have been border clashes between Nigeria and the Cameroon Republic, but there too one can argue that they are the consequence of a late shift in the frontier in 1960 - following the UN administered plebiscite - when the northern Cameroons chose to remain as part of Nigeria whereas the southern districts opted to join the newly independent Republic of Cameroon.[2] Where, by contrast, the boundaries between African states were established over a discernible period of colonial rule, they have become acceptable, *faute de mieux*, despite the absurdities of the partition boundaries. Perhaps we should make two further exceptions - Tanzania's attack on Uganda, and Gaddafi's claim to the northern strip of Chad? But Nyerere's war against Amin did not lead to any seizure of territory: as the next chapter shows, it simply evicted Amin whose forces had imprudently entered Tanzania. As for Colonel Gaddafi - well, no one can easily discern his intentions whether in relation to Chad or to any other interest. What is said today may be contradicted tomorrow.

Yet one should pause a little over Libya. Under Gaddafi's rule, the republic has a certain fervour of intent, an ideology which extends beyond its boundaries. Morocco, too, has dynastic ambitions of a pre-colonial origin which places it apart from most African states. Although this book's focus is on sub-Saharan Africa, the point is made only to note the contrast since African governments (other than Somalia, Libya and Morocco) are primarily concerned not to advance an ideology, or to extend their territory, but to uphold their national claims to govern within their colonial borders. They are the offspring of colonial rule, born within colonial frontiers. Do communities create out of a shared culture a state as the expression of their history; or do states impose a unified control, through which a sense of nationalism is inculcated? The answer varies across the world - the Germans, for example, created a state out of a congerie of German speaking principalities - but across the greater part of the African continent the state - the colonially created state - has somehow to engender a new nationalism among diverse societies. There is no other way forward. The African past breeds

Pax Africana?

confusion, the future can only be built on the colonial past. And despite the rhetoric of African socialism there is little of the ideological ferocity of, say, Vietnam or Kampuchea. Moreover, only Libya, Morocco and South Africa have any great capacity in arms or money for foreign wars: Ethiopia has a powerful standing army but it is fully engaged at home. Few African governments, therefore, have the ability to sustain military campaigns beyond their border: Tanzania is still enduring the cost. Nor are there strong economic reasons for aggression. The burden of annexing, say, Benin to Nigeria or Mali to Senegal, is hardly worth the candle: it would only add the problems of the destitute to those of the poor. It is true that Morocco's desire for the Western Sahara, and Libya's occupation of northern Chad, owe something to the iron and phosphate deposits beneath the sand but, in each instance, there are more than economic reasons for war ... In general, therefore, African governments lack both the means and the motive for wars between themselves, in marked contrast (one may hope) with the history of Latin America.[3] The result may be absurd - sovereign mice and sovereign elephants, forever Djibouti and Zaire? - but it is an absurdity which gives some assurance for the future by embalming the colonial past.

Pax-Africana between (most) governments, war within (many) states? If the number of African countries is unlikely to be reduced by annexations,[4] might it not be increased by division? The persistent fear of many regimes is the threat of secession by armed dissident movements under a banner of liberation. There is scarcely an African country whose leaders are not troubled or whose citizens are not plagued by the problem: the post-colonial state is in fact creaking and groaning in its internal structures of control, pulled this way and that by regional disaffection under local war-lords.

Here is a different threat, not external aggression and annexation but secession and dismemberment. A pax-Africana that cannot prevent the armed creation of new states out of the existing map of OAU members is no king of peace at all. But how serious a threat is it?

The present array of rebel movements can be divided into three broad categories.

1. *Neo-traditionalists*, whose case rests on the

obvious artificiality of the frontiers - states determined not by national sentiment but chance. If the early adventurers who tracked their way through the mephitic swamps of the Upper Nile, and who concluded treaties with as many chiefs as they could waylay, had altered their itinerary, bringing in this area rather than that, or foregoing a particular claim to possession, then both the treaty settlements at Berlin and the frontiers of modern African states would have been different: villages which became British might instead have come under French or Belgian or Portuguese rule. Accident determined their history. So, the traditionalists argue, the mischance of past events where fate - for some - took the wrong turning, ought to be remedied. The neo-traditionalists point to a history distinct from that of the colonial period, and assert the need to have states more closely aligned with pre-colonial societies: Ashanti, Yoruba, BaCongo, Ndebele, Barotse and Buganda, for example, instead of colonially-fashioned, polyglot states - unstable because ill-founded - such as Ghana, Nigeria, Zaire, Zimbabwe, Zambia and Uganda.
2. Closely aligned - perhaps one should call them *proto-nationalists* - are those who argue (with a gun) that particular regions of existing states - Katanga, 'Biafra', southern Sudan, Casamance - constitute defined territories whose inhabitants, linked as much by a common dislike of those who rule them as by any historical unity, ought to form their own state out of Zaire, Nigeria, the Sudan, Senegal. They employ the idiom of self-determination for what are in effect secessionist claims.
3. *Revolutionary populists*, very often under communally-based commanders, who struggle by armed revolt to wrest control of the state, or part of a state, from its rulers. A particularly brutal example was the civil war in 1972-3 between the Hutu subjects and the Tutsi ruling class in both Rwanda and Burundi: the former were successful in Rwanda, the latter

in Burundi, both conflicts coming close to genocide. Uprisings in southern Angola under Savimbi, dissident groups in Mozambique, Tigre rebels in Ethiopia, guerrilla forces in Uganda make nonsense of the 'sovereign state' since the government controls only part of its territory, while its opponents - and refugees - move in and out of the 'liberated areas' and across the frontier.

The list of such troubles is long. But one must be careful not to exaggerate. There are obstacles, too, in the way of secession.

An obvious problem (as it is for would-be aggressors) is that of international recognition. Bangladesh succeeded, but in unusual circumstances. Others have failed. In the days of colonial wars, rebel-governments-in-exile were occasionally given recognition by (some) countries, but rebel provinces of a sovereign state face a much harder task. The international world will recognise revolution, or a *coup d'état*, or treason when it is successful, but not secession: yet without that seal of approval, rebel leaders are doomed, like the Kurds, Armenians and Basques, to the limbo of perpetual struggle.

In addition, a number of African states have external patrons who have been willing (at least in the past) to go to some lengths to protect their dependants: Cuban troops to Angola, French forces to Chad, Russian advisers in Ethiopia, Benin and Mozambique, American advisers in rival capitals, training teams from Britain in Commonwealth countries. Mozambique was obliged to seek South African protection against South Africa itself under a treaty arrangement which purports to safeguard not only the government of Samora Machel but the territorial integrity of Mozambique itself. And as Anthony Clayton argues in Chapter Eight, France in particular watches over many of its former colonies and may still be prepared, despite its uncertain record in Chad, to sustain both government and state of a friendly Francophone member.

Then there are the actual intentions of many of the 'secessionists'. At first blush, the claims put forward by dissatisfied minorities seem plain enough. The Nigerian civil war was a serious affair. Zaire was dismembered in the 1960s, with further outbreaks of civil violence in the 1970s.

The examples one could take are legion, and about most African states there is an air of permanent uncertainty - nervous governments confronting dissatisfied citizens. When however we look at the record of liberation movements and civil wars, the failure of secession has to be explained not only by the balance of military power but by difficulties which go to the heart of the problem.

The first is something of a paradox - the strength of the colonial state. Whereas allegiance to the politics of African rule is conditional, experience of living in the colonical state runs deep. The indifference among the population is about regimes rather than the state as such, and it is not difficult to understand why. There is now a post-colonial elite accustomed to the language, economy and ways of the colonial state. There is a colonially derived civil service. There are habits ingrained over at least two generations of leaders and followers. The post-colonial state stands guarantor, therefore, of a good many interests built up over the past fifty or more years.

It is true that an anti-Nigerian sentiment ran high in the 1960s among the Ibo of the eastern region, as did dissatisfaction among the Katangese with the newly independent state of Zaire. But there was then the daunting problem - a second and fundamental difficulty to any bid for secession - of finding a clear identity for the alternative. To be Ibo-speaking was not enough to engender a loyalty to the region as the basis for a separate Biafra state, for if the Ibo distrusted the Hausa and Yoruba, the peoples of the Delta within the former eastern region also took a jaundiced view of the Ibo. It was in fact the dismantling of the four cumbersome regions and the promises of twelve smaller states that did much to win support for the federal government among anti-Ibo minorities. Similar problems have always faced the leaders of a would-be Katanga or Shaba state, or other bids for statehood, in the former Belgian Congo. The provinces are too divided internally, too diverse, too incoherent, to sustain a 'state-within-a-state' as the foundation for a new nation. The history of caravanserai states, which seem periodically to disintegrate and from which a sizeable number of its citizens try from time to time to escape is hardly one of stability; but a non-colonial map of Zaire is even less plausible - there are no unifying ties strong enough among its mixed ethnic societies to support any alternative arrangement of the huge territory. Disintegration in the capital simply leads to disintegration in the interior.

Thirdly, perhaps surprisingly, many who demand the right to secede are perhaps only at one end of a scale of complaints from which they may retreat if the opportunity presents itself. Protests against the boundaries of the state may be only the extreme expression of discontent with the actual incumbents of the state. The history of dissident movements in the Sudan is very illustrative. It is one of guerrilla war and periodic negotiation. A peace treaty was actually signed in 1972, then fighting restarted when Nimairi curtailed the autonomy of the provinces and introduced Sharia law in the Christian South.[5] It is arguable that even the Eritreans, who are divided among themselves, might be reconciled to a reconstituted Ethiopia if there were a change of regime in Addis Ababa.[6] Precisely because African regimes are vulnerable, the guerrilla in the bush may always hope that his time will come, if only to occupy a more congenial place within, rather than outside, the ex-colonial state.

Africa, therefore, for the ex-colonial Africans. Enforced change to any of the boundaries is frowned upon, and a pax-Africana is sustained by the alliance of those whose interests are congruent with the post-colonial map. Do not disturb. And in fact very little *has* been disturbed, despite the extraordinary whirligig of change within almost every one of the fifty or so states. Pax-Africana is colonial Africa under new managers, and in their weakness lies an uneasy peace.

Two last puzzles remain - the effect of international rivalry on African states, and the dilemmas of South African policy south of the Limpopo. Will either disturb the uneasy peace between African governments or alter the existing map of sovereignty?

From the early 1960s foreign intervention re-engaged its interests in Africa from new as well as old sources of power. The effect today is clear - the independence of African states is heavily qualified. In theory, all governments are equal in status within the world of international relations, but status has little bearing on their actual position. The permanent factor is dependence. The external world has drawn closer to Africa to the point where one can now map out rival zones of influence between Moscow, Washington, Havana, Paris, London, the EEC, COMECON, the IMF and related agencies. As yet there is no parallel to the concert of powers at the end of the nineteenth century; there is no agreement on 'partition'. Indeed, the danger has been that great power rivalry is tempted to use Africa as a trial ground of competition in order to mark out new frontiers for the Western world or for Marxist-Leninism. The exacerbation of local conflicts by external intervention can be seen in Chad, Ethiopia, Mozambique and Angola, but these new spheres of dependence have not altered the map of sovereignty, and do not seem likely to do so. Even in the worst years of the cold war, American, Soviet or European involvement tended either to reinforce the existing states or to bring them under new management. And should some kind of accommodation be reached between these external powers, that too might actually confirm the map. It would not be the first time that a regional peace - in this instance an African peace - was enforced by external restraints.

South of the Limpopo, however, the clouds are gathering that may yet break in disaster. From the limited standpoint of this chapter, one can see (very uncertainly) two or three outcomes from the present unrest.[7] One is that white South Africa will succeed in holding itself intact, penning unrest back within the black townships,[8] and thus assuaging external fears, while moving forward along its own peculiar path of repression and reform. An independent Namibia might be the price Pretoria needed to pay to ensure its own security; but that would not greatly affect the international map of Africa, though it would add a substantial element to a pax-Africana by the cessation of fighting along the Namibia/Angola border.

At the other end of the spectrum, South Africa might be turned upside down - Blacks on top, Whites underneath. It is hardly likely to be as simple as that, but if against the odds 'Azania' replaced the Afrikaner republic no-one could be sure what view an African government might take of Namibia or, for that matter, Lesotho and Swaziland. (One could be absolutely sure what opinion it would have of the present array of 'independent' republics and 'national' states). The map of southern Africa might therefore be redrawn over time by a strongly

Pax Africana?

confident, powerfully endowed, black South African government.

At a more sombre level of possibility, South Africa may lapse into civil war, of which the outcome could again be very different from the intentions of either side. It is in keeping with the riddle of southern Africa that the unexpected may actually occur, namely fragmentation. There are always the long odds of partition to any irreconcilable bloody conflict, as in Indo-China, the Middle East, the Indian sub-continent, or Cyprus. How strange it would be if the most strongly armed region of the continent failed not only to preserve any kind of peace, whether a pax-Africana or pax-Afrikaner, but to uphold the boundaries of colonial Africa.

NOTES

1. For detailed accounts of two such cases, see Woodward, P., Sudan: Threat to Stability (London: Institute of Conflict Studies, No. 173), and Hodder-Williams, R., Conflict in Zimbabwe: The Matabele Problem (London: Institute of Conflict Studies, No. 151).
2. The most recent study is by Nyamndi, N., International Politics and British Cameroons (unpublished Ph.D. dissertation: London University, 1984).
3. See, especially, Calvert, P., Boundary Disputes in Latin America (London: Institute of Conflict Studies, No. 146).
4. The likelihood of *voluntary* amalgamation on the lines of Zanzibar and Tanzania in 1964 seems unlikely in present conditions. The stress is on sovereignty. The most one can hope for is 'functional cooperation' and that, too, is marred by disputes between neighbouring states, as in the expulsion from Nigeria of some two million migrants early in 1983. For further discussion on the subject, see Mayall, J., 'Africa in the International System', Government and Opposition, 14, 3 (Summer 1979), pp. 349-72.
5. See Woodward, Sudan: Threats to Stability, pp. 12-13.
6. Eritrea, once an Italian colony, was incorporated into Ethiopia by decision of the United Nations, which also proposed a federal basis of unity that was never implemented.
7. A fuller analysis of these scenarios appears in the author's South Africa 1984 (London:

The Royal Institute of International Affairs, Chatham House Paper No. 26, 1985).

8. For discussions on the mechanics and impact of police and military action in the townships, see Baynham, S.J., 'The Sledgehammer and the Nut: Riot Control and the South African Security Forces', <u>Indicator South Africa</u>, 3, 1(Winter 1985), and 'Protest, the Police and Public Order', <u>Reality</u>, 17, 3 (May 1985).

Chapter Seven

ARMIES ON LOAN: TOWARD AN EXPLANATION OF TRANS-
NATIONAL MILITARY INTERVENTION AMONG BLACK AFRICAN
STATES: 1960-85

Arnold Hughes
Roy May

INTRODUCTION

In recent years considerable academic interest has been shown in the growing part played by the armed forces of black Africa in the political and governmental processes of their countries. By today a substantial literature exists, both at a general theoretical level and on a country basis, on the causation and mechanics of military intervention. There is also much interest in evaluating the performance of military governments, and some scholars (including Goldsworthy and Welch in this volume) have addressed themselves to the thornier topics of military containment and disengagement. At the same time there has been a recognition of the importance of external military intervention in sub-Saharan Africa. The continuing interventionist role of France has spawned a passionately denunciatory literature. Conspiracy theorists of the right have attacked Soviet and Cuban intervention equally vehemently. In the last few years the military activities of Morocco, Libya and South Africa (and for a while the Smith regime in Rhodesia) have been subjected to critical scrutiny as well.
    But there has been another dimension of military intervention of a transnational character in sub-Saharan Africa which has largely escaped academic attention. Apart from brief news reports, usually based on single-country incidents, there is virtually nothing to be found on what has become an increasingly frequent occurrence: the use of African armies as an instrument of foreign policy in relations between states (as opposed to being used to promote liberation movements in colonial and settler regimes).[1] Yet since

1960 some 30 instances of the deployment of military forces in pursuit of foreign policy objectives can be identified, and, but for the clandestine nature of some of these activities, more undoubtedly could be added to this increasing list. Of the 43 independent states of black Africa, 31 have been involved as providers or recipients of such military deployment.

This study confines itself largely to one form of the use of military power in inter-African relations: the deployment of elements of the armed forces in open support of foreign policy objectives on the territory of other countries in the region. Conventional warfare, border disputes and guerrilla operations all have a relevance and intrinsic interest to this study and we intend to pursue these linkages in future work. Similarly, while we recognise alternative means of using military resources - funding, training, logistical support etc. - we are unable to go into detail here. Space and the geographical scope of this book also necessitate limiting our coverage to sub-Saharan Africa. We also refer in a few specific instances to extra-regional intervention but not as a major dimension as there already exist numerous studies on this subject.

We have adopted James Rosenau's definition of military intervention '...coercive military involvement in civil and regional conflict [or in anticipation of such conflict], which is intended to, or does, affect internal political outcomes'.[2] The numerous episodes of military intervention are analysed in respect of OBJECTIVES, MODALITIES and MOTIVATIONS. A conclusion offers some more general and tentative reflections on the use of the armed forces in inter-state relations in post-colonial black Africa.

OBJECTIVES

An analysis of nearly 30 cases of military intervention reveals three broad objectives; though it must be recognised that the stated purpose of involvement may conceal a different aim and a particular act of intervention might lead to a result different from that intended. The first and most widespread objective - 18 of the 29 cases examined - is what may be termed *Regime-Supportive*. Here, the purpose of intervention is to provide military assistance (usually with other forms of support) to a threatened regime or government.

Armies on Loan

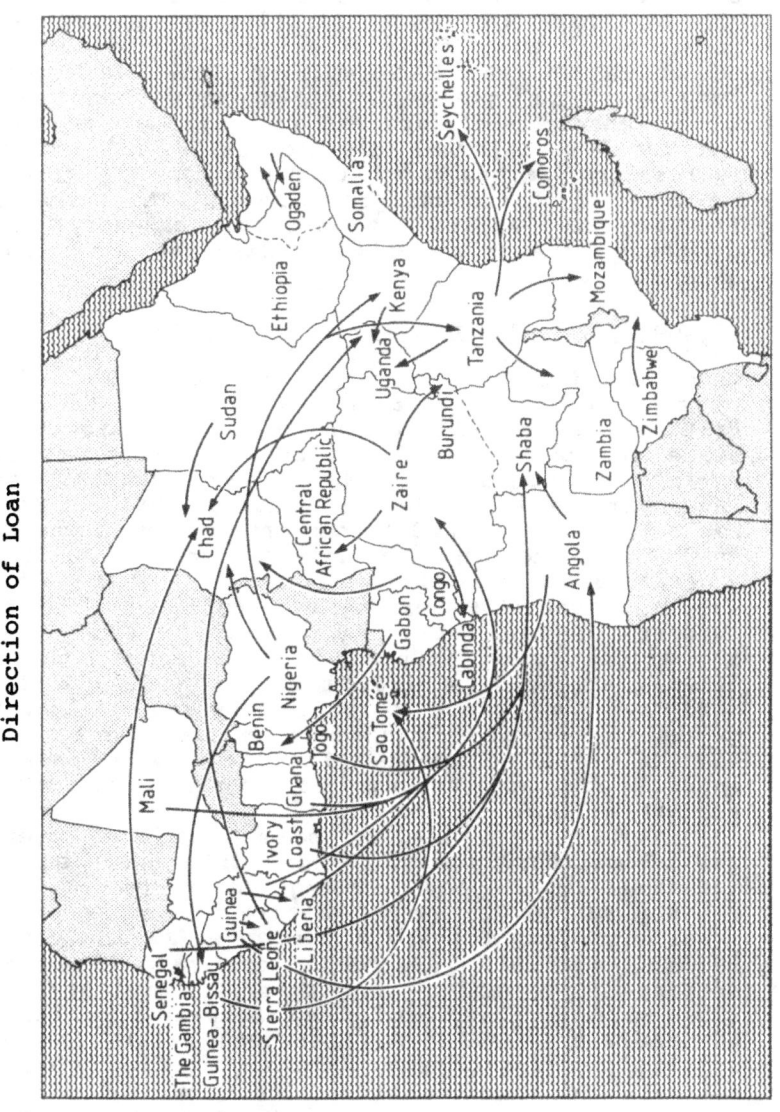

Regime-Opposing interventions, the second of our categories, seek the opposite objective, namely the overthrow or destabilisation of a regime or government. Six of our cases appear to fit this category. The third category we term *State-Supportive*, for here the purpose of external intervention is to ensure the survival of the very state in the face of internal disintegration and external aggression, rather than to maintain a particular regime or government in power. The remaining five of our examples fit into this category. Each of these categories will be discussed in greater detail.

Regime-Supportive Military Interventions

This form of transnational military activity was made familiar to the new rulers of black Africa by their colonial mentors. While it is true that Britain has only intervened once on a significant scale in post-colonial Africa - to suppress army mutinies on behalf of the governments of Kenya, Tanganyika and Uganda in January 1964 - France has deployed its armed forces on numerous occasions. As Clayton notes in a separate chapter, it maintains several bases on African soil for this purpose and is currently providing logistical military support to the Habre government in Chad though its troops have withdrawn. In a sense, the new African states have indigenised a technique first used by the former colonial powers. A handful of these - Guinea, Tanzania, Zaire, Senegal and Nigeria - are responsible for most cases of intervention and account for nearly all regime-supportive interventions.

Guinea is the leading exponent of the external use of military power. It has intervened on five occasions to support endangered regimes. Twice it has rushed troops to Sierra Leone to protect President Siaka Stevens (once an exile in Guinea): in 1971 some 300 paratroops were sent in to help restore order after an attempted military coup (the Bangura plot) and they remained in reduced numbers until 1973. A subsequent crisis in 1977, sparked off by student unrest, obliged Stevens to call in Guinean troops once more.[3] In the same year Touré was the first to despatch troops to Benin when the Kerekou regime came under attack from a mysterious mercenary force ('Operation Omega') in January. The airborne raiders flew off before Guinean help arrived.[4] In April 1979 Touré came to the aid of another neighbour -

President Tolbert of Liberia. A tense political situation existed after the 'rice riots' in which a number of people were killed by the security forces, and the presence of Guinean troops probably deferred a military coup by another year. Surprisingly, Touré did not send in troops when the Tolbert regime was overthrown by the Liberian army in 1980. On this occasion he limited himself to a verbal denunciation.[5] Finally, Touré claimed also to have sent Guinean forces to aid the MPLA in Angola.[6]

Another radical interventionist state is *Tanzania*, a seemingly incongruous record given President Julius Nyerere's gentle and anti-militaristic reputation. In each case of regime-supportive intervention the Tanzanian army has come to the assistance of governments broadly sharing the same radical, non-aligned ideology as Tanzania. Following the overthrow of the Abdallah government in the Comoros in August 1975 by white mercenaries under the notorious Colonel Bob Denard, Tanzania despatched about 100 soldiers to back the new and increasingly 'radical' regime of Ali Soilih and to help train his 'revolutionary' forces. Though few in number the Tanzanian soldiers are reputed to have helped put down a rising on Anjouan Island. Comoron exiles in France demonstrated at the Tanzanian embassy in Paris on this occasion, denouncing the 'annexation aims' of the Nyerere government and its support for repression. The Tanzanian force may well have been depleted by May 1978 when Denard returned with his mercenaries and this time overthrew and killed Soilih before handing over power to Abdallah. The remaining Tanzanian soldiers were withdrawn and France re-assumed its protective role in the islands.[7]

Tanzania also lent military support to the radical government of Albert René in the Seychelles. Some of those who took part in the *coup d'état* of June 1977, in which the conservative Mancham government was deposed, had received military training in Tanzania. While there is no proof of Tanzanian involvement in the coup, Nyerere sent some 400 troops to the Seychelles after the insurrection in order to train its new security forces and provide protection against several plots organised by the exiled Mancham. A mutiny in August 1982 is thought to have been put down by Tanzanian soldiers. The Tanzanian garrison may have been reduced recently but joint manoeuvres have taken place between Tanzanian, Malagasy and Seychellois forces.[8]

Tanzania's most extensive supportive role has been in Mozambique. Even before independence in 1975, FRELIMO received considerable military assistance and sanctuary from the Tanzanian government. When it faced a serious threat from Rhodesian-backed anti-government guerrillas in the Cape Delgado region, FRELIMO obtained substantial Tanzanian support: two battalions, comprising some 1,500 men, were deployed in the restless Macua and Makonde areas and at the Cabora Bassa dam site. They were withdrawn in 1979 when the guerrilla threat was deemed to have abated; also by then Tanzanian forces were heavily committed in Uganda.[9]

Finally, Nyerere also sent troops to help his old friend Kenneth Kaunda of Zambia in 1980. Because of the poor performance of the Zambian army, Tanzanian forces were 'borrowed' to patrol the Copperbelt during the disturbances of that year.[10]

From a rather different and more controversial political position *Zaire* has also used its military forces on external missions, notwithstanding the fact that twice Mobutu had to call in external military assistance to save his own regime in 1977-79. Mobutu sent troops to Burundi in 1972 during the savage fighting between the Tutsi-dominated government and the Hutu populace.[11] In 1979 Zairean forces were involved in another controversial and brutal supportive role in the Central African Empire. Some 200-300 Zairean soldiers reinforced the Emperor Bokassa's forces during the repression of student protestors and were accused by a Senegalese jurist, sent to investigate the atrocities, of taking part in the killing of school children.[12] Mobutu has also sent fighter aircraft and some 2,000 ground troops to Chad to assist the Habre faction in its struggle against Libyan-backed rivals. Earlier a small air-liaison unit was stationed in Chad during the Tombalbaye period and Zaire also contributed to the Inter-African Force sponsored by the OAU in 1981.[13] Zaire has come to be regarded in many quarters as a Western proxy force in black Africa, trading limited military intervention in return for military and economic support from such countries as France and the USA.

A certain amount of political controversy has surrounded the external activities of the *Senegalese* armed forces as well. Domestic critics of the Diouf government accuse it also of being a proxy force for Franco-American interests; certainly its two supportive interventions were anti-leftist, if not necessarily furthering the interests of these two external powers. It is likely that Senegal's participation with Morocco and a number of other black African countries in the Inter-African Force sent to replace the departing French and Belgian paratroops in Zaire's Shaba province in mid-1978 was at the behest of the French, though it must be stated that Senegal previously supported the idea of a pan-African defence force to respond to local crises.[14] In the case of the Gambia, Senegal intervened twice, in October 1980 and July-August 1981, in response to appeals from the Gambian government. The first incident involved nothing more than a brief show of strength - some 150 Senegalese soldiers were flown to the Gambian capital to discourage a rumoured mutiny among the local para-military police force. The second intervention, 'Operation Foday Kabba II', was a more serious affair. Some 3,000 Senegalese forces, drawn from all three services, were rushed into the neighbouring country to put down by force an uprising engineered by self-styled civilian leftists and disgruntled para-military police. Many casualties occurred during the week-long campaign to restore to power the temporarily deposed Gambian head of state, Sir Dawda Jawara. Several hundred Senegalese soldiers remain in the Gambia as part of a confederal defence force following the decision to form a Senegambian Confederation in December 1981.[15]

Surprisingly, despite its vast military establishment and declared regional power aspirations, *Nigeria* has not deployed its substantial military power externally to any great extent. It agreed to replace British forces in Tanganyika after the 1964 mutiny and had earlier taken part in the UN Congo operation. Civil war prevented it from engaging in external military activities for a number of years but even under the assertive foreign policy of the Murtala-Obasanjo military administrations, with an inflated army and treasury, it has been cautious in its external deployment of armed force. Supportive actions have been few: Soviet-built heavy artillery was reputedly sent to assist the PAIGC in its struggle against the Portuguese;[16] military transport aircraft, two C-130 Hercules, and a civilian Boeing 707 are reported to have been sent to assist the MPLA in Angola in 1979;[17] and Nigeria has sent ground forces to Chad twice in pursuit of a peace settlement in that country rather than to promote a particular faction (though Thompson and Adloff observe that the FROLINAT Third Army, based in the Lake Chad area, was subsidised by the Nigerian government and an American oil company!).[18] Nigeria seems more committed to an OAU defence force, and to a general opposition to settler power in South Africa and external intervention in black African affairs, than to more narrowly bilateral involvement on behalf of individual countries.[19]

Of the few remaining regime-supportive military interventions, several have been directed toward assisting radical states by other radical countries. Thus *Angola* and *Guinea-Bissau* sent troops to Sao Tomé in 1977 to ward off a reported *coup d'état* being planned against the Pinto da Costa government by political rivals and exiles in Gabon.[20] Between 1,000 and 1,500 Angolan troops are believed to have been despatched and there was also promise of fighter aircraft for off-shore patrol duties.[21] In 1982, once more under pressure from MNR (Renamo) guerrillas, this time sponsored by South Africa, and reputedly supported from Malawi and the Comoros, the Mozambique government appealed to an independent *Zimbabwe* for military aid. A battalion of the Fifth Brigade was sent for a period to guard the Sofala-Mutare common oil pipe-line. Fighter aircraft may also have been sent by Zimbabwe.[22] By late 1985 the Zimbabwean military presence in Mozambique had increased considerably.

Reference has been made to Senegal's participation in the rescue mission to Zaire's Shaba province in 1978. In addition to 1,500 Moroccans and 500 Senegalese, token units were sent by *Ivory Coast* (a medical detachment), *Togo* and *Gabon*. Central African Republic was reported to have agreed to participate as well but no record of its involvement exists. Sudan agreed to provide air support but it is not clear whether this was actually accepted. The Inter-African Force is believed to have been withdrawn by August 1979 as a result of improved relations between Zaire and Angola (from whose territory the FLNC guerrillas had launched their attack on Shaba) and the re-training of Zairean forces.[23]

Regime-Opposing Military Interventions
One reason why there are fewer demonstrated instances of the deployment of African military force

to overthrow or undermine regimes is that it is much more difficult to obtain information about activities which may be politically embarrassing if more widely known. African leaders frequently accuse neighbouring governments of harbouring their political opponents and giving them military assistance but such charges are usually denied. Besides, even if true, they seldom involve the 'loan' of military units to fight outside their national borders. Ghana's former head of state, Kwame Nkrumah, was widely thought by his more conservative neighbours to be plotting their overthrow by providing clandestine military training and support to dissidents. Whatever the truth of these accusations, Nkrumah never sent his army on foreign expeditions, save with the UN to the Congo in 1960-64. In other situations, such as the war between *Ethiopia* and *Somalia*, which has been going on intermittently since 1976, both sides deny using their national forces on each other's territory. Instead, they claim that Somali dissidents are fighting the Somali government forces, albeit backed by Ethiopia; or that the Western Somali Liberation Front is confined to Ogaden Somalis. Independent accounts testify to the involvement of regular troops by both sides.[24]

Mystery surrounds two other alleged oppositional military interventions in central Africa. In the case of *Zaire* there is less uncertainty perhaps as several accounts exist of regular Zairean troops fighting with Holden Roberto's FNLA during the tripartite struggle for power in Angola at the time of the Portuguese withdrawal in the mid-1970s. Zairean forces are also alleged to have fought alongside FLEC, the Cabinda separatists, at the same time. The MPLA government claimed of a plot, 'Cobra 77', involving the Mobutu government and local separatists in Cabinda and northern Angola, together with dissidents from Sao Tomé, to overthrow it.[25] Zaire, in turn, claimed that the MPLA were organising rebel Katangese 'gendarmes', the FLNC, to invade Shaba (formerly Katanga) in 1977-8. Both antagonists also alleged great power involvement - Angola the French and the Americans, Zaire the Soviets and the Cubans. While there is good reason to believe that the MPLA might have used the Katangese exiles as a counter to Zairean backing for FLEC and FNLA and may have provided logistical support in order to overthrow Mobutu's pro-Western government, there is no evidence of MPLA units fighting alongside the

FLNC during the two invasions of Shaba.[26]

Yet another example of military destabilisation of dubious provenance is the mercenary attack on the *Benin* capital, Cotonou, on 16 January 1977. The Kerekou government blamed not only Benin exiles and mercenary accomplices for carrying out the brief raid, but claimed that the raiders had been trained by the Moroccans, backed by the French and flown to Cotonou from Libreville, the capital of Gabon with the blessing of its government. Togo, Ivory Coast and Senegal were also accused of complicity but no supporting evidence was produced. Indeed, the main charges rested on the evidence of a Guinean-born Senegalese mercenary. Neither the OAU nor the UN got to the bottom of the mystery. But here too, there was no evidence of Gabonese forces, or indeed those of other countries, taking part in the attack. All accounts spoke of foreign-backed mercenaries.[27]

Lack of concrete evidence prevents us from accepting the accusation made by President René of the *Seychelles* that the Kenyan government - or elements within it, particularly Minister for Constitutional Affairs, Charles Njonjo - were implicated in the abortive mercenary plot of November 1981. René asserted that former Seychellois President, James Mancham, was in league with South African and Kenyan interests and, had the coup succeeded, would have brought in Kenyan military units to replace the Tanzanians. The Kenyan government denied these allegations, though Njonjo has suffered political eclipse subsequently and has been the subject of an official enquiry, which found him guilty of complicity in the Seychelles affair.[28]

The most clear-cut case of regime-opposing military intervention was the *Tanzanian* army's overthrow of the Idi Amin regime in Uganda in early 1979. Responding to Ugandan attacks on the Kagera salient, some 20,000 Tanzanian soldiers backed by over 1,000 men loyal to ex-President Milton Obote of Uganda, drove back the invaders and within a few weeks had over-run the whole of the country. Nyerere's motives were doubted in some quarters, where it was believed he was out to restore Obote to power and turn Uganda into a grateful client-state. While personally and ideologically close to Obote, Nyerere does seem to have acted from less partisan motives and though Obote eventually was elected back to power, his government does not appear to be kow-towing to that of Tanzania. By 1981 most of the Tanzanian expeditionary force had been withdrawn, leaving only a training unit working as part of a Commonwealth programme for reconstituting the Ugandan army.[29] However in July 1985, elements of the army overthrew Obote for the second time.

State-Supportive Military Interventions
The earliest example of inter-state military deployment in black Africa took place in the former Belgian Congo (now Zaire) in 1960-64. The political disintegration and large-scale communal violence which followed on the precipitate Belgian withdrawal at the end of June 1960, together with the presence of mercenaries and the possibility of great power confrontation, led the United Nations to send in a large multi-national expeditionary force 'to take vigorous action in the restoration of law and order throughout the territory...and to safeguard its unity, territorial integrity and political independence in the interests of international peace and security'.[30] During the next four years a total of 93,000 men from 35 member countries served at one time or other in the Congo. Among the black countries which agreed to send contingents were several black African ones. The most imporant and valuable contributions came from *Ghana* and *Nigeria*, each of which sent an army brigade and a police unit. *Ethiopia* provided a brigade as well, though its performance fell short of that of the Nigerians and Ghanaians. Smaller contingents came from *Liberia*, *Guinea* and the Mali Federation.[31]

Though the UN Congo operation met with considerable military success in preventing the secession of Katanga and in restoring order, it did run into a number of problems; such difficulties were to afflict the OAU-backed Inter-African Force intervention in Chad two decades later. Among them may be mentioned the financial cost of mounting such a large and lengthy operation - US$411 million; effective communications, logistics and transport provision; co-ordinating military contingents drawn from a wide number of countries with different military as well as cultural characteristics; containing political and military interference by external vested parties; and agreeing on a common set of objectives. Radical critics of the UN operation blamed the world organisation for 'betraying' Prime Minister Lumumba and allowing him to be killed by his opponents - Guinea and Mali withdrew their small contingents quite early, partly because of disagreements over the role of the UN forces. Right-wing critics of the UN in western Europe, in their turn, disapproved of military action against the Tshombe secessionist government in Katanga. Lacking a permanent military capacity of its own, the UN had to rely on the willingness of member-states to carry out its military instructions. Originally it had hoped to mount its operation using the military resources in African states, but these lacked the necessary manpower and technical capacity to operate in such a vast and difficult terrain as that of the Congo. It became clear that practical assistance and financial backing were needed from either of the super powers or one of the middle-ranking countries. In the event it was the United States, for reasons of its own as well as from a belief in the UN principles, that provided these.

The *OAU* attempts to bring the warring factions together in Chad and end external military intervention faced in more severe forms the difficulties encountered by the UN in the Congo.[32] OAU attempts to resolve the long and destructive factional strife in Chad by military intervention (there was an equally unsuccessful attempt to resolve it through diplomatic means within the OAU itself) took three forms. In 1979 Nigeria - as an interested party with a shared frontier with Chad and believed to possess the necessary military and financial means to intervene - acted semi-independently to try and resolve the crisis. In addition to summoning conferences in Kano and Lagos, the Nigerian military government sent a military force to Chad in March 1979 to try and uphold the Kano agreement of the same month. The 1,600 strong force could achieve little by way of maintaining the peace and its task was made more difficult by complaints about the behaviour of individual soldiers and the resentment of the major Chadian factions headed by Hissen Habre and Goukouni Oueddei at what they felt to be Nigerian attempts to foist their own candidate - Mahamat Chona Lol - on the other leadership contestants.

Although the military operation had to be abandoned in June 1979, the Nigerians persisted in their attempts to get France and Libya to withdraw from Chad and to get a government of national union set up. A Transitional Government of National

Union (GUNT) was formed in November and a second multi-national OAU force was created to provide a peace-keeping role while the new Chad administration sought to create a national army. This force was to be provided by *Congo-Brazzaville, Benin* and *Guinea* but only the first of these actually sent a detachment of some 600 soldiers. They achieved nothing for they only stayed a week and were confined to their barracks for most of the time. Guinea and Benin pleaded lack of funds (though there may have been political disagreements over OAU policy toward Chad as well) and the OAU itself lacked money to pay for the operation. Inevitably, Nigeria had to become the principal paymaster of any OAU peace-keeping force in Chad. Only US$600,000 out of the US$6 million promised was paid up by member states.

The temporary political and military eclipse of Habre in 1981 and the gradual withdrawal of Libyan and French forces led to a third attempt at OAU military involvement. Six countries agreed to participate under a Nigerian commander, General Geoffrey Ejiga. *Guinea*, *Benin* and *Togo* failed to send troops and peace-keeping duties devolved on *Nigeria* (2,000 troops), *Zaire* (800-2,000) and *Senegal* (500?). Although units were deployed to various parts of the country (unlike the two earlier interventions, which had been confined to N'Djamena - the Chad capital) this second multi-national force was unable to achieve anything and it was withdrawn by late June 1981. Not even Nigeria could, or was prepared to, fund the operation and, despite its objective of keeping foreign powers out of collective military operations as well as excluding them from direct intervention in African states, Nigeria had to turn to the USA for financial assistance. The Zaireans and Senegalese were also dependent on American financial and logistic support. Financial shortcomings were compounded by a lack of political direction - the peace-keeping force refused to fight on the side of Oueddei and the GUNT, seeing its role as a neutral one, but at the same time the GUNT lacked the means to prevent the Habre faction reconstituting itself to eastern Chad. Promises of an election were given by Oueddei but this was never held as fighting recommenced which this time led to success for Habre. Once more the Libyans and the French, with their superior resources, became the main external military interveners in Chad and by the late summer of 1983 the country

189

was effectively partitioned between their protégés - Oueddei and Habre. Neither individually, nor collectively, it would appear, were the member-states of the OAU in a position to resolve the Chad conflict. The Chad imbroglios offer sombre lessons to advocates of a pan-African defence force.

The decision to send a Commonwealth Training Force to Uganda following the overthrow of the Amin regime and the withdrawal of the Tanzanian army in 1981, in order to help reconstruct the discredited and demoralised Ugandan army, is the last example of 'neutral' external military intervention. Here again though, it should be noted, the training mission is composed of a number of non-African elements and most of the funding is from non-African sources. *Tanzania*, *Kenya* and *Sierra Leone* comprise the African component of the training mission. The persistence of political violence on a substantial scale in Uganda and the lack-lustre record of the new national army (now installed in office) suggest that much remains to be achieved in restoring its discipline and efficiency.[33]

MODALITIES

The means of exercising military power in a transnational context varies as the survey of the 30 case studies shows. One distinction is that between *bilateral* and *multilateral* intervention. Collective intervention in black Africa is far less common than bilateral assistance. Only five examples of multilateral military intervention can be found although it is true that several bilateral actions may involve covert assistance from third parties. This is particularly the case with so-called 'proxy interventions', where another country with an interest in the crisis and the means to assist, may prefer to channel its support through a local state. The technical, financial and political problems encountered in mounting a multilateral operation are formidable and it should be noted in the case of the UN Congo operation and the Shaba rescue mission in 1978 (also the earlier one of 1977 which involved forces from non-black African countries - principally Morocco and France), both successful operations, unlike the OAU ventures in Chad, that considerable backing was made available either by certain member states of the UN or by external powers anxious to resolve the crisis.

Bilateral intervention, particularly when countries are adjacent and the external military assistance required is small, often proves more effective. At least in the short-term, bilateral supportive interventions have been extremely successful.

This chapter has concentrated on the 'loaning' of military units in pursuit of national foreign policy objectives. However, other means of deploying military resources are available to black African states. Some of these may be considered. *Training* agreements are common - brief reference has been made to Tanganyika and Uganda in this respect. A state with a 'surplus' military capacity may deploy some of it as training teams to other countries. But it is not always easy to distinguish between active service and training teams; 'training missions' are frequently euphemisms for covert combat support or internal policing. Tanzanian intervention in the Comoros and Seychelles included a training function and the Senegalese contingent in the Gambia is engaged in training a new National Gendarmerie as well as in providing security cover while the new forces are being trained. Training may take place at the donor country's military academies as well as abroad. Nigeria and Ghana's defence academies at Kaduna and Teshie provide (or did provide) places for cadets from other African states. The up-grading of Nigeria's defence college may enable it to provide advanced forms of instruction in future, which can only be obtained overseas at present. Francophone African states have a number of agreements regarding transnational training of military personnel and, following the mercenary raid on Cotonou in 1977, Nigeria and Benin signed a training agreement whereby Beninois officer cadets would receive instruction in Nigeria. In the main, specialised training is still provided by non-African instructors, either overseas or through training missions in Africa.

Funding is another area where military assistance may be provided but here again lack of funds is a problem. In 1963 the newly-formed OAU agreed to create a Liberation Committee to channel financial and other resources from member-states to anti-colonial liberation movements. It is evident that many members have failed to keep up their payments to the Liberation Fund or to the OAU general levy. Non-black African states, the Western alliance, the Soviet bloc and the Arab world are still the major sources of funds for upgrading and expanding African armed forces. Individual states such as Nigeria under the Murtala-Obasanjo administrations have deployed financial resources to overseas military support but principally in respect of southern Africa. Widespread poverty and pressing domestic needs set limits to military funding of other countries on the sub-continent.

The same applies to the *supply of weapons and military equipment*. Few African states have a surplus and are themselves dependent on outside powers for their own materiel. Nigeria and Zimbabwe are the only black states with a capacity to fabricate materiel but this is very limited at present. Here again, Nigerian governments have committed themselves to increasing their country's military self-sufficiency but, with the exception of South Africa, there is no integrated defence industry in sub-Saharan Africa.

Finally, there have been attempts at creating *regional defence organisations* - in the case of the Francophone African states these may be continuations or adaptations of earlier arrangements during the colonial period. Attempts by Kwame Nkrumah and others to create an African High Command during the early 1960s have never borne fruit despite the obvious attraction of a continental collective defence force capable of keeping out external powers and lending effective military assistance to the 'front-line states' of southern Africa. The problems encountered have been discussed elsewhere [34] but they centre on funding; the absence of an indigenous defence industry; lack of logistical, communications and transportation facilities; political rivalries and suspicions; existing arrangements with external powers (such as France, cited above). Even the political will to make a determined effort to overcome them seems lacking. Agreement on a common objective and the presence of a regional 'super-power' to give direction and practical assistance also seem to be missing, though Nigerian designs in the latter direction inevitably arouse the suspicion of small states. Even so, a modest beginning has been made in West Africa through the ECOWAS military defence council established in 1981. To date, little of substance has emerged from its deliberations but there is no reason to believe that resolving regional, as opposed to continental defence and security problems, is any easier.

MOTIVATIONS

Some further attention needs to be given to the reasons why black African states have engaged in external military intervention. Why is it that countries which are themselves politically unstable and economically weak involve themselves in sometimes costly and possible politically embarrassing military adventures? A number of reasons are suggested, which may operate singly or in combination.

If we look at the radical group of African countries there is a strong element of ideological solidarity at play. Nyerere's supportive military activities embrace fellow 'front-line states' and Indian Ocean microstates sharing his radical non-aligned position. Angola and Guinea-Bissau's defence of Sao Tomé, and Guinea's military support for Benin and Angola, also reflect this sense of ideological solidarity. However, attachment to radical ideologies has not prevented Ethiopia and Somalia from seeking to destabilise each other. The prolonged fighting between Ethiopia and local left-leaning liberation movements in Eritrea also reveals a lack of socialist comradeliness.

Threats from a common enemy may also explain some military interventions. Fear of South African machinations in the southern African and Indian Ocean regions reinforces any ideological affinity between the countries involved. Tanzanian and Zimbabwean intervention in Mozambique is a case in point; Angolan support for Sao Tomé derived in part out of fear of a plot to subvert both countries. Senegalese intervention in the Gambia was dictated by fears of a leftist take-over there leading to instability in Senegal itself. Fear of Libyan expansion has played a part in the intervention in Chad by Nigeria, Senegal and Zaire.

Racial solidarity and a common hatred of racialist or colonial regimes is seen in the military support given by countries of different ideological persuasion to the 'front-line states' and liberation movements. Nigerian support for PAIGC and MPLA cannot be said to spring from a common ideology; neither can Nigeria feel more than a vague threat to itself from distant antagonists. Related to this is an old-established belief in keeping imperialism out of Africa. France and the United States figure largely here, but conservative African states see the Soviet Union, together with Cuba and Libya, as the main threat. The

Shaba II intervention of 1978-9 owed something to Mobutu's portrayal of the invasion as a crypto-Soviet/Cuban venture.

Personal friendships between national leaders should not be ignored in some cases of military intervention. Mobutu's friendship with Bokassa may explain his willingness to send troops to Bangui in 1979 (when the French were rapidly abandoning the eccentric Emperor). Sekou Touré's friendship with Siaka Stevens and William Tolbert may help us understand why this acclaimed radical African leader helped shore-up two governments of a decidedly unradical character. This is not to exclude fears of a 'domino-effect' of course should the Sierra Leonean army have toppled Stevens or the young leftists in Monrovia overthrown Tolbert.

The use of African armies in a 'proxy' role has already been referred to. Convergence of interest, as much as blind allegiance to external powers, may explain the motives of a ruler such as Mobutu. The ideological ambivalence and shifting loyalites of some African leaders courted by external powers urge caution in attributing their external involvements solely to a 'proxy' relationship.

Personal or national aggrandisement may be a contributing factor in some cases of external military intervention. The activities of Nkrumah, Mobutu and Nyerere have been interpreted in this light, as has Nigeria's bid for leadership on the African continent. Yet very few acts of military intervention have as their direct object the increase in national territory of the country concerned. Somalia's support of Somali dissidents in the Ogaden region of Ethiopia is almost the sole exception in sub-Saharan Africa. The Angolan government claimed that Zaire had designs on Cabinda at the time of the 'Cobra 77' plot but this was never confirmed by independent sources. Libya's designs on the Aouzou strip of northern Chad is more authentic but its military intervention is that of a non-black African state rather than a sub-Saharan power.

Pachter suggests another reason for sending armies out of a country. To her it is a means of reducing military interference in domestic politics. She interprets Tanzanian and Guinean external interventions principally in this light.[35] This is doubtful as only a very small part of the armed forces of these countries saw service abroad (with the exception of the invasion of

Uganda in 1979, when an estimated half of the Tanzanian army was so engaged). It is also likely that Nyerere and Touré would have been aware of the problems created by Nkrumah in sending a sizeable part of the Ghanaian army to the Congo and by threatening to send it against the Smith regime in Rhodesia, following UDI in 1965. Afrifa mentioned these acts as contributing to the 1966 military coup against Nkrumah.[36]

CONCLUSION

This chapter has sought to draw attention to a surprisingly neglected tendency in post-colonial Africa: the widespread external involvement of African armies. The survey of actual interventions reveals some unexpected findings. Civilian regimes are more likely to use national armies on external missions than military ones. It also discloses that self-designated radical countries have engaged in external military adventures more frequently than states that regard themselves as moderate. Another interesting finding is that the most interventionist states have been economically impoverished ones. Tanzania, despite its chronic economic circumstances, has managed to increase its army from 4,000 in 1961 to over 50,000 today; and has assumed the enormous burden of invading Uganda as well as deploying military units elsewhere in the region. Guinea, another impoverished country, has also been prepared to fund several foreign interventions. Unlike Senegal or Zaire, whose interventions have in part been subsidised by external powers, Tanzania and Guinea seem to have had to foot their own bills.

Compared with this somewhat ostentatious resort to external intervention by these poorer countries, the richer states of the sub-continent have a pallid record. Ivory Coast and Kenya have only involved themselves once in external military activity: a small medical contingent sent to Zaire with the Inter-African Force in 1978 and a training unit attached to the Commonwealth Training Force in Uganda in 1981. Nigeria has never quite lived up to the expectations of those of its citizens who eagerly anticipated a dramatic interventionist foreign policy following the rise to power of General Murtala Mohammed. Its major external military involvement, the Congo intervention with the UN operation, took place under what is now regarded as a conservative civilian government. It is true that the soldier-rulers adopted an assertive and militant rhetorical and diplomatic posture but their intervention in Chad was a bruising experience. Will that experience lessen the present military government's appetite for similar adventures or lead it to try and rectify the technical and logistical shortcomings that were exposed?

It would appear that financial constraints need not prevent external military intervention in black Africa. Technical constraints may be more important. Another restraining factor may be the unpopularity of sending troops overseas. Opponents of the Senegalese government have strongly criticised the use of troops in the Gambia and Zaire so that their use in 'proxy' situations may prove politically too embarrassing. The actual treatment meted out to soldiers serving abroad may also discourage further interventions. Nigerian soldiers in Chad and Tanzanian troops in the Seychelles were not universally welcome. The removal from power of an interventionist leader may also affect a country's desire to intervene externally. The death of Sekou Touré is a case in point.

Yet there is no reason to expect a rapid decline in transnational military intervention among black African states. We are compelled to agree with James Rosenau that 'the developing nations and black Africa in particular appear destined to be the primary forms of this form of international behaviour'.[37] Domestic political instability and economic crisis encourage military intervention, not only by the super-powers or other non sub-regional middle powers, but also by aspirants to regional power status in black Africa and, as we have noted, by countries with resources normally felt to be insufficient to sustain such a posture. At the same time, this survey supports MacFarlane's conclusion that external military intervention is not necessarily a destabilising activity, or one that need lead to a loss of domestic sovereignty.[38] Just as military irruption within individual African states is now commonplace so we contend that the trend toward intra-style intervention by African armed forces will continue as a characteristic of international relations in the sub-continent for some time to come.

APPENDIX

TRANSNATIONAL MILITARY INTERVENTION IN BLACK AFRICA: 1960-85

	Target Country	Intervening States
1960-64	Congo-Leopoldville	UN operation included Nigerian, Ghanaian, Liberian, Ethiopian, Guinean, Senegalese and Malian units.
1964	Tanganyika	OAU negotiated Nigerian and Ethiopian assistance following British departure.
1971-73	Sierra Leone	Guinea
1972	Burundi	Zaire (and France).
1975(?)	Angola	Guinea
1975-79	Angola/Cabinda	Zaire
1975-78	Comoros	Tanzania
1976-79	Mozambique	Tanzania
1976-	Somalia	Ethiopia
1976-	Ethiopia	Somalia
1977	Zaire/Shaba	Angola(?)
1977	Benin	Gabon(?)
1977	Benin	Guinea
1977	Sierra Leone	Guinea
1977-	Seychelles	Tanzania
1977-	Sao Tomé	Angola
1977	Sao Tomé	Guinea-Bissau

Armies on Loan

	Target Country	Intervening States
1978-79	Zaire/Shaba	Inter-African Force included Senegal, Gabon, Ivory Coast, Togo, Central African Republic (and Morocco).
1978-81	Uganda	Tanzania
1979	Central African Empire	Zaire
1979	Liberia	Guinea
1979	Angola	Nigeria
1979	Chad	Nigeria
1980	Chad	Inter-African Force: only Congo-Brazzaville sent units.
1980-81	The Gambia	Senegal
1981-82	Chad	Second Inter-African Force: Nigeria, Senegal, Zaire.
1981	Uganda	Commonwealth Training Force: included Tanzania, Kenya and Sierra Leone.
1982	Mozambique	Zimbabwe
1983	Chad	Zaire, Sudan.
1985	Mozambique	Zimbabwe

NOTES

1. MacFarlane, S.N. 'Intervention and Security in Africa'. *International Organisation*, 60, 1 (1983/84) confines his principally to *outside* intervention in a handful of black African states. His table (p. 68) of the incidence of military intervention lists only 15 examples between 1975 and 1982. Clapham, C., in a more recent book, *Third World Politics: An Introduction* (London: Croom Helm, 1985), p. 115, cites only four interventory states.

2. Rosenau, J., 'Intervention as a Scientific Concept'. *Journal of Conflict Resolution*, 23, 2 (June 1971), pp. 149-71.

3. For Guinean intervention in Sierra Leone, see *Africa Confidential*, 12, 7 (2 April 1971), p. 2; 12, 14 (11 July 1971), p. 6; Keegan, J. (ed.), *World Armies* (London: MacMillan, 1983), pp. 239-40, 517-8; *Africa South of the Sahara: 1983/84* (London: Europa Publications, 1983), p. 713.

4. *Africa Contemporary Record: 1976/77* (London: Rex Collings, 1977), p. B.551. See, too, Baynham, S.J., 'Praetorian Politics and the Benin Raid' *The Army Quarterly and Defence Journal*, 107, 4 (October 1977), pp. 422-34.

5. For Guinean intervention in Liberia, see *Africa Contemporary Record: 1978/79*, pp. B.680, B.684; *Africa South of the Sahara: 1983/84*, p. 495; *Africa Research Bulletin*, 1-31 January 1979, p. 5118; 1-30 April 1979, p. 5200; 1-31 May 1979, p. 5268.

6. *Africa Contemporary Record: 1978/79*, p. B.646.

7. For Tanzanian intervention in the Comoros, see Keegan, *World Armies*, pp. 124-5; *Africa Contemporary Record: 1977/78*, pp. B.189-91; *Africa Contemporary Record: 1978/79*, pp. B.186-93.

8. For Tanzanian intervention in the Seychelles, see Keegan, *World Armies*, p. 516; *Africa Research Bulletin*, 1-30 June 1977, pp. 4465-7; 1-31 May 1978, p. 4053; 1-31 May 1979, p. 5269; 1-31 August 1982, p. 6566; 1-31 August 1983, p. 6954; *Africa Confidential*, 19, 9 (17 March 1978), p. 6; *Africa South of the Sahara: 1983/84*, p. 705; *Africa Contemporary Record: 1976/77*, p. B.317; 1977/78, pp. B.3635, B.367, B.415-6; 1979/80, pp. B.295-8, B.335; 1981/82, p. B.282.

9. For Tanzanian intervention in Mozambique, see Pachter, E.F., 'Contra-Coup: Civilian Control

of the Military in Guinea, Tanzania, and Mozambique', *Journal of Modern African Studies*, 20, 4, (December 1982), pp. 609-610; Keegan, *World Armies*, pp. 407-8; *Africa Contemporary Record: 1976/77*, p. B.360; *Africa Research Bulletin*, 1-30 June 1976, p. 4055; 1-31 January 1980, pp. 5533-4.
  10. Keegan, *World Armies*, pp. 769-80.
  11. Ibid., p. 90.
  12. Ibid., pp. 100-1; *Africa Contemporary Record: 1978/79*, p. B.519.
  13. *Africa Contemporary Record: 1981/82*, p. B.390; *Africa South of the Sahara: 1983/84*, p. 293; *Africa Confidential*, 24, 15 (20 July 1983), pp. 1-3; *West Africa*, 11 July 1983, p. 1630.
  14. *Africa Research Bulletin*, 1-31 August 1978, p. 4964; 1-28 February 1979, p. 5166; 1-31 August 1979, p. 5585.
  15. Senegal's intervention in the Gambia is discussed in *Africa Contemporary Record: 1981/82*, pp. B.410-12.
  16. It is not known whether gun crews accompanied them. They were located in the border areas of Senegal and Guinea.
  17. Georgewill, H.A., *Nigeria and the Liberation of South Africa* (unpublished M.A. dissertation: Birmingham University, 1981), pp. 14-15.
  18. Thompson, V. and Adloff, R., *Conflict in Chad* (London: Hurst, 1981), pp. 92-3.
  19. For a discussion of Nigerian policy, see Ofoegbu, R., 'Foreign Policy and Military Rule', and Akinyemi, A.B., 'Mohammed/Obasanjo Foreign Policy' in Oyediran, O. (ed.), *Nigerian Government and Politics under Military Rule 1966-79* (London: MacMillan, 1979).
  20. According to one source, the majority of Angolan troops have been sent home following a shift away from doctrinaire Marxism on the part of the Sao Tomé government. *Guardian*, 9 April 1985.
  21. Angola and Guinea-Bissau support for Sao Tomé are discussed in Keegan, *World Armies*, pp. 239-40, 501; *Africa South of the Sahara: 1983/84*, pp. 684-5; *Africa Contemporary Record: 1977/78*, p. B.584; 1978/79, pp. 567-8; 1979/80, p. B.447.
  22. Keegan, *World Armies*, pp. 681-4.
  23. Details of the Inter-African Force are found in sources for note 13, and *Africa Contemporary Record: 1977/78*, pp. B.589-94; 1978/79, pp. B.571-80.

24. *Africa South of the Sahara: 1983/84*, pp. 729-831.
25. *Africa Contemporary Record: 1977/78*, pp. B.526-8; Dos Santos, D., 'Cabinda: the Politics of Oil in Angola's Enclave' in Cohen, R. (ed.), *African Islands and Enclaves* (Beverley Hills/London/New Delhi: Sage, 1983).
26. *Africa Contemporary Record: 1978/79*, pp. B.498-500. The Angolan government moved the Shaba refugees away from the Zaire border and later expelled the FLNC leader to Guinea-Bissau.
27. Some attempts at unravelling 'Operation Omega' are to be found in Keegan, *World Armies*, p. 56; *Africa Confidential*, 18, 9 (18 March 1977), pp. 6-7; 17, 8 (29 April 1977), pp. 1-2; *Africa South of the Sahara: 1983/84*, p. 209; *Africa Contemporary Record: 1976/77*, pp. B.549-52, B.557; 1977/78, pp. B.616-7; Baynham, 'Praetorian Politics and the Benin Raid'.
28. *Africa Contemporary Record: 1981/82*, pp. B.187-8.
29. Tanzania's campaign in Uganda is discussed in *Africa South of the Sahara: 1983/84*, pp. 829-30; *Africa Contemporary Record: 1978/79*, pp. B.393-7; 1979/80, pp. B.350-2. See, also, Avirgnan, T. and Honey, M., *War in Uganda: The Legacy of Idi Amin* (Dar es Salaam: Tanzanian Publishing, 1982), which provides the most detailed though partisan account of the war.
30. Rikhye, I.J., Harbottle, M. and Egge, B., *The Thin Blue Line: International Peacekeeping and its Future* (New Haven and London: Yale University Press), pp. 87-8.
31. Full details are given in Higgins, R., *United Nations Peacekeeping 1946-67. Documents and Commentaries. 3 Africa* (London: RIIA/Oxford University Press, 1980), Annex. I, pp. 91-5.
32. Thompson and Adloff, *Conflict in Chad*, chs. 4 and 5.
33. Keegan, *World Armies*, pp. 598-600.
34. Imobighe, T.A., 'African defense and security: an overview' *Nigerian Forum* (April 1981), pp. 66-71; Imobighe, T.A., 'An African High Command: the search for a feasible strategy of continental defence', *African Affairs*, 79, 315 (April 1980), pp. 241-54; Wornoff, J., 'The Case for an African Defence Organization' *Africa Report* (June 1971); Meyers, R.D., 'An Analysis of OAU's Effectiveness at Regional Collective Defence' in El-Ayouty, Y., (ed.), *The Organisation of African Unity After Ten Years. Comparative Perspectives*

(New York: Praegar, 1975) pp. 118-51.
  35. Pachter, 'Contra-Coup'.
  36. Afrifa, A.A., <u>The Ghana Coup</u> (London: Frank Cass, 1966).
  37. Rosenau, J., <u>The Scientific Study of Foreign Policy</u> (New York/London: The Free Press/Collier-MacMillan, 1971), p. 302.
  38. MacFarlane, 'Intervention and Security in Africa', pp. 56-60.

Chapter Eight

FOREIGN INTERVENTION IN AFRICA

Anthony Clayton

INTRODUCTION

The militarisation of post-independence Africa, a theme of much of this work, has been enhanced by the international setting of global ideological confrontation. From the death of Stalin in 1953 the Soviet Union embarked on a global strategy, wishing to assert a voice on any international issue and so challenging the United States, already in a position to do so. The Soviet strategy received massive new impetus in the 1960s with the emergence of the Soviet Union as a major surface naval power with a balanced fleet of large ocean-going warships capable of posing an out-of-NATO-theatre threat to Western maritime interests. Few corners of the globe were any longer to be spared some attention from the superpowers, the USSR and the USA, or their respective allies. Africa with its three strategic seaways, Suez, the Horn of Africa and the Cape, inevitably began to attract such attention. African governments in response sought and continue to seek to turn such attention to their advantage, very often in the military field, usually for their own domestic security but sometimes for external relations reasons.

Linked to the global ideological confrontation and the need perceived by the superpowers to arm themselves to the teeth were and are other factors serving also to increase militarisation in newly independent African countries. Weaponry requires certain strategic raw materials; any form of naval or military training adds vastly to a nation's fuel bills. African countries began, therefore, to figure in superpower and other nations' access strategies. In Western countries where defence estimates are the subject of open debate and controversy, weapons sales, the training of foreign personnel and contributions by Third World countries to research and development costs, are all seen as useful in easing the burden of the defence budget on home taxpayers. Some countries, notably France, deliberately design equipment for its sales value and tell their own armies that this must do for them also; as a consequence, many African regimes are buttressed by Panhard armoured cars. In the Soviet Union, where defence estimates are not the subject of debate and where production of tanks and armoured personnel carriers can run such riot that even the Russians themselves may not know the total numbers produced, there are always vast quantities of last year's equipment, obsolescent for European battlefields but adequate for anywhere else, available for issue to liberation movements or to the armies of newly independent countries - on appropriate terms.

Most of the new states are impoverished, only a few have any arms manufacturing capacity, and these are very recent and mainly limited to small arms. Many are beset with internal problems liable to erupt into violence; an increasing number of border disputes call for military force. The stage for mischief is well set, but it must also be noted that without foreign military support in one form or another, or on occasions provision by a friendly foreign government of intelligence concerning the activities of an unfriendly rival, many African governments would be overthrown by ethnic, labour or other forms of street or palace coups. This chapter therefore is not a text in demonology.

Foreign military intervention and interest in black Africa has taken and can take a variety of traditional forms. These can range from overt, uninvited military intervention to invited military intervention; formal garrisons; defence and co-operation treaties; the provision of military equipment, technical staffs and training support; covert, clandestine military intervention; and intelligence gathering operations. More recently, and especially since the Iranian Revolution, a new variant has appeared: the needs of the United States to secure safe routes for the transport of a Rapid Deployment Force to the Middle Eastern oil-producing areas. It is tempting to set out the various nations' activities under these headings and make comparisons; the result would, however, be confusing to a general reader wishing to understand the overall policies and activities of one or other particular nation. Further, details on covert operations and intelligence activities are necessarily sketchy, making the whole subject too conjectural for adequate comparison - though it should also be stated that the mere presence of a foreign country's intelligence personnel in an African country does not in itself necessarily predicate intervention. For these reasons this chapter will initially follow a structure based on the activities of individual nations, in turn France, the Soviet Union, the United States and Britain.

FRANCE

Paradoxically in the context of a world-wide ideological confrontation, it is France rather than either of the superpowers that has consistently played the most widespread interventionist role. The role has generally (but not always) also served wider Western interests even if pursued for immediate interests entirely French; it has in consequence attracted criticism in France as a departure from *la France seule*.

The reasons for France's proprietorial attitude - at least in the 1960s - in African affairs are complex, but they straddle both the right and the left in France's domestic politics. Francois Mitterrand for example, although a life-long socialist, was also once a staff sergeant in a *Régiment d'Infanterie Coloniale*. Origins may be seen deep in French metropolitan history, in Braudelian perceptions of an essential unity of Mediterranean France with North and West Africa, and in the centralist Roman Law style of France's colonial policies. More recently, French towns and cities saw the massive contribution of North and black African military manpower to the armies of Juin and de Lattre de Tassigny in 1944-45, and later to the French cause in Indochina from 1946 to 1954. These impressions reinforced the belief among many French leaders, political as well as military, that one of the foundations of their country's position in the world was a hegemony role in, at least, Francophone Africa.

While de Gaulle, whose priorities were nuclear, did not fully share these views, they greatly influenced French thinking on the nature of independence in black Africa. Independence, to many

British academics more correctly termed 'flag independence', was to be based on treaties of co-operation; these included military agreements aimed at securing a French garrison in a number of ex-colonies (especially those of strategic or mineral significance) and a monopoly for the provision of military aid and training facilities for the armed forces of the new state.[1] These latter the French saw as useful for internal order, and perhaps as auxiliaries in wider French designs.[2] It was precisely the rejection of these paternalistic concepts by Sekou Touré's Guinea that so profoundly rankled the French. Further, as the 1960s progressed, the hitherto well-balanced French metropolitan economy ran into its first major fundamental weakness, oil. France found a new reason for interest in Africa, in particular territories that were either oil-producing or which were strategically important to a French naval presence, to secure Middle Eastern oil supplies, in the Indian Ocean.

In pursuit of these interests, France, alone among the world's great powers, developed substantial forces especially trained and equipped for general Third World intervention but with particular reference to Africa. In 1958, the *Régiments d'Infanterie and Artillerie Coloniale*, the famous *marsouins* (dolphins) and *bigors* (molluscs) were returned to their pre-1900 title as *Troupes de Marine*;[3] after the end of the Algerian campaign they and the surviving units of the *Légion Etrangère* were reconstituted as the nucleus of France's Intervention Force.[4] At the time of writing in 1985, this force reflects the 1976 reorganisation and expansion and comprises the 11th Parachute Division, the 9th Marine Infantry Division, and a smaller mechanised 31st Brigade tasked for Mediterranean roles. Under the 1984-85 French Defence Programme, a Rapid Action Force of five divisions (47,000 men), the existing 9th and 11th together with a mountain, an air mobile and a light armoured division, is to be created. The Rapid Action Force is seen as suitable for an intervention in northern Europe, the Mediterranean or in Africa. But a major reason for this new expansion is France's - largely bipartisan - resolution neither to allow a Soviet/Cuban monopoly of military intervention in Africa, nor to allow the United States to be the only counter to the Russians. The programme when complete will provide France with Europe's finest intervention army, complete with its own air transport and logistic support. The British Army's equivalent is one brigade with totally inadequate air support.

The *Troupes de Marine* have a very high percentage of volunteer regulars, the *Légion* is entirely volunteer; the regiments are therefore freed from the legislative constraints that exist for traditional metropolitan conscript regiments, though not all the new Divisions will be so uninhibited. The *Légion* was moved to Corsica, later to Aubagne in the south of France; the main ceremonial avenue of their new depot was carefully laid out to point towards their old one at Sidi Bel Abbès in Algeria. *Marsouin* units provide the garrisons in Senegal, Ivory Coast, Gabon and Réunion, the *Légion* in Djibouti and Mayotte. At the time of writing the *Troupes de Marine* total 33,800, one fifth of France's entire army, and the *Légion* some 8,500.[5]

Clear indication of France's views of independence was to be seen as early as 1959 in Tunisia, where popular pressure against the retention by France of the Bizerta naval base led to the dropping of one *Marine* parachute battalion to reinforce another already garrisoning the base under treaty arrangements. In post-independence black Africa, France from the outset enjoyed an advantaged position in her former colonies through cadres trained in the last colonial years (mostly at Fréjus or Cherchell in Algeria) and through the French language, French-speaking cadres not unnaturally preferring contacts with France as no language difficulties arose. France's policies in the 1960s reflected her own self-confidence and the enormous respect in which de Gaulle, 'the Man of Brazzaville', was held in Africa. After the retirement of de Gaulle and with Pompidou's declining health, some of the confidence briefly evaporated. The accession to power of Giscard and the challenge presented to France by Soviet/Cuban activity, however, led to resumption of French military interest and action.

The record of formal interventions over the years is a remarkable one. French garrisons, before their departure in some cases, maintained stability at the delicate moment of independence and its first months, intervening to restore order in Cameroon in 1960-61, in Congo-Brazzaville in 1960 and Mauritania in 1961 to end ethnic conflict, in Gabon in 1962 and in Chad in 1960-63 to maintain order, and in Niger in 1963 to put down a military revolt.[6] In 1964 the small French garrison in Libreville, Gabon, supported by reinforcements flown in from Dakar rescued and restored to his authority President M'ba, who had been seized by a group of soldiers and gendarmerie. In the late 1960s units of the French garrison in Cameroon were again used to assist government forces in suppressing an uprising among the Bamileke. In 1968 the prolonged French counter-insurgency involvement in Chad, set out in succeeding paragraphs, opened. In 1977 and early 1978 a French Air Force squadron of Jaguar strike aircraft supported Moroccan troops in Mauritania against vigorous assaults by the POLISARIO insurgent movement which was destabilising the weaker of its two opponents, following the rash Mauritanian-Moroccan accord to partition the former Spanish Sahara. A change of regime in Mauritania in 1978 withdrew the country from active military operations, the withdrawal ending any further need for overt French help. In 1979, in 'Operation Barracuda', parachute troops of the *Marine* ejected the infamous Emperor Bokassa, restoring Dacko as President of the Central African Republic. Although Zaire had not been a French colony the territory is often viewed in Paris as part of *le monde francophone,* a view contributing to noteworthy French action in both 1977 and 1978 in Zaire. In both years a largely Lunda insurgency movement supported by the radical Angolan regime launched an incursion into Zaire's Shaba province, incursions which the Zaire Army was unable to arrest. In 1977 French military aircraft transported a Moroccan military force supported by French logistic staffs to the rescue. The more serious 1978 incursion, during which some 200 Europeans were massacred in the city of Kolwezi, led to a more overtly French intervention, that of *Légion Etrangère* parachute troops; these were carried (for technical reasons connected with the parachutes) in United States military aircraft. Ongoing French interest in Zaire is evidenced by French cadres and training teams serving in parachute and logistic units selected by President Mobutu as being among the more reliable in his dubiously loyal army. Occasions on which France did not intervene must also be noted; in Togo in 1963 following the assassination of Olympio; in Congo-Brazzaville and Dahomey (now Benin) on the resignations of Youlou and Maga; in Madagascar to buttress Tsiranana in 1971 and 1972; and in Niger in 1974. The reasons for the first three would appear to be the relatively low importance of the territories; in the case of Madagascar distance, limited French air lift capability (at the time), and a perception that the cause was lost anyway; and in the case of Niger a paralysis in decision-making caused by the death of Pompidou and the pre-election situation.[7]

The complex history of France's intervention in Chad has its origins at the turn of the century, when French strategists assessed Chad as being the key hinge-territory linking North, East and West Africa (a perception whose validity was dramatically proved by General Leclerc in his epic 1941-42 march and thought to be re-emphasised by the Soviet presence in North-east Africa), and also in the summer of 1940 when the colony rallied to de Gaulle, the first African colony to do so. The state, however, is an artefact encapsulating a largely Moslem nomad population in the North and Christian or animist negro agriculturalists in the South and West.[8] These latter provided the ruling groups at independence but were faced from 1968 with an insurrectionary movement, FROLINAT, drawing increasingly on Libyan support, in the North. The distracted and unbalanced President, Tombalbaye, appealed to France for help and a French garrison was despatched, later reinforced substantially and placed under the command of a general, Cortadellas. Considerable fighting took place in the North in 1969, 1970 and 1971; among the 50 or so French soldiers killed was Cortadellas's son.

From 1973 onwards France began to modify her policy in Chad; de Gaulle was gone and a need for some form of working relationship with Libya in France's wider energy interests was perceived. French troops were largely withdrawn from the combat areas, though some teams fought on in Chad uniforms. This withdrawal led to bitter reproaches from Tombalbaye and his successor in 1975, General Malloum, who was installed as a result of a coup in which France was almost certainly involved. Malloum even demanded a French withdrawal, a demand clearly intended to mean the reverse rather than be taken literally. A new agreement in 1976 provided for a returned presence of several hundred French 'advisers', in theory not to be involved in battle. In practice they were so involved on several occasions, and equally important they served to buttress General Malloum's somewhat shaky position.

On this basis, and aided by emerging divisions

within FROLINAT, only limited French military assistance was necessary until 1978 when one of the FROLINAT grouping occupied Faya-Largeau, the last centre of Chad government authority in the North. A substantial French reinforcement of 1,500 troops together with air-to-ground strike aircraft operations contained the insurgents, but the number of French casualties introduced a new dimension to the Chad question for France, effective political criticism in Paris of the involvement.[9]

One result of this criticism and the overall cost of military action was a new government, led jointly by Malloum as Head of State (and the leader of one of the more moderate FROLINAT groups) and Habre, as Prime Minister, which was formed under French military auspices. The majority of FROLINAT, under Goukouni Oueddei, however, rejected compromise and determined to continue fighting to secure the removal of the French. The French Army commander, Bredeche, favoured an offensive against FROLINAT but was replaced by another general, Forest, under whom the lines of a more limited French policy commitment began to appear. It was one in which Libya's forcible annexation of the North-western Aouzou area and FROLINAT domination of much of the North was tacitly accepted, but a French military force of some 2,000 supported by Jaguar strike aircraft secured the South under the authority of the capital, N'Djamena. This arrangement's chances of success appeared at the time also to be strengthened by divided counsels in Tripoli.

The local political situation, however, worsened, with a rift opening between Habre and Malloum, the latter falling under the influence of a hardline southern officer, Colonel Kamougué. Violent fighting broke out, Habre's forces entering N'Djamena in early 1979 with French troops confined to their barracks. At this point the country was effectivly divided into three, a North once again divided into rival factions, the capital and centre under Habre, and the South under Malloum and Kamougué; in the latter area reprisal pogroms of Moslems began.

Habre next made common cause under a mediatory figure, Chona Lol, with Oueddei, still the most effective if not undisputed northern leader. The withdrawal of the French and their replacement by an all-African force was proclaimed as the aim, one that attracted much African support, especially from Nigeria who provided the bulk of the troops.[10] This possible basis of settlement was, however, undermined by Libya, even to the extent of arming the resentful southerners as well as supporting insurgency in the North. Chona Lol once more found French military support essential for suvival.

The French in their turn assessed that Chona Lol was not capable of restoring unity to the country and by exceedingly skilful negotiation engineered a national coalition which provided for Oueddei as President, Kamougué as Vice-President and Habre as a senior minister. Once again a possible basis of settlement was to be wrecked by factionalism. Oueddei dismissed Habre, apparently in the belief that if he promised to keep the Libyans out the French would tolerate Habre's removal. In the event Oueddei proved incapable in other fields as well and by mid-1980 Chad was once more rent by a dozen armed factions operating in different areas of the territory including Habre in the East and Kamougué in the South. Oueddei himself was forced back on to massive Libyan military support in the North.

Surprisingly, Habre emerged the winner. After a shaky start he concluded an agreement with Kamougué. This appears to have qualified him in French eyes for a measure of resumed French military support more in terms of equipment and training aid than French soldiers.[11] Habre's success was also assisted by yet further rifts ending in fighting in the North, Oueddei trying to stave off total Libyan domination. Success led to success, the OAU force in these circumstances found it impossible to support Oueddei and in 1982 Habre entered the gutted wreck of what had been Chad's capital city in triumph, forming a new government of national unity.

But Libya refused to accept this settlement and after a brief wound-licking period of military withdrawal and eclipse, opened up new insurgency activity in central Chad in 1983, setting up an alternative government at Bardai under Oueddei. Habre was once again obliged to seek French military help - 'Operation Manta' - to bolster his illassorted and only half-formed army. The 3,000 French troops (*Marine* and parachute *Légion*) were given some of the latest of France's anti-tank, anti-aircraft, missile and electronic warfare equipment.[12] In the event their presence alone secured the desired result, the Libyans withdrawing themselves and their clients very rapidly.

In 1984 President Mitterrand sought and reached an understanding with the Libyan leader, Gadaffi, by which both France and Libya withdrew their troops under arrangements including international observers. The issue of Libya's annexation of Aouzou was politely avoided. France honoured its side of the agreement, the Libyans failed to do the same. The situation at the time of writing (in 1985) is obscure, and the Mitterrand government is under sharp domestic political criticism. Whether the French government will react against Libyan duplicity by a reinforcement rather than a withdrawal of its few remaining training advisers, or whether the French have decided to end their ever more costly Chad commitments is unclear. Continued support for the southern half of a Chad partitioned along the 16th Parallel seems the most likely possibility, as complete abandonment would have wider implications for the whole credibility of France's African military policies, intervention, aid and garrisons.

By the various 1960 independence treaties of co-operation already mentioned, France retained garrisons in Cameroon, Gabon, Ivory Coast, Madagascar, and Senegal throughout the 1960s.[13] Those of Cameroon and Madagascar were withdrawn in 1974 and 1971 respectively, following demands for the re-negotiation of the treaties. France maintained a small garrison in the Central African Republic in the late 1960s at the request of President Bokassa; following 'Operation Barracuda' a garrison of some 1,100 *Marine* infantry is in the territory, divided between Bangui and Bouar. A small garrison force was despatched to Niger in the early 1970s at a time of Libyan-backed internal unrest. There is no doubt that the garrisons of Senegal (2,250 to the mid-1970s, thereafter some 600)[14] and Ivory Coast (600) have by their presence contributed to the political stability of these two states.

On attaining independence in 1977, Djibouti signed an agreement providing for a French garrison of two regiments and an air force squadron. Although under the terms of the agreement the French garrison is expressly forbidden to intervene in any internal issues, its role being limited to defence against an external threat, the effect of its presence is to underpin the political order left by the French, an order in which Djibouti's two main communities, Afars and Issa Somalis, despite their links with communities in neighbouring Ethiopia and Somalia, agreed locally to work together for the territory's independence. This at one and the same time preserves the territory from the larger-scale conflict that would undoubtedly arise if one neighbour or the other attempted to take over Djibouti; it also for the present secured France a military, air and naval presence in an area of crucial strategic importance.

The 1960 independence co-operation agreements met differing fates.[15] The Ivory Coast alone has kept absolutely loyal to France as the sole source of equipment and training facilities for its ground (though not its air) units. The agreement with Benin, Madagascar and Mali soon lapsed, though the French appear still to retain a few contacts. The agreements negotiated and later re-negotiated with Cameroon, Central African Republic, Gabon, Niger, Senegal, Togo and Upper Volta (now Burkina Faso) provide for French training assistance, including joint exercises and the provision of military equipment, but France no longer has a monopoly position. Niger briefly attempted to end its arrangements with France, but soon found this impracticable. After the fall of the Youlou government in Congo-Brazzaville in 1963 all military contacts between France and the country ceased. Moving away from former French territories, France concluded an agreement in 1969 with Burundi, French equipment and contract personnel playing a role in the unattractive inter-ethnic conflicts of 1972. Another agreement provided a similar facility for Rwanda.

Covert military activity, by any nation, is very rarely exposed in terms irrefutable; a measure of surmise must always surround the topic. It is, however, reasonable to suggest certain areas of covert French military and intelligence activity in post-independence Africa. The *Service de Documentation Exterieure et de Contre Espionage* (SDECE) and its linked *Service d'Action Civique*, the redoubtable 'Foccart machine' (so named after its director, and using diplomats, business and aid personnel) have kept Paris well-informed of internal, Soviet - and American - activities. In the 1960-62 turmoil in Zaire, at that time Congo-Kinshasa, France appeared to have anticipated the disintegration of the state, a situation to be turned to the advantage of France and her clients. She hoped to attach the north bank of the Congo (Zaire) River area to Youlou's Congo-Brazzaville, at that time a very subservient client state. She also supported the break-away of Tshombe's Katanga, covert French government assistance being given to the recruitment of former French military personnel for the secessionist regime. Later, at the time of the collapse of Portuguese rule in Angola, some French Intelligence activity took place in Cabinda. In 1966-67 France was to play an equally unfortunate, and equally unsuccessful, role in Nigerian affairs. To de Gaulle, much influenced by a leading intelligence adviser of marked anti-anglophone views, Nigeria appeared to be an African Canada, a British artefact; further, Nigeria's size disturbed several of France's West African clients and Nigeria's oil provided a strong economic temptation.[16] The army of Biafra began the war with consignments of rifles supplied by the Ivory Coast and Gabon, at the time France's two most dependable African client states and one example of French military intervention by means of surrogates. The Moroccan force sent to Zaire in 1977 represents a second example.[17] The inter-African force assembled in Zaire after the 1978 incursion, a force composed of units from, again, Morocco, Senegal, the Ivory Coast, the Central African Empire and a small contingent from Egypt can also be advanced as a third instance, France being heavily involved in the logistics. A perhaps less obscure example of French covert military intervention in an African state can be seen in the change of regime in Bangui, Central African Republic, in September 1981 when President Dacko was removed by General Kolingba to evident French approval.[18]

One final area of French military assertion must be noted before concluding any overview of French action, the Comoro Islands. These islands lie near the northern end of the Mozambique Channel, the major European/Middle East oil route. Of the four main islands Mayotte, the largest, differs from the largely Arab culture of the others by its possession of a culture more Roman Catholic and Malagasy oriented; Mayotte also possesses a deep-water harbour. The other islands opted for full independence in 1974, Mayotte opposing this option, wishing to continue under French control. Murky events followed. The remaining islands, in protest, declared independence under President Ahmad Abdallah whose regime lasted only a few weeks, being overthrown by a force led by a French mercenary soldier, Colonel Denard, who installed a new government headed by a President Ali Soilih. Although France recognised Soilih initially, when he attempted to land on Mayotte he was rebuffed and all French aid withdrawn, so creating acute economic hardship. Soilih in response embarked on radical policies applied with great ferocity, to such an extent that he was overthrown and killed in another Denard-led coup in 1978. This coup, after various manoeuvrings, restored Ahmad Abdallah to his original authority over all the islands, except Mayotte. In this latter island France has stationed a detachment of the *Légion Etrangère* as a permanent garrison with other units, military, air and naval, also frequently in post. A further 2,000 French troops are stationed in Réunion. While the United Nations recognises Abdallah's government as the lawful authority for all the islands, Paris seems set on policies that could make Mayotte, at present still a French Overseas Territory, into an Overseas Department of France itself, though France might grant Mayotte full independence if the Comoros were to permit permanent French bases.

THE SOVIET UNION

The only other country to match the French in overt military activities in post-independence Africa is the Soviet Union, together with its principal surrogate, Cuba. Soviet foreign policy is a compound of traditional Russian interests such as the Baltic and Poland, her newer priority concerns in glacis areas such as Eastern Europe and the Far East, her access strategy,[19] her assertion as a superpower, her role in the advancement of Marxism-Leninism and in Africa a measure of assistance to 'countries of socialist orientation', a tendency to over-react to trump Chinese initiatives, and an old-fashioned plain caution in respect of the United States if the latter is in a mood of resolution. The weighting of the various ingredients vary from time to time; they contain a measure of continuity larger than in a free election democracy, though the absence of significant public debate makes prediction and analysis on specific issues virtually impossible.[20] Policy tends therefore to be pragmatic. It is a matter of what can be gained for the Soviet Union at any one particular moment if an opportunity presents itself; nothing suggests an overall comprehensive African strategy.[21] And at the outset of any survey of Soviet activities it is useful to bear in mind the fact that Africa is low in Soviet overall priorities. In respect of Southern Africa, for example, the Soviets must have drawn the lesson that too militant policies will draw the West together rather than serve the priority Soviet aim of decoupling the rest of NATO from the USA. France's limited return to NATO military commitments is at least in part a consequence of her suspicions about Soviet military activities in Africa, (though France would never accept that her African policies were in any way any part of NATO-out-of-theatre area policy). Furthermore, many Russians as individuals are negrophobe and aid to Africa is unpopular with the general public.

The military results of these attitudes and processes of policy formulation vary according to the weighting attached by different Russian leaders to the situation at any one time. Krushchev, presiding over the Soviet Union in the period of formal decolonisation, saw political and ideological opportunities that for the most part did not in fact exist and were later to form part of the charge of 'adventurism' raised against him. Assessing Africa as in a revolutionary situation, Krushchev sought to support Nkrumah in Ghana with equipment and training assistance for the President's Own Guard Regiment, Nkrumah's *Waffen SS*.[22] He also promised Lumumba lorries with which to transport forces to suppress Kalonji's Kasai uprising; later he was to support an even more dubious Lumumbist cause, the 1964 *Simba* uprising, with military weaponry flown in aboard Soviet aircraft overpainted with Sudanese emblems. On the occasion of the 1964 Zanzibar Revolution, a small part of a consignment of light armoured vehicles and automatic weapons destined for Somalia was delivered to Karume's regime. Although after the fall of Krushchev, also belonging to this early era of crude, naive attempts to intervene was the attempt to supply (very obsolete) tanks to Kenya in 1965, an offer refused by the Kenya government. The provision of these tanks was almost certainly part of a wider project to advance the political interests of the militant radical Luo politician Oginga Odinga, a number of Luo officer cadets trained in Bulgaria together with a Soviet military team all appearing in Nairobi at the same time.

More successfully and sensible from the Soviet

point of view were the beginnings, in the Krushchev era, of the provision of weaponry and training to the emerging insurgency movements in Portuguese Guinea (Guinea-Bissau), Angola and Mozambique. Advantage was also taken of France's abandonment of Guinea to instal a permanent maritime air reconnaissance base; this lasted until 1979 when Touré's mounting suspicion of Soviet African designs led him to close it down.

With the fall of Krushchev Soviet policy became less active for several years, a reflection of the weakness of Brezhnev's authority in his first eight years. Aid for FRELIMO, PAIGC and MPLA was, however, maintained. Initiatives that reappeared in 1968-69 were much more professional and calculating, and on much less of a heady and ideological basis. Artillery and aircraft, in the event little used, were supplied to the Nigerian Federal government in the civil war, earning the USSR much goodwill.[23] More tangibly rewarding was the greatly increased Soviet military aid and support given to the post-1969 Siyad Barre government in Somalia, as in return the Soviets acquired air and maritime reconnaissance facilities in a strategic area.[24]

The mid-1970s saw Brezhnev at the height of his political and physical powers, with the USA in its post-Vietnam, post-Watergate irresolution. This tilted world balance led the Soviet Union to its two most spectacular interventions, those in Angola and in Ethiopia. The intervention in Angola in favour of the Marxist liberation movement, MPLA, was justified on the grounds of Western and South African efforts in favour of the non-Marxist FNLA;[25] a possibility of Chinese support for FNLA was also significant. The intervention took the new form, a partnership with Cuba (held by many Third World countries to be non-aligned and so giving the Soviet intervention a spurious repute) and also with the GDR.[26] The Cubans had for long had their own interests in Africa, training insurgents and militants. These now coincided with those of the USSR, for its own domestic reasons not willing to commit conscript soldiers. The Soviets provided direction, heavy lift and training staffs, the East Germans technical specialists ranging from helicopter pilots to medical personnel, and the Cubans a mass of soldiery. An important contribution to the success of the operation was the use of the port of Luba, in Equatorial Guinea, where the Soviets had been granted a facility by Macias Nguema.[27] Although the FLNA was quickly defeated in early 1976 the more resolute joint South African military and UNITA insurgency movement operations continue to dominate much of the southeast and centre of Angola, and are argued to justify an increase in the Cuban military presence from the original 14,000 to a (1985) total of some 25,000 or more. In the mid-1970s Cuban units were used to try and contain the South Africans but they performed poorly. The next pattern was one of mixed Angolan and Cuban ground units, supported by East German-manned helicopters. This proved little better. The latest pattern provided for the withdrawal of Cuban units to garrison roles, the actual ground fighting being left to Angolan units (now equipped with some very recent Soviet weaponry), very closely supported by East German and Russian training logistic cadres. Without this massive Soviet-Cuban commitment the MPLA regime, neither popular politically nor ethnically well-balanced, would not survive. The Cubans are also an important instrument in the Soviet Union's - exceedingly cautious - policies towards Namibia and South Africa. Immediate Soviet profit again takes the form of a Southern Atlantic maritime reconnaissance facility, replacing that closed by Touré in Guinea. Relations between the Cubans and the Angolans are said to be poor; in the years 1976 to 1984 some 2,000 Cuban soldiers have been killed and over 4,000 wounded.[28]

In 1977 the Soviets decided to support the 'creeping revolution' in Ethiopia, in particular its militant leader, Colonel Mengistu who shot his way to power in that year. Massive Soviet and other military aid was poured into Ethiopia to enable Mengistu to defeat the Somalia-supported Western Somali Liberation Front (WSLF) invasion of 1977. The aid followed Angolan patterns: Soviet transport aircraft and ships, Russian command and training cadres (including at least three generals), a number of East German - and South Yemeni - specialists, in particular East German helicopter personnel, and some 15,000 Cuban troops. At the same time Soviet advisers assisted the Ethiopian regime in reorganising the rabble of a 'peasant army' into a militia, and in reorganising and retraining the surviving Ethiopian regulars. The combined Ethiopian and Soviet/Cuban forces then took the field against firstly the Eritrean and later the Tigrean internal rebel forces. Both suffered heavy defeats in violent fighting, but neither has been destroyed. The Ethiopian forces and supporting Soviet/Cuban cadres continue counter-insurgency operations against them, the Eritreans alleging Soviet use of nerve gases. Recently they have been engaged in bombing starving refugees fleeing into the Sudan.[29] Some 6,000 Cubans are thought to remain in Ethiopia.[30] Latest reports in mid-1985 suggest the Cubans are deployed only against the Somalis, being unwilling to combat their erstwhile protégés among the Eritreans. Further, it suits the Soviets very well that the Ethiopian regime is dependent on their continued military support. The price the Soviets have had to pay for their ascendancy in Ethiopia, and with it, of course, maritime facilities,[31] was, however, the complete write-off of their gains and installations in Somalia, all to the advantage of the USA.

A less easily explicable exercise in the mid-1970s was the military aid given to Idi Amin in Uganda, aid (including as it did amphibious armoured vehicles and load carriers) that was clearly intended to assist Amin's designs on Tanzania. One can only surmise that a mixture of opportunism, a wish to harm a friend of China, and ideological confusion as being the ingredients of the Soviet decision.

Soviet interventions, weapon sales, military agreements and intelligence activities are perhaps more closely interlocked than those of other countries. A comprehensive recent agreement with Mozambique appears to include maritime air reconnaissance and harbour facilities for the Soviet forces.[32] On various occasions - in Mali in the 1960s, in Zaire in 1963 and 1972, in Lusaka in 1979 - reports of activities by KGB officers appear; on other occasions African countries deport Soviet diplomatic or commercial officials believed to be KGB members. Some of these reports are no doubt true; equally true would it be to assert that the KGB interests itself in one way or another in most African territories. Hard evidence is, however, not available. East Germany often provides secret service security training as a Soviet surrogate, two well-known examples being Nkrumah's Ghana in the early 1960s and Karume's Zanzibar in 1964.[33] Other recipients include Angola, Ethiopia, Mozambique, Somalia (in the early 1970s) and Zambia.[34] The case of Zambia is almost bizarre; GDR security personnel secure Kaunda against organised massive industrial labour unrest that could overthrow him - a protection more in the interests of the West than of the USSR.[35]

The Soviet preference for the use of Cubans as a surrogate may extend also to training teams. Cubans are certainly at work in Congo-Brazzaville where an air-staging post for the Cuban forces in Angola, with a small local defence garrison, exists, and also in Benin, Sierra Leone and Tanzania. They have also been at work in Guinea. Reports impossible to confirm suggest Cuban missions are at present working in a number of other countries.[36]

THE UNITED STATES

Compared with these massive involvments, those of other countries are small-scale. The United States has traditionally been chary of overt military involvements outside the American hemisphere, a chariness strongly reinforced by the Vietnam experience.[37] With the exception of Liberia (see below), no regular US Army units have either intervened in or been based in post-independence black Africa. US Air Force aircraft lifted the Belgian parachute unit that rescued American hostages in Stanleyville (now Kisangani), Zaire, in 1964, an intervention limited to rescue and entirely justifiable under international law. The American Air Force was also involved in the evacuation of the last of Ethiopia's 'Black Falashas' from the Sudan early in 1985. The USA has, however, specific military interests which are advanced by other means. The first field of these military interests is intelligence and covert operations; the second is weapon sales, influence and in particular goodwill in states that lie athwart the route of any emergency US military force deployed in the Middle East.

Covert operations remain an obscure area. The Central Intelligence Agency has an African department; a number of Americans at work in Africa in one capacity or another are on retainers. Probably the most useful academic detection of CIA activities is that offered by René Lemarchand.[38] Lemarchand claims that CIA activities in former French territories (he in particular cited CIA interest in overthrowing M'ba in Gabon in 1964 and Tsiranana in Madagascar in 1971) had often been frustrated by the French. He did however believe the accession to (short-lived) power of Colonel Ratsimandrava in Madagascar in 1975 owed much to CIA influence.

Lemarchand contends that the CIA has been most successful in former Belgian territories where it was often able to take over existing Belgian systems. He alleges in respect of Rwanda and Burundi that CIA activities contained and reversed the spread of Chinese influence in the mid-1960s. But his most striking claims for CIA involvement concern Congo-Kinshasa, where he alleges a CIA dimension successively in President Kasavabu's decision to dismiss Prime Minister Lumumba in September 1960, in the 1961 murder of Lumumba, in the hiring of mercenaries and aircraft to defeat the 1964 *Simba* uprising, in the hijacking of Tshombe in 1967 and in further assistance to Mobutu once in power.[39]

Another success, again brief-lived, claimed for the CIA by Lemarchand was the funding of pro-Western Somali Youth League members to ensure the return to power of Mohammed Egal in the 1967 Somalia elections. A major failure, however, was CIA efforts to prevent the accession to power of the MPLA in Angola in 1974-76.

It is easy to cast the CIA as a leading figure in popular demonolgy.[40] In the opinion of this writer, Lemarchand's cited instances of CIA activity are probably correct, but this writer would not necessarily subscribe to Lemarchand's overall conclusions - that covert intelligence activities have a negative effect on African development. Intelligence work is an inevitable fact of life for any government anywhere not wishing to be overthrown; foreign co-operation is often necessary where governments lack their own resources.

In terms of aid and training facilities, three countries attracted especial US favour until the mid-1970s: Ethiopia, Zaire and Liberia. The former received massive credits for American equipments; in return the US received a large radar surveillance facility at Kagnew, now closed down.[41] Zaire was granted access to considerable training facilities in the USA; Liberia only received miniscule help, but was the one territory with a permanent, uniformed, US Army training team. Further assistance to the other countries was until 1967 constrained by the provisions of the 1961 Foreign Assistance Act, which imposed tight limits on military aid; these limits, only slightly eased, remained until 1973. Other recipients of substantial US assistance included Nigeria, which sent numbers of specialist personnel to the USA for training in the mid-1970s, Ghana and Kenya. Small numbers of military students were also accepted from the Ivory Coast and Senegal in the early 1970s.

Most significant of recent developments, planned before the Iran Revolution but given urgency following it, has been the formation in 1980 of the Rapid Deployment Joint Task Force, which under current plans is to evolve from an initial two divisions to a force even larger than the one in France.[42] Its designated area of operations is to be 'South West Asia', for which transport and access facilities have been arranged with Kenya (under a 1980 agreement) and with Somalia, defence credits being offered in return.[43] Both agreements have attracted domestic criticism - in Kenya muted and in Somalia voiced externally - as an intervention. They have, further, impinged one upon the other in view of Somalia's irredentist claims on North-east Kenya, some Kenyans sharply criticising any US strengthening of Somalia as double-dealing. Lastly, US military aid has been given to Cameroon in return for overflying and access facilities on a possible Rapid Deployment Force route.

GREAT BRITAIN

For Great Britain, independence meant military independence.[44] No permanent garrisons in ex-African colonies were ever envisaged, nor did independence or Commonwealth membership imply any guarantee of British military support against an aggressor. While Britain was willing to offer newly independent African states training aid she never sought a monopoly position. Covert operations have been only very rarely, and then generally improbably, alleged against her.

Following the independence of Kenya (and by agreement with the Kenyatta government), a British brigade-size garrison remained in Kenya for a few months. In January 1964, at the invitation of the Kenyan and Ugandan governments, British troops suppressed army mutinies. In revolutionary Zanzibar however, the British presence, a frigate with a company of infantry on board (but not landed) was there simply to safeguard British lives and not to intervene.[45] In Tanganyika, where riots followed the Zanzibar Revolution and an army mutiny,

Royal Marines from an aircraft-carrier restored order - again by invitation. Only on three occasions was military intervention without invitation considered. Briefly in 1960 consideration was given to the despatch of units to the Congo on a life-saving mission. One platoon was actually sent to Stanleyville. In 1965 plans were drawn up for an intervention in Rhodesia but these were abandoned when it became clear that intervention would neither command bi-partisan Parliamentary support nor a military force of the necessary morale and enthusiasm. Finally, in 1972 airborne units were alerted for a possible operation in Uganda to rescue Asians.

Elsewhere British armed forces have figured very little. The Royal Navy maintained, in respect of ships thought to be carrying fuel and other imports for Rhodesia, a blockade of Mozambique ports; this blockade was of political rather than economic significance. An RAF squadron was stationed briefly in Zambia after Rhodesia's UDI but it was not committed operationally.

By far the most important British military contribution to post-independence Africa, however, was the support given by Britain, despite sharp domestic, Commonwealth and West European political criticism, to the Federal Nigerian cause in the 1967-1970 civil war. This support was decisive, without it the Federal cause would almost certainly have been lost. The Soviets produced the showy weapons, guns and aircraft, but it was with British small arms that the war was won and Lagos's authority preserved.[46]

The remaining formal British military activity in Africa has been very low key. Under a 1964 agreement one British Army unit trains in a remote area of Kenya for a few weeks each year; other units have from time to time trained for two or three weeks in Ghana (once in 1967), and in the Gambia. These are arrangements of minimal political and military significance.[47] RAF aircraft assisted in the evacuation of Portuguese from Angola in 1976. The British Army organised, and in part staffed, a small Commonwealth military force of teams that supervised the emergence from the bush of the two Zimbabwe insurgent movements, ZANLA and ZIPRA, and the 1980 election.

British training activity has been considerable, initially all African Commonwealth countries using British cadet and specialist military schools and staff colleges. As time passed some territories, notably Tanzania and Zambia, found British facilities to be unsuitable for the type of politically linked army that they were creating;[48] others opened their own colleges, sometimes with British, Canadian or Indian assistance. From the mid-1960s Zaire sent small numbers of military personnel to Britain for training; Senegal began to do so in the late 1970s and Mozambique is to do so this year (1985). In addition, British Army Training Teams have been at work in several countries, notably in Kenya, Ghana and Zambia in the early independence years. At the time of writing small British Army Training Teams are also at work in Zimbabwe and Uganda, with a handful of advisers in Kenya and Swaziland. British officers also instruct at the Ghanaian and Nigerian Staff Colleges. The British Army has made such personnel available under 'loan service' arrangements since independence; they figured in the cadres of the Ghana, Kenya, Nigeria and Sierra Leone Armies in the early years of independence, in the Tanganyika and Uganda Armies to 1964 and in the Malawi and Zambia Armies to 1965. However, the British government refused to allow them to participate in any conflict with Rhodesia and in consequence Zambia dispensed with their services.[49] The British Ministry of Defence has also on some occasions assisted in the recruitment of former British Armed Services personnel on contract to African governments. Britain has of course also sold military, air and naval equipment to a number of states. On occasions, she has also intervened to secure speedy help from other suppliers, a notable example being negotiation with India to supply urgently needed ammunition to Tanzania at the time of Amin's first aggressions in 1971-72.

OTHER COUNTRIES

Belgium intervened twice in post-independence Zaire. The first intervention was within a few days of independence, as law and order collapsed following the mutiny of the Congolese Army; its purpose was simply to save Belgian lives. The second was in 1969 when Belgian paratroops dropped from US aircraft to rescue Belgian, American and other Western hostages held by the *Simba* rebels. Portugal's colonial campaigns are outside the scope of this chapter but the raid by Portuguese military personnel on Conakry in 1971 provides an example of intervention. Portugal also gave some covert assistance to the Biafran cause in the Nigerian civil war.[50] Portuguese intelligence and covert activities in African states also occurred in these years, notably the assassination of Dr Mondlhane, the FRELIMO leader, in Dar es Salaam in 1969. Spain is thought to have played some covert role in the coup that led to the fall of President Macias Nguema in Equatorial Guinea in 1979.

China, like the USSR, assessed Africa in unreal terms in the early 1960s and, disillusioned and pre-occupied with her own internal problems, except for a brief spell of diplomatic activity caused by tension with the USSR in the early 1970s, lost interest for a number of years. Recent signs suggest a cautious return to African interests. In detail, China provided some assistance to Nkrumah's camps for insurgents,[51] some weaponry to the 1964 revolutionary regime in Zanzibar and, because the Soviets were helping the Bamileke, support for insurgents in southern Cameroon in 1960. More realistically China later moved to support for insurgency movements in Portuguese territories. Chinese military engineers built the Tazara (Tanzania-Zambia) railway, and Tanzanian military personnel were sent to China for tank training in the 1960s. In the 1970s Chinese activity, apart from Tanzania, was more modest. Training arrangements, either by visiting Chinese teams or in Chinese military schools, were made with Cameroon, Congo-Brazzaville, Guinea, Mali, Mozambique, Sierra Leone, Somalia, Togo, Zaire and Zambia, but these arrangements were all very small in scale.

Two other states that have pursued forward military policies in Africa also merit brief mention. Both have non-African reasons for their activities. North Korea, living as it does with a frontier with both Russia and China, has good reasons to look for international regard as well as the more maverick ones associated with the former Kim ll Sung's idiosyncracies. North Korean training teams have been and are at work in Zimbabwe and Uganda, and on a smaller scale, Togo and Equatorial Guinea and possibly Madagascar, their role often being the creation of *Waffen SS* -type units politically linked to the regime.

Israel has always attempted to look for allies beyond the ring of Arab nations that encircle her. Military training assistance on a very large scale was provided to Imperial Ethiopia in its initial campaign against Moslem Eritrean secessionists,[52] and briefly (until the 1973 agreements) to the Southern Sudanese Christian secessionists, both as facets of Israel's anti-Moslem policies. In the 1960s Israel also provided considerable training facilities for Uganda, Tanzania and Zaire with a more limited facility for Kenya and Sierra Leone.[53] Her post-1967 international unpopularity served to end these, but the first half of the 1980s has seen a renewed Israeli attempt to seek friends in Africa, the 1979 Camp David agreement having restored her to a measure of international respectability. An Israeli team is reported to be at work again in Zaire. Such evidence as was available in early 1985 suggested a considerable Israeli military involvement in the movement of the Falasha community from Ethiopia to Israel, Israeli covert military aid to Ethiopia, and Israeli Intelligence once again operating in Addis Ababa.

Other states involved in the training field include Australia, which occasionally trains Nigerians; Belgium, for historic reasons, at work in Zaire at present; Canada, which trained Ghanaian, Nigerian and Tanzanian personnel in the 1960s; West Germany, which trains a few African personnel, notably from Gabon, Guinea (from the late 1970s) and Nigeria;[54] India which trained Ghanaians in the 1960s and Nigerians in the 1970s, and is training Botswana personnel at present; Iraq which introduced Zambians to Soviet equipments from 1979; Ireland which trained small numbers of Kenyans and Zambians in the 1960s; Pakistan which has trained Nigerian personnel and is now assisting the Zimbabwe Air Force; Romania, always in need of friends, which assisted training Mozambique cadres in the 1970s; and Spain, at work in Equatorial Guinea in the 1960s. A number of countries, including Bulgaria, China, East Germany, North Korea, the USSR and Yugoslavia, have provided training facilities for Portuguese African and Southern African liberation movements, in a mix of ideological solidarity and hopes for a subsequent advantaged position.

ARMS TRANSFERS

Any brief attempt at an overview of foreign weapon supply meets other difficulties besides that of sheer space.[55] Information is incomplete and not always reliable. The supplying source may

- in non-communist countries - be a private company rather than a state ordnance factory, though government permission to export weapons is nearly always required. Precise sources of Warsaw Pact weaponry may not be clear, but it can be assumed that prior Soviet approval had been secured. Weapons, too, can arrive from sources other than their manufacturer - capture or purchase from a previous owner. Transport aircraft and helicopters, not noted in this chapter, are sometimes acquired in this way.

Some attempt at an overview, however, is necessary as arms supply can constitute a form of intervention, sometimes carrying with it the donor nation's wish to establish an ascendancy over the recipient's defence policy, or conversely, a wish by a donor country to deny such an ascendancy to other donor countries. Quite often though, the provision of arms is seen by the giving (or selling) nation in less dramatic form, little more than the ensuring of a basic political stability within the territory of the recipient. All forms imply that the providing country approves of the recipient's regime, a legitimisation which can on occasions be of the very greatest importance for the recipient. Britain's military transfers to the Federal Nigerian government during the civil war provide a very clear example of such legitimisation. Purely commercial considerations played an increasing role from the mid-1970s.

Table 8.1 may serve to provide the reader with a synoptic view.[56] From this table it is interesting to contrast the limited sales of US equipments in the 1970s, when the USA was in its period of eclipse and self-doubt, with increased sales in the 1980s under the assertive Reagan administration. Similar contrasts apply to the USSR whose world status, as well as that of Brezhnev himself, may well be said to have peaked in the mid-1970s; at the end of the decade the USSR replaced China and Britain respectively as the main source of arms for Tanzania and Zambia. But also by the end of the decade leadership succession problems were already beginning to inhibit Soviet actions. By the 1980s these had worsened, with added to them the issues of Afghanistan, Poland and the West's nuclear reassertion in Western Europe. France can be seen as pursuing an increasingly aggressive weapon sales policy, Nigeria becoming an especial target and one well calculated to please those asserting *la France seule*. West

Table 8.1 : The Supply of Arms by Non-African Countries to Sub-Saharan Africa
(Excluding South Africa)

Country of Origin (a)	Country of Destination (b)	1960s (c)	1970s (d)	1980s (e)	Notes (f)
AUSTRIA	NIGERIA		50 apcs	20 apcs	Light tank assembly plant order under consideration. See Note 3
BELGIUM	BURUNDI	A few anti-tank RLs			
	CAMEROON RWANDA	A few anti-tank RLs	Field howitzers	ATGW	
	ZAIRE	Infantry weapons			
BRAZIL	GABON			16 armoured cars	Also two maritime reconnaissance aircraft
	NIGERIA			100 armoured cars	See Note 3

Foreign Intervention in Africa

(a)	(b)	(c)	(d)	(e)	(f)
BRAZIL (cont)	TOGO				COIN aircraft
	ZIMBABWE			18 Cascavel armoured cars	
CHINA (Peoples Republic)	CAMEROON	Light anti-aircraft guns. Infantry RLs. Light anti-tank guns			
	CONGO		15 medium tanks, 14 light tanks		
	GABON		Automatic weapons		
	GAMBIA		Automatic weapons		
	LIBERIA				
	MADAGASCAR				Unconfirmed
	MALI	30 light tanks	10 light tanks	20 jeeps	
	TANZANIA		30 medium tanks, artillery pieces of various sizes, armoured vehicles	A few light tanks	Also combat aircraft

229

(a)	(b)	(c)	(d)	(e)	(f)
CHINA (cont)	ZAIRE				
	ZIMBABWE		50 (?) light tanks	30 medium tanks	
CUBA	CONGO		35 medium tanks, 37 armoured vehicles, 68 apcs; artillery weapons, artillery RLs, light anti-aircraft guns		Precise source uncertain. Possibly Soviet but Cuba more likely
CZECHO-SLOVAKIA	GUINEA	Infantry weapon			
	UGANDA	30 apcs			
FINLAND	GHANA		20 large mortars		
FRANCE	BENIN	Infantry weapons incl. mortars, a few 105 mm howitzers			

(a)	(b)	(c)	(d)	(e)	(f)
FRANCE (cont)	BURKINA FASO	Infantry weapons, mortars	15 armoured cars, 13 apcs, a few field guns, mortars, infantry RLs		
	BURUNDI			27 armoured cars	
	CAMEROON	Infantry weapons incl. mortars. Field howitzers			
	CAR	Infantry weapons, mortars			
	CHAD	Infantry weapons, mortars	Infantry weapons, mortars, ATGW	Infantry weapons, ATGW	
	CONGO	Infantry weapons (at independence), a few guns			

(a)	(b)	(c)	(d)	(e)	(f)
FRANCE (cont)	DJIBOUTI		10 armoured cars, infantry and artillery mortars, anti-tank guns		
	GABON	Infantry weapons, mortars	15 armoured cars, 12 apcs		More armoured cars and artillery said to be on order. Also Mirage COIN aircraft
	IVORY COAST	Infantry weapons, mortars	5 light tanks, 16 armoured cars, 22 armoured vehicles, 4 howitzers, large mortars, light anti-aircraft guns	7 armoured cars	5 COIN aircraft
	KENYA		60 armoured cars, some apcs		
	MADAGASCAR	Infantry weapons, mortars. Some light artillery pieces			

(a)	(b)	(c)	(d)	(e)	(f)
FRANCE (cont)	MAURITANIA	Infantry weapons, mortars	65 armoured cars, some apcs, mortars, anti-tank RL.		
	NIGER	Infantry weapons, mortars, RLs	36 armoured cars, 14 apcs	10 armoured cars	
	NIGERIA		35-90 armoured cars, some apcs	50 anti-aircraft vehicles	See Note 3
	RWANDA		27 armoured cars, a few light artillery pieces and mortars		
	SENEGAL	Infantry weapons, mortars, RLs	54 armoured cars, apcs	Mortars, ATGW	
	TOGO	Infantry weapons, mortars, RLs	10 armoured cars, 5 apcs		

Foreign Intervention in Africa

(a)	(b)	(c)	(d)	(e)	(f)
FRANCE (cont)	ZAIRE		140 armoured cars, 80 apcs, light field guns		
GERMANY (FRG)	BENIN			30 scout cars. 6 load carriers	
	GHANA		100 armoured cars		
	NIGERIA			Ground to air missile units. See Note 3	COIN aircraft. Frigate
	SIERRA LEONE TANZANIA	Some limited small arms in early 1960s	10 apcs		
	TOGO ZIMBABWE		30-60 apcs	50 apcs A number of apcs	COIN aircraft

(a)	(b)	(c)	(d)	(e)	(f)
GERMANY (GDR)	CAPE VERDE			8 armoured vehicles, a few infantry RLs	Possibly Soviet?
GREAT BRITAIN	BOTSWANA		Infantry weapons, mortars, grenade launchers		
	BURKINA FASO	A few scout cars			
	CAR	A few armoured cars.			
	GAMBIA	Small arms	Small arms	Small arms	
	GHANA	Infantry weapons, incl mortars and RL. A few armoured cars			
	KENYA	Infantry weapons, incl mortars, a few armoured cars	60 medium tanks, 56 guns, 12 armoured cars	ATGW	Anti-aircraft missiles on order. 17 COIN aircraft

Foreign Intervention in Africa

(a)	(b)	(c)	(d)	(e)	(f)
GREAT BRITAIN (cont)	LESOTHO				
	MADAGASCAR	A few scout cars	Infantry weapons		
	MALAWI	Infantry weapons, mortars	12 armoured cars, light field guns.	SAM missiles	
	NIGERIA	Infantry weapons, mortars, field guns, armoured cars	50 light tanks, 70 armoured cars	55 light tanks (a few have Belgian turrets), 35 medium tanks, anti-aircraft missiles	COIN aircraft. See Note 3
	SIERRA LEONE	Infantry weapons, mortars, field guns, armoured cars			
	SWAZILAND				
	TANZANIA	Infantry weapons, mortars	36 light tanks	Small arms	

236

Foreign Intervention in Africa

(a)	(b)	(c)	(d)	(e)	(f)
GREAT BRITAIN (cont)	UGANDA	Infantry weapons, mortars, a few apcs		Infantry weapons	
	ZAMBIA	Infantry weapons, mortars, a few scout cars	Light anti-aircraft missiles		
	ZIMBABWE	(As Rhodesia and before UDI), infantry weapons, mortars, armoured cars, artillery		COIN aircraft	Also before UDI. Bomber and fighter aircraft
ISRAEL	CAR		Automatic weapons		
ITALY	GHANA				
	NIGERIA			25 SP medium guns	12 COIN aircraft in late 1960s See Note 3

(a)	(b)	(c)	(d)	(e)	(f)
ITALY (cont)	SOMALIA			Armoured vehicles	Number unknown
JORDAN	SOMALIA		40 medium tanks (British made)		
KOREA (North)	EQUATORIAL GUINEA			Chinese made infantry RLs	Unconfirmed report
	ZIMBABWE			A few medium tanks and armoured vehicles, 8 field guns, apcs, mortars, SAM-7	For the North Korean trained 5th Brigade
POLAND	ANGOLA ETHIOPIA		Part of the USSR supplies to these two countries emanated from Poland		
SPAIN	EQUATORIAL GUINEA		Infantry small arms		

Foreign Intervention in Africa

(a)	(b)	(c)	(d)	(e)	(f)
SWEDEN	CAMEROON				Light anti-aircraft guns on order
	NIGERIA			30 medium guns	See Note 3
SWITZERLAND	ANGOLA				Pilatus training aircraft on order
	CAMEROON				Light anti-aircraft guns on order
USSR	ANGOLA		100-150 T34 tanks, 120-150 T54 tanks, a few T62 tanks, 50-60 PT 76 and 200 BRDM armoured vehicles, 150 BTR 60 and BTR 152 apcs, 200 artillery pieces, 50 BM 21 artillery RLs, infantry grenade launchers and ATGW, ZSU 23-4 and ZSU	New equipment include machine grenade launchers (Plamya) and SAM-9 missiles	In addition the USSR has supplied in small number combat aircraft as follows : MIG21, MIG17: Angola, MIG17 : Congo, MIG21, MIG17: Ethiopia, MIG21, MIG17: Guinea

239

Foreign Intervention in Africa

(a)	(b)	(c)	(d)	(e)	(f)
USSR (cont)					
	BENIN		57-2 anti-aircraft vehicles, SAM-3, SAM-6, SAM-7. Infantry mortars, automatic weapons		MIG21, MIG19, MIG17 : Mali, MIG21, MIG19, MIG17:Mozambique, MIG21 : Nigeria
			8 BRDM 1, 10 PT 76 armoured vehicles. Infantry weapons, incl mortars, grenade launchers		Bombers, MIG21, MIG17: Somalia, MIG21, MIG17: Tanzania, MIG21, MIG17, MIG15: Uganda
	BOTSWANA		Some infantry automatic weapons. SAM-7. Possibly BTR 60 apcs.		
	BURUNDI		A few mortars and light anti-aircraft guns		
	CAR		Light mortars and anti-tank RLs. Possibly 20 light armoured vehicles		

240

Foreign Intervention in Africa

(a)	(b)	(c)	(d)	(e)	(f)
USSR (cont)	CONGO			Possibly artillery RLs	
	DJIBOUTI			Some apcs	Precise origin obscure. Possibly Libya
	EQUATORIAL GUINEA			10 armoured vehicles, 10 apcs. Infantry grenade launchers	
	ETHIOPIA			From 1975: 500 medium tanks, 200 armoured vehicles, artillery pieces, artillery RLs, anti-aircraft	Some of Czech origin. Others Polish

241

(a)	(b)	(c)	(d)	(e)	(f)
USSR (cont)					
	GUINEA-BISSAU		12 medium tanks, 30 apcs, small number of field guns, RLs, SAM-7	guns. SAM-3, SAM-7, ATGW, infantry weapons	
	GUINEA	45 medium tanks, 35 armoured vehicles, 40-60 apcs, small numbers of artillery pieces and anti-tank guns. Infantry weapons. SAM-7			Some may be Chinese or Czech in origin. New military credits approved late 1984

(a)	(b)	(c)	(d)	(e)	(f)
USSR (cont)	MADAGASCAR		A few armoured vehicles		Origin may not be Soviet
	MALAWI		A few armoured vehicles		
	MALI	45 medium tanks, 40 apcs, light artillery pieces, infantry weapons	20 armoured vehicles, SAM-3	8 apcs	Unconfirmed
	MAURITANIA		A few anti-aircraft guns		
	MOZAMBIQUE		350 medium tanks, 150(?) armoured vehicles, 200 apcs, 200 artillery pieces, artillery RL, ATGW, anti-aircraft guns, SAM-3, SAM-7	Further limited deliveries in 1981	The 1981 deliveries followed South African air attack

Foreign Intervention in Africa

(a)	(b)	(c)	(d)	(e)	(f)
USSR (cont)	NIGERIA		From 1968: 100(?) medium tanks, some 250 field guns, anti-air-craft guns	Anti tank RLs. Air-craft missiles	See Note 3
	SOMALIA		Estimated totals to 1975: 150 medium tanks, 75-100 armoured vehicles, 250 apcs, 200 Soviet artillery pieces, anti-aircraft artillery, SAM-2, SAM-3, mortars, infantry weapons		
	TANZANIA		Armoured vehicles, apcs, artillery pieces numbers not known, SAM-3, SAM-6, SAM-7, mortars, infantry weapons		Although Soviet designs may have been purchased elsewhere–perhaps Czechoslovakia

(a)	(b)	(c)	(d)	(e)	(f)
USSR (cont)	TOGO			2 medium tanks	Probably from Libya
	UGANDA		Small numbers of medium tanks, armoured vehicles, apcs, field guns, anti-aircraft guns, SAM-7, mortars, infantry weapons and RLs		
	ZAIRE		Small numbers of apcs and artillery pieces		Some may be of Chinese origin?
	ZAMBIA		34 medium tanks, over 100 armoured vehicles, 12 apcs, field artillery, artillery RLs, anti-aircraft guns, SAM-7, possibly SAM-3		Deliveries commenced in 1978-79 as a result of Rhodesian air attacks

(a)	(b)	(c)	(d)	(e)	(f)
USSR (cont)	ZIMBABWE		A few medium tanks		These also may be North Korean
UNITED STATES	BOTSWANA			20 light armoured cars	
	BURKINA FASO	A few armoured cars			
	CAMEROON	A few armoured cars and apcs		26 light armoured vehicles	
	ETHIOPIA	To 1975: 35 medium tanks, 90 apcs, artillery weapons, infantry weapons			
	GABON			6 armoured vehicles	

Foreign Intervention in Africa

(a)	(b)	(c)	(d)	(e)	(f)
UNITED STATES (cont)	KENYA				COIN aircraft, anti-tank and assault helicopters (See Note 4)
	LIBERIA	Infantry weapons, light artillery	A few additional light artillery weapons		Mostly obsolete
	MADAGASCAR	A few apcs			
	NIGER	A few armoured vehicles			
	NIGERIA	Infantry weapons		Heavy machine guns	See Note 3
	SENEGAL	A few field guns	Six field guns		
	SOMALIA			Armoured vehicles	Number unknown

247

(a)	(b)	(c)	(d)	(e)	(f)
UNITED STATES (cont.)	TOGO	10 armoured cars	Six field guns		
	ZAIRE	Infantry weapons	10 medium tanks	A number of apcs ordered	
	ZAMBIA		A few medium guns		
YUGOSLAVIA	ETHIOPIA		30 USA built medium tanks		

Notes :

1. Abbreviations : apc   Armoured personnel carrier
                   ATGW   Anti-tank guided weapon
                   COIN   Counter-insurgency aircraft
                   RL   Rocket launcher
                   SAM   Surface-to-air missile
                   SP   Self-propelled

2. In addition, Angola and Mozambique may have some old equipment left by the Portuguese still in service.

3. In the case of Nigeria some orders may have been cancelled or delayed on account of economic problems. The ground-to-air missile units are of a joint Franco-German design and manufacture.

4. Kenya's strategic problems, that of a large area of territory with possible threats on remote borders - those with Somalia, Tanzania and Uganda - led to the nation deciding in favour of a small but rapidly transportable army. Great Britain was unable to offer the credits necessary for the large transport and assault helicopter and aircraft force required by this 'Air Cavalry' strategy. The USA was willing to do so as a complement to its own Rapid Deployment Force requirements.

Germany began sales in the 1960s to counter threats of sales by East Germany and generally in order to assist Western strategic interests; her concerns are now almost entirely commercial.

Sometimes arms transfers are linked to specific political conditions, but generally African states have been able to exercise some preference against such conditions. One indicator of this is the way donor countries have had on occasions to be content with access, in emergency, to recipient country facilities rather than permanent installations. Recipient countries, too, can and do play possible donors off against each other, magnify domestic or international political situations to obtain better terms, or encourage massive military investment almost as an economic hostage. Leverage can operate in both directions.

CONCLUSIONS

A bouquet then of both flowers and weeds. What string binds them? Few paradigms, even if desirable, are possible. One can suggest interventions 'regime supportive' and 'regime destructive', but a foreign intervening country can rapidly change roles. More usefully, perhaps, one may remark upon the roots, sometimes long, of foreign intervention and action as all lying in the domestic histories of the intervening powers. France's policies have been a facet of her quest for *gloire*, a quest made necessary as a unifying factor after colonial defeats as well as revolutionary social divisions of two hundred years ago. The Soviet government, whose two major concerns are the problems caused by the straightjacket of an obsolete ideology and by ethnic micronationalism, with great emphasis parades successes in Angola and Ethiopia as the triumphs of Leninism. In the later 1980s and in the 1990s a more aggressive policy is likely, as at home the Soviet Union overcomes its generation-change leadership problem but faces mounting and frustrating domestic issues, and the mineral economic attractions of Southern Africa prove even more attractive.[57] Cuba is faced with unemployment, which it resolved in part by retaining a large army, but the army has to have a role; Cuba also desperately needs economic aid from its Soviet patron. The GDR has been in chronic need of international recognition. Britain with, apart from the 1967-70 Nigerian issue, only limited domestic political interests or constraints upon policies towards former black African colonies, is able to pursue policies of enlightened self-interest. The United States, caught between historic isolationist and anti-colonial attitudes precluding overt intervention on the one hand and the problems of ideological conflict nevertheless perceived as calling for some action on the other, exhibits a marked preference for covert activities, sometimes 'overtly covert'. Israel and North Korea, both faced with - very different - problems of acceptability on the world stage pursue forward policies. Chinese interventions tended to reflect both Mao's unrealistic political philosophies and the Sino-Soviet split. Success attends, to quote a nineteenth century American admiral, 'who gets there fustest with the mostest' - the philosophy of any intervention force. The remaining nations, those simply concerned with the sale of weaponry, reflect domestic pre-occupations of arms industry viability and employment. Albeit somewhat improbably, then, an historical survey of foreign intervention in black Africa produces a striking reinforcement of Maitland's 'seamless web' view of history.

NOTES

This chapter is primarily concerned with military interventions into the affairs of sub-Saharan African states by countries not forming part of the African continent. Military actions by interventionist African nations (South Africa, Libya, Tanzania and others) are not therefore covered. Nor, primarily for reasons of space, can the UN military intervention in the Congo (Zaire) or in Cameroon be included.

1. *Coopération* as a concept, replaced the earlier 1958 *Communauté* project. This latter had envisaged France retaining total control of African states' defence policies.
2. When in October 1916 the elite *Régiment d'Infanterie Coloniale de Maroc* fought its way to the recapture of the symbolic Fort Douamont at Verdun, it was in fact composed of two battalions of white Frenchmen, one battalion of *Tirailleurs Sénégalais* and two companies of Somalis. There is a continuity of military thinking to be seen here.
3. It should be noted that the *Troupes de Marine*, with their autonomy preserved

by Parliamentary legislation, equate more to the United States Marine Corps than the British Royal Marines, for whom the French equivalent are the *Fusiliers Marins*.

4. The original 1963 intervention force had been a brigade, entirely of *Troupes de Marine*; the brigade was quickly expanded in 1964 to form the 11th *Division d'Intervention*. This in 1971 became the 11th Parachute Division from which in 1976 the Marine units were excised to form a second intervention formation.

5. The *Troupes de Marine* comprise four motorised infantry regiments, a mechanised infantry regiment (Leclerc's famous *Régiment de Marche de Tchad*), an armoured reconnaissance regiment (the RICM, the *Régiment Infanterie - Chars de Marine*, formerly the *Régiment d'Infanterie Coloniale de Maroc*, the French Army's most decorated unit), four parachute units, five artillery regiments and a small number of additional batteries; seven *Inter-Armes* regiments and two additional battalions, five regiments of *Service Militaire Adapté* tasked with minor development work in France's overseas departments in the Antilles, and a number of miscellaneous logistic units. Of the 33,800, 21,500 are regulars, and 12,300 conscripts. Some units are mixed in with France's garrisons in Germany or France itself; a number are permanently posted overseas. One *Inter-Armes* Regiment is in Djibouti. The bulk, however, are available for intervention commitments.

The *Légion*, at the time of writing, comprises the 1st, 2nd and 4th *Régiments Etrangers d'Infanterie* (REI) and the 2nd *Régiment Etranger de Parachutists* (REP) all stationed in France; the 3rd REI (the *Régiment de Marche de la Légion Etrangère*, second only to the RICM in honours) in French Guiana, the 13th *Demi-Brigade* (with traditions of Bir Hakeim, Italy and the Liberation together with most of the 1st *Régiment Etranger de Cavalerie* in Djibouti, the 5th *Régiment Mixte du Pacifique* stationed and partly recruited in the Pacific, and the small *Detachement de Légion Etrangère de Mayotte*.

In this footnote the names of regiments have been specifically included to illustrate the powerful symbolism Africa still holds for France and her army. Edith Piaff's song *Je ne regrette rien* was adopted by the *Légion*; at the end of ceremonial parades the *Troupes de Marine* still dismiss with a mass shout *Au nom de Dieu, vive la Coloniale*.

6. Pierre Lellouche and Dominique Moisi in an article entitled 'French Policy in Africa',

International Security 3, 4 (October 1979), pp. 108-133. The authors draw on a statement by the French Minister for Information, Peyrefitte, that appeared in Le Monde on 28 February 1964.
Formal Treaty obligations figured little in French calculations, there being no intervention agreement with Cameroon.

7. See Higgott, R. and Fuglestad, F., 'The 1974 Coup d'Etat in Niger', Journal of Modern African Studies, 13, 3 (September 1975), pp. 383-98.

8. The account of events in Chad that follows is a shortened version of the author's entry in respect of Chad in Keegan, J. (ed.), World Armies (London: Macmillan, 1983), pp. 102-03.

9. Chad focused increasing unease in France over the nation's African policies, seen by right-wing critics who favoured European and nuclear roles for France as 'Gendarmisme', and by left-wing critics as 'Otanisation'.

10. The force included also contingents from Senegal and Zaire. Britain provided some financial help for the Nigerian contingent, and France and the USA transported the Senegal and Zaire contingents respectively.

11. Other countries with no love for Libya, notably Egypt and Sudan also offered Habre facilities, equipment and assistance.

12. The Guardian (London), 20 November 1984. Article written by Paul Webster 'In Africa, all the President's men'.

13. In detail the 1960 agreements provided for both technical assistance and French intervention in the cases of Senegal, Mauritania, Togo, Ivory Coast, Dahomey, the Central African Republic, Chad, Gabon, Congo-Brazzaville and Madagascar, and for French military intervention if both France and the host country agreed. Togo and Dahomey qualified any direct intervention by France, and Upper Volta limited French military rights to access and transit facilities. All the former French colonies signed military technical assistance agreements except Guinea, though Mali ended her agreement a little after independence.

14. It is perhaps worth noting that the commander of the *Marine* unit in Dakar at the time of writing in 1985 is a black French *Marine* parachute officer from the Antilles.

15. Full details of the sources of equipment and training arrangements of the armies of African states appear in the various national entries

in Keegan, World Armies.

16. Yet one more ingredient, even more difficult to quantify, was the 'Catholic dimension'. Iboland had traditionally possessed a number of Roman Catholic missions, including a number of French Canadian and Irish priests.

17. It should, however, be noted that the operation also suited Moroccan policy aims, their conflict with the POLISARIO movement rendering them willing to oppose any Marxist movement in Africa.

18. If allegations of SDECE involvement are correct, the attempt to overthrow the government of Benin in 1977 would represent a French failure in a parallel covert operation. There may also have been French covert support for an unsuccessful attempt to overthrow Mobutu in 1977. Allegations have also been made that only Soviet naval intelligence warning precluded French covert support for a coup in the Seychelles in late 1979.

19. Access strategy for non-military resources may in fact have implications for Soviet military strategies. While it is impossible to quantify or assess, it is reasonable to claim that, for example, Soviet fishing interests in the Southern Atlantic (45 per cent of the world's total catch of 1.5m tons in the early 1980s) must have a voice in Soviet Southern African policies and strategies; one may surmise the voice to be advising against any rocking of the fishing boat.

20. Debate, probably fierce, undoubtedly takes place in the Soviet Union on foreign policy formulation - but behind closed doors. A useful summary of Soviet ideological thinking and its development appears in Gorman, R.F., 'Soviet Perspectives on the Prospects for Socialist Development in Africa', African Affairs, 83, 331 (April 1984), pp. 163-87.

21. Nevertheless one of the most interesting essays in attempting to analyse Soviet policy into some form of pattern appears in Brayton, A.A., 'Soviet Involvement in Africa', Journal of Modern African Studies, 18, 2 (June 1979), pp. 253-69. Brayton suggests penetrations based on:

(1) Colonial Penetrations, where the USSR has assisted liberation movements; (2) Leverage states, where the Soviets have filled a gap abruptly left by an outgoing colonial power or regime; and (3) Targeted states of unstable poverty areas.

22. In return, the Soviets were permitted

to begin construction of a large military airfield for their own use at Tamale, in northern Ghana. The Soviets were withdrawn after the 1966 coup.

23. The Soviet Union's Middle Eastern policies necessitated support for the side that included the Moslem North in the Nigerian conflict, despite that side's linkages to the West.

24. The facilities included use of the airfields at Uanle Uen, Hargeisa and Galcao, with radar and/or maritime reconnaissance facilities at Agfoi and Birikao.

25. It is useful to recall that defence of full socialist countries is one of the Soviet Union's official criteria for a just war, such a war being mandatory. Preserving gains of socialism against counter-revolutionary threats, although correct, is not seen as mandatory however, and the amount of force committed may be discretionary.

26. Both Cuba and the GDR had their own motives. Cuba seeks prestige, a hegemony role among American hemisphere liberation movements. The GDR, despite UN membership, still seeks to assert its own personality in world affairs, and also welcomes Soviet economic favours.

27. The facility has now been closed down, following the fall of Macias Nguema.

28. Janes Defence Weekly, 8 December 1984, p. 1018 estimates just over 30,000 Cuban military personnel in Angola, the contingent comprising sixteen motor rifle regiments, an anti-aircraft brigade, a medium artillery regiment and logistic, air force and training cadres.

29. The Times, 19 December 1984.

30. Janes Defence Weekly, 8 December 1984, p. 1019. A small reduction of some 2,000 was effected in 1984. The Cuban units are stationed in the Harar and Diredawa areas.

31. These facilities include a major air, naval and missile installation on Dahlak Island, near Massawa.

32. There is a possibility that the Soviet Union has received some concession from Tanzania also; it is however reported that Soviet requests for naval facilities in Cape Verde and Guinea-Bissau have been rejected.

33. Karume's Zanzibar also drew briefly on the services of Chinese and Cuban security personnel.

34. See, for example, David, S.R., 'Third World Interventions', Problems in Communism, 32 (May-June 1984), pp. 68-69.

35. Laurance, E.J., 'Soviet Arms Transfers in the 1980s', in Arlinghaus, B.E. (ed.), Arms for Africa (Lexington, Mass.: Lexington Books, 1982). This curious information is provided on p. 67. Kaunda is seen by Moscow as 'of socialist orientation' and therefore to be secured.

36. The usually reliable Janes Defence Weekly of 8 December 1984, for example, published South African military intelligence claims of large Cuban missions in Guinea, Guinea-Bissau, Congo-Brazzaville, Madagascar, Mozambique, Nigeria, Sao Tomé, Sierra Leone, Uganda and Zambia, with smaller teams in Benin, Cape Verde, Lesotho and Tanzania.

Such a report cannot be entirely discounted. Countries with Soviet equipment may very well prefer Cubans to either East Germans or Russians, the latter being additionally unpopular on personal grounds.

37. A commonly held US view also argues that while communist countries may briefly gain ascendancy and advantages in individual territories, the Soviets and their allies will sooner or later be ejected. Egypt, Somalia and Guinea are cited as examples.

38. Lemarchand, R., 'The C.I.A. in Africa', Journal of Modern African Studies, 14, 3 (September 1976), pp. 401-26. It should be noted that Lemarchand was Professor of Political Science at the University of Florida.

39. Tshombe, according to Lemarchand, was to be returned to Zaire for trial as a boost to the Mobutu regime, a project paradoxically including the blaming of the CIA. The project misfired as the Algerians refused to release him and Mobutu became more overtly dependent on the CIA after the coup attempt by unpaid mercenaries a little later.

Mobutu's accusations against the CIA in 1975 were, according to Lemarchand, again a double bluff, to conceal his continuing dependence.

40. An example of blame heaped upon the CIA for an alleged conspiracy - to overthrow the revolutionary government in Zanzibar in 1964 - appears in this author's The Zanzibar Revolution and its Aftermath, (London: Hurst, 1981), pp. 148-49. There was no conspiracy; but the allegation, almost certainly fostered by GDR intelligence personnel, had disastrous implications for US relations with Tanzania.

41. A figure of $US275 million of military

assistance to Ethiopia from 1952 to 1976 appears in Keegan, World Armies, pp. 178-79.

42. The RDJTF is to comprise the 101st Air Assault, 82nd Airborne and 24th Infantry Divisions, the 6th (Army) and 7th (Marine) Brigades, together with massive naval and air support centring around three naval carrier and one surface action groups and five fighter wings.

43. In practice Kenya had provided these facilities for some considerable time previous to the agreement.

44. For an overall view of the British military legacy and post-independence policies, see this author's chapter 'The Military Relations between Great Britain and Commonwealth Countries, with particular reference to the African Commonwealth Countries' in Morris-Jones, W.H. and Fischer, G., Decolonisation and After, The British and French Experience (London: Cass, 1980), p. viii.

45. HMS *Rhyl's* very presence, however, did have the effect within the Zanzibar Revolutionary Council of strengthening the position of Abeid Karume against the genocidal 'Field Marshal' John Okelo. See this author's Zanzibar Revolution, pp. 86-90.

46. The intense criticism of the British government's pro-Lagos policy imposed certain constraints on the Wilson government. The Foreign Office found itself limited to supplying only the weapons that it had supplied before the war began rather than more powerful and destructive ones; it was not however constrained in the quantities. The result was what the Nigerians most needed, a steady supply of small arms and ammunition. See St John Jorré, J., The Nigerian Civil War (London: Hodder and Stoughton, 1972), pp. 297-98.

47. The basis of the arrangements is the need to provide varied training to retain the services of volunteer recruits in a non-conscript army, the retention of tropical experience on the British side, and the chance to earn hard currency on the part of the host government.

48. Despite the ideological difference and the breach in diplomatic relations, Tanzania still sent cadets to Sandhurst until 1967.

49. Kenya first appointed a Kenyan as army commander only in 1969. Zambia was not able to appoint a Zambian as a battalion commander until 1970. The Malawi Army retained a British commander until 1972. Sometimes, for example the case of

Nigeria which retained a British general as army commander until 1965, local ethnic jealousies led governments to prefer a British officer.

50. Other supporters (in a very limited form only) of this cause included China and Israel.

51. Major R. Alers-Hankey, interview with the author, January 1972. Major Alers-Hankey was the last British officer serving with the Ghana Army.

52. Nadelmann, E.A., 'Israel and Black Africa: A Rapprochement?' Journal of Modern African Studies, 19, 2 (June 1981), pp. 194, 203. The relationship with Ethiopia extended to small bases on two Ethiopian islands in the Babel Mandeb straits, (p. 215).

53. Jacob. A., 'Israel's Military Aid to Africa', Journal of Modern African Studies, 9, 2 (June 1971), pp. 165-87, asserts that direct military aid was also provided to Ghana and Upper Volta, aid for police work to Dahomey and Madagascar and para-military training aid for national (youth) service schemes to Cameroon, Central African Republic, Chad, Congo-Kinshasa, Dahomey, Gabon, Ghana, Ivory Coast, Kenya, Liberia, Malawi, Niger, Senegal, Tanzania, Upper Volta and Zambia in this period.

54. West Germany, curiously matching the GDR in this respect, has also assisted several African states with police training, notably Somalia, Niger and (pre-1974) Ethiopia.

55. A useful guide to the literature appears in a commendable overview, Arlinghaus, Arms for Africa. This otherwise excellent work is marred by the absence of any analysis of British assistance policies and arms sales, and virtually no mention of the specialised activities of North Korea.

56. This table is compiled from entries in Keegan, World Armies; those entries themselves are based on material published in issues of Afrique Defense, Africa Confidential, and the International Institute of Strategic Studies annual, The Military Balance (London: IISS); together with other information available for contributors.

57. At present the USSR has no forces specifically trained or earmarked for Third World intervention - as the difficulties experienced in the 1979-80 Afghanistan operation revealed. Soviet forces do, however, have a capacity to lift five, perhaps six divisions, together with a massive (and expanding) naval assault landing capability. The Angolan and Ethiopian commitments strikingly illustrate Soviet military logistic capabilities.

Chapter Nine

ARMS CONTROL IN AFRICA

Abbott A. Brayton

INTRODUCTION

Emerging regions composed of newly-sovereign nations historically have experienced high levels of international violence. Consequently, they expand their security systems substantially, often provoking arms races and new wars.
   Africa is more than an emerging region - it is an emerging continent composed of one-third of the world's sovereign states, almost all of which have attained independence within the past generation. Independence has brought new armaments to Africa: the US Arms Control and Disarmament Agency reported that military expenditures among African countries rose 154 per cent in the decade 1969-78. To the inexperienced observer it appears that the African peoples have descended into a Hobbesian abyss, and that misguided governments are squandering their national resources on armaments rather than on programmes for human development.
   Research suggests otherwise: there are heartening signs amid disheartening news. Empirical evidence indicates that *most* African countries are engaged neither in conflict with neighbouring states, nor in an arms race; indeed, there emerges, for whatever reason, a pattern of military restraint. This is not to deny the presence of conflict in Africa. Fifty-three sovereign and semi-sovereign newly-emerging states are not likely to coexist without contention (as Hughes and May indicate in their chapter), and this compounded by extraordinary border problems, the legacy of a century of conflict and compromise among the colonial powers. Rather, it is suggested here that while some African states may be squandering

some national resources on armaments, many are not.

There must be reasons why many African states, newly emerging into an imperfect, often hostile world, renounce large security systems. It appears that some form of arms limitation is functioning among many African states and that rapid growth of armaments is confined to a few countries.

TRENDS IN AFRICAN ARMAMENTS

African nations since independence of course have expanded their armed forces, from the small local security forces appended to the colonial regimes into independent national security forces. Not surprisingly, this causes an increase in armaments. Much of the misperception about the magnitude of African armaments, however, is caused by ignoring or distorting statistical data.

Several reliable data sources on African armaments aid the researcher, including the *United Nations Statistical Yearbook,* the publications of the International Institute for Strategic Studies, the Stockholm International Peace Research Institute, and the US Arms Control and Disarmament Agency. Ruth Leger Sivard's *World Military and Social Expenditures, 1983,* is especially useful because of its reliability and comprehensiveness. It portrays a pattern of armaments activity since 1960 - the year generally regarded as the independence year, since more African states gained independence at that time than in any other year. Thus, for many, 1960 symbolises the end of colonialism in Africa and the beginning of nationhood.

There is a need for caution, however, when examining statistical data for this period. Tables 9.1 and 9.2, adapted from Sivard's compilation, reveal an apparently dramatic growth in the level of military activity among 'developing' countries, including Africa. Whereas the gross national products (GNPs) of 'developing' countries rose a very respectable 223 per cent in constant (non-inflationary) dollars from 1960 to 1979, military expenditures (MILEX) during the same period rose 300 per cent. This is in contrast to the 70 per cent increase among the developed countries. The knowledgeable observer, however, will recall that many new countries for the first time established armed forces during this period. The military growth from little or nothing for a new nation

Table 9.1: World Socio-Economic Trends, 1960-1979*

	Population (millions)			GNP (constant $billions)			GNP/Per Capita (constant $)			Foreign Economic Aid (constant $billions)		
	1960	1979	Percent Increase	1960	1979	Percent Increase	1960	1979	Percent Increase	1960	1979	Percent Increase
World	3,047	4,389	31	3,831	9,770	122	1,260	2,230	57	5.2	30.4	485
Developed Countries	879	1,045	16	3,148	7,573	141	3,581	7,246	102	5.0	24.2	384
Developing Countries	2,168	3,344	35	681	2,197	223	316	658	108	.2	6.2	3000

* All dollar figures are in 1979 US constant dollars
Source: Adapted by the author from data supplied by Sivard, R.L., *World Military and Social Expenditures, 1981* (Leesburg, VA: WSME Publications, 1981), p. 24.

Table 9.2: World Military Trends, 1960-1979*

	Military Expenditures (constant $billions)			Armed Forces (thousands of men)			Arms Exports (constant $billions)			Arms Imports (constant $billions)		
	1960	1979	Percent Increase	1960	1979	Percent Increase	1960	1979	Percent Increase	1960	1979	Percent Increase
World	259	432	60	18,550	24,435	76	2.4**	23.7	888	2.4**	23.7	888
Developed Countries	235	336	70	9,851	9,501	(-4)	2.3**	22.6	883	1.3**	5.3	308
Developing Countries	24	96	300	8,699	14,934	58	.1**	1.1	1000	1.1**	18.4	1573

* All dollar figures are in 1978 US constant dollars

** Figures are for 1961

Source: Adapted by the author from data supplied by Sivard, R.L., *World Military and Social Expenditures, 1981* (Leesburg, VA: WSME Publications, 1981), p. 24.

in 1960 to a very modest armed force thereafter statistically would produce a large percentile increase. In contrast, the large military budgets of the developed countries became significantly larger during this period, yet the percentile increase appeared to be more modest. Thus, percentile figures alone may be misleading.

The same is true with arms sales. The African countries, like other 'developing' countries, do not possess major armaments industries, and therefore must purchase arms abroad. As no significant purchases were recorded before independence, any subsequent purchase would cause a dramatic percentile increase in arms imports (Table 9.2). The developed countries, continuing to trade voluminously in armaments, present a more modest, but deceptive percentile increase.

The African countries, even more than other new states (Tables 9.2 and 9.3), increased the size of their armed forces somewhat above the rate of population growth, again not an alarming statistic when one recalls that these often are new countries establishing armed forces for the first time. In contrast, the developed countries decreased in both the comparative and the actual size of their armed forces, this trend being driven primarily by international political developments in the United States, Western Europe and the Pacific. It is regrettable that much of the impressive growth in the size of the GNPs among the 'developing' countries during this period was eroded by population growth.

While actual military expenditures have increased throughout the world (Table 9.2), comparative military expenditures (MILEX/GNP) and comparative manpower levels have decreased. The 19 per cent decrease in world MILEX/GNP is due primarily to the sharp constant dollar growth (69 per cent) of the world GNP, 1969-1978, which outpaced the actual increase (17 per cent) of the world MILEX. Similarly, a 31 per cent world population growth rather than an actual decline in military manpower levels accounts for the 11 per cent decrease in the world armed forces per 1000 people. Yet, even for the 'developing' countries, the four per cent increase in armed forces per 1000 people fell behind the 18 per cent population increase, a moderately bright note.[1] It is evident from Table 9.3 that the sharpest increases in spending have occurred in the OPEC and Middle East countries, followed by

Table 9.3: Regional Military Expenditures (MILEX): 1977 Actual Figures (and percentile increase, 1969-78*)

Region	a. MILEX (in billions of constant US $**)	b. MILEX/GNP (%)	c. MILEX/Capita (in 1974 constant US $)	d. Armed Forces/ 1000 People
World Total	446.7 (17%)	5.4 (-19%)	107 (-4%)	6.2 (-11%)
Developed Countries	344.7 (8%)	5.3 (-2%)	324 (0%)	10.1 (-16%)
Developing Countries	102.0 (62%)	5.50 (-8%)	31 (29%)	4.9 (4%)
North America	105.0 (-23%)	4.8 (-41%)	435 (-27%)	9.0 (-43%)
Europe	238.9 (29%)	6.5 (-5%)	304 (17%)	12.4 (-4%)
Latin America	6.9 (53%)	1.6 (-6%)	20 (25%)	4.4 (-7%)
OPEC Countries	27.9 (171%)	7.9 (32%)	87 (112%)	3.9 (-5%)
Oceana	3.0 (-3%)	2.5 (31%)	142 (-31%)	4.2 (-33%)

Table 9.3 (cont'd)

Region	a. MILEX (in billions of constant US $**)	b. MILEX/GNP (%)	c. MILEX/Capita (in 1974 constant US $)	d. Armed Forces/ 1000 People
East Asia	51.6 (37%)	3.9 (-24%)	33 (14%)	5.4 (-2%)
South Asia	4.5 (50%)	3.3 (0%)	5 (20%)	11.9 (27%)
Middle East	30.3 (203%)	13.4 (37%)	245 (138%)	2.4 (-8%)
Africa	6.6 (43%)	3.1 (6%)	6 (7%)	3.3 (43%)

* Figures in parentheses are percentile increase/decrease, 1969-78
** Percentile increase are based on 1977 constant dollars

Source: US Arms Control and Disarmament Agency, *World Military Expenditures and Arms Transfers, 1969-1978* (Washington, D.C.: December 1980), pp. 33-37, as revised by the author.

Latin America and South Asia, then Africa. The East Asian and Pacific countries have increased their miliary forces at the smallest rates, even decreased in some categories, a reflection of declining hostilities in the Southeast Asian region during the 1970s, after decades of conflict. For Africa the MILEX increased 43 per cent, well below the GNP constant dollar growth of 66 per cent.[2] In actual figures, however, the African countries remain at or near the lowest levels in all armaments categories. The percentile figures thus may appear to be more alarming than they really are. To verify this, the statistics must be broken down by country.

A summary of the 46 African countries for which comprehensive data is available through 1978 (Table 9.4), reveals 21 countries with no growth or actual declines in one or more columns. Deleting three of these (Gabon, Libya, and Zaire) as statistical aberrations (significant military growth was outpaced by GNP expansion) and adding seven countries with such insignificant military forces that they are not listed in the table, leaves 21 African countries out of a total of 53 (approximately one-half) whose military systems in 1978 remained approximately at or below levels of the decade earlier: Algeria, Cameroon, Central African Republic, Cape Verde, Chad, Comoro Islands, Egypt, Ghana, Guinea-Bissau, Kenya, Lesotho, Liberia, Maldive Islands, Mauritius, Niger, Nigeria, Réunion, Rwanda, Sao Tomé, Senegal, Seychelles, Sierra Leone, Swaziland, Tunisia and Uganda.

The remaining 28 countries which have increased their military systems, some of them quite modestly, reflect the internal conflicts, civil and border wars which have characterised African politics during the past decade. Significantly, however, these countries maintain military forces well below both the world average and the 'developing' countries average. In the relative size of the armed forces (Table 9.4, fourth column), only nine countries (Angola, Congo-Brazzaville, Egypt, Equatorial Guinea, Ethiopia, Gabon, Libya, Mauritania, and Somalia) exceeded the world average of 6.2 soldiers per 1000 population while only one other (Morocco) exceeds the average of all developing countries (4.9). It is significant that seven of the nine countries often are perceived to have served as Soviet client states, with close military ties to the Soviet Union and Soviet support for expansion of their military system. The remain-

Table 9.4: African Military Expenditures (MILEX): 1977 Actual Figures (and percentile increase, 1969-78)

African Countries	MILEX (in millions of constant US $)	MILEX/GNP (%)	MILEX/CAPITA (in constant US $)	Armed Forces/ 1000 people
Algeria	401.00 (48%)	2.0 (-9%)	22 (10%)	4.3 (-28%)
Angola	*	*	*	7.3 (4%)
Benin	12.00 (71%)	2.0 (18%)	3 (1%)	1.2 (50%)
Botswana (1974-78)	*	*	*	4.3 (21%)
Burundi	12.00 (140%)	2.2 (47%)	3 (200%)	2.0 (233%)
Cameroon	51.00 (34%)	1.6 (-20%)	6 (20%)	1.4 (14%)
CAR	9.00 (-10%)	2.2 (-29%)	4 (-20%)	1.8 (6%)
Chad	18.00 (0%)	3.4 (-11%)	4 (-20%)	2.1 (50%)
Congo-Brazzaville	39.00 (86%)	5.2 (37%)	26 (100%)	7.3 (193%)
Egypt	1,261.00 (78%)	8.5 (-11%)	31 (48%)	8.8 (23%)
Equatorial Guinea (1969-76)	* (0%)	4.6 (-12%)	15 (-34%)	10.0 (203%)
Ethiopia	94.00 (47%)	2.8 (8%)	3 (50%)	7.5 (316%)
Gabon	8.00 (38%)	0.5 (-67%)	13 (-50%)	6.7 (235%)
Gambia (1975-78)	* (0%)	* (0%)	* (0%)	1.3 (19%)
Ghana	64.00 (-80%)	0.4 (-85%)	5 (-86%)	1.7 (-56%)
Guinea-Bissau	*	*	*	*
Guinea	20.00 (-20%)	2.3 (-36%)	4 (33%)	3.5 (52%)

Table 9.4 (cont'd)

African Countries	MILEX (in millions of constant US $)	MILEX/GNP (%)	MILEX/CAPITA (in constant US $)	Armed Forces/ 1000 people
(1969-75)				
Ivory Coast	141.00 (220%)	2.2 (83%)	18 (125%)	1.1 (10%)
Kenya	72.00 (140%)	1.6 (45%)	4 (100%)	0.9 (50%)
Lesotho	* (0%)	* (0%)	* (0%)	0.8 (0%)
(1974-78)				
Liberia	9.00 (50%)	1.1 (-21%)	5 (0%)	4.1 (74%)
Libya	436.00 (47%)	2.4 (26%)	156 (0%)	17.9 (36%)
Madagascar	49.00 (88%)	2.8 (75%)	6 (50%)	2.5 (79%)
Malawi	18.00 (800%)	2.1 (32%)	3 (200%)	0.9 (18%)
(1974-78)				
Mali	23.00 (130%)	3.5 (59%)	3 (50%)	1.3 (7%)
Mauritania	27.00 (440%)	7.1 (344%)	19 (375%)	8.6 (244%)
Mauritius	1.00 (0%)	0.1 (0%)	1 (0%)	0.4 (*)
Morocco	421.00 (148%)	3.7 (42%)	21 (100%)	5.8 (29%)
Mozambique	*	*	*	*
Niger	7.00 (0%)	0.8 (-20%)	1 (0%)	0.8 (-20%)
Nigeria	1,742.00 (-77%)	4.2 (-57%)	24 (-29%)	2.8 (-40%)
Rwanda	13.00 (30%)	1.6 (-16%)	2 (0%)	0.8 (-27%)
Senegal	35.00 (17%)	2.2 (5%)	6 (-14%)	2.4 (50%)
Sierra Leone	6.00 (50%)	1.0 (3%)	2 (100%)	0.3 (-80%)

Table 9.4 (cont'd)

African Countries	MILEX (in millions of constant US $)	MILEX/GNP (%)	MILEX/CAPITA (in constant US $)	Armed Forces/ 1000 people
Somalia	60.00 (233%)	13.8 (171%)	17 (183%)	15.9 (137%)
South Africa	1,618.00 (110%)	4.2 (56%)	59 (67%)	2.9 (16%)
Sudan	217.00 (92%)	4.0 (54%)	12 (50%)	4.0 (138%)
Swaziland (1974-78)	4.00 (300%)	1.4 (57%)	8 (166%)	4.0 (100%)
Tanzania	148.00 (604%)	4.2 (367%)	8 (700%)	3.8 (216%)
Togo	20.00 (300%)	2.8 (155%)	8 (300%)	2.0 (233%)
Tunisia	88.00 (166%)	1.6 (-23%)	14 (130%)	3.2 (-36%)
Uganda	124.00 (85%)	3.1 (63%)	9 (3%)	0.5 (-71%)
Upper Volta	21.00 (250%)	3.4 (183%)	3 (200%)	0.9 (3%)
Zaire	30.00 (-79%)	0.7 (-79%)	1 (-83%)	1.9 (-10%)
Zambia	71.00 (273%)	3.1 (210%)	13 (225%)	3.6 (25%)
Zimbabwe	203.00 (463%)	6.8 (325%)	28 (367%)	3.4 (70%)
Africa Average	6.6 (43%)	3.1 (6%)	6 (7%)	3.3 (43%)
Developing Countries' Average	102.0 (62%)	5.5 (-8%)	31 (29%)	4.9 (4%)
World Average	446.7 (17%)	5.4 (-19%)	107 (-4%)	6.2 (-11%)

Table 9.4 (cont'd)

* Data reflects inconsistencies or inadequacies and is thus unreliable.
** Percentile increases are based on 1977 constant dollars.

Source : US Arms Control and Disarmament Agency, *World Military Expenditures and Arms Transfers, 1969-1978* (Washington, D.C.: December, 1980), pp. 33-116, as revised by the author.

ing two (Gabon and Mauritania) reflect statistical distortions due to the small size of their populations. (The magnitude of Soviet involvement in the African arms trade is clearly demonstrated in Table 9.7). In the category of MILEX/GNP (second column), all but four African countries (Egypt, Mauritania, Somalia, and Zimbabwe) are below the averages of both the world and of 'developing' countries; each of those four recently have been engaged in serious conflict.

Looking at the armed forces of African states somewhat differently, here in terms of raw material power as measured by manpower and equipment, 23 countries have accomplished significant (over 50 per cent) growth in the size of their forces during the decade of 1969-1979: Algeria, Angola, Burundi, Chad, Congo-Brazzaville, Egypt, Ethiopia, Guinea, Kenya, Libya, Madagascar, Malawi, Mauritania, Morocco, Somalia, South Africa, Sudan, Tanzania, Togo, Uganda, Upper Volta (now Burkina Faso), Zambia, and Zimbabwe.[3] In perspective, eight of these countries now have armed forces totalling less than 10,000 men.

Only a handful of African countries have armed forces which presently possess even modest cross-border capabilities (Table 9.5): significant forces could be moved into neighbouring countries to conduct military operations with a logistical support system. These forces, which would be considered significant by international standards, are limited to South Africa, Ethiopia, Nigeria, Somalia, and the North African states. Because of the relative size of these few states (population, military, and economic power), they distort the averages of all African states. Concomitantly, the size of military expenditure as a percentage either of GNP or of governmental expenditures has been rising at the greatest rate among these more heavily armed African states in recent years.[4]

It is these same countries which are the primary importers of armaments into Africa (Tables 9.6 and 9.7). Egypt alone imported almost half of the US $5,928 million in arms transferred to Africa between 1965 and 1974. Nigeria, South Africa, and the Arab states of North Africa, a total of eight countries, imported US $5,001 million in armaments in the same period, almost 85 per cent of the total. Six other states imported three-fourths of the balance. Thus, one-fourth of all African states imported 95 per cent of all armaments in the decade from 1965 to 1974.

Table 9.5: Size of African Armed Forces, 1983

Under 5,000	5,000–10,000	10,000–25,000	25,000–50,000	50,000–100,000	Over 100,000
Benin	Burundi	Ghana	Angola	Libya	Algeria
Botswana	Cameroon	Kenya	Tanzania	Somalia	Egypt
Cape Verde	Congo-Brazzaville	Madagascar	Tunisia	South Africa	Ethiopia
CAR	Guinea	Mozambique	Zimbabwe	Sudan	Morocco
Chad	Guinea-Bissau	Uganda			Nigeria
Comoros	Ivory Coast	Zaire			
Djibouti	Liberia	Zambia			
Eq. Guinea	Mauritania				
Gabon	Rwanda				
Lesotho	Senegambia				
Malawi					
Mali					
Mauritius					
Niger					
Sao Tomé					
Seychelles					
Sierra Leone					
Swaziland					
Togo					
Upper Volta					

Table 9.5 (cont'd)

Note : Does not include reserves, paramilitary, or police gendarmeries.

Source : International Institute for Strategic Studies, *The Military Balance, 1983-84* (London: IISS, 1983), pp. 66-81. Those countries not listed are placed in the 'Under 1,000' column.

Table 9.6: Arms Transfers to African States, 1974-78

Primary Recipients

$10-50 Millions	$50-100 Millions	$100-300 Millions	$300-1,000 Millions	Over 1,000 Millions
Benin	Ghana	Mali	Angola	Algeria
Botswana	Ivory Coast	Mozambique	Morocco	Egypt
Burundi	Kenya	Nigeria	Somalia	Ethiopia
Cameroon	Mauritania	Sudan	South Africa	Libya
Chad	Tunisia	Tanzania		
Congo-Brazzaville		Uganda		
Equatorial Guinea		Zaire		
Gabon		Zambia		
Gambia				
Guinea				
Guinea-Bissau				
Madagascar				
Malawi				
Niger				
Senegal				
Togo				
Zimbabwe				

Table 9.6 (cont'd)

Arms Suppliers

Soviet Union	56%	USA	4%
France	11%	PRC	1%
West Europeans	9%	All Others	15%
East Europeans	8%		

Total Arms Transfers, 1974-78: $14,300 Million (Current year dollars)

Source: US Arms Control and Disarmament Agency, *World Military Expenditures and Arms Transfers, 1969-1978* (Washington, D.C.: December 1980), pp. 160-161.

Arms Control In Africa

Table 9.7: Value of Arms Transfers as a Percentage of Total Arms Levels*

	Total Arms Level**	Received From Colonial Power	Received From USA	Received From USSR
Algeria	$1,500	$10 (1%)	—	$1,200 (80%)
Angola	725	—	—	410 (57%)
Benin	30	10 (33%)	—	20 (67%)
Botswana	10	10 (100%)	—	—
Burundi	10	5 (50%)	—	5 (50%)
Cameroon	30	—	10 (33%)	—
Chad	10	—	—	10 (100%)
Congo-Brazzaville	40	—	—	30 (75%)
Egypt	1,200	110 (9%)	60 (5%)	430 (36%)
Equatorial Guinea	10	—	—	10 (100%)
Ethiopia	1,600	—	1 (1%)	1,300 (87%)
Gabon	30	10 (33%)	—	—
Ghana	90	10 (11%)	—	—
Guinea	50	—	—	50 (100%)
Guinea-Bissau	10	—	—	10 (100%)
Ivory Coast	90	70 (78%)	—	—
Libya	5,000	330 (6%)	5 (1%)	3,400 (68%)
Madagascar	30	—	—	20 (67%)
Mali	110	—	—	100 (90%)
Mauritania	80	40 (50%)	—	—
Morocco	950	470 (49%)	170 (18%)	20 (2%)

Table 9.7 (cont'd)

	Total Arms Level**	Received From Colonial Power	Received From USA	Received From USSR
Mozambique	180	–	–	130 (72%)
Nigeria	200	30 (15%)	30 (15%)	80 (40%)
Senegal	40	10 (25%)	–	–
Somalia	500	20 (4%)	–	300 (60%)
South Africa	600	–	20 (3%)	–
Sudan	110	–	30 (27%)	30 (27%)
Tanzania	180	–	–	110 (61%)
Togo	40	10 (25%)	–	–
Tunisia	80	10 (13%)	20 (25%)	–
Uganda	120	–	–	100 (92%)

* Cumulative 1974-1978 totals of arms transfers.
** In 1978 constant US $ millions.

Source: US Arms Control and Disarmament Agency, *World Military Expenditures and Arms Transfers, 1969-1978* (Washington, D.C.: December, 1980), pp. 160-161.

To keep this in perspective, however, it should be noted that African countries imported only four per cent of the world's arms trade during that period, and possessed no significant armaments industry of their own. In the brief four years thereafter, African arms imports rose substantially, accounting for US $4.8 billion (25 per cent) of the world total of US $19 billion in 1978 (1977 constant US dollars). This is an average increase of 100 per cent per year, again confined largely to those same few countries.[5]

A recent volatile five year period confirms essentially the same few countries as the major arms importers, with Ethiopia replacing Nigeria near the top of the list (Table 9.6). The highest eight importers continue to receive almost 85 per cent of the total arms imports; the next eight receive almost two-thirds of the balance. Thus, one-third of the African states imported 95 per cent of all armaments between 1974 and 1978. It is disturbing, nevertheless, to realise that the African states now are receiving 17.5 per cent of the world arms trade, up from four per cent earlier. It is evident that the rate of arms limitation is decreasing somewhat.

Competition among the arms suppliers for lucrative sales contracts is increasing (see below), especially in the secondary market for used equipment. Arms dealers from the Western nations compete among themselves and the Western nations compete with the Soviet Union to minimise where possible Soviet arms sales or gifts. As most Western governments agree on the need to limit arms sales to African states, Western arms dealers are constrained in their sales efforts. No such constraints impair Soviet arms deliveries.

The African states which have been engaged in arms escalation in recent years are the North African states, South Africa, Zimbabwe, the oil producers and Soviet-sponsored governments/ movements. There is no direct correlation between the relative increase/decrease in armaments and the relative geographic proximity of these states to major areas of conflict or liberation. Thus, increased armaments levels normally are due to factors other than the geographic proximity to violence.

In summary, the above data clearly demonstrates that the popular perception of African countries fiercely engaged in an arms race is essentially a myth, although recent developments among a few countries are cause for concern. This is not to deny that some African states are developing and utilising military power, perhaps even squandering resources in that attempt. Rather, the data indicates that very few African states have been engaged in significant arms escalation, while at least half the states are content with a very modest *status quo*. In general, the data shows Africa to be among the least armed regions of the world, especially among the independent states south of the Sahara. Therefore, it appears that some form of arms limitation policy is in actual practice among the African states and that public pronouncements to that effect are not mere propaganda. There is no singular explanation for the presence of military systems of such modest size among African states, but rather an amalgam of reasons.

A BACKGROUND OF LIMITED MILITARISATION

A historical reason for the presence of only modest military systems in Africa is that Africa experienced very little militarisation during its colonial era, somewhat in contrast to its pre-colonial history, because there was no need until the twentieth century to arm the colonies.[6] An important distinction must be made in the pattern of colonial conquest, however, for it influenced subsequent national military systems and international politics. The French, like the Italians, Spanish, and Belgians, pursued a traditional pattern of direct conquest and subjugation of successive African societies until a region was consolidated into an exploitable colony under a single administrative centre.

In contrast, the British employed considerably smaller forces, instead preferring to juxtapose one society against another, often using the victorious group as its proxy. Rather than just territory, the British sought strategic positions, bases, and entrepôts from which it could dominate a region; these were linked to traditional British command of the seas. Hence, local security forces (usually officered by British professional soldiers) sometimes were larger, while British military forces were smaller, normally being used to tilt the balance of power in favour of a preferred proxy group. Should that proxy fail, prove unsuccessful in containing its rivals, or revolt against British rule, a powerful expedition would then be mounted to restore the relationship (e.g., the Kitchener Expedition to Khartoum[7] or the Boer War). The former British colonies thus have experienced somewhat greater international conflict, partly due to these political juxtapositions. The post-independence development of the armed forces of former British colonies was affected by the lack of African officers who possessed senior-level schooling and experience.

In all colonial cases, the Africans were kept unarmed or lightly armed to avoid an uprising against European rule. Of particular importance, military technology was denied to Africans. The African security forces thus remained small, lightly armed and ruled largely by the threat that resistance would bring deadly results from the imperial European forces.

The First World War changed African military patterns. The European powers, desperate for manpower to fill the trenches, recruited substantial forces from the colonies. Compounding the threat to the Allied Powers was the successful campaign of the German commander Von Lettow Vorbeck, who led a German/African force against the British in East Africa.[8] Stretched to its limits, the British government responded primarily with local military forces composed of British and Dutch settlers from South Africa.[9] Although largely disarmed after the war, African troops nevertheless acquired considerable knowledge of military organisation, equipment and tactics.

This trend continued during World War II. African troops fought not only in the campaigns of North and East Africa, but also in France, Italy, India and Burma. More importantly, this was a war of technology, unlike the comparatively simple infantry battles of World War I. This war required all forces to possess higher skill levels in firepower, mobility, communications, and logistics, not to mention operations at sea or in the air. A much greater level of training and technological proficiency was required, hence also a broader educational base. Returning from war, African troops had experienced modernity and nationalism and would never again be content with colonial rule.

The period of transition saw the more settled territories of Rhodesia, South Africa, and Egypt (independent after 1922, but with British influence) retaining large military forces after demobilisation (as they do today), whereas other colonial forces were disarmed to pre-war levels. Indigenous African leadership emerged, however, particularly during the post-war struggles for independence. The French granted commissions to African soldiers, even promoting some through the rank of major (such as Thomas d'Aquin of the Ivory Coast). The British, however, did not award full (Queen's) commissions, instead granting only a governor's commission, the equivalent rank of a warrant officer (such as to Idi Amin of Uganda).

Thus, the desire to avoid internal revolts, the absence of struggle between the colonial powers except for the World Wars, and the general assumption that Africans were militarily and technologically inept (reinforced by the victory of Italy over Ethiopia in 1935, in retrospect an exeedingly unfair contest), combined to limit the size and capability of African military forces during the colonial era. Very little military institutionalisation was passed on to the new national governments, which in all cases initially were civilian governments. In most cases the new independent civilian rulers had little or no military background and were confronted primarily with non-military problems. Once the immediate post-independence period had passed and internal security was assured, the role of the military dissipated until some event, usually domestic, again brought it to the fore. Those states with the larger armed forces (over 25,000 men in Table 9.5 or above 4.0 armed forces/1000 population in Table 9.4) reflect internal unrest, including successful military coups, more than transnational aggression. Ironically, the military forces over whom the new governments assumed control were often the very enemies the new civilian leaders opposed in the pre-independence jockeying for positions of political power.

THE ECONOMIC FACTOR

Economic forces also resisted the development of armaments, including the prodigious costs of manpower and equipment. Because the urgent need upon independence was to provide socio-economic development, a legacy of limited investment during the colonial era, governments lacked the resources to pursue a 'guns and butter' policy. The burden of overarmament has been well documented in other newly emerging nations with strong socio-economic demands and limited financial resources. In most newly emerging African states, the legacy of diminutive colonial security forces was promptly converted upon independence into diminutive national security forces.

Most governments resisted the temptation to acquire the tangible, flashy symbols of armed independence represented by tanks or jet fighters. These are costly to procure and, even if donated, require a level of technical expertise often unavailable in newly emerging states; repair parts also are costly. Thus, a decade after independence (1970), the only tanks found in independent sub-Saharan Africa were in the Ivory Coast (five French), Guinea (12 Soviet), Ethiopia (50 US), Somalia (150 Soviet) and Mali (ten Soviet). Similarly, jet fighters were delivered to Guinea (eight Soviet), Mali (six Soviet), Nigeria (15 Soviet), Ethiopia (26 US/UK), Somalia (18 Soviet) and Uganda (seven Soviet).[10] Much of this equipment soon became inoperable because of maintenance problems or unutilised for lack of operators, a lesson not lost on other states.

Since 1970 there have been only modest increases in these equipment levels, confined largely to those states involved in transnational conflicts and supported by outside arms suppliers. Ethiopia, Somalia, Angola, and Zambia are the exceptions among independent sub-Saharan states, with significantly increased equipment levels, all heavily armed by the Soviet Union. The North African states continue to be well armed, although significant hardware increases in recent years have occurred only in Libya. During the next decade one should expect to find some increase in the jet fighter capability among states south of the Sahara. Presently limited only to symbolic quantities (usually under 20 aircraft) in 15 other sub-Saharan states, used jet fighters increasingly will flow into 'developing' nations' arsenals as they are excessed from developed nations' arsenals. Several aircraft manufacturers are preparing major sales campaigns to sell rebuilt aircraft at comparatively low prices to African governments. Possessing both offensive and defensive capabilities, it will be hard for governments to resist the sirens' song of military modernity and prestige if a rival nation has purchased jets. Similarly, most coastal states will purchase light naval craft to protect shipping and off-shore oil deposits. It is unlikely that many states will be attracted to expensive heavy ground-combat equipment in the immediate future, other than those which now have this capability.

Two new factors have emerged to threaten the economically-imposed limitation upon armaments: the willingness of the Soviet Union to provide Cuban troops and armaments to client states (see Table 9.6), and the growth of sophisticated armaments in the hands of the minority government of South Africa, despite arms embargos by many other governments, including Britain and the United States. Most of the larger armies listed in Table 9.5 received the preponderance of their heavy military equipment from the Soviet bloc.[11] The presence of comparatively large armaments in the hands of one nation of course gives potential adversaries the incentive to acquire similar armaments, thus fuelling an arms race.

Some adventurist national leaders have not been deterred by the high cost, the inability to operate or maintain, the lack of threat, or the coup potential of armaments, and have eagerly sought arms on the world market. In some cases they have been successful. In many cases, however, the reluctance of responsible foreign governments to supply arms to adventurist governments has impeded arms transfers (Table 9.7). For most African governments, Table 9.6 reveals considerable moderation and an unwillingness to expend limited national resources on armaments in view of pressing socio-economic needs. Moderation often evaporates, however, following a successful military coup.

MILITARY COUP POTENTIAL

Large and proficient armed forces present the threat of coups against established governments. For Africa, this seems to have peaked in the mid-1960s when successful military coups averaged four per year.[12] Thereafter it declined to an average of two successful coups per year, a level at which it has remained to this day, despite a larger number of sovereign states. Political leaders naturally have been reluctant to deliver powerful armed forces into the hands of potential adversaries, including ethnic rivals from the early years of independence. Interestingly, the number of unsuccessful attempted coups increased during the late 1960s and early 1970s, reaching a constant level of four to five unsuccessful attempts annually, indicating enhanced survivability of established governments.

Coups and attempted coups by junior officers and NCOs have increased during the 1970s and early 1980s, supplementing senior and middle-ranking officer coups. The former often pose the greatest problems, for the new national leaders usually have little political experience or a sense of fiscal responsibility. Recent coups in Ghana, Burkina Faso (Upper Volta), Liberia and Mauritania reflect the growing frustrations and impatience of these younger groups.

There appears to be some statistical correlation between the size of the armed forces and the number of coups/coup attempts. Those African nations with the larger armed forces generally have a higher incidence of coups, attempted coups, and related anomic disturbances than do other states, perhaps both a cause and effect relationship. The post-coup leaders usually increase military expenditures both to buy loyal supporters with pay raises and technology, and to enlarge the security forces against counter-coups. These expenditures often have impacted seriously upon the national economies, including countries such as Liberia, Ghana, Uganda and Zaire.

Besides limits upon the size and complexity of armed forces, experienced African national leaders have resorted to a variety of means of reducing the coup potential of their armed forces, including the presence of protective foreign troops (French troops in Chad, Djibouti, Gabon, Ivory Coast and Senegal; Soviet bloc/Cuban troops in Angola, Ethiopia and elsewhere). Other measures include special presidential guard forces, countervailing gendarmeries and civic action responsibilities for the armed services which occupy the attention of would-be plotters.[13] The OAU decision to accept existing borders, mentioned below, may well be regarded as the pragmatic recognition by civilian leaders that to open the borders issue could bring about armed conflict, leading to the need for larger armed forces, resulting in a greater threat from military coups.

TRANSNATIONAL AGGRESSION

Africa, and especially the sub-Saharan region, has been remarkably free of *major* transnational aggression. Although there were several cross-border military actions in the 1960s, these have dwindled to a few isolated cases during the past decade. The Ogaden dispute, the Angola/Namibia situation, the Western Sahara controversy, the Libyan invasion of Chad and the Tanzanian invasion of Uganda to topple Idi Amin are the major occurrences. Cross-border guerrilla operations involving Senegambia, Zimbabwe or the Shaba incursion more properly would be categorised as indigenous rather than transnational conflicts.

Actions by Libya's Gaddafi, however, threaten to destabilise this pattern. His willingness to use military force to influence political events in nearby countries is distinctly atypical. The recent use of Libyan forces in Chad, Tunisia and Uganda has sent an alarm throughout Africa. Significantly, however, he is yet to succeed in any of these endeavours.

Similarly, the risk of armed conflict over the issue of majority rule in South Africa is very real. South Africa's continued willingness to employ its armed forces in the 'front-line' states (as demonstrated by the Cabinda and Botswana incursions in mid-1985) could galvanise several African states into some form of united armed action against South Africa, although indigenous urban guerrilla warfare seems more likely in the immediate future.

The continued presence of an estimated 36,000 Cuban troops in Angola and Ethiopia, the threat of further foreign involvement in Mozambique, plus miscellaneous East European involvement in several other countries, continue to be destabilising factors. Unlike much of the French military presence, the size of the Cuban forces presents a cross-border capability, although they apparently have not yet been used to cross recognised borders. The emergence of a majority-ruled Zimbabwe in 1980, however, appears to have deflected the use of Cuban troops in that region of Africa.

In summation, while very real risks persist, mainly from Cuba, Libya, and South Africa in the near term, it appears that African states have largely avoided major transnational aggressions, further defusing the need to maintain large military forces.[14]

THE OAU IN CONFLICT MANAGEMENT

The Organisation of African Unity (OAU) also has played a role in arms limitation. Most scholars concede that the OAU since its inception in 1963 has not been particularly successful in managing conflict among African states. Some consider it to be an abject failure in this role.[15] Others are more charitable, attributing to the OAU some small successes in specific peace-keeping tasks. These include a major role in the resolution of the Algerian-Moroccan crisis (1963), the Somalian-Ethiopian conflict (1967 and 1973), the Ugandan-Tanzanian dispute (1973), the Somalian-Kenyan conflict, the Congo crisis (1964-65), the Ghana-Guinea dispute, the Biafran civil war, the Guinea-Senegal conflict (1971), the Guinea-Ivory Coast dispute and the Chad-Sudan border conflict.[16] In perspective, of course, these alone are not insignificant achievements.

Quick judgements on the failure of the OAU are misleading - the organisation upon examination appears to be more durable and more effective than commonly believed.[17] Too many scholars focus on the official OAU peace-keeping body, the Commission of Mediation, Conciliation and Arbitration, without considering the effects of less-visible endeavours. The private efforts of African leaders working through the OAU informal apparatus have successfully avoided or resolved conflicts. It has not only resolved a number of specific border disputes, but has clearly stated the intent of African states to accept all existing borders established by the colonial powers; artificial borders, perhaps, but very real today. To attempt to adjust borders would open all Africa to competing claims and conflict with perfidious results, as noted above.

Perhaps the OAU's greatest achievement, from the perspective of non-African states, has been its success in preventing regional conflicts from becoming international conflicts.[18] This clearly reduced the responsibilities of an over-burdened United Nations during the period 1965-75. The Angola crisis of 1975, however, signaled an end to major power restraint in Africa. Later, the war between Somalia and Ethiopia, plus the Zaire conflict in Shaba Province, included active participation by non-African military forces. The OAU has responded without success to this new facet of transnational conflict, although this has been addressed in numerous sessions.

As an institution which included conflict management as one of its charter purposes (Article III), the OAU in general has had mixed success. Most important, it adheres to a theme of peaceful conflict resolution, a principle which is probably more important than specific actions or policies.[19]

It provides a single voice for member states in world affairs and has aided some liberation movements (the primary goal in its early years[20]). It certainly cannot be regarded as a total failure from the perspectives of the member states themselves.

On a number of occasions, several African leaders have sought the creation of a multi-national security force under the OAU which would aid any victim of transnational aggression, thus precluding the need for military expansion among individual states. Haile Selassie first made this proposal at the 1973 OAU Conference. While not developed through the OAU, a number of Francophone states have developed an informal security arrangement of this nature without extensive publicity. It was evident that such an arrangement functioned during the 1978 Shaba crisis in Zaire when Belgium, France, Morocco, and several smaller Francophone African states sent troops to oust the attackers and restore order; a similar force was proposed for Chad, but was not adopted, although French troops re-entered Chad in 1983 to stabilise the Habre government following an overt Libyan invasion. The Francophone arrangement reflects a common pattern that, when threatened, newly independent African states often have turned to the former colonial power for military assistance. While the United Nations has played a role in the resolution of some African disputes, most notably in the Congo during 1960-64, its multilateral decision-making apparatus has proven unreliable in swiftly responding to security threats. Thus, African states often have relied upon unilateral support from a larger outside power for real security.

CONCLUSION

The evidence on African armaments patterns is clear: some African nations are increasing their armaments beyond the levels of a decade ago; a few are increasing these levels at a dramatic rate. Most, however, are not: their increases are modest by any standard or, indeed, are decreases. A number of social, political and economic forces explain the limitation of armaments in Africa. Should any of these factors be disrupted by events which give the perception of serious threat, other African states could join the few now embarked on an arms race.

Arms limitation in Africa cannot succeed without the cooperation of the major powers. If major power involvement in Africa increases in the late 1980s and in the 1990s, increased African armaments will surely result. Similarly, unrestricted arms sales has not been noticeably restrained. This is not to suggest that all foreign arms sales necessarily are wrong - only provocative or uncontrolled sales, especially those which aid armies' cross-border capability.

The future of African armaments is unclear. Certainly the active guerrilla groups in selected locations (not discussed here) have demonstrated little concern about arms control, which potentially threatens sovereign states. More important, however, some of the more extremist African political leaders have demonstrated a desire to rule with the traditional instruments of military power, reflecting a mixture of ego and the appetite for political control.

The major powers, however, could perform a responsible role in African arms limitations. If the Organisation of African Unity charter principle of inviolate existing borders (Article III) is reaffirmed by member states, the withdrawal of military forces from border areas (100 km) would be an important confidence-building measure. This could be accomplished with verification, which is beyond the existing technical capabilities of the African states. Outside powers could perform the verification service with various technical means, under the direction of an OAU military information committee. Once assured of reliable verification, enhanced border security, greater arms control and disarmament would be possible. Similarly, regional security arrangements such as that of the Francophone states would obviate the need for large security forces, even if a neighbouring state were perceived as a threat. Certainly the major powers, through self-restraint and by working to resolve the majority rule/equal rights disputes of southern Africa can aid in the arms control process. It is conceivable that the OAU, as the forum for reasoned minds, could replace the battlefield for the peaceful resolution of conflict in Africa.

NOTES

My thanks to Anthony Iheukwu of Arondizugu, Imo, Nigeria, for his help in preparing the tables for this chapter.

1. US Arms Control and Disarmament Agency, World Military Expenditures and Arms Transfers, 1969-1978 (Washington, D.C.: US Arms Control and Disarmament Agency).
2. Ibid.
3. International Institute for Strategic Studies, The Military Balance, 1983-84 (London: IISS, 1984), pp. 66-81.
4. Ibid. Some of the reasons for this rise are discussed in Legum, C., 'The Organisation of African Unity - Success or Failure?' International Affairs, 51, 2 (April 1975), pp. 208-19.
5. US Arms Control and Disarmament Agency, World Military Expenditures, 1966-75, pp. 78-79; 1969-78, p. 117.
6. Welch, C., 'Continuity and Discontinuity in African Military Organizations', Journal of Modern African Studies, 13, 2 (June 1975), pp. 229-48. For further discussion of the colonial legacy and the transformation to nationhood, see Lee, J.M., African Armies and Civil Order (New York: Praeger, 1969).
7. For a personalised account of this expedition, including an account of the employment of African troops, see Churchill, W., The River War (New York: Universal Publishing Co., 1964).
8. Vorbeck, General P., My Reminiscences of East Africa (London: Hurst and Blackett, 1920).
9. Crowe, General J., General Smuts' Campaign in East Africa (London: Murray, 1918).
10. Booth, R., The Armed Forces of African States, 1970 (London: IISS, Adelphi Paper No. 67, 1970).
11. International Institute for Strategic Studies, The Military Balance, 1983-84, pp. 66-81.
12. Gutteridge, W.F., Military Regimes in Africa (London: Methuen, 1975), ch.1.
13. Further discussion on the question of civilian control mechanisms is found in Goldsworthy's chapter in this volume as well as in his 'Civilian Control of the Military in Black Africa; African Affairs, 80, 318 (January 1981), pp. 49-74. For single regime case-studies, see Brayton, A., 'Stability and Modernisation: the

Ivory Coast Model', World Affairs, 141, 3 (Winter 1979), pp. 235-39; and Baynham, S.J., 'Quis Custodiet Ipsos Custodes?: the case of Nkrumah's National Security Service', Journal of Modern African Studies, 23, 1 (March 1985), pp. 87-103.

14. But see the chapter by Hughes and May in this volume. For earlier work on the problems of transnational and internal conflict, see Mazrui, A.A., 'The Anatomy of Violence in Contemporary Black Africa', in Kitchen. (ed.), Africa: From Maze to Mystery (Lexington, Mass.: D.C. Heath, 1973).

15. El-Ayouty, Y. (ed.), The Organization of African Unity after Ten Years (New York: Praeger, 1975).

16. See, Cervanka, Z., The Organization of African Unity and Its Charter (New York: Praeger, 1969), especially ch.4.

17. Legum, 'The Organization of African Unity', pp. 208-19.

18. Meyers, B.D., 'Intraregional Conflict Management by the Organization of African Unity', International Organization, 28, 3 (Summer 1974), pp. 345-73.

19. Mayall, J., 'African Unity and the OAU: The Place of a Political Myth in African Diplomacy', Yearbook of World Affairs, 27 (1973), pp. 110-33.

20. Matthew, K., 'The Organization of African Unity', India Quarterly, 33, 3 (July-September 1977), pp. 307-24.

Chapter Ten

SOUTH AFRICA'S MILITARY RELATIONS WITH ITS
NEIGHBOURS

J.E. Spence

The events leading to the signing of the Nkomati Accord between South Africa and Mozambique have been interpreted, indeed justified, by the South African government as a straight forward exercise in coercive, regional diplomacy: à la Clausewitz, this involved the application of military force in pursuit of a political objective, the realisation of which was finally achieved by a flurry of semi-secret diplomacy between representatives of the two states concerned.
Thus according to the 1984 Defence White Paper, South Africa's pursuit of 'a successful strategy of deterrence', its pursuit of 'forceful military action' during the last decade has 'created the climate in which ... peace initiatives in the southern African region became possible.'[1] In passing, it is worth remarking on the curious and ambiguous use of the term 'deterrence' in this context; 'compellence' - to cite Thomas Schelling's term - might be a better description insofar as South Africa's policy of military intervention has involved '*initiating* an action ... that can cease, or become harmless, only if the opponent responds.'[2]
The Accord was hailed both within the Republic and Western capitals as a major coup for Mr Botha's government: its origins, terms and long-range implications have generated considerable discussion by commentators and politicians alike; this chapter is a contribution to the debate over these issues, and in particular the role of South Africa's military elite in the formulation and conduct of foreign policy in southern Africa.[3] At the same time, the claim - asserted in the 1984 Defence White Paper - that the Nkomati Accord represented a self-conscious, goal-directed strategy leading

to a desired political outcome will also be tested.

THE FOREIGN POLICY CONTEXT: 1959-1974

Any examination of a state's defence policy must - if it is not to be exclusively concerned with purely technical issues of capability, structure and military expertise - require prior consideration of the state's *political* goals, the interests it seeks to defend and assert and, most important, the perceptions of the external environment entertained by decision makers. It is a truism, but one nonetheless well attested in the literature of civil-military relations that defence policy is the handmaiden of foreign policy: the military instrument - in terms of this thesis - is one among several designed to protect and enhance state interest in the unceasing search for security in a competitive and potentially dangerous international system. Economic leverage and diplomatic pressure are two such instruments, although their use - either singly or in combination, with or without the threat or application of military force - will depend on the capabilities available, the perception of the opponent's strength and credibility and, most crucial of all, the nature and scope of the challenge at any one time to the state's core values of survival and the maintenance of internal stability.

South Africa's foreign policy in the last four decades has proved no exception to these general propositions, though the role, status and use of the military in pursuit of political objectives has varied depending upon the incentives open to policy makers and the constraints imposed by circumstances. In the 1950s, for example, as Kenneth Grundy has pointed out, 'the defence forces were not involved deeply in policy consideration or implementation, and not at all in policy making.'[4] There was no immediate regional threat to counter, the white-ruled territories to the north of South Africa's borders constituted an effective buffer against attack from without, and this remained the case well into the 1960s, although there was some relatively modest involvement by the South African defence and police forces in support of Rhodesian and Portuguese counter-insurgencies. Foreign policy concentrated on maintaining and increasing economic ties with Western countries, Britain in particular, on the assumption that the more integrated into the international economy South Africa became, the less likely that effective international action would be taken against apartheid by the Commonwealth or the United Nations where Eric Louw (South Africa's Minister for External Affairs) and his successors offered a fierce defence of their country's policies.

In the early 1960s, however, defence expenditure began to mount rapidly: in 1958/59 the defence budget was R.36m; six years later, after a formidable burst of expansion, the figure was R.210m. This suggests a growing awareness that the combination of economic strength (the growth rate at its highest point in the boom of the 1960s reached 8 per cent), and its corollary of enhanced value to Western traders, investors and governments under pressure from the UN and elsewhere to defy sanctions, together with legislation spawning more refined bureaucratic and political instruments of social control and an aggressive diplomacy abroad, were deemed sufficient to provide security. At this stage, i.e. the 1960s, a more sophisticated military posture was perceived as contributing to the maintenance of internal security; spurred on by the arms embargo of 1963, self-sufficiency in arms production became a major goal of policy, and where that proved difficult in certain weapons categories such as military aircraft and submarines, diversification of supply sources was actively promoted, the French becoming a major supplier.[5]

Increased defence spending also serviced policy objectives beyond the Republic's borders: the outbreak of guerrilla war in Rhodesia and the Portuguese colonies in the late 1960s, and the danger that such conflicts might spill over into the Republic via the infiltration of insurgents, led to the creation of a South African counter-insurgency capability. It is significant that the threat of African National Congress penetration from Zambia across Rhodesia led, in 1967, to the despatch of two police battalions to aid the Smith regime's campaign against black nationalist insurgency. Related but subordinate objects of defence policy were: (1) deterrence against any conventional attack by the African states, or alternatively, (2) economic and military sanctions by the UN - both remote contingencies, but useful (especially in the context of domestic political rhetoric) and inexpensive by-products of the main thrust of defence policy. Finally, defence preparations were part of a wider campaign to impress the West with the contribution South Africa might make to the security of the 'Free World' as a formally recognised ally - incorporated either within NATO or some new defence arrangement (e.g. SATO - South African Treaty Organisation) based on co-operation with other hemispheric powers. What must be emphasised, however, is that the primary role of military capability was internal. As the author wrote over a decade ago:

> South Africa's internal military posture must therefore be seen as part of a wider framework of security involving complex legal and bureaucratic procedures endorsed by a high degree of consensus on the part of the white minority. It is this combination of non-military factors which gives the configuration of the defence forces on a counter-insurgency basis a degree of credibility lacking in their counterparts elsewhere, in Rhodesia in particular. Indeed, the structure of power in SA as it has been elaborated over the last two decades suggests in some respects the notion of a 'garrison state' in which the civil and military instruments of coercion have been fused together to inhibit *in advance* any threat to its integrity rather than be compelled to improvise the necessary techniques of social and military control after the event.[6]

During the late 1960s and early 1970s there were frequent allegations that South Africa was giving military assistance to both Rhodesian and Portuguese governments in their counter-insurgency campaigns against indigenous guerrilla governments. In the latter case the allegation has never been proved conclusively, but there is little doubt that the Republic was an important source of economic and military assistance to the Smith regime and contributed greatly to the Rhodesian capacity to lessen the worst effects of sanctions.[7]

But in the pursuit of the 'outward movement' of foreign policy that began in the mid-1960s, the military instrument played an insignificant role. This was, after all, the heyday of the Department of Foreign Affairs. Much was made of the economic contribution the Republic could make to the development of poorer African states in the regional hinterland; there was talk of establishing, in due course, a Southern African

Economic Community with the Republic as the guarantor of order and generator of economic growth. This objective of foreign policy was in particular designed to improve the country's standing in the eyes of Western decision makers. As Dr Hilgard Muller, South Africa's Foreign Minister, put it:

> ... As the West becomes aware of our fruitful co-operation with other African states, their attitude towards us improves. I believe that it will happen to an increasing degree because we must simply accept that our relations with the rest of the world are largely dependent on our relations with the African states.[8]

Thus the motives behind the policy were economic and diplomatic, and relatively little reference was made to an interventionary role for the military - apart from the occasional and studiously vague outburst during the post-UDI period about 'putting out one's neighbour's fires' and the threat - voiced by Mr Vorster - 'to hit [Zambia] so hard that they will never forget it.'[9] Indeed, direct military intervention in Rhodesia and the Portuguese colonies, although urged by some right-wing elements in the Republic, would have been counter-productive, running the risk of the 'Vietnamisation of Southern Africa' as the Republic's forces found themselves sucked into an ever-widening confrontation in the buffer zone of Rhodesia and the Portuguese territories. In fact, from the point of view of the liberation movements in these territories, the substitution of military force for economic penetration made sense. This, however, was a temptation the Republic resisted - partly because of the impact large-scale military involvement would make on the Great Powers (the Soviet Union and China included) and the damage this would do to the idea of a Pax Afrikaner in the southern African region and the notion that 'racial groups with different policies can live together alongside one another in the same geographical area.'[10]

Thus direct military intervention on a substantial scale in either Rhodesia or the Portuguese colonies was - after 1974 - regarded as the worst alternative; to do so would certainly have strengthened the argument of South Africa's opponents that apartheid constituted a threat to the maintenance of international peace and security. And at this stage the Republic's leaders were bent on establishing their government's credibility as a loyal and much misunderstood ally of the West, desperately counting on a Conservative victory in the 1970 British election, a reversal of the arms embargo and recognition as a state well placed to help guard the security of the southern oceans.

Through the 1960s and early 1970s, then, South Africa's foreign policy was dominated by an obsession with diplomatic respectability, an aspiration to qualify as a candidate for the American sponsored Nixon Doctrine which after 1969 sought to identify and to reward states which cultivated a regional, hegemonic role.

THE RISE OF THE MILITARY AND ITS IMPACT ON FOREIGN POLICY

The analysis so far has attempted to prove a negative: that in the period 1960-1974 an orthodox diplomacy prevailed varying between the defiant posture of the 1950s to the confident thrust of the 'outward movement' of the 1960s; the state's growing military capability was designed for the twin functions of internal defence (Namibia included) and external deterrence, and there was little positive incentive (apart from isolated incursions in support of the Smith regime) to deploy force abroad in an aggressive pursuit of political objectives. The South African state was, after all (following the shock administered by the Sharpeville crisis of 1960), secure and the economy generating enough wealth to produce both 'guns and butter'. In a climate of 'liberalism abroad and repression at home', the military role was confined in practice to underpinning the second half of that equation.

The military under the efficient guidance of P.W. Botha, then the Defence Minister, were in the meanwhile subjected to intense modernisation and exposure to modern theories of counter-insurgency of the sort produced by French soldier-scholars such as Roger Trinquer and André Beaufre. It is true that until the late 1960s and the beginning of low intensity warfare against SWAPO in Namibia, the armed services had little operational experience. But Botha's long period of office (1966-1978) meant that the defence force had the great advantage of continuity of administration and, more important, consistent direction of purpose under a minister with very clear ideas about the Republic's security needs at home and abroad.

Between 1970 and 1974, for example, defence expenditure doubled from R.329m to R.692m; by

1980, defence costs had already trebled to R.1,970m. This astonishing rise during the 1970s was largely the result of three major developments in the southern African region - two external and one internal: first, the independence of Angola and Mozambique (1975) and Zimbabwe (1980), and the increase in commitment required to deal with the war against SWAPO; secondly, after a decade of quiescence, the outbreak of widespread disturbances in Soweto (1976) which rapidly spread to the other major black urban areas of the Republic. Indeed, the years 1974-1976 might be seen as a watershed for South African foreign and defence policies: the emergence of two independent, Marxist-inclined states on the Republic's borders, coupled with a major internal challenge to the apartheid system required a reorientation of foreign policy and an appropriate adjustment in military capability. Infiltration of ANC guerrillas from neighbouring sanctuary states was no longer the remote contingency of the 1960s; indeed, hundreds of young black refugees from Soweto et al. found their way to training camps in Tanzania, Mozambique and Algeria. The disturbances - it is true - were quickly put down, but their outbreak demonstrated all too clearly that the traditional demarcation between foreign and domestic policy no longer held.

The 'detente' policy launched jointly by Mr Vorster and the front line states in the wake of Portugal's collapse as a buffer power was designed to compel Mr Smith to come to terms with his black nationalist opponents: the former's calculations were brutally realistic: white rule in Rhodesia was expendable if the price was a breathing space for South Africa to put its own house in order. But a commitment to domestic political reform did not imply any slackening of the state's resolution to defend itself and - if necessary - take the offensive against enemies operating from neighbouring states. Hence the government embarked between 1975 and 1979 on a major programme of modernisation and re-equipment of its conventional forces designed to give it a capability 'to conduct large-scale pre-emptive and punitive raids against guerrilla bases in neighbouring countries'[11] and to deal with any conventional retaliation. Thus the traditional posture of counter-insurgency was to be supplemented by one involving the operation, abroad if necessary, of a powerful conventional capability with the threat of going nuclear as a last resort.

The first indication of a more aggressive policy came with the Republic's military intervention in the Angolan civil war in August 1975. A precise reconstruction of the political and bureaucratic infighting that occurred, both before and during the intervention, cannot be made in the absence of archival evidence and the secrecy which still surrounds crisis decision-making. However, Deon Geldenhuys, Robin Hallett and Kenneth Grundy all offer helpful, if at times speculative, accounts and what does emerge is the extent to which the military dominated key decisions at least in the early stages of the operation.[12] Geldenhuys provides a telling summary:

> The Department of Foreign Affairs from the outset found itself largely excluded from decision making on South Africa's Angolan venture. The foreign ministry's religious adherence to the principle of non-interference in other countries' internal affairs was the very antithesis of the Defence Force's belief that South Africa should take a hand in shaping Angola's destiny. Foreign Affairs wanted South Africa to adopt the same 'hands off' attitude it had (ostensibly) displayed when the Portuguese left Mozambique. The military saw major differences between the situations in Mozambique and Angola: in Angola three rival liberation movements were fighting for political power and creating opportunities for communist involvement and for a SWAPO presence on Namibia's northern border. In Mozambique FRELIMO had been the sole heir to political power.[13]

The failure of the Angolan intervention had four important consequences: (1) the refusal of the West, and in particular of the United States, to support the Republic confirmed Mr Vorster's view that 'when it comes to the worst, South Africa stands alone'[14]; (2) paradoxically, Mr Botha's position and that of his senior military and intelligence advisers was strengthened because if Mr Vorster was correct, then clearly military capability and the will and skill to use it effectively was bound to become increasingly important in the very different regional environment in which the Republic found itself after 1974; (3) Mr Botha was therefore well placed to assert a military definition of his country's security needs against the more orthodox 'diplomatic' style of the Foreign Affairs bureaucracy, sometimes disparagingly referred to as 'cocktail diplomacy'. (And here Mr Botha was greatly assisted in his rise to the premiership by the Information Scandal and the contribution that made to Mr Vorster's ultimate downfall): and (4) more alarmingly from Pretoria's perception, it could be argued - though not proved conclusively - that events in Soweto and elsewhere in 1976 were related to the Republic's ill-fated venture in Angola. It is true that the Republic's forces withdrew in good order without suffering undue humiliation at the hands of their Cuban opponents. The predominant black perception was, however, very different: for the first time the much-vaunted, seemingly impregnable military arm of the state appeared to suffer a major reverse. This led to a revival of black militancy and a willingness to challenge the security forces of the state in the streets of Soweto.

GOVERNMENT REORGANISATION AND THE CONCEPT OF TOTAL STRATEGY

When Mr Botha became Prime Minister in 1978 he attempted a managerial revolution in the structure and process of government modelled on the reforms he had instituted in the military bureaucracy during the preceding decade. His style of government is profoundly different from that of his predecessor: to quote Grundy, 'P.W. Botha is a manager, an organisational virtuoso, a leader who places great stock in expert advice, planning, preparation, structure, and follow through.'[15] Nowhere is this personal style better reflected than in the organisation and role of the State Security Council, a body originally established in 1972 but which - under Botha's direction - has steadily gained in influence on decision making in a variety of fields, both military and civil.

Its membership includes, *inter alia*, the State President as Chairman, the Ministers of Foreign Affairs, Defence, and Law and Order, and it meets fortnightly before cabinet meetings. The SSC has been aptly described (by Kenneth Grundy) as the apex of 'a security establishment'[16] designed to provide a 'total strategy' to cope with the 'total onslaught' which the government has defined as a Marxist conspiracy using a variety of instruments ranging from the black African states to front organisations, e.g. trades unions and churches. All these are perceived as undermining white power in the Republic and promoting the expansion of Soviet influence in the process. Thus, ANC sabotage, township unrest, labour disputes and overseas propaganda are all part of the same insidious design - a total war involving political, diplomatic, religious, cultural and social instruments of coercion by South Africa's enemies, whether domestic or external.

Clearly, once 'total onslaught' is defined in these apocalyptic terms, 'total onslaught', requires that every aspect of state policy be perceived in terms of its significance for the maintenance of white security. Thus the SSC has the all-embracing task of assessing domestic policy: 'regional planning, economic planning, manpower planning, constitutional planning - the whole gamut is influenced by security and internal stability considerations.'[17] Hence, the enhanced role of the military in the SSC and in particular that of General Magnus Malan, the Minister of Defence, and one of Botha's most able military advisers during his tenure as Minister of Defence.

It has, however, been argued - by John Seiler, for example - that this interpretation of 'total onslaught', while valid enough in the period 1978-1983 no longer holds to the same degree. On the evidence of interviews conducted in 1983 with senior defence force and police officers he detected a growing belief that the concept is 'an exaggerated and counterproductive rubric for strategic planning.'[18] Thus according to Seiler, the Soviet Union is no longer perceived as giving high priority to the destruction of the Republic, while the forces available to neighbouring states - cited as a threat by both Magnus Malan and P.W. Botha 'to justify additional military expenditure - is no more than a "paper" threat, given the enormous problems of maintenance, driver training, and ineffective political direction in those countries.'[19] Seiler acknowledges, however, that senior defence force personnel 'assume Moscow *control* of ANC and SWAPO, rather than *influence* over them, and ... remain unfathomably apprehensive of all Soviet regional presences, unable yet to make analytical judgements about varying threats in different regional situations.'[20]

Seiler' argument is a timely reminder against exaggeration of the role of ideology in moulding perception of the outside world. Yet as Frankel has ably demonstrated, a generation of SADF officers have been influenced - though not entirely, he is careful to stress - in the course of their military education by the doctrines of thinkers such as André Beaufre, with his emphasis on the crucial relationship between the political and military dimensions of counter-revolutionary strategy. Thus 'the concept of strategic action, therefore, necessarily stems from political analysis.'[21] The effect of this intellectual exposure is to produce a cast of mind in which 'the ostensible onslaught against South Africa is total and "instigated by monolithic organizations ... in absolute control of all the means available to their states".' Therefore the response must be 'total', and 'the means to defend the state must be similarly all-encompassing in strategic nature.'[22]

The changes in perception cited by Seiler may well have occurred, but they represent not so much an abandonment of the concept, but rather a more sophisticated understanding of its limitations and the need to adjust one's perception of the role of individual actors in the total strategy of the 'enemy', which, in the last analysis, is defined as the aggressive ideological motivated foreign policy of the communist powers. And it is in this context that the SSC role is pivotal for it appears to have set the parameters for policy making: as Grundy remarks, 'the military ... benefits from a government that effectively accepts its framework of analysis and its strategic-ideological mind set.'[23]

Yet Seiler and others are right in their refutation of the view that South Africa is ruled by a hidden praetorian caste. What has happened during the last decade is that the military has greatly expanded its influence on the decision making process. Its senior personnel have been profoundly influenced by the literature on counter-insurgency in the Third World and, in particular, the doctrine that success requires an 80 per cent political and 20 per cent military capability. At a micro-level this is reflected in the Civic Action programme in which servicemen take on civilian roles as doctors, teachers, engineers and administrators both in Namibia and black areas of the Republic. Yet another example would be the institution of nine regional management centres covering the major regions and designed to promote co-operation between the military and the civilian bureaucracies.

Thus a commitment to limited reform of the kind enshrined in the new constitution - to win the 'hearts and minds' of the Coloured and Indian minorities - is not inconsistent with an enhanced role for the military both as social engineers concerned with filtering economic and social policy through a security lens and as an increasingly visible presence to deter and defend against the threat of black violence. Thus, when ministers justify military action in the black townships (as in October 1984 and during much of 1985) or destabilising raids against South Africa's neighbours, they invariably talk of rooting out 'revolutionary elements' - a conception which it is easy to square with the assumption that South Africa *is* threatened by 'total onslaught'.

Yet we must be careful not to exaggerate the role of the military: influence is not domination, as Grundy reminds us:

> ... although the SSC has been regarded as a sounding board for SADF views, in a way it is also a check on the SADF. It reinforces a reliance on the principle of civilian supremacy over the military and to political paramountcy in the decision making process. The military voice is clear and, as ... well placed, but in the end it, too, must come to accept that this is an elected government answerable to an exclusive electorate, but nonetheless answerable.[24]

The military, it is true, have the support of 'certain technologically-minded bureaucrats ... who ... [identify]... with the rationalising thrust of military policy',[25] but there are other elites - as Frankel particularly reminds us - in Foreign Affairs, for example, and other 'civilian' areas of the bureaucracy who resent the

> tendency of government to centralise major decision-making in a system of committees surrounding the [President's] office ... This is exacerbated by the fact that the hub of the system, the State Security Council, is basically dominated by military, civilian and bureaucratic personnel with demonstrably scant regard for established bureaucratic procedures.[26]

These arguments suggest that it would be mistaken to describe South Africa as heading rapidly towards the creation of a garrison state ruled by a soldier-elite imposing an exclusively military definition of social and political reality on discredited and incompetent civilian politicians and bureaucrats. The SADF, despite a fashionable commitment to systems analysis and the modern paraphernalia of 'technological decision making' remains reluctant to cast aside the Western tradition of civil-military separation. Indeed, as Seiler sensibly remarks:

> ironically, the misplaced accusation ... [i.e. of militarisation ... that government decision-making is controlled by the SADF] ... ignores a more hazardous reality: cabinet ministers, civilian officials and military officials are in general agreement about coercive regional policies.[27]

It is to these policies, their objectives and implications, that the remainder of this paper will be devoted.

DESTABILISATION: MEANS AND ENDS

In the 1980s a more aggressive military posture was adopted by the Republic towards its black neighbours in the region. The pattern for military intervention had been set as early as 1977 as the Republic - following the abortive 1975 invasion of Angola - launched a series of raids on Angolan territory designed primarily to weaken SWAPO's capacity to operate from its bases there. These increased in magnitude in the 1980s, involving a combination of air power and army units and led to occupation of areas within southern Angola. The UNITA movement served as a proxy for this intervention and one which, since 1975, under the leadership of Jonas Savimbi, has been fighting a counter-revolutionary war against the MPLA government in Luanda. Pretoria has actively supported UNITA with significant military assistance and advice and this explains the movement's success in gaining control of a substantial part of the territory.

A similar strategy operated with respect to Mozambique and Lesotho. Here the military target was the African National Congress which, from the late 1970s onwards, followed an urban guerrilla strategy involving cross-border infiltration and sabotage attacks on symbolic targets of apartheid such as police stations, power and communications systems, and the more dramatic manifestation of the state's industrial military power (the SASOL plant, the Voortrekkerhoogte base, and the air force headquarters in Pretoria). This strategy was in essence a form of 'armed propaganda' in support of 'mass politicisation through demonstrations, boycotts, strikes and confrontations' leading ultimately to the achievement of 'mass based armed insurrection aimed at seizing political power.'[28] From Pretoria's perspective, this level of guerrilla activity did not represent a major threat to the security of the state. It did, however, contribute to that condition of 'violent equilibrium' which complicated the efforts of a reform-minded Nationalist government to convince its supporters of the need for change.

Retaliation quickly followed against ANC sanctuaries in neighbouring states: two attacks were made against Mozambique in May 1983 and June 1983, and in December 1982 against Lesotho from where, it was alleged, military aid was being given to the Lesotho Liberation Army, a movement hostile to the government of Chief Jonathan Lebua. Coupled with this intervention was military aid for the Mozambique Resistance Movement (MNR or Renamo), a motley collection of Portuguese and disgruntled Mozambiquans intent on bringing down the FRELIMO government. During this period there were also allegations of border incursions into Botswana, Zambia and Zimbabwe.

This combination of 'offensive defence' and support for anti-government proxies has been described as 'destabilisation' by South Africa's critics on the grounds that its primary motive is to '[undermine] the stability of African governments' in the region.[29] The difficulty with this definition is to render it precise; to separate primary goals from subordinate ones and at the same time establish the extent to which the policy demonstrates a 'coherent inner logic' [30] rather than a series of *ad hoc* responses to developments abroad. In the 1960s and early 1970s, for example, it was sufficient to maintain a policy of deterrence against conventional attack from the north and revolution from within, but the post-1974 environment - for reasons already made clear - called for a strategy of 'compellence' involving the use of force to contain opponents committed to guerrilla infiltration and insurgency.

Thus the question at issue is how far 'destabilisation' by military means was designed to achieve more than the neutralisation of the ANC threat emanating from beyond South Africa's borders. That this was achieved at least for the first few months following the signing of the Nkomati Accord in March 1984 and the agreement of the parties to clamp down decisively on their respective proxies (the ANC and the MNR) is not in dispute. What requires further examination is how far this military strategy was subordinate to the achievement of wider regional goals for foreign policy and, if so, with what success.

A variety of political objectives have been ascribed to the destabilisation strategy: (1) to demonstrate to neighbouring states the Republic's determination to resist external attack on its domestic order; (2) to demonstrate in forceful terms Republican hegemony and undermine the efforts of alternative 'constellations' such as the Southern African Development and Co-ordination Conference (SADCC) to escape Pretoria's economic domination and in the process compel neighbouring states to pay a price in terms of resources devoted to coping with the danger caused by destabilisation and otherwise available for positive economic development; (3) to 'actively turn back the tide of foreign or Marxist influence in the subcontinent', [31] and as the 1984 Defence White Paper emphasised, to allow 'black African states to experience the dangers of Russian involvement in their countries, as well as the suffering and retrogression that follows upon the revolutionary formula.'[32]

None of these objectives are necessarily inconsistent with one another, and indeed might be subsumed - as Robert Price has reasoned in a closely argued analysis - under the wider rubric of a long-standing ambition to create a Constellation of Southern African states. First enunciated by Mr Vorster in 1974, the concept was refined by Mr P.W. Botha and his Foreign Minister, Mr Pik Botha in 1979 to provide for 'a common approach in the security field, the economic field, and even the political field.'[33] The constellation was perceived as including the BLS states (Botswana, Lesotho and Swaziland); Rhodesia, Namibia and South Africa; the four TBVC 'independent' homelands (Transkei, Bophuthatswana, Venda and Ciskei);

and possibly Zambia and Mozambique as well.

This grandiose vision - yet another version of the 1960s' dream of a Southern African Economic Community - failed to materialise as the independent states in the region served notice on Pretoria that apartheid was an insuperable obstacle to co-operation beyond that forced upon them by economic necessity. Instead, a counter-constellation in the form of SADCC emerged, designed primarily (admittedly over the long-term) to reduce dependence on the Republic by promoting economic co-operation among member states and enhancing their bargaining power for investment and increased aid from the outside world.[34]

The future of the constellation after 1980 is a matter of debate between analysts. Deon Geldenhuys, for example, claims that P.W. Botha has been compelled to scale down the enterprise to a 'device to restructure relations, politically and economically, between present and former parts [i.e. the 'independent' homelands] of the South African state.'[35] Price, by contrast, carefully distinguishes between long, medium and short-term objectives of policy, arguing that the achievement of a constellation remains Pretoria's long-term goal for the region. He cites the following advantages that would accrue if the objective were realised: (1) the neighbouring black states would be locked 'even more firmly into the South African economic system'[36]; (2) a wider constellation would mean 'indirect recognition, by at least some black African states ... of the independence and sovereignty of the South African homelands-cum-states'; (3) the OAU would be badly split on the South African issue and lose its effectiveness as a potential source of military opposition to the Republic; (4) relations with the West would improve as the latter and 'their international firms would find themselves under less pressure to demonstrate opposition to minority rule in the Republic.'[37]

Price interestingly distinguishes between two strategies employed by Pretoria in the late 1970s and early 1980s: first, the *destabilisation* of antiSouth African states through the use of proxies (MNR, UNITA, the LLA) in pursuit of the longterm objective of establishing client regimes sympathetic to Pretoria and which might in time have become candidates for admission to a Constellation of Southern African States - the ultimate goal of policy. Secondly, the *neutralisation* of these states through the use of military attacks (on ANC bases, etc.) and economic leverage, techniques which seek '·to prevent the existing regimes in her neighbouring states from adopting policies that are directed towards ending white rule in the Republic.'[38] This is a medium-term objective, a second-best solution forced upon the Republic because the difficult task of establishing new regimes - the object of destabilisation by proxies - takes time and there can be 'no guarantee that successor regimes, once installed, will be willing to co-operate with Pretoria to the extent that it desires.'[39] In a compelling passage Price argues that:

> Pretoria's long- and medium-term strategic objectives ... interact and support each other. The policies of forward defence and economic leverage, whose main objective is the neutralization of neighbouring states, have the secondary effect of undermining the credibility and economic viability of existing regimes. In so doing, they contribute to the destabilization of these states. Destabilization, whose primary objective is to alter the political character of neighbouring states, has the secondary effect of maintaining and increasing Pretoria's economic leverage. The policies complement each other while being directed at different primary objectives.[40]

Finally Price claims that the short-term objective of the Republic is the *'maintenance not the removal of the Soviet/Cuban presence'* [41] on the assumption that Western countries, especially the United States, will be constrained from hostile action by a recognition of South Africa's contribution to the protection of their common interest in containing the Soviet threat. This resolves the contradiction 'between its domestic and external efforts to repress the black liberation movements on the one hand, and its need to avoid pressure from the Western industrial countries on the other.'[42]

This is a perceptive hypothesis which appears to confirm the argument put forward earlier in this chapter that the 'total onslaught' thesis advanced by Pretoria as justification for its foreign and defence policy in the region is designed to promote domestic mobilisation rather than reflecting a deeply held passionate fear of Soviet policy on the part of the key military and political elites. Thus the real threat posed by the Soviet Union to South African interests is not conventional attack, but the support given to liberation movements. It follows, therefore, that destabilisation keeps this threat (the real one) at bay, and at the same time maintains the Soviet presence until pro-South African governments are in power in the neighbouring states and the way clear for the establishment of a constellation of Southern African states.

Price's analysis has been cited at some length because it is (in this writer's view) a serious and impressive attempt to explain - rather than simply describe - the aspirations of Pretoria's foreign policy makers. It relates military means to political objectives, detecting in the process a coherent logic in South Africa's regional policy. This view contrasts with those who in the early 1980s saw destabilisation as an end in itself (in Geldenhuys's words, 'let us destabilize them lest they really succeed in destabilizing us'[43]), providing clear evidence that military considerations were paramount in Pretoria's strategic thinking with all that it implied for a shift in the balance of power in the civil-military structure of South African politics.

My disagreement with Price concerns the importance he attaches to the notion of a long-term objective, self-consciously articulate and determining both the parameters and substance of policy. I accept his definition of medium and short-term objectives with this difference: that the neutralisation of neighbouring states has been pre-eminent in Pretoria's strategy and I am therefore sceptical about the constellation as constituting anything more than an aspiration lacking the concrete import and significance which Price ascribes to it.

Furthermore, the assumption of a long-term goal (the creation of a Constellation of Southern African states) to which medium and short-term strategies are subordinate, implies a monolithic unity of purpose in decision making between military and civilian decision makers and leaves out of account changes in the regional environment outside Pretoria's control which have compelled a scaling down of objectives. A capacity to pursue long-term objectives through thick and thin is rare in international politics, and as Price himself admits, there are formidable obstacles to South

Africa's realisation of the goal he cites as central to its policy. It is surely, therefore, not unreasonable to assume that Pretoria, too, has become aware over time of these obstacles and has in effect abandoned the prospect of building a wider constellation beyond that which includes the 'independent' homelands.

And it is in this context that the Nkomati Accord and the 1982 Security Agreement with Swaziland have significance. Difficult as it was for both these states to enter into non-aggression treaty relations with South Africa, the step could nonetheless be taken insofar as neither agreement implied formal incorporation within a constellation dominated by the Republic. In other words, what the latter gained from Nkomati was the neutralisation of the ANC as a cross-border threat capable of undermining Mr Botha's attempts at domestic reform. True, much was made of the prospect of military co-operation spilling over into economic linkage of a mutually profitable kind, but what was at stake for Pretoria was relief from an irritating and domestically damaging external pressure. Thus Price's medium-term objective - 'altering the policies of existing regimes' - was (and still is) the primary goal of policy and one on which military and political elites could agree: the former because their capability could be put to effective use; the latter because political benefits were seen to accrue from the use of that capability.

The aspiration to build a constellation may still survive among some members of the Nationalist elite, but accepting this is very different from postulating a long-term goal against which every strategy - military, political and economic - is tested for relevance and conformity. As politicians everywhere know to their cost, the press of events, the world of 'telegrams and anger', inevitably absorbs their time and energy, smothering efforts to conduct foreign policy on the basis of long-term planning and goal setting.

Moreoever, South Africa's policy makers have, over the last two decades, demonstrated a ruthless pragmatism in their conduct of regional relations - an attitude which does not square easily with an unchanging commitment to grandiose external visions of the future. The military, in particular, I suspect, show little enthusiasm for a Pax Afrikaner which goes beyond the maintenance of regional security by means other than the threat or use of force when neighbouring states prove hostile. If they are concerned with non-military, i.e. economic and political, techniques for enhancing the Republic's security, it is primarily as an aspect of that counter-insurgency strategy which the more perceptive amongst their ranks have always acknowledged as crucial to maintaining white rule *within* the Republic.

Thus we may conclude that regional policy over the last five years has been designed to buy time to put the Republic's house in order, to create a 'shield of stability' behind which the task of internal reform can be undertaken free of external attempts at disruption. And if we do feel obliged to posit a long-term goal of policy, this might be it - with this difference, that it is a goal of policy deriving from current perceptions and is therefore capable of being expressed in action in both the short and medium-term.

BEYOND NKOMATI

Since the signing of the Accord in March 1984, events have conspired to lower the expectations originally entertained by both parties to the agreement. No other state in the region has chosen to follow the Mozambique example and the MNR has continued its campaign of disruption despite several South African attempts at mediation between the latter and the Machel government. There is evidence of disenchantment in Mozambique at Pretoria's failure to bring the MNR to heel, and President Botha has so far not been willing to contemplate military intervention in pursuit of this objective.

This seems unlikely for several reasons: (1) it would stretch South Africa's military resources which still remain committed to defending Namibia against SWAPO; (2) equally, it would deplete domestic capability, increasingly visible as a deterrent in support of police action in the black townships where violent protest has continued unabated since September 1984; (3) such intervention would be unpopular with government supporters who quite rightly fear a Vietnamisation of South Africa's role in the region - or to use another analogy - have observed the high costs, both internal and external, that Israel has incurred in the Lebanon; (4) intervention, even at the express invitation of the Machel government, would be open to profound mis-interpretation abroad the longer the exercise continued. Indeed, military involvement in the Mozambique civil war would be different in kind and degree from the destablisation strategy which has been successful precisely because there was a well defined political objective and one which could be achieved by short, sudden bursts of military activity followed by rapid withdrawal.

Nor has the promise of economic regeneration been fulfilled as businessmen are naturally reluctant to invest in a state which cannot guarantee their operations the necessary order and stability. Moreover, the private sector of the economy is unlikely to risk capital while the economic recession persists, although 'transport diplomacy' will no doubt continue, which is, according to its leading exponent, Dr J.G.H. Loubser (retired in 1983), 'the art of applying the transport potential of the country to perform a maximal role in its relations with other countries for its own benefit as well as that of others.'[44] In the last analysis, however, repairing Mozambique's infra-structure and improving port facilities will not reap political and economic rewards unless and until the MNR is brought under control.

In addition, Nkomati has not led to a settlement of the Namibian issue, assuming, of course, that was ever South Africa's intention, and in the light of recent events that seems doubtful. The Accord coincided with the initiative on Namibia from which resulted an Angola-South African joint military commission designed to monitor withdrawal of South African forces from the southern part of Angola. This was completed in April 1985, but two months later South Africa unilaterally established a transitional government under the auspices of the Multi-Party Conference of internal parties. The prospect of a settlement - whether regional, i.e. excluding tha UN, or in terms of Resolution 435 of the Security Council - seems to have receded and Pretoria has no doubt reasoned that the domestic costs of 'decolonising' Namibia are too high. And here the military appear to be confident of their ability to maintain control indefinitely, despite the counter-arguments that the Orange River is the Republic's natural strategic boundary and that Namibia is, by virtue of its terrain and geographical position, hardly a suitable sanctuary for the prosecution of guerrilla activity against the Republic.

Finally, after a brief lull, ANC sabotage attacks started again: some 30 to 40 occurred between January and June 1985 - almost as many as the number of incidents attributed to the ANC during 1984. This suggests either that the latter has stockpiled weapons, etc., *in* the Republic and has the trained personnel to use them or, alternatively, that states other than Mozambique and Swaziland are still providing sanctuary from which infiltration can take place. (These two possibilities are not, of course mutually exclusive.) It is also significant that the external threat proved to be sufficiently serious for the South African military to attack Gabarone, the Botswanan capital, in order to destroy ANC cells. And this despite the fact that the US Congress had in June 1985 passed two potentially damaging sanction resolutions against the Republic. This indifference to Western opinion suggests that domestic security factors weigh more heavily in political calculations than any constraint arising from the need to demonstrate a commitment to constructive engagement with Western governments.

CONCLUSION

This chapter has attempted to chart the influence of military factors on South Africa's regional policy. In the short term at least, the Republic's strategy appears to have paid off: the continued deployment of troops in Namibia has prevented a SWAPO victory, and deterred the Cubans from military action hostile to South African interests. Further afield, military intervention has compelled at least two neighbouring states to cut their support for the ANC guerrillas, and the threat of further destablisation remains should that threat reassert itself - witness the attack on Botswana in June 1985.

In the long run, however, military solutions may not be enough if, that is, the ultimate objective is to provide the government with flexibility and security at home to promote reform. Despite the apparent neutralisation of enemies abroad, there has been a resurgence of guerrilla activity with a sustained pattern of domestic unrest unprecedented in South Africa's post-war history. Faced with these difficulties, it is unlikely that President Botha's government will be able to build on the foundations laid by the Nkomati Accord; a grand constellation of states remains a remote aspiration as black pressure increases in the towns and cities and refuses to be bought off by anything less than meaningful participation in the central structures of the state. And this President Botha cannot easily, if at all, concede if he is to keep faith with his supporters on the vital issue of ultimate white control over any new political dispensation that may emerge.

It, therefore, seems improbable that radical new initiatives will be taken in the sphere of regional policy while domestic unrest and economic recession persists. In the past such initiatives only occurred when the domestic base was secure and black opposition quiescent; in the past, too, South Africa had the resources both to deter against violent challenge and defend effectively whenever the political system was threatened. In the mid-1980s that deterrence capability is much weaker, though few doubt the capacity of the state to defend effectively when violence does occur. It is in this context that the military will be increasingly visible both at the level of policy making and the implementation of measures required to prevent the spread of civil disorder and any threat to the maintenance of white power. In other words, domestic imperatives rather than regional aspirations will largely dictate the role of the military in South Africa politics.

Whether in a climate of continued social unrest that elite will be content to remain a subordinate arm of civil government, whether its leaders will exercise a reformist rather than a reactionary influence on policy, can only be a matter for speculation.

NOTES

1. The Times, 13 April 1984.
2. Schelling, T.C., Arms and Influence (New Haven and London: Yale University Press, 1966), p. 72.
3. Recent contributions to this debate include the following: Grundy, K.W., The Rise of the South African Security Establishment: An Essay on the Changing Locus of State Power (Johannesburg: South African Institute of International Affairs, 1983); Geldenhuys, D., The Diplomacy of Isolation: South African Foreign Policy Making (Johannesburg: MacMillan/South African Institute of International Affairs, 1984); Frankel, P.H.,

Pretoria's Praetorians: Civil-Military Relations in South Africa (Cambridge: Cambridge University Press, 1984); Price, R.M., 'Pretoria's Southern African Strategy', African Affairs, 83, 330 (January 1984), pp. 11-32). The author acknowledges a debt to these works in the preparation of this chapter.

4. Grundy, The Rise of the South African Security Establishment, p. 3.

5. Spence, J.E., The Strategic Significance of Southern Africa (London: Royal United Services Institution, 1971), p. 26.

6. Spence, J.E., The Political and Military Framework: Study Project on External Investment in South Africa and Namibia (London: African Publications Trust, 1975), pp. 61-62.

7. Note Geldenhuys's contention that '... Since the early 1970s, South Africa had been covertly supplying arms and helicopters and also a limited number of pilots to the Portuguese forces fighting the Angolan guerrilla movements.' Geldenhuys, The Diplomacy of Isolation, p. 75.

8. Quote in Minty, A.S., South African Defence Strategy (London: Anti-Apartheid Movement, 1969), p. 15.

9. See Spence, J.E., 'South African Foreign Policy: the Outward Movement' in Potholm, C.P. and Dale, R. (eds.), Southern Africa in Perspective (New York: The Free Press, 1972), pp. 46-58.

10. South African Parliament, House of Assembly, Debates (speech of the Prime Minister), Vol. 17, 21 September 1968, col. 2606.

11. Jaster, R.S., Southern Africa's Narrowing Security Options (London: International Institute for Strategic Studies, Adelphi Paper 159, 1980), pp. 27-28. For an account of South African nuclear potential, see Spence, J.E., 'South Africa: The Nuclear Option', African Affairs, 80, 321 (October 1981), pp. 441-52.

12. See also Spence, J.E., 'Detente in Southern Africa - an Interim Judgement', International Affairs, 53, 1 (January 1977), pp. 1-16.

13. Geldenhuys, The Diplomacy of Isolation, p. 79.

14. Ibid., p. 81.

15. Grundy, The Rise of the South African Security Establishment, p. 15.

16. Ibid.

17. Ibid., p. 35, quoting Harry Schwarz, Financial Mail, 86, 2 (1982), p. 144.

18. Seiler, J., 'The South African State

Security System: Rationalization to what ends?', unpublished paper, 1984. See also Geldenhuys, D., Grundy, K.W. and Seiler, J., 'South Africa's Evolving State Security System', paper presented to Study Group on Armed Forces and Society of the International Political Science Association, West Berlin, 15 September 1984.

19. Ibid.
20. Ibid.
21. Frankel, Pretoria's Praetorians, p. 52, quoting Beaufre, A., Strategy of Action (London: Faber & Faber, 1967), p. 130.
22. Ibid., p. 54, quoting from White Paper on Defence and Armaments Production (Pretoria: Department of Defence, WPD-1973), p. 1.
23. Grundy, The Rise of the South African Security Establishment, p. 35.
24. Ibid., p. 34.
25. Frankel, Pretoria's Praetorians, p. 147.
26. Ibid., p. 147.
27. Seiler, 'The South African State Security System'.
28. Karis, T., 'The Resurgent African National Congress: the struggle for hearts and minds in South Africa', in Callaghy, T.M. (ed.), South Africa in Southern Africa (New York: Praeger, 1983), p. 192.
29. Price, 'Pretoria's Southern African Strategy', p. 18.
30. Ibid., p. 27.
31. Barratt, J., 'The Outlook for Namibian Independence: some domestic constraints', International Affairs Bulletin, 71, 1 (January 1983), p. 23.
32. The Times, 13 April 1984.
33. Quoted in Geldenhuys, The Diplomacy of Isolation, p. 41.
34. For an illuminating account of SADCC, see Maasdorp, G., SADCC: A Post-Nkomati Evaluation (Johannesburg: South African Institute of International Affairs, 1984).
35. Geldenhuys, The Diplomacy of Isolation, p. 41.
36. Price, 'Pretoria's Southern African Strategy', p. 15.
37. Ibid., p. 15.
38. Ibid., p. 21.
39. Ibid., p. 21.
40. Ibid., p. 25.
41. Ibid., p. 25.
42. Ibid., p. 26.

43. Geldenhuys, *The Diplomacy of Isolation*, p. 145.
44. *Ibid.*, p. 154.

INDEX

A

Abdallah, A., 214, 215
Abdallah government, 181
Abidjo, A., 99
Acheampong, I., 55, 76, 77
Adeksen, J.B., 87
Africa
  armaments: statistics, 260
  armed forces: training, 191
  armed forces, 1983, 272 (fig)
  armed forces: funding, 191
  armed forces: materiel supplies, 192
  arms limitation, 260
  arms trade, 287, 288
  arms trade (value), 276, 277 (fig)
  arms trade, 1974-78, 274 (fig)
  colonial state boundaries and nationalism, 168
  coups d'état (1958-84), 89 (fig)
  destabilising factors, 285
  economic problems, 167
  foreign intervention, 173, 174
  militarisation (colonial period), 280, 281
  militarisation: economic factors, 282, 283
  military aspects, 259
  military expenditures, 1977: statistics, 267, 268, 269 (fig)
  military intervention, 198 (fig), 251
  military intervention, 1960-1985, 197 (fig)
  partition boundaries, 167, 168
  peace question, 166
  regional defence organisations, 192
  secession problems, 169, 170, 171
  socio-economic development, 281
African Independence Front (FREINA), 144
African military forces, 106
  composition, 46
  ethnic aspects, 48
  ethnic divisions, 50
  officers, 49
  post-independence era, 47-49
  pre-independence era, 47
  recruitment, 48
African National Congress (ANC), 18, 303, 315n28
  sabotage attacks, 312
  Soviet control, 300
African National Congress of South Africa, 147
African National Congress, 'new', 130
Afrifa, A.A., 77
Afro-Marxism, 50, 59

317

Index

Akuffo, F., 76, 77
Alers-Hankey, R., 258n51
Algeria, 1, 16, 92
  armed forces, 266, 271
  coup d'état (1965), 89
  military regime, 71
  training bases, 130
  war with Morocco, 167
All People's Congress (APC) (Sierra Leone), 73
Amin, I., 24, 44, 48, 53, 61, 71, 104, 111, 186, 201n29, 281
Anglo-Boer War, 280
Anglo-French Convention, 1890, 35
Angola, 16, 17, 18, 19, 23, 35, 171, 174, 201n26
  armed forces, 185, 266, 271, 282
  arms trade, 28
  civilian rule, 98
  coup d'état attempt (1977), 112
  Cuban forces, 116
  leadership succession, 99
  military aid by East Germany (GDR), 218
  military aid by Soviet Union, 217, 218
  military aid to Sao Tomé, 184, 193, 200n20
  military equipment, 249 (fig)
  military intervention by Cuba, 218
  military intervention by Guinea, 197
  military intervention by Nigeria, 198
Angola/Namibia problem, 284
Ankrah, J., 75, 77
anti-colonialism, 132
Anti-Corruption Revolutionary Movement (Sierra Leone), 74
apartheid, 306
Argentina, 33
armed forces
  as instrument of foreign policy, 177-180 (map)
  internal organisation, 6
<u>Armed Forces and Society</u>, 69

Armed Forces Revolutionary Council (Ghana), 78
arms imports, 2
arms supplies, 227
arms trade
  Africa, 1974-78, 274 (fig)
  Africa (value), 267-77 (fig)
  statistics, 263
ARMSCOR, 17
Ashanti, 170
Austin, D., 20, 75
Australia
  training assistance: Nigeria, 226
Austria
  arms trade, 228 (fig)
'Azania', 19
Azikiwe, N., 76

B
BaCongo, 170
Bahro, R., 100
Banda, H., 14, 99, 104, 122
Barotse, 170
Barre, S., 29n4
Beaufre, A., 296, 301
Beira, 25
Beira-Mutare railroad protection, 156
Belgian Congo, 4
  military intervention (1960-1964), 187, 188
Belgium
  Africa policy, 224
  arms trade, 228 (fig)
  colonial policy, 279
  military aid to Zaire, 226
Benin, 4-5, 25, 50, 61, 62, 87, 90
  coup d'état (1963), 89
  coup d'état (1965), 89
  coup d'état (1967), 89
  coup d'état (1969), 89
  coup d'état (1972), 89
  mercenary plot, 1977, 186
  military intervention

Index

by Gabon, 197
military intervention
  by Guinea, 197
Benin see also Dahomey
Benin Raid, 36, 199n4, 201n27
Benjedid, C., 92
Berlin Conference, 1884-85, 2, 19
Biafra, 170, 172
Biya, P., 99, 111
Bizerta naval base, 207
BMATT see British Military and Advisory Training Team
Bokassa, J-B., 44, 48, 55, 61, 104, 194
Bophuthatswana, 29n3, 305
Botha, P.W., 291, 296, 305
Botha, Pik, 305
Botswana, 2, 18, 305
  armed forces, 163n63
  civilian rule, 98
  leadership succession, 99
Boumedienne, H., 92
Brazil, 33
  arms trade, 228 (fig)
Bredeche, P., 210
Brezhnev, L., 217
British Military and Advisory Training Team (BMATT), 151
  training of ZNA, 153
Buganda, 170
Buhari, M., 53, 58, 78
Burkina Faso, 2, 10, 34, 53, 61
  corruption, 58
Burkina Faso see also Upper Volta
Burundi, 2
  armed forces, 271
  coup d'état (1966), 89
  coup d'état (1976), 89
  democratisation, 72
  Hutu-Tutsi conflict, 170
  military intervention by Zaire, 197
  relations with France, 213
Busia, K., 75, 76

C

Cahora Bassa dam project, 131, 135
Cameroon, 1, 11, 22, 99, 253n6

armed forces, 266
border disputes, 168
civilian rule, 98
coup d'état, 51
coup d'état attempt (1984), 111, 112
relations with France, 213
Canada
  military training assistance, 226
Cape Verde
  armed forces, 266
Cartwright, J.R., 73, 104
Casamance, 170
Central African Republic (CAR), 48, 53
  armed forces, 266
  coup d'état (1966), 44, 55, 89
  coup d'état (1979), 90
  coup d'état (1981), 90
  economic policy, 59
  military intervention by Zaire, 198
  relations with France, 213
Chad, 2, 22, 43, 44, 50, 174, 200n18, 201n32, 253n8&n9
  armed forces, 49, 266, 271
  armed forces: officers, 51
  corruption, 57
  coup d'état (1974), 60
  coup d'état (1975), 89
  military intervention, 196
  military intervention (1979), 188, 189
  military intervention (1981), 189, 190
  military intervention by France, 211, 212
  military intervention by Inter-African

319

Force, 198
military intervention by Libya, 211, 212
military intervention by Nigeria, 198
military intervention by Sudan, 198
military intervention by Zaire, 198
China, 23, 65, 258n50
  Africa policy, 225, 251
  aid to ZANU, 132
  arms trade, 229 (fig)
  military assistance: Africa, 225
Chipande, A., 163n56
Chissano, Vice-Pres., 141
Chitepo, H., 133
Chona Lol see Lol, M.C.
Ciskei, 29n3, 305
City Youth League of Salisbury, 130
civil-military relations, 68, 77, 97-8, 105-6, 115, 119, 122, 125n8, 126n25, 163n63, 177
civilian regimes, 97
  ideological factors, 119
  leadership characteristics, 100
Clapham, C., 25
'Cobra 77' plot, 194
Colombia, 33
colonial rule, 101
  effect on post-colonial states, 172
Commonwealth Training Force, 190, 198
Comoro Islands, 24, 29n1, 214
  armed forces, 266
  coup d'état (1978), 89
  military intervention by Tanzania, 197
Congo-Brazzaville, 5, 22, 50, 53, 59, 61, 62
  armed forces, 266, 271
  coup d'état, 60
  coup d'état (1963), 89
  coup d'état (1968), 89
  coup d'état (1969), 60
  coup d'état (1977), 89
  coup d'état (1979), 90
  democratisation, 72
  military aid to Chad, 189
  relations with France, 213
Congo-Leopoldville
  military intervention by UN, 197
Constellation of Southern African States, 305
COREMO, 132, 138, 144
corruption, 56, 57
counter-insurgency, 301
coups d'état, 4, 5, 38, 39, 97, 127n41, 283
  causes, 7, 32, 40, 41, 42, 43, 45, 49, 51, 68 results, 284
Cox, T.S., 73, 74, 109
Creoles (Sierra Leone), 73
Cristina, O., 147
Cuba, 21, 22, 255n26
  Africa policy, 116, 215, 217, 250
  armed forces, 256n36, 283
  arms trade, 230 (fig)
  military aid to Angola, 26, 171, 218, 255n28, 285
  military aid to Ethiopia, 219, 285
Czechoslovakia
  arms trade, 230 (fig)

D

d'Aquin, T., 281
Da Costa, P., 184
Dabengwa, D., 153
Dacko, D., 44
Dahomey, 4, 44, 48, 55, 66, 95
  armed forces: officers, 51
  coup d'état, 60
Dahomey see also Benin
de Gaulle, C., 22, 205
Decalo, S., 101, 119
Denard, B., 181, 214
Dhlakama, A., 147

Index

Dias, M., 144
Diouf, A., 99
Djibouti, 14, 22
   civilian rule, 98
   French garrison, 212
Doe, S., 5, 53, 55, 61, 81, 82
Dos Santos, M., 163n56

E

East Germany see Germany, East (GDR)
Egypt, 1, 92, 253n11, 256n37
   armed forces, 266, 271
   military regime, 71
Ejiga, G., 189
Equatorial Guinea, 2, 43, 61, 225
   armed forces, 266
   coup d'état (1979), 90
Eritrea, 173, 175n6
Ethiopia, 2, 26, 34, 61, 87, 171, 174, 175n6, 258n52
   armed forces, 169, 266, 271, 282
   arms trade, 278
   conflict with Somalia, 185, 193
   coup d'état (1974), 89
   military aid to Belgian Congo, 187
   military intervention by Somalia, 197
   police training, 258n54
   Russian advisers, 171
   secession problem, 173
   war with Somalia, 167
Eyadema, G., 54, 59

F

Falashas, Black, 220, 226
FAM see Mozambique armed forces (post 1975)
Fernandez, E., 147
Finer, S.E., 39, 68, 72, 97
Finland
   arms trade, 230 (fig)
'Foccart machine' see Service d'Action Civique
France, 26
   Africa policy, 21, 22, 116, 171, 177, 205, 213, 214, 250
   armed forces, 206
   arms trade, 28, 227, 230-33 (fig)
   assistance to Chad, 171
   colonial policy, 279
   intelligence service (SDECE), 22
   Légion Etrangère, 206, 207, 215, 252n5
   military aid, 251n1
   military aid to Cameroon, 208
   military aid to Central African Republic, 208
   military aid to Chad, 180, 189, 208-11
   military aid to Djibouti, 212
   military aid to Gabon, 208
   military aid to Mauritania, 208
   military aid to Zaire, 208
   military interventions in Africa, 207, 208
   military regimes, 68
   military technical assistance agreements, 253n13
   Rapid Action Force, 206
   relations with Tunisia, 207
   SDECE, 213, 254n18
   Troupes de Marine, 206, 207, 251n3, 252n4&n5
Franco, F., 69
FRELIMO, 18, 129, 130, 131, 133, 134, 135, 159n15, 160n24&n27
   armed forces, 140, 141
   internal tensions, 137, 138
   Marxism-Leninism, 139
   post-independence, 143
   post-independence changes, 144

relations with Smith government, 144, 145, 146
relations with South Africa, 144
relations with Tanzania, 182
FRELIMO Partido, 145
FROLINAT, 209, 210
Front for the Liberation of Mozambique (FRELIMO) see FRELIMO
'frontline' states, 17
aid to liberation organisations, 133
control of guerrilla organisations, 134
Fulani emirates, 3
FUNIPAMO, 138

G

Gabarone, 312
Gabon, 2, 11, 14, 22, 26, 99
armed forces, 51, 266
civilian rule, 98
coup d'état attempt (1964), 111
leadership succession, 98
military aid to Zaire, 184
relations with France, 213
Gaddafi, H., 168, 212, 285
Gambia, The, 2, 11
civilian rule, 98
coup d'état, 51
coup d'état attempt (1981), 112
military intervention by Senegal, 198
Garang, J., 26
Geldenhuys, D., 306
Germany, East (GDR), 255n26
arms trade, 235 (fig), 250
secret service security training: Africa, 219
technical assistance, 217
technical assistance: Ethiopia, 26
Germany, West (FRG), 65, 258n54
arms trade, 234 (fig), 250
military training assistance, 226
Gethi, B., 108, 109

Ghana, 4, 5, 9, 10, 30n7, 33, 43, 50, 53, 61, 64, 65, 86, 94, 95, 170
armed forces, 49, 258n51, 266
corruption, 56, 57
coup d'état (1966), 44, 55, 60, 75, 89, 202n36
coup d'état (1972), 55, 89
coup d'état (1978), 90
coup d'état (1979), 90
coup d'état (1981), 71, 90
democratisation, 75, 77
economic policy, 58, 59
elections (1969), 76
military aid to Belgian Congo, 187
military training assistance, 191
Gichuru, J., 107
Gold Coast, 3
Goldsworthy, D., 71
Gorongoza rebel base, 25
Gowon, Y., 83
Great Britain, 23
Africa policy, 222, 250
arms trade, 28, 227, 235-237 (fig), 257n46
colonial policy, 279
foreign policy, 257n44
military aid to Nigeria, 223
relations with Kenya, 222
relations with Tanganyika, 223
training assistance, 223-224
Greece
military regime (1973), 69
Grey's Scouts, 151
Grundy, K., 292, 299, 302
guerrilla liberation

Index

armies, 15, 16
guerrilla warfare, 34
  international aspects, 132
Guinea, 2, 24, 43, 65, 66,
  161n42, 199n3, 200n9, 256n37
  armed forces, 120, 195,
    271, 282
  civilian rule, 98
  corruption, 58
  coup d'état, 51
  coup d'état (1984), 60, 90
  military aid to Angola, 193
  military aid to Belgian
    Congo, 187
  military aid to Benin, 180,
    193
  military aid to Liberia, 181
  military aid to Sierra Leone,
    180
  military takeover (1984), 99
  relations with France, 206
Guinea-Bissau, 2, 16
  armed forces, 266
  coup d'état (1980), 51, 90
  military aid to Sao Tomé,
    184, 200n21
Gumane, P., 138
Gwambe, A., 138
Gwenjere, M., 144

H
Habre, H., 188, 210, 211
Haidallah, O., 58, 66
Hausa, 172
Hausa city-states, 3
Hodder-Williams, R., 122
Houphouët-Boigny, F., 14,
  99, 104
Huntington, S.P., 69, 86
Hutu-Tutsi conflict, 170, 182

I
Ibadan University confe-
  rence, 1964, 3
Ibo, 172
Income per capita, 2, 117,
  118 (fig)
India, 65
  military training as-
    sistance, 226
Indian Army, 64

Inter-African Force, 183,
  184, 187, 198
International Institute
  for Strategic Studies,
  260
Intervention, 21, 23, 24
  motivations, 26
Iranian Revolution, 204,
  222
Iraq
  military training as-
    sistance: Zambia, 226
Ireland
  military training as-
    sistance, 226
iron deposits, 169
Islam, 1
Israel, 23, 65, 258n50,
  n52, n53
  Africa policy, 251
  arms trade, 237 (fig)
  military aid: Ethio-
    pia, 225, 226
Italy
  arms trade, 237-238
    (fig)
  colonial policy, 279
Ivory Coast, 1, 11, 14,
  123
  armed forces, 51, 195,
    282
  civilian rule, 98
  military aid to Zaire,
    184
  relations with France,
    213
  secession, 20

J
Jackman, R.W., 45
Jackson, R.H., 100, 101,
  123
Janowitz, M., 70
Jardim, J., 144
Jawara, Sir D., 99, 183
jet fighters, 282
Jordan
  arms trade (fig), 238
Juxon-Smith, A., 74, 93

Index

K
Kaduna defence academy, 191
Kalenjin group, 107
Kamba group, 107
Kamougué, Col, 210, 211
Kanyotu, J., 108
Kawawa, R., 124n2
Karume, A., 257n45
Katanga, 170, 172
Kaunda, K., 14, 99
Kavandame, L., 144
Keita, M., 55
Kenya, 1, 2, 11, 15, 23, 125n11, 126n20, 127n34, 128n51, 257n43
   armed forces, 195, 257n49, 266, 271
   civil-military relations, 106, 107, 108, 109
   civilian rule, 98
   coup d'état attempt (1971), 112
   coup d'état attempt (1978), 113
   coup d'état attempt (1982), 110, 112-114
   ethnic groups, 107
   General Service Unit (GSU), 107, 110
   leadership succession, 98
   military equipment, 249 (fig)
Kenyatta, J., 104, 107
Khama, S., 104
Kikuyu group, 107, 108
Kilson, M., 73
Kinshasa, 4
Kirk-Greene, A.H.M., 71
Kitchener Expedition to Khartoum, 280
Korea, North, 23
   Africa policy, 251
   arms trade, 238 (fig)
   military aid: Equatorial Guinea, 225
   military aid: Uganda, 225
   military aid: Zimbabwe, 225
   training of ZNA, 153
Korea, South, 68, 69
Kouandété, M., 55
Kountché, Gen, 53, 59

Krushchev, N., 216

L
Lamizana, S., 79, 80
Lancaster House conference, 142
Landgren-Bäckström, S., 28
Lansana, D., 73
leadership, 125n12
leadership succession, 98, 123
Lebua, J., 99, 304
Lellouche, P., 252n6
Lemarchand, R., 220
Leopoldville, 4
Lesotho, 17, 18, 99, 305
   armed forces, 266
   civilian rule, 98
Lettow-Vorbeck, P.E. von, 25, 280
Levy, M., 41
liberation organisations
   armies, 140
   diplomatic offensives, 132
   international aspects, 134
   international recognition, 135
Liberia, 5, 10, 53, 61, 80, 199n5
   armed forces, 266
   coup d'état (1980), 55, 90
   democratisation, 81, 82
   military aid to Belgian Congo, 187
   military intervention by Guinea, 198
Libya, 1, 61, 168, 253n11
   armed forces, 169, 177, 266, 271, 282
   coup d'état (1969), 89
   military intervention, 285
   military intervention: Chad, 189, 210, 211-12, 285
Limann, H., 33, 78

Index

Lol, M.C., 188, 210-211
Loubser, J.G.H., 311
Luba, 218
Luckham, R., 109
Lumumba, P., 4, 187, 216
Lusaka Agreement, 137

M
Mabunda, J., 138
MacFarlane, S.N., 196
Machel, S., 23, 119, 122, 138, 145
Machiavelli, N., 102
Machungu, M., 163n56
Maclean, S., 151
Madagascar, 1, 29n1, 61
　armed forces, 271
　coup d'état (1972), 89
　coup d'état (1975), 89
Maji Maji rebellion, 3
Malan, M., 300
Malawi, 2, 11, 14, 25, 126n25
　armed forces, 110, 163n63, 257n49, 271
　civilian rule, 98
Maldive Islands
　armed forces, 266
Mali, 55, 61
　armed forces, 282
　coup d'état (1966), 60
　coup d'état (1968), 44, 89
　military aid to Belgian Congo, 187
Malloum, Gen, 57, 209
MANC see Mozambique African National Congress
Mancham, J., 181, 186
MANU, 130, 138
Margai, A., 73
Marxist-Leninism, 215
Mashona, 139
Masuku, L., 153
Matabele, 139
Matabeleland, 16, 18
　guerrilla warfare, 133
　security problems, 154
Matsinhe, M., 163n56
Matzangaissa, A., 147
Mauritania, 22, 61, 167, 266
　armed forces, 271
　corruption, 58.
　coup d'état (1978), 90
　coup d'état (1979), 90
　coup d'état (1980), 90
　coup d'état (1984), 90
Mauritius, 38
　armed forces, 266
Mayotte, 214
Meiring, G., 35
Mende, 73
Mengistu, Col, 218
Mexico, 33
　military regime, 68
Mgagao Declaration, 135
militarisation
　Africa, 27
military expenditures (MILEX), 1960-1979, 262 (fig)
military expenditures (MILEX), African, 1977, 267-69 (fig)
military expenditures (MILEX), regional, 1977, 264-65 (fig)
military institutions
　civilian control, 12, 13, 14, 15
　social organisation, 31
military intervention
　bilateral, 191
　ideological factors, 193
　personal connections, 194
　technical constraints, 196
military power, 4
Military Recovery Committee for National Progress (Upper Volta), 80
military regimes, 33, 53-4
　disengagement from politics, 9-10, 67-72, 85, 86, 88
　permanence, 61
　socio-economic development, 58
　stability, 59

325

Index

military training, 191
Millinga, J., 138
Mitterrand, F., 22, 205, 212
Mmole, M., 138
MNR (or RENAMO), 16, 18, 25, 119, 146-148, 161n39, 162n54, 184, 304, 310
   aid from South Africa, 148
   effect on Zimbabwe economy, 155
Mobutu, S., 4, 29n4, 53, 54, 194, 256n39
Mohammed, M., 108, 115, 195
Moi, D.A., 108, 113
Moisi, D., 252n6
Mondhlane, Dr, 138, 225
Monrovia, 56
Morocco, 1, 26, 168
   anti-Marxist policy, 254n17
   armed forces, 169, 177, 266, 271
   war with Algeria, 167
Mowoe, I.J., 90
Mozambique, 1, 5, 15-18, 65, 158n1&n3, 159n10, 160n17, 160n22&n29, 161n42, 162n43, 174, 200n9
   armed forces, 35, 119
   armed forces (post 1975), 144, 145
   armed forces: training, 36
   civil-military relations, 109
   civilian rule, 98
   coup d'état attempt (1975), 110, 112, 145
   defence budget, 147
   economic factors, 144, 148
   economic problems, 128n42, 162n52
   guerrilla warfare, 130, 131, 133, 135, 137
   military equipment, 249 (fig)
   military intervention by Tanzania, 197
   military intervention by Zimbabwe, 198
   oil pipeline protection, 25
   Portuguese emigration, 144
   post-independence, 144
   relations with South Africa, 148, 171
   scientific-socialism, 139
   security arrangements (post independence), 144
   security problems, 148, 149, 156
   transition to independence, 143
   ZNA presence, 165n84
Mozambique African National Congress (MANC), 138
Mozambique Common Front (FRECOMO), 144
Mozambique Institute, Dar-es-Salaam (FRELIMO), 134
Mozambique National Resistance (MNR or RENAMO) see MNR
Mozambique People's Liberation Army organisation, 140
Mozambique Revolutionary Council (MORECO), 138
Mozambique United Group (GUMO), 144
Mubarak, H., 92
Mugabe, R., 16, 133, 135, 140, 159n16, 161n36
Mulinge, J.K., 108, 109, 115
Mungai, N., 113
Murtala, M., 82, 83, 84, 86
Musinyi, A.H., 11
Mutare refinery, 25
Muzorewa, A., 13

N

Namibia, 18, 19, 24, 35, 174, 305, 311, 315n31
Nasser, G.A., 92
National Advisory Council (Sierra Leone), 74
National Democratic Party, 130

National Liberation Council
   (Ghana), 4, 75
National Reformation Council
   (NRC)(Sierra Leone), 73, 93
naval craft, 282
Ndebele, 170
Ndlovu, A., 153
Ndolo, J.M., 107, 112
neo-colonialism, 116
Nguema, M., 104, 218, 225
Nhongo, R., 151
Niger, 22, 43, 53, 61
   armed forces, 266
   coup d'état (1974), 89, 253n7
   economic policy, 59
   police training, 258n54
   relations with France, 213
Nigeria, 2, 5, 10, 24, 53, 61, 65, 82, 86, 94, 95, 170, 175n4, 200n17&n19
   armed forces: Angola, 183
   armed forces, 30n7, 31, 49, 64, 126n25, 195, 258n49, 266
   arms trade, 278
   border disputes, 168
   corruption, 56
   coup d'état (1966), 89
   coup d'état (1975), 83, 89
   coup d'état (1983), 71, 90
   defence expenditures, 84
   democratisation, 82, 83, 85
   economic factors, 84, 85
   economic policy, 58
   election (1979), 92
   military aid, 257n46
   military aid to Angola, 183
   military aid to Belgian Congo, 187
   military aid to Chad, 184, 188-9
   military aid to Tanganyika (1964), 183
   military equipment, 249 (fig)
   military training assistance, 191
   oil revenues, 82
   reforms, 83
   secession problem, 172
Njonjo, C., 108, 127n35, 186

Nkomati Accord, 1984, 18, 148, 291, 305, 309-10
Nkomo, J., 16, 130, 139
Nkrumah, K., 4, 44, 64, 75, 94, 185
Nordlinger, E.A., 50, 88
Nuer, 3
Nyerere, J., 11, 19, 24, 99, 104, 124n2

O
OAU, 1, 37, 136, 160n18, 167, 184, 188, 201n34, 290n15-n20
   Commission of Mediation, Conciliation and Arbitration, 286
   conflict management, 285, 286
   secessions, 20
   security force, 287
Obote, M., 44, 71, 111, 186, 187
Odinga, O., 216
Ogaden dispute, 167, 185, 284
oil price, 59
oil trade, 204
Okelo, J., 257n45
OPEC, 84
'Operation Barracuda', 208, 212
'Operation Foday Kabba II', 183
'Operation Omega', 180
Organisation of African Unity see OAU
Oueddei, G., 188, 210, 211
Ouedraogo, G., 80
Ovambo, 19
Oyediran, O., 83

P
Pachter, E.F., 109, 120, 194
Pakistan, 10
   military training assistance, 226
Party of National Coalition (PCN), 144

Index

People's Redemption Council (Liberia), 81
Perlmutter, A., 40
personalised rule, 101, 102, 103, 104
phosphates, 59, 169
Poland
   arms trade, 238 (fig)
POLISARIO guerrillas, 167
political systems, 2
population statistics, 2
Portugal, 159n17
   Africa policy, 225
   coup d'état (1974), 137
   military regime (1974), 69
praetorianism, 4, 5, 60
Price, R., 305, 306, 307, 308
Provisional National Defence Council (Ghana), 78

Q
quasi-military regime, 29n4

R
Radio Truth (radio station), 164
Rapaport, D.C., 60
Rawlings, J., 33, 53, 58, 76, 77, 78
redemocratisation, 69
RENAMO see Mozambique National Resistance
René, A., 181, 186
Réunion, 215
   armed forces, 266
Revolutionary Committee of Mozambique, 132
Rhodesia, 16, 305
   relations with Mozambique, 146
Rhodesia see also Zimbabwe
Rhodesian African Rifles, 151
Rhodesian Front party, 130, 143
Rhodesian Light Infantry, 151
Romania
   military training assistance: Mozambique, 226

Ronen, D., 90
Rosberg, C.G., 100, 101, 123
Rosenau, J., 178, 196
Rwanda
   armed forces, 266
   coup d'état (1973), 89
   democratisation, 72
   Hutu-Tutsi conflict, 170
   relations with France, 213

S
Sadat, A., 92
SADCC see Southern African Development and Co-ordination Conference
Saffu, Y., 115
Samori Touré, 3
Sankara, T., 53, 80
Sao Tomé, 29n1
   armed forces, 266
   military intervention by Angola, 197
   military intervention by Guinea-Bissau, 197
Savimbi, J., 18, 171, 303
Sawe, J.M., 108
scientific-socialism, 157
SDECE see Service de Documentation Exterieure ...
secession
   international recognition problem, 171
Security Agreement, 1982 (Swaziland: South Africa), 309
Seiler, J., 300
Sekou Touré, A., 99, 194, 206
Selous Scouts (Rhodesia), 16, 151
Senegal, 1, 11, 51, 170, 253n10
   armed forces, 195, 266
   civilian rule, 98
   leadership succession, 99

Index

military aid to Chad, 189
military aid to the Gambia, 183, 200n15
relations with France, 213
Senghor, L.S., 99, 104
Sergeants' Revolt (Sierra Leone), 72
Service d'Action Civique ('Foccart machine'), 213
Service de Documentation Exterieure et de Contre Espionage (SDECE), 213
Seychelles, 24
armed forces, 266
coup d'état (1977), 89, 181
mercenary plot, 1981, 186
military intervention by Tanzania, 197
Shaba see Katanga, Zaire/Shaba
Sierra Leone, 10, 11, 30n7, 72, 86, 87, 94, 126n25, 199n3
armed forces, 266
coup d'état (1967), 55, 89
coup d'état (1968), 89
democratisation, 73, 74
military intervention by Guinea, 197
Sierra Leone People's Party (SLPP), 73
Sigauke, S., 138
Simao, J., 144
Sithole, N., 131, 135
Sivard, R.L., World Military and Social Expenditures 1983, 260
Smith, I., 143
Sobhuza, King, 99
socio-economic trends, 1960-1979, 261 (fig)
Sofala-Mutare oil pipeline protection, 156, 184
Soglo, C., 4, 48
Soilih, A., 181, 215
Somalia, 23, 29n4, 61, 256n37
armed forces, 266, 271, 282
conflict with Ethiopia, 185, 193

coup d'état (1969), 89
military intervention by Ethiopia, 197
police training, 258n54
war with Ethiopia, 167
South Africa, 200n17
alleged assistance to ZAPU dissidents, 153
and MNR, 147, 162n51
armed forces, 169, 177, 271, 283, 297
armed forces: Angola (UNITA), 218
arms trade, 28, 278
assistance to Matabeleland dissidents, 164n73
border incursions, 18, 304
civil-military relations, 299-303, 314n3
defence policy, 17-18, 293, 296
Defence White Paper, 1984, 291
destabilisation strategy, 305, 306, 308
'detente' policy, 297
economic policy, 17, 305
economic pressures on Zimbabwe, 155
economic problems, 313
foreign policy, 19, 306-307
foreign policy, 1959-1974, 292-294
internal problems, 174-175, 176n8
internal reforms, 310, 312
military aid to Angola (UNITA), 218
military intervention, 295
military intervention in Angola, 298, 303
military intervention in Botswana, 285

329

military intervention in Mozambique, 310
regional security policy, 309
relations with Mozambique, 147, 171
relations with Zimbabwe, 153, 155
State Security Council (SSC), 299, 301
'total onslaught' concept, 300
unrest problem, 313
South African Defence Force, 35
 statistics, 17
South African Treaty Organisation (SATO), 294
South America, 4
Southern African Development and Co-ordination Conference (SADCC), 155, 305, 315n34
Soviet Union, 22, 23, 65, 255n32
 Africa policy, 215, 250
 aid to FRELIMO, 132
 aid to ZAPU, 133
 armed forces, 258n57
 arms supply to Angola, 217
 arms supply to Guinea-Bissau, 217
 arms supply to Mozambique, 146, 217
 arms supply to Nigeria, 217
 arms supply to Somalia, 217
 arms trade, 28, 227, 239-245 (fig), 256n35
 assistance to Benin, 171
 assistance to Ethiopia, 171
 assistance to Mozambique, 171
 defence policy, 255n25
 fishing industry (South Atlantic), 254n19
 foreign policy, 215, 216
 foreign policy, 254n20&n21
 foreign policy: Namibia, 218
 foreign policy: Nigeria, 255n23
 foreign policy: South Africa, 218
 ideological confrontation, 203
 intelligence service: Africa, 219
 military aid to Ethiopia, 218, 219
 military aid to Mozambique, 219
 military aid to Uganda, 219
 military assistance, 266, 282-283
 military training assistance, 216
 relations with Ghana, 216
 relations with Kenya, 216
Soweto disturbances, 1976, 297
Spain, 65, 69, 94, 167
 Africa policy, 225
 arms trade, 238 (fig)
 colonial policy, 279
 military training assistance: Equatorial Guinea, 226
Special Air Service (Rhodesia), 16
Stevens, S., 73, 75, 180, 194
Sudan, 2, 3, 5, 11, 23, 61, 70, 170, 175n1&n5, 253n11
 armed forces, 271
 armed forces: officers, 51
 coup d'état, 60
 coup d'état (1958), 89
 coup d'état (1969), 89
 dissident movement, 173
 secession problem, 173
Sudan People's Liberation Army, 26
Sudan, Southern, 170
Supreme Military Council (Ghana), 76
Supreme Military Government (Nigeria), 82

Index

SWAPO, 297, 303
  guerrilla forces, 18
  Soviet control, 300
Swaziland, 2, 305
  armed forces, 266
  civilian rule, 98
  leadership succession, 99
Sweden
  arms trade, 239 (fig)
Switzerland
  arms trade, 239 (fig)

T
Tamarkin, M., 110
Tanganyika, 3
  military intervention by OAU, 197
  relations with Great Britain, 223
tanks, 282
Tanzania, 11, 15, 24, 65, 124n2, 131, 161n42, 175n4, 200n9
  armed forces, 120, 195, 271
  civilian rule, 98
  leadership succession, 98
  military aid to Comoros, 181, 199n7
  military aid to Mozambique, 147, 182, 199n9
  military aid to Seychelles, 181, 199n8
  military aid to Uganda, 186-7, 210n29
  military aid to Zambia, 182
  military intervention: Uganda, 285
  military training assistance, 257n48
Tazara railway (Tanzania-Zambia), 225
Tekere, E., 133
Temne, 73
Teshie defence academy, 191
Tete Province, Mozambique, 135
Thailand, 70
Tigre dissidents, 171
Togo, 2, 11, 50, 54, 61, 64, 72
  armed forces, 271
  coup d'état (1963), 89
  coup d'état (1967), 89
  economic policy, 59
  military aid to Zaire, 184
  relations with France, 213
Tolbert, W., 81, 194
Tombalbaye, N., 44, 209
Tongogara, J., 143
Touré, A.S., 99, 194, 206
Transkei, 29n3, 305
'transport diplomacy', 311
Traoré, M., 55
Trinquer, R., 296
Tshombe, M., 256n39
Tunisia, 1
  armed forces, 266
Turkey
  military regime, 68
Tutsi-Hutu conflict, 170

U
UDENAMO, 130, 138
UDV-RDA party (Upper Volta), 80
Uganda, 5, 11, 24, 30n7, 48, 50, 53, 65, 70, 72, 170, 201n29
  Amin regime, 55
  armed forces, 195, 266, 271, 282
  armed forces, training (1981), 190
  coup d'état (1971), 44, 89
  coup d'état (1980), 90
  coup d'état (1985), 187
  economic policy, 59
  military intervention by Commonwealth Training Force, 198
  military intervention by Tanzania, 198
  secession, 20
UNAMI, 130, 138
'Union Government' (Unigov), 76
Union of the Peoples of

Index

Mozambique (UNIPOMO), 144
UNITA, 18, 23, 303
   armed forces, 218
United Nations, 286
   intervention: Belgian Congo, 187
<u>United Nations Statistical Yearbook</u>, 260
United Popular Anti-Imperialist Front of the Africans of Mozambique, 138
United States, 22, 23, 81, 171
   Africa policy, 220, 251
   armed forces: Belgian Congo, 188
   arms trade, 227, 246-48 (fig)
   Central Intelligence Agency, 220, 256n38-40
   Foreign Assistance Act, 1961, 221
   foriegn policy, 203
   foreign policy: Liberia, 220
   foreign policy: Madagascar, 221
   military aid to Ethiopia, 221
   military aid to Ghana, 222
   military aid to Kenya, 222
   military aid to Liberia, 221
   military aid to Nigeria, 222
   military aid to Zaire, 221
   military intelligence: Africa, 220
   Rapid Deployment Task Force, 23, 204, 222, 257n42
   weapon sales: Africa, 220
Upper Volta, 10, 76, 86, 95
   armed forces, 271
   coup d'état (1966), 89
   coup d'état (1974), 89
   coup d'état (1980), 90
   coup d'état (1982 & 1983), 90
   coups d'état, 80
   democratisation, 79, 80
   elections, 71
   relations with France, 213
Upper Volta <u>see also</u> Burkina Faso
uranium, 59
US Arms Control and Disarmament Agency, 260

USSR <u>see</u> Soviet Union

V
Venda, 29n3, 305
Venezuela, 33
Viljoen, C., 162n51
Voice of Free Zimbabwe (radio station), 164
Vorbeck, Von Lettow - <u>see</u> Lettow-Vorbeck, P.E. von
Vorster, B.J., 305

W
Walls, P., 151
Waugh, E., 3
<u>West Africa</u>, 38, 53, 57, 80, 84
Welch, C., 71
Western Sahara dispute, 285
Western Somali Liberation Front (WSLF), 218
World War, 1914-18
   African troops, 280
World War, 1939-45
   African troops, 3, 280

Y
Yoruba, 170, 172
Yugoslavia, 65
   arms trade, 248 (fig)

Z
Zaire, 2, 23, 29n4, 37, 53, 54, 61, 170, 253n10
   armed forces, 195
   coup d'état (1960), 89
   coup d'état (1965), 89
   military aid to Burundi, 182
   military aid to Central African Republic, 182
   military aid to Chad, 182, 189
   secession problem, 20, 172
Zaire <u>see also</u> Belgian Congo

Index

Zaire/Shaba
　military intervention by Angola, 197
　military intervention by Inter-African Force, 198
Zambia, 11, 14, 17, 24, 126n25, 133, 170
　armed forces, 257n49, 271, 282
　civilian rule, 98
　security problems, 220
ZANLA, 131, 161n36
　guerrilla army, 16
　organisation, 141
　statistics, 161n33
ZANU, 129-33, 136, 154, 163n59
　armed forces, 141
　election results, 143
　internal tensions, 134, 139-40
　scientific-socialism, 140
Zanzibar, 175n4, 255n33, 256n40
　coup d'état (1964), 89
　coup d'état attempt (1982), 112
Zanzibar Revolution, 223, 257n45
ZAPU, 129-33, 136
　armed forces, 141
　dissidents in Matabeleland, 154
　election results, 143
　internal tensions, 134, 139-40
Zartman, I.W., 21, 117
Zia ul Huk, Gen, 10
Zimbabwe, 2, 15, 16, 17, 24, 170, 159n8,n14&n16, 160n19&n28, 161n32&n34, 163n57
　Air Force, 163n64
　Air Force: Thornhill incident, 165n76
　armed forces, 25, 110, 163n63, 271
　armed forces (post-independence) see Zimbabwe National Army
　armed forces integration (1980), 143, 150
　arms trade, 278
　black politics (pre-1962), 158n2
　civilian rule, 98
　economic factors, 150, 163n58
　election, 143
　Fifth Brigade, 153, 165n77
　guerrilla warfare, 131, 133, 136, 137
　independence constitution, 142
　Matabele problem, 175n1
　military aid to Mozambique, 184
　'Operation Merger', 150
　relations with South Africa, 153
　scientific-socialism, 140
　security problems, 151, 152, 153
　'Soldiers Employed in Economic Development' (SEED) programme, 152
　transition to independence, 143
Zimbabwe African National Liberation Army see ZANLA
Zimbabwe African National Union see ZANU
Zimbabwe African People's Union see ZAPU
Zimbabwe National Army (ZNA), 149-51
　effect of unrest, 154-55
Zimbabwe People's Army (ZIPA), 134
Zimbabwe People's Liberation Army (ZIPRA), 131, 153, 164n70&n75
　statistics, 161n33
Zolberg, A.R., 38, 39

For Product Safety Concerns and Information please contact our EU representative GPSR@taylorandfrancis.com
Taylor & Francis Verlag GmbH, Kaufingerstraße 24, 80331 München, Germany